MODELING FOR
LEARNING ORGANIZATIONS

MODELING FOR
LEARNING ORGANIZATIONS

JOHN D.W. MORECROFT
JOHN D. STERMAN

EDITORS

Foreword by Arie P. de Geus

Publisher's Message by Norman Bodek

SYSTEM DYNAMICS SERIES

Productivity Press
Portland, Oregon

Productivity Press
P.O. Box 13390
Portland OR 97213-0390
Telephone: (503) 235-0600
Telefax: (503) 235-0909
E-mail: service@ppress.com

Portions of this work were previously published as "Modelling for Learning," a special issue of the European Journal of Operational Research 59, no. 1 (May 26, 1992). Reprinted by arrangement with Elsevier Science Publishers, Amsterdam, The Netherlands.

Cover design by Teutschel Design Services, copyright © 1994 by Productivity Press
Composition by Frank Loose Design
Printed and bound by Edwards Brothers in the United States of America

Library of Congress Cataloging-in-Publication Data

Modeling for learning organizations / John D.W. Morecroft, John D. Sterman, editors.
       p.   cm.
     "Portions of this work were previously published as 'Modelling for learning,' a special
  issue of the European journal of operational research, 59, no. 1 (May 26, 1992)"--T.p. verso.
     Includes bibliographical references and index.
     ISBN 1-56327-060-9 :
     1. Management--Study and teaching--Simulation methods. 2. Decision-making--Simulation
methods. 3. Executives--Training of--Simulation methods. 4. Computer Simulation. I. Morecroft,
John D.W. (John Douglas William) II. Sterman, John.
    HD30.4.M626 1994
    658.4'0352—dc20   94-17395
                                                                             CIP

02 01 00 99 98 97   9 8 7 6 5 4

CONTENTS

CONTRIBUTORS

EDITORS

John D.W. Morecroft
London Business School
Sussex Place
Regent's Park
London NW1 4SA
U.K.

John D. Sterman
Sloan School of Management
Massachusetts Institute of Technology
Cambridge MA 02142
U.S.A.

CONTRIBUTING AUTHORS

David F. Andersen
Graduate School of Public Affairs
State University of New York at Albany
135 Western Avenue
Albany NY 12222
U.S.A.

Bent Bakken
Norwegian School of Management
Elias Smith Vei 15
1300 Sandvika
Norway

Brian Dangerfield
Department of Business & Management
    Studies
University of Salford
Salford M5 4WT
U.K.

Pål I. Davidsen
Department of Information Science
University of Bergen
5020 Bergen
Norway

Ernst W. Diehl
Microworlds, Inc.
Kendall Square
P.O. Box 1400
Cambridge MA 02142
U.S.A.

Robert L. Eberlein
Ventana Systems, Inc.
60 Jacobs Gate Road
Harvard MA 01451
U.S.A.

Jay W. Forrester
Sloan School of Management
Massachusetts Institute of Technology
Cambridge MA 02142
U.S.A.

Arie P. de Geus
London Business School
Sussex Place
Regent's Park
London NW1 4SA
U.K.

Janet Gould
Sloan School of Management
Massachusetts Institute of Technology
Cambridge MA 02142
U.S.A.

Alan K. Graham
Product Development Consulting
8 Story Street
Cambridge MA 02138
U.S.A.

Jan W. Gubbels
Department of Research Methodology
University of Nijmegen
P.O. Box 9108
6500 HK Nijmegen
The Netherlands

Anthony M. Hodgson
Idon Ltd.
Edradour House
Pitlochry PH16 5JW Scotland
U.K.

William Isaacs
Sloan School of Management
Massachusetts Institute of Technology
Cambridge MA 02142
U.S.A.

Daniel Kim
Sloan School of Management
Massachusetts Institute of Technology
Cambridge MA 02142
U.S.A.

David C. Lane
City University Business School
Frobisher Crescent
Barbican Centre
London EC2Y 8HB
U.K.

James M. Lyneis
Pugh-Roberts Associates
41 William Linskey Way
Cambridge MA 02142
U.S.A.

David W. Peterson
Ventana Systems, Inc.
60 Jacobs Gate Road
Harvard MA 01451
U.S.A.

Steve Peterson
High Performance Systems, Inc.
45 Lyme Road, Suite 300
Hanover NH 03755
U.S.A.

Kimberly Sklar Reichelt
Pugh-Roberts Associates
41 William Linskey Way
Cambridge MA 02142
U.S.A.

George P. Richardson
Graduate School of Public Affairs
State University of New York at Albany
135 Western Avenue
Albany NY 12222
U.S.A.

John Rohrbaugh
Graduate School of Public Affairs
State University of New York at Albany
135 Western Avenue
Albany NY 12222
U.S.A.

Peter M. Senge
Sloan School of Management
Massachusetts Institute of Technology
Cambridge MA 02142
U.S.A.

Todd Sjoblom
Pugh-Roberts Associates
41 William Linskey Way
Cambridge MA 02142
U.S.A.

Kees A.J.M. van der Heijden
Strathclyde Graduate Business School
University of Strathclyde
130 Rottenrow
Glasgow, Scotland G4 0GE
U.K.

Jac A.M. Vennix
Department of Research Methodology
University of Nijmegen
P.O. Box 9108
Nijmegen 6500 HK
The Netherlands

Eric F. Wolstenholme
Department of Management Science
School of Management
University of Stirling
Stirling, Scotland FK9 4LA
U.K.

PUBLISHER'S MESSAGE

Business and other human endeavors are bound by invisible fabrics of inter-related actions, which often take years to fully play out their effects on each other. Since we are part of that lacework ourselves, it's doubly hard to see the whole pattern of change. Instead, we tend to focus on snapshots of iso-lated parts of the system, and wonder why our deepest problems never seem to get solved.

–Peter Senge, *The Fifth Discipline: The Art and Practice of the Learning Organization*

It is no longer possible to ignore the complexity of the systems we are part of, nor can we deny the need to improve our ability to function effectively within them. Understanding complex, dynamic organizational systems requires different tools than the ones managers typically have been given. Managers need methods for recognizing their own assumptions about how their organization works and for improving that understanding. They need to know which policies and practices have the desired outcomes, and which have no impact or negative results.

Our most significant learning often occurs as the result of the discoveries we make through errors. But in business organizations and human systems, errors may undermine viability over time, rather than promote learning, simply because we are unable to recognize or directly experience the results our actions have produced. Building models is a tried and true method used by inventors and product designers to test the functionality of a new idea. Architects build models to detect flaws in their building designs before beginning construction. Managers, too, need models of how their organization works in order to test their policies, discover flaws in thinking, and understand hidden sensitivities and leverage points within the com-plex systems they must manage.

John Morecroft and John Sterman, the editors of *Modeling for Learning Organizations,* have gathered together the leading system dynamicists from around the world to articulate the latest thinking and practice on how modeling can support learning in organizations. We encourage you to discover in this volume the many ways system dynamics modeling can be approached and the many purposes it can serve. You will find penetrating discussions of teamwork, a multitude of case stud-ies, and a review of the most recent simulation software available for building com-puter-based models of organization behavior.

We at Productivity Press are proud to offer our readers *Modeling for Learning Organizations* as the newest addition to our System Dynamics Series. In this series we have made available the classic textbooks in system dynamics, the field of inquiry founded by Jay Forrester at MIT. Peter Senge's recent best-selling book, *The Fifth Discipline,** has introduced the basic concepts of systems thinking and described a valuable role for system dynamics in managing organizations. Morecroft and Sterman answer many of the important questions being raised by readers of Senge's book: Where do I go from here? How do I apply it in my organization? What questions should I be asking? How do I identify high-leverage policies? How can I survive the short-term pressures to initiate policies with long-term positive outcomes?

We wish to thank the distinguished editors and contributors for the privilege of publishing this volume in North America. Both editors are leaders in the private corporate sector and the academic worlds where they teach. John Morecroft, professor at London Business School, for many years has led organization modeling programs at Royal Dutch/Shell and other major corporations while building thie field of system dynamics in British and European academia. John Sterman, now director of the MIT System Dynamics Group founded by Jay Forrester, works tirelessly to shape the system dynamics program at the Sloan School of Management to address the needs managers face in the private and public sectors. Both Morecroft and Sterman are committed to articulating the relevance of system dynamics without sacrificing the rigor that makes this field so critical for serious managers today.

We also wish to thank the many people who contributed to the excellent production of this book: Karen Jones for managing the manuscript preparation; Bill Stanton for art direction; Susan Swanson for overseeing the production process and printer relationships; Jennifer Albert for copyediting; Mary Junewick for proofreading; Frank Loose Design for text design, art preparation, and page composition; and Teutschel Design Services for the cover design.

Norman Bodek, Publisher
Diane Asay, Series editor

---

*Peter M. Senge (1990), *The Fifth Discipline: The Art and Practice of the Learning Organization,* New York: Doubleday/Currency.

MODELING TO PREDICT
OR TO LEARN?

ARIE P. DE GEUS
EXECUTIVE IN RESIDENCE, LONDON BUSINESS SCHOOL

The future cannot be predicted and, even if it could, we would not dare to act on the prediction.

Most people accept this thesis in a cool, academic debate. Nevertheless, in real life there is an insatiable demand for predictions. The yearning for some certainty about the future is so strong that most of us, at times, will act against our better judgment and demand some precise information about the future: a prediction.

Where there is a demand, there is a supply. From fortune-tellers and astrologers to planners and academics, a worldwide industry exists to supply information about the future. It is an industry rich in euphemisms, in which predictions become forecasts, and in which the product is often wrapped in sheets of fine print and jargon that normally is not read by the customer. But the fine print does not matter anyway, because few people with real responsibilities dare to make decisions based on the information, even though they had asked (and sometimes paid) for it in the first place.

Some of the suppliers employ sophisticated means of prediction, to which has been added modeling since the advent of the modern computer. Computer-based modeling seems attractive because it carries the promise that someday our knowledge of all the interrelationships and the power of the computer will allow a complete and precise representation of reality.

It appears to me that we are still a long way from this ideal. For a model to produce reliable predictions of living systems such as companies, markets, and national economies, such a model must be:

- *indeed complete*

- *a precise representation of reality*

Then for a manager to act on such predictions, he or she must *recognize* the model as a complete and precise representation of reality.

None of these conditions is likely to be fulfilled. Even the simplest business has so many internal and external interrelationships, to which new ones are added all the time, that it is most unlikely that the model describing a company will ever be finished. This point came home to me strongly when participating in Peter Senge's Leadership and Mastery course. During this course the participants are asked to list all the important facets and relationships that describe a simple one-product manufacturing firm in Milwaukee. After half an hour the whole wall was covered from floor to ceiling and it was clear that the group was still a long way from completing the description of this relatively simple entity and of its relevant relationships with its environment.

In my Shell career I have never seen a model that fully describes all the relevant relationships of a business unit or a business situation. The trouble is that an incomplete model will only give predictions surrounded by so many limiting conditions that no decision maker will be prepared to act on its predictions.

Apart from these practical reasons, there are theoretical ones as well. No model can ever be a precise representation of reality. In the living world, as in the world of inanimate objects, the observation of reality is influenced by the position of the observer. This makes it impossible to construct a model that represents reality well enough that a reliable prediction can be made from it and, anyway, it is unlikely that the manager will acknowledge the model as either complete or precise.

Each one of us has participated in discussions like, "Life is not as simple as you make it look in your model," or, "You must realize that from my vantage point, I see other (more distant) things that are the really important driving forces." And it leads to a useless discussion for the modeler to argue that he had looked at these distant things but discarded them as not (sufficiently) relevant. Even if the manager cannot point out glaring omissions in the model, he is more than likely to start a discussion on the modeling methodology in order to discredit it.

I have not met a decision maker who is prepared to accept anybody else's model of *his/her* reality, if he knows that the purpose of the exercise is to make him, the decision maker, make decisions and engage in action for which *he/she* will ultimately be responsible. People (and not only managers) trust only their own understanding of their world as the basis for their actions. "I'll make up my own mind" is a pretty universal principle for everyone embracing the responsibility of their life, whether private or business life.

If the future is unpredictable—if models are unlikely to be useful as instruments for prediction—and if the chances of a manager acting on someone else's prediction are rather remote, what could be the role of modeling in company management? Here the deeper meaning of Pierre Wack's (1985) remarks about "changing the manager's microcosm" come into focus. Models and computer modeling can play an important role in facilitating a manager or a group of managers "to make up their own minds."

Then, however, we are talking about a quite different category of models. We are no longer talking about the model, the understanding of this world as it has been acquired by a modeler or planner. We are no longer talking about a modeled understanding of this world as it has been acquired by an academic or some institute like a planning bureau to be used to make predictions. We are talking about the understanding of *his/her* world as it has been acquired by this manager or this management group—however incomplete or deficient their model may be. By computer modeling their world, we give them a "toy" (a representation of their real world as they understand it) with which they can "play," i.e., with which they can experiment without having to fear the consequences.

The work of John Holt, Seymour Papert, and the Tavistock Institute has shown that in the process of playing with a representation of the real world, children change their understanding of that world—they *transit* into the next phase of development—they *learn.*

Experientially, these principles have been known to work as well for adults as they work for children; witness the use of flight simulators for pilots, pilot plants for chemical process engineers, or flow models in hydraulic engineering. All are good examples of representations of real worlds with which the pilots and the engineers can experiment without having to fear the consequences. In the process they learn—and only then do they go and apply into practice their new and now confirmed understanding of this part of their world, accepting the responsibility for their actions.

It is a matter of some concern that as a rule we do not give managers equally powerful means to learn their trade. The work of many managers has human consequences with potential for disaster equal to malfunctioning airplanes, chemical plants, dikes and dams. Nevertheless, we find it perfectly normal to send managers into positions of responsibility to learn by experience—by trial and error. We ask them to learn "by experimenting with reality." Being intelligent people, they will recognize and fear the consequences—*and learn a lot less and slower* than they would have done otherwise.

Further clues come from neurobiology. In 1985, David Ingvar published an article called "Memory of the Future," in which he describes work done at the University of Lund on how the human brain deals with the future. Ingvar reports that one part of the brain is constantly occupied with making action plans—*sequences of events into an anticipated future,* from the next moment and minutes, to the coming hours, days, weeks, years, and so on. The healthy brain does not make one such time path, it makes several of these sequences of actions under different anticipated futures (in well-balanced people, usually a little more than half are "favorable" futures). The interesting thing, says Ingvar, is not only that the brain makes those alternative time/action paths, but also that it stores them: We have a memory of the future.

Note that in dealing with the future, the brain does not rely on predictions. It figures out what the human being would *do* under *several* anticipated futures: "*If* the train arrives late, I'll call by phone from the station and then take a cab, rather than the subway," but also, "*If* the train is on time, I'll take the subway halfway and walk the rest, so I can pass by the bookshop and see whether there is something interesting to buy."

From Ingvar's work we are beginning to get a better perspective what the end product of "modeling for learning" should be, especially if it is done with management teams, rather than individuals. Such a group should be playing with their own, computer-based representation of their real world to work out a number of action sequences (options) to be taken by their business unit or company under several anticipated futures.

Scenarios (internally consistent descriptions of possible futures, as Pierre Wack calls them) would be a useful input into this play process. We would normally expect a management team to come up with seven to ten options for two to three scenarios. This is already a major improvement over the traditional situation in which a company has at best one plan, one strategy: The Corporate One-Track Mind is a dangerous thing to have!

At this stage, we have now had about eight years of experimentation with these and connected ideas. Several of the people who have actively contributed in this process can be found in this work. A lot of work remains to be done, but as, hopefully, the reader will conclude, there is now sufficient evidence that we have more than a promise. We may have come a little closer to the vision expounded by Jay Forrester as far back as 1961.

REFERENCES

Forrester, Jay W. (1961), *Industrial Dynamics*, Portland, Ore.: Productivity Press.

Holt, J. (1964), *How Children Fail*, London: Pitman Publishing Corp., reprinted by Pelican Books, Penguin Books Ltd., Harmondsworth, U.K., 1969.

Holt, J. (1967), *How Children Learn,* London: Pitman Publishing Corp., reprinted by Pelican Books, Penguin Books Ltd., Harmondsworth, U.K., 1970.

Ingvar, D.H. (1985), "Memory of the Future: An Essay on the Temporal Organization of Conscious Awareness," *Human Neurobiology* 4: 127-36.

Papert, S. (1980), *Mindstorms: Children, Computers, and Powerful Ideas*, New York: Basic Books.

Wack, P. (1985), "Scenarios: The Gentle Art of Re-Perceiving," *Harvard Business Review* September-October, 1985.

Winnicott, D.W. (1971), *Playing and Reality,* London: Tavistock, reprinted by Pelican Books 1974, reprinted by Penguin Education, 1980.

INTRODUCTION AND BACKGROUND

JOHN D.W. MORECROFT AND JOHN D. STERMAN

In 1987 one of us (JM) wrote a paper called "System Dynamics and Microworlds for Policymakers," which reviewed developments in the field of system dynamics over the previous ten years. At the time, JM had just returned to England and joined London Business School after more than a decade at MIT's System Dynamics Group in the Sloan School of Management. The mid-1980s were a time when many new and exciting developments in the area of feedback modeling and simulation were just beginning to emerge in academic journal articles, seminars, working papers, doctoral dissertations, and consulting practice. The 1987 paper reviewed these developments and set forth a vision for the effective use of system dynamics tools with managers, an approach now known as "modeling for learning."

Shortly after the publication of the article in the *European Journal of Operational Research* in 1988, the editors invited JM to edit a special issue of the journal expanding the themes covered in the review article. Due to the scope of the effort and our common research focus, JM invited JS to participate as a co-editor. The special issue, titled "Modelling for Learning," was published in May 1992 (vol. 59, number 1). The popularity of the special issue, and the growing interest in and development of the "modeling for learning" approach has now led us to update and reprint the special issue in this volume. Twenty-seven authors have contributed eighteen articles covering the process of building, using, and learning from models.

The authors share a "modern" view of modeling. Models should capture the knowledge and mental data of policymakers; models should blend qualitative mapping with friendly algebra and simulation; models can be small; their purpose is to support team reasoning and learning; they encourage systems thinking and scenario planning. Simulations provide consistent stories about the future, but not predictions. This modern view repositions the role of the model and the modeler. Models are "owned" by policymakers, not by technical experts. They are created in a group process. The policy insights from models are disseminated throughout an organization in hands-on workshops, not presentations. Such workshops are designed to mimic the learning process of the original modeling team. The modeler is, in part, a facilitator, one who designs and leads group processes to capture team knowledge. The modeler designs and delivers learning laboratories that embed models in an overall learning context of group dialogue and experimentation.

The first concrete step in producing the special issue and now the book was to bring together a group of modelers and business people who shared this modern view of modeling. JM organized a mini-conference at London Business School on the theme "Computer-Based Learning Environments for Business and Social Systems," which took place in July 1989. The conference was attended by about twenty-five academics and business people. Their papers and ideas provided the raw material and inspiration for the special issue. Thereafter followed the long and sometimes arduous process of communicating, writing, peer review, and rewriting that produced the collection of papers you now see. For publication in this volume several new software articles are included, all the software articles and a number of the main articles have been revised, and we have also added an annotated bibliography of the rapidly growing literature on modeling for learning.

While the special issue was in its formative stage in 1988 and 1989 there were many influences on our thinking that came to shape the choice, content, and organization of the articles. Foremost was the role played by Shell's Group Planning department and Arie de Geus who was then the Head of Planning for the Royal Dutch/Shell Group of companies. Arie was fascinated with new approaches to planning that could influence the mind-sets of senior managers and accelerate organizational learning. Both of us had worked with Shell, as teachers of system dynamics and facilitator/consultants. Group Planning was a ferment of ideas and talented people. Arie challenged us (and others, including David Kreutzer) to experiment. We taught modeling and simulation to senior managers throughout the firm. We built models with senior management teams in areas as diverse as gasoline retailing, global oil markets, and biotechnology. We experimented with group processes for eliciting and mapping team knowledge. We introduced a training program to disseminate systems thinking. We tried out new soft modeling methods, such as Hexagon Modeling, that we first encountered at Shell (see Chapter 18).

It was also through Shell that JM was fortunate enough to become involved in the Learning Conference Series. This fascinating series of meetings took place from May 1987 through October 1989, sponsored by Royal Dutch/Shell, Volvo, and AT&T, and organized by Stewart Brand. The purpose was to explore the learning of individuals and organizations by diverse analogies to evolutionary learning, biological and ecological adaptation, computer-based learning, and artificial intelligence. The conferences brought together 20 international participants made up of academics, independent thinkers, and senior executives from the sponsoring companies. The yeasty mix included Marvin Minsky and Seymour Papert from MIT's Media Lab, biologist Peter Warshaw, immunologist Francisco Varela, anthropologist Catherine Bateson, computer scientist Danny Hillis, independent scientist James Lovelock, and independent consultant Peter Schwartz. The executives included Arie de Geus and Kees van der Heijden from Royal Dutch/Shell, Bo Ekman and Berth Jonsson from Volvo, and Jim Pagos from AT&T. Of course the group's discussion ranged over topics far wider than systems thinking and modeling. The effect was to broaden the group's appreciation of learning and the many guises in which learning processes present themselves. The conferences also generated some new vocabulary. "Microworlds" is a term first coined by Seymour Papert to describe computer-based learning environments. It has now been adopted by system dynamicists and more generally in business education. The term seems to fit uniquely the style and purpose of business models and simulators that are instruments for strategic change.

On the other side of the Atlantic, JS and colleagues in the MIT System Dynamics Group were experimenting with "real-time modeling" where teams of managers worked with modelers to develop their own working simulations of important strategic issues. Building on classic system dynamics work such as the Beer Distribution Game and the simulation games developed by Dennis Meadows, we created "Management Flight Simulators"—microworlds embodying a system dynamics model of a particular managerial or strategic issue. The first of these, the People Express Management Flight Simulator, described in Part 3, is now in use in hundreds of institutions around the world. Many simulators have since been developed at MIT and elsewhere for use in education and in corporations.

Two other streams of thought came together during this time to stimulate our thinking on the role of modeling in organizational learning. First, a series of experimental studies conducted by JS and doctoral students in the MIT group employed management flight simulators as laboratories to study how people make decisions in complex dynamic environments. The experiments showed that people make large, systematic, and persistent errors in environments with even modest levels of dynamic complexity. The tried and true Beer Distribution Game provides an example: Despite its simplicity compared to real production-distribution systems, participants consistently generate large, costly cycles in production, orders, and inventories, even though customer demand is essentially constant. These errors arise from what are now known as "misperceptions of feedback"—the mismatch between people's mental models and the complexity of the environment. People tend to focus on event-level explanations and assume cause and effect are closely related in time and space. Such linear, short-term, open-loop thinking is ill suited to a world of multiple feedbacks, stocks and flows, time delays, and nonlinearities. The experiments identified the particular difficulties people have and suggested ways to overcome them through training with management flight simulators and modeling.

The second stream involved interpersonal and group-process barriers to effective interventions with management teams. For several years JS, along with Peter Senge and William Isaacs, participated in an ad hoc "learning seminar" with Chris Argyris of Harvard, Ed Schein and Donald Schön of MIT, and several other leading thinkers in the area of process consultation, action science, and organizational learning. We met monthly to explore the relationships and differences among our various approaches to organizational interventions. These extraordinary sessions, where we often experimented on ourselves through role-plays and simulations, and where transcripts of our own dialogue often served as the data for subsequent analysis, led to a much deeper appreciation of the role of individual and group processes in modeling and learning. Overcoming the misperceptions of feedback that limit individual understanding of complexity is not sufficient. The defensive routines, scripts, and perceptual filters people bring to what should be opportunities for learning, such as management team meetings, can destroy any chance for learning to take place, cover up that failure, and make the cover-up undiscussable.

The learning seminar and the experimental work together posed a double challenge as we sought to develop better methods to enhance individual and organizational learning. On the one hand, there are fundamental cognitive limitations on our understanding of dynamic complexity in the various systems in which we live. Tools for modeling and simulation are essential for effective learning in these settings. On the other hand, deeply embedded defensive routines prevent us from functioning and learning well in teams. There can be no purely technical solution— no improvements to software or modeling methods alone—to the damaging open-loop thinking so prevalent in society today. The mutual necessity of better tools and better processes is the central theme in the papers of this volume.

The book is divided into four parts. Part 1 presents perspectives on the modeling process as a group activity that builds on team knowledge. The opening paper, "Executive Knowledge, Models, and Learning," sets the scene and previews the other papers in the book. Part 2, titled "Feedback Modeling in Action," presents four in-depth case studies of the model-building process with particular emphasis on conceptualization, mapping, and team involvement. Part 3, "Learning from Modeling and Simulation," illustrates developments in model-supported case studies and workshops. It also describes the efforts now being made to understand obstacles to group learning and to measure rigorously improvements in learning that derive from the use of models and gaming simulators. Part 4, "New Ideas in Representation and Software," reviews new developments in modeling software and raises the broader issue of representation—the symbols and media available for capturing group knowledge and supporting systems thinking. These papers have been completely revised and several new ones added as new software for simulation continues to emerge.

ACKNOWLEDGMENTS

A long project goes through critical phases where personal ideas become a shared agenda, plans are implemented, and deadlines imposed. Several people have helped us move this project through its critical phases. David Andersen encouraged JM to organize the London Business School conference that brought together many of the contributing authors, and helped outline the themes from which the final volume arose.

JM's colleagues at London Business School in the Strategy area, and Decision Sciences, including Ann van Ackere, Derek Bunn, Gary Hamel, Erik Larsen, John Stopford, Kim Warren, and Peter Williamson, created an environment where interest in systems thinking and model-supported learning have flourished. JS's colleagues at Sloan, the System Dynamics Group, and the Organizational Learning Center have all contributed greatly to our emerging understanding of these issues, including Chris Argyris, Gabriel Bitran, John Carroll, Bill Isaacs, Janet Gould, Fred Kofman, David Kreutzer, Ed Schein, Don Schön, Peter Senge, and many others.

Arie de Geus provided the initial opportunity for us both to work with Shell. He has been a constant source of encouragement and advice. Other members of Shell have contributed in many ways, including Graham Galer, Peter Hadfield, Kees van der Heijden, Donald Kalff, Brian Marsh, and Basil South.

We have a special debt of gratitude to Jay Forrester. He started the field in which so many of us now enthusiastically work. He created the environment at MIT that allowed others to discover and share his insights about feedback systems, modeling, and simulation. It is amazing to think that many ideas now generating excitement in modeling and computer-based learning were clear in his mind over thirty years ago. Jay's foresight is clearly illustrated in his paper "Policies, Decisions, and Information Sources for Modeling," in Part 1. The paper builds on material that first appeared in *Industrial Dynamics* in 1961. Yet with its emphasis on models that use the mental data base, structure that portrays the information limitations of management decision making, and simulations that challenge intuition, the paper fits perfectly with contemporary ideas on team model building.

Tony Hodgson of Idon has been a great source of ideas on facilitation, group work, and mapping. David Kreutzer generated enormous enthusiasm each time he appeared in London to lead Shell's Systems Thinking Workshop. David Lane was a close collaborator in our Shell activities, and continues to engage us in interesting conversations about modeling with management teams now that he has joined academia. Linda Morecroft took an active interest in the compilation of the special issue. Her MIT degree came from a research group founded by Seymour Papert, where she built a Logo microworld—the first microworld JM had ever seen.

We also thank the many referees who participated in the peer review of the full-length articles. In alphabetical order they are: Ann van Ackere, David Andersen, Derek Bunn, Pål Davidsen, Andrew Ford, David Green, Alan Graham, Roger Hall, Jack Homer, David Kreutzer, William Isaacs, Henry Mintzberg, Alistair Nicholson, Mark Paich, Larry Phillips, George Richardson, John Rohrbaugh, John Stopford, Venkat Venkatraman, Jac Vennix, Peter Williamson, and Eric Wolstenholme.

We thank our secretaries, Karen Moss and Kelley Donovan. Karen helped organize the mini-conference that launched the project. She handled mailings to authors and referees and mastered software to create several diagrams that appear in Part 1. On the other side of the Atlantic, Kelley handled the correspondence, disks, manuscripts, revisions, and frequent last-minute mailings to England with grace and skill.

Finally, we thank our editors at Productivity Press, Diane Asay and Karen Jones, who were effective advocates for the project and solved the many problems that arose during production. This book would not exist without them.

John Morecroft
John Sterman
December 1993

MODELING FOR
LEARNING ORGANIZATIONS

1

EXECUTIVE KNOWLEDGE, MODELS, AND LEARNING

JOHN D.W. MORECROFT

ABSTRACT: Over the last decade modeling and simulation have come of age, extending their influence beyond the mind and desktop of the analyst into the boardroom and the mental models of managers. In the past, business computer models were thought of as technical tools for tightly structured problems of prediction, optimization, or financial planning. But increasingly, models are seen to have a different and more subtle role as *instruments* to support strategic thinking, group discussion, and learning in management teams. In this respect they are quite similar to qualitative problem structuring approaches used by strategy advisers and process consultants. In this chapter, models are described in terms of three attributes that support different cognitive and group processes in management teams. Models can be viewed as maps that capture and activate knowledge. They can also be viewed as frameworks that filter and organize knowledge. Finally, they can be viewed as microworlds for experimentation, cooperation, and learning. The paper explains how the modeling process fits into conventional management team meetings, and then contrasts the value-chain methodology and system dynamics in order to illustrate the variety of group and cognitive support provided by different maps and frameworks. The final section provides a brief review of the companion articles in this work.*

*The author is grateful to two anonymous referees for their very helpful comments and criticisms on an earlier draft of the paper. The ideas presented here have been evolving for some time. They first appeared in "Maps, Frameworks and Microworlds for Policy and Strategy Debate," London Business School discussion paper GS-24-87, presented at the Inaugural Meeting of the British Academy of Management, University of Warwick, U.K., September 1987.

INTRODUCTION

Recent developments in system dynamics and systems thinking have included group model-building with management teams, the process of eliciting knowledge and mental models, misperceptions in dynamic decision making, learning, and gaming simulation. All these developments share in common a concern with the question, how do models come to influence thinking and actions in management teams? Increasingly, modelers have turned their attention to the mental models of managers and the learning processes of individuals and groups. From these concerns come several basic messages. Management teams are much more likely to use models when it is clear to team members that their ideas and knowledge are represented in the model, and when the models do not seem to overly restrict team thinking. So, at some level, managers must build models. Learning takes place when people discover for themselves contradictions between observed behavior and their perceptions of how the "world" should operate. So, managers must experiment with models, try their own what-ifs, and use simulations to trigger wide-ranging discussion.

Understanding of mental models and learning is improving based on recent work of cognitive psychologists such as Johnson-Laird (1987), Norman (1976), and computer scientists such as Minsky (1986). Appreciation is growing of the relevance to everyday affairs of cognitive processes such as perception, interpretation, attention, memory, and knowledge representation (see for example Norman [1990] on design and cognition). The importance of cognitive and group processes is being recognized in the management literature too, in strategic management and in branches of operational research and information technology that deal with group decision support systems.

In the strategic management area, there is increasing interest in the ways that managers conceptualize their business and make critical strategic decisions. Prahalad and Bettis (1986) talk about a *dominant general management logic,* which they define as "a mind set or a world view or conceptualization of the business... stored as a shared cognitive map" among the dominant coalition of a top management group. They discuss how this dominant logic might explain the elusive connection between performance and diversification in multi-business firms. Their line of argument is that good performance comes from good management, and that good management depends on the adequacy of the management team's dominant logic relative to the characteristics and variety of the core businesses.

Starting from a behavioral decision-making perspective, Zajac and Bazerman (1991) probe the rationale of competitive decision making to reveal managerial "blind spots" that can help explain persistent but poorly understood strategic phenomena such as industry overcapacity, new business entry failures, and acquisition premiums.

The concept of dominant logic and mental models is finding broad applicability in the strategy area. By using a variety of cognitive mapping methods, researchers have investigated causes of business decline (Narayanan and Fahey 1990), the rationale for joint ventures (Fiol 1990), and management perceptions of competitive positioning (Hodgkinson and Johnson 1994; Birnbaum-More and Weiss 1990). There is increasing attention to mapping tools. Huff (1990) has usefully classified maps into five categories ranging from verbal maps that register concepts and frequency of word use, to more complex graphical maps that reveal influence and causality, the structure of argument, and the schemas and frames that guide cognition. As yet, little has been written in the strategy literature about the *process* of mapping mental models with live management teams, though Prahalad and Bettis (1986) report that they have "had experience in trying to construct the dominant logic of a firm by in-depth interviewing of the top management team."

Interestingly, the most informative work about the process of mapping with management teams has appeared in the literature on group decision support. In particular, recent European literature has focused on facilitated problem structuring methods (Rosenhead 1989) to support groups. (This is in contrast to most U.S. decision support literature, which has emphasized the provision of computer hardware and software to support group communication [Kramer and King 1988]). Eden (1989 and 1990) describes a process of Strategic Options Development and Analysis, SODA, with computer support from a cognitive mapping package called COPE. Phillips (1990) uses decision analysis for group problem structuring and mapping, with computer support from a package called HiView. Checkland (1989) has developed his well-known soft systems methodology which uses graphical mapping methods (but no computers) to structure group problems.

System dynamics models are now viewed as instruments to support cognitive processes and group problem structuring. In one sense they are maps—diagrams, words, and friendly algebra—to activate and capture team knowledge. In another sense they are frameworks to help organize, filter, and structure the vast amount of knowledge that an experienced team shares. They are also microworlds, microcosms of reality, learning environments that managers can use to test, challenge, and refine their own mental models. By examining and comparing system dynamics with other strategy frameworks the paper shows the range of group and cognitive support that is available from graphical modeling and from simulation.

STRATEGIC CHANGE, MENTAL MODELS, AND MEETINGS

Consider for a moment the conventional management team meeting as a basis for initiating important strategic change. People are sitting around a table, debating, listening, reflecting, viewing a slide, watching the other members of the team. Before the meeting they may have received a report (usually a text document plus some figures and charts) that outlines goals and strategic options and proposes alternative courses of action. Figure 1-1 is a cognitive view of such a meeting. It shows the process, at the executive level, of adapting the company's activities to a changing business environment. Several steps are involved as indicated on the left of the diagram. First, there is the need to recognize a strategic issue. The business environment is changing: technology is advancing, new products are being developed and launched, competitors are responding, the economic climate is becoming better or worse. Managers cannot respond to all these changes. They need to be selective. A *recognized* strategic issue is a management team's *perception* of an important opportunity or threat to the company, coming from a change in the business environment. Given the variety of change taking place, the *quality* of the management team's perception is crucial to successful adaptation.

Once the team members have recognized a strategic issue then further executive debate and dialogue is required to generate action plans. For implementation to occur, the debate must include those individuals who have the power to act. The end product is a set of action plans intended to bring about changes in products, services, systems, or structure.

The right-hand side of Figure 1-1 shows the management team in terms of knowledge and mental models (not very flattering to the executive ego, but nevertheless instructive!). Inside each box, the dots represent the huge list of business facts that any experienced person carries in his head: names of competitors, market

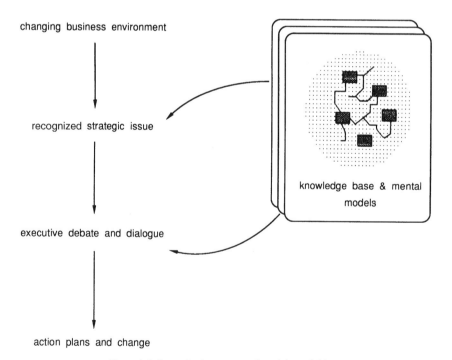

Figure 1-1. Strategic change, mental models, and debate

segments, product types, product prices, trends in demand, channels of distribution, suppliers, business objectives, budgets, manufacturing sites, employee skills, etc. The small rectangles represent learned concepts (from formal education or experience) such as competitive advantage, the product life cycle, net present value, or reinforcing feedback. Rectangles could also represent perceptions of social and political factors such as personalities, coalitions, and procedures for negotiation. This knowledge base of facts and concepts is extensive (Forrester 1980 and Chapter 3 of this volume) and is shaped by a person's career path (whether they rose through the ranks in marketing, finance, or production), by their educational background, and by a host of other experiential factors.

The term *mental model* means the conceptual model that each member of the management team carries in his or her head to explain the way the business (or more generally, the outside world) operates. As Johnson-Laird (1987) has noted: "If you understand inflation, a mathematical proof, the way a computer works, DNA, or a divorce, then you have a mental representation that serves as a model of an entity in much the same way as, say, a clock functions as a model of the earth's rotation." A mental model is shown in Figure 1-1 as a network of facts and concepts. The structure and content of a given network contains our understanding of social and physical phenomena. (Such networks are similar to "schemas" described by Norman [1976] and used by Huff [1982]).

Mental models give us answers to questions like: What will be the impact on oil price of a war in the Gulf; or even, Why is the sky blue? Each question, of course, evokes a different network. Moreover, the longer we think about a topic, the more facts and concepts we remember, and the more complex the network becomes. So it is useful to think of mental models as a dynamic pattern of connections comprising a core network of "familiar" facts and concepts, and a vast matrix of potential connections that are stimulated by thinking and by the flow of conversation. We base our models on whatever knowledge we have, real or imaginary, naive or sophisticated. Not surprisingly, the members of a management team may carry around quite different mental models of the business. It is these varied models that enter the debate and determine the quality of action plans.

Mental models play two roles in a strategy meeting. First, they are involved in the recognition of strategic issues or environmental scanning (Hambrick 1982). A given change in the business environment receives attention only if it is known to a management team *and* if, when analyzed with the team's mental models, it seems to pose a threat to the business or to offer an opportunity. Consider the example of the British motorcycle manufacturer Norton-Villiers-Triumph, facing the entry of Japanese motorcycles into the U.K. market in the 1960s and 1970s (University of Virginia Case Services 1980). The Japanese manufacturers began by selling low-displacement (50-100cc), easy-to-run and maintain mopeds, while Norton-Villiers was selling high-performance motorcycles that demanded care and attention from mechanically minded enthusiasts. Initially, the management team at Norton-Villiers did not perceive a threat to their business from the entry of Japanese products—in fact quite the reverse. They felt that mopeds would give many people a taste for motorcycle riding, some of whom would eventually "graduate" to Norton-Villiers' large and serious motorcycles. The collective mental models of the executive team saw no threat from the changing environment and therefore took no action to counter the growth of Japanese sales.

Mental models shape executive debate and dialogue. Given a strategic issue, the individuals in the management team use their mental models to generate opinions on appropriate courses of action. One can imagine the problem-processing of Norton-Villiers executives in the following chain of reasoning: Japanese mopeds—more interest in motorcycles—more demand for large motorcycles—no threat to Norton-Villiers—perhaps an opportunity to expand capacity. Here we have an opinion which indicates a course of action. A completely different opinion is possible if mental models include concepts such as manufacturing experience, strength of distribution network, and product-line evolution. With these concepts in mind, the growing presence of Japanese mopeds in the U.K. motorcycle market is perceived as a threat, because a moped manufacturer who has a strong distribution network and lots of manufacturing experience is quite capable, in the future, of producing and selling large motorcycles in direct competition with Norton-Villiers. The recognized issue changes, the focus of debate and dialogue shifts, and a whole new set of action plans emerges.

So far we have outlined a cognitive perspective on strategic change that highlights the role of executive knowledge and mental models in generating change. The main assumptions of this perspective are:

- Strategic change results from a group process of debate and dialogue among those who have the power to act (the top management team in an operating company or business unit).

- The mental models of the management team shape strategic change through issue recognition and debate which lead to action plans.

- Mental models are networks of facts and concepts that mimic reality and from which executives derive their opinions of strategic issues, options, courses of action, and likely outcomes.

- The quality of action plans depends on both the adequacy of mental models (how well they mimic reality) and the use made of participants' knowledge and mental models (whether participants are truly engaged in the debate).

- An important function of management team meetings is to activate the participants' knowledge and mental models.

WHERE FORMAL MODELING FITS IN—ACTIVATING AND CAPTURING MANAGEMENT TEAM KNOWLEDGE

What does this cognitive perspective of change imply for the use of formal modeling? To be effective, models must become an integral part of executive debate and dialogue. They should help to activate and capture executive knowledge. They should improve communication between members of the management team. They should allow executives to experiment with their knowledge in order to improve their mental models, and thereby learn.

Many modelers, particularly people who build mathematical simulation and optimization models, have great difficulty imagining models as an integral part of debate and dialogue (except perhaps when presenting "answers"). How can managers be involved in building models if they are not familiar with calculus or algebra? The problem here is not with managers, but rather with a limited view that many people take of a formal model and the process of model building. To expand the traditional view of models let me introduce three new terms: maps, frameworks and microworlds, which, when added to the picture of strategic change in Figure 1-1, result in the new picture shown in Figure 1-2.

In the lower right of the figure is a rectangle labeled "MAPS" which is connected to executives' knowledge of the business. Maps include lots of different ways of representing what a management team knows about the business. The simplest maps are made of just words—say a list that you could write on a flipchart or blackboard. Such maps give a limited though sometimes insightful view of people's knowledge. Imagine writing a list of the factors that you think would most affect the growth of a fledgling software company, or a list of factors that affect competition in the airline business. One thing you will notice if you try such an exercise is that creating a list prompts new thoughts—in other words, maps both capture and activate knowledge. A map could also be made of text phrases written on sticky notes. More complex maps are combinations of words and symbols such as causal diagrams which use words and arrows to denote connections between cognitive elements. A map might also be a diagram composed of modeling symbols (stocks, flows, converters, and information flows) to represent the operating structure of a business. One step further in complexity would take you to a map composed of friendly algebra!

Enclosing MAPS is a larger shaded rectangle labeled "FRAMEWORK" which combines maps with concepts and theory. A framework adds structure to a map by imposing logical or spatial constraints on the arrangement of text or symbols. It is a map whose layout is guided by theory. Whereas a simple list just captures items of knowledge, a framework packages and organizes knowledge. A framework also filters knowledge because some ideas won't easily fit within the constraints of the framework. Consider for example the Boston Consulting Group's famous growth-share matrix as a way of thinking about resource allocation in a multi-business firm.

The growth-share matrix is a kind of map. If you conjure up an image of the well-known "bubble chart," you will recall two labeled and scaled axes and labeled circles with which to represent a portfolio of business units. The structure of the map builds on the concepts of the experience curve and the product life cycle. The experience curve leads to the choice of relative market share as an axis to show the internal strength of a business, and the life cycle leads to the choice of market growth rate as an axis to show the external attractiveness of a given market. Together the two axes define a space in which to display the attractiveness of a firm's portfolio of businesses, in terms of their contribution to corporate growth and

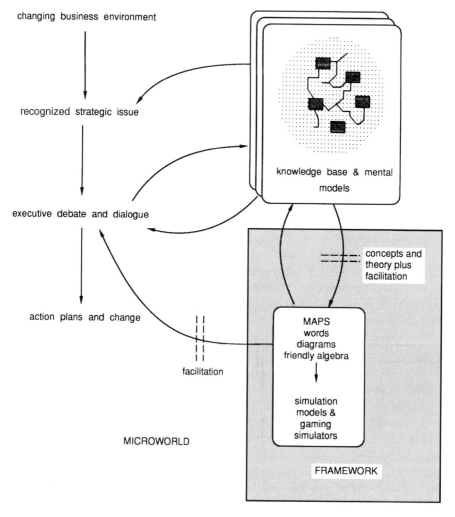

Figure 1-2. Maps, frameworks, and microworlds

profitability (Hax and Majluf 1991, ch. 7). It is a structured map. A consultant using the growth-share matrix knows which questions to ask and what information to gather about the business portfolio. By contrast, if you were to ask an executive to merely list the factors that he would intuitively use to allocate resources to business units, the resulting map would undoubtedly be radically different. (It is worth noting that the growth-share matrix was traditionally used in a prescriptive "expert" mode to back the consultants' recommended portfolio changes. But there is no reason why it could not be used in a participative mode to structure management team discussion about resource allocation.)

Computer simulation models also combine maps with theory. The model builder has certain rules for linking symbols and writing algebra that impose constraints on the way management knowledge is organized. So although modelers often say nowadays that they are mapping mental models, really they are not. They are filtering and organizing knowledge from mental models to fit the modeling framework.

A microworld (the last of the 3 new terms in Figure 1-2) is an environment for learning and encompasses all the labels and connections in the diagram. The expression *microworld* comes from computer scientist Seymour Papert (1980) in a fascinating book called *Mindstorms*. A fundamental premise of his work is that people learn effectively when they have transitional objects to play with in order to develop their understanding (or refine their mental models) of a particular subject or issue. The combination of transitional objects, learner, and learning process is what Papert calls a microworld. For example, child psychologists think of building blocks as transitional objects for young children. Playing with the blocks enables children to form the mental constructs needed to stack blocks into a tower and to recognize and build arches. The combination of child, building blocks, and play is a microworld.

In an executives' microworld the transitional objects are maps of their knowledge—words, diagrams, and computer models. "Play" and learning take place in the interaction of maps and mental models (de Geus 1988). The effectiveness of the learning cycle depends in part on facilitation: the skill with which knowledge is elicited, and the skill with which options and consequences are debated. Effectiveness also depends on characteristics of the framework: how easy it is to "fit" knowledge and information into maps, and the scope for challenging mental models through "hands-on" exercises that involve reconfiguring maps or making simulations.

TWO CONTRASTING EXAMPLES OF MAPS AND FRAMEWORKS

Let us take a closer look at the meaning and use of maps and frameworks with two examples: the value chain and system dynamics modeling. These two examples are deliberately chosen for their striking differences—the value chain is purely descriptive and graphical, whereas system dynamics involves algebra and simulation. The contrast allows us to think about the content of maps (the type of mental spaces and building blocks they provide), the differing possibilities they offer for play, and the effort and skills required to use them in management teams.

The Value Chain

The value chain is a framework for thinking about how a company can build and sustain a unique advantage over its competitors that will ensure long-term profitability and survival. The value chain builds on microeconomic theory of the firm that views the firm as a collection of discrete but related production functions. Although the label "production function" conjures up the image of machines producing widgets, the theory uses the label to encompass a whole range of business activities (like distribution, marketing, and service) in which economic inputs (such as labor, materials, and equipment) are combined into goods or services. The theory focuses on how these activities create value and what determines their cost, giving the firm considerable latitude in determining how activities are configured and combined.

The theory is quite intricate and involved and so in its raw form is unsuitable for direct entry into management team dialogue. What management teams use is a value-chain diagram that provides some of the theory's labels, concepts, and mental discipline to determine how business activities are configured and combined to generate profitability (and hence competitive advantage). The most widely known value-chain diagram comes from Porter (1985). His major contribution has been in designing a visually compact map that retains some of the organizing power of the theory, together with numerous guidelines and examples to show how the map is used to analyze competitive advantage.

Figure 1-3 is a blank value-chain diagram that might be given to a management team. Consider its visual layout and labels. It is a matrix of boxes and labels that depict the value activities of a firm. Within this framework every firm is viewed as a collection of activities that are performed to design, produce, market, deliver, and support its products. Value activities are divided into two broad types, *primary* activities and *support* activities. Primary activities, listed along the bottom of the figure, are the activities involved in the physical creation of the product and its sale and transfer to the buyer as well as after-sale assistance. The primary activities that Porter has selected are "inbound logistics" (like material handling, warehousing, inventory control), "operations" (like machining, assembly, equipment maintenance), "outbound logistics" (like order processing, scheduling, delivery vehicle operation), marketing, sales, and service. Support activities, listed in the top half of the figure, support the primary activities and each other by providing purchased inputs, technology, human resources, and various firmwide functions.

The basic diagram contains 21 boxes and 11 labels with which to categorize and organize the activities of a firm that together support its competitive advantage.

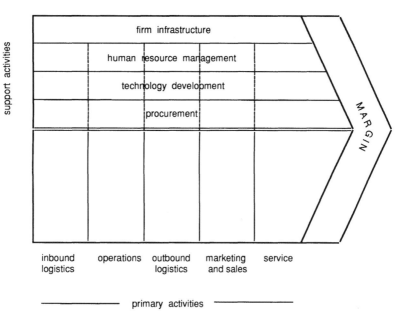

Figure 1-3. A blank value-chain diagram (based on Porter, 1985)

Moreover, the diagram can easily be extended to include more boxes and labels by subdividing a primary activity into component activities. For example, one might subdivide marketing and sales into marketing management, advertising, and sales force administration. So the diagram has a hierarchical structure to its boxes and labels. It uses an arrow shape with the arrowhead labeled margin as a clear visual reminder that the primary activities and the support activities are responsible for generating and sustaining margin.

What possibilities does such a diagram offer for support in a management team discussion? It provides a working space of boxes and labels in which executives (and/or consultants) can categorize the facts they know (or gather) about the operation of the business. Once the diagram is filled in it provides a tangible focus for debate and discussion in the management team. Moreover, if the diagram leads to extended debate, then gradually the value-chain framework becomes a part of the team's mental models, and the contents of its boxes can be modified as the discussion continues. (In fact it is only recently that consultants have started to use frameworks like the value chain and "5-forces" in facilitated group processes. More often such frameworks have been used to deliver answers and recommendations.)

Figure 1-4 shows a value chain filled in for a no-frills airline that is pursuing a strategy of cost-focus (i.e., low cost leader in a limited segment of the air transportation business). I should point out that this particular filled-in diagram is very simple and does not do full justice to the organizing power of the framework. It is just an illustration. Here the diagram is used to select and display important activities in the business that taken singly and in combination seem most responsible for sustaining the company's unique image of a focused cost leader. One can scan the diagram and begin to appreciate how the strategy builds on detail activities. One can also begin to question whether the increased cost of providing a new service could be recovered through higher prices and higher margins without endangering the company's unique appeal to its customers (e.g., should the company offer seat reservations instead of first come - first serve seating?).

What skills are required to use the value chain in management teams? The value-chain diagram is not difficult to explain. The crucial skill is to guide the filling in and the interpretation of the diagram. One might provide some written guidelines, but these left alone with a management team are highly unlikely to lead to full use of the framework. What is needed in addition is a facilitator who is familiar with the intricacies of the diagram and its labels. (The facilitator will likely be familiar with the microeconomic theory behind the diagram, but not necessarily a theory expert.) The role of the facilitator is to translate the operating knowledge of the management team into the language of labels and boxes used in the diagram and then prompt the interpretation of the diagram. A good facilitator can draw out a lot of facts and knowledge from the team by being intimately familiar with the many elaborations of the framework, hints, guidelines, and examples that Porter provides in his book.

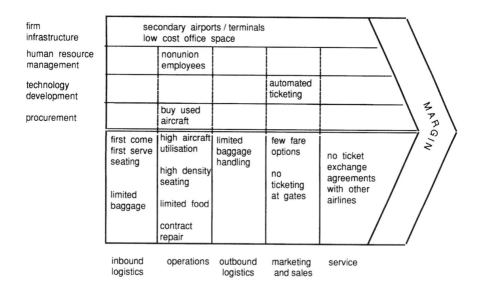

Figure 1-4. A value chain for a no-frills airline

SYSTEM DYNAMICS MODELING AND SIMULATION

System dynamics is a framework for thinking about how the operating policies of a company and its customers, competitors, and suppliers interact to shape the company's performance over time (Forrester 1961). System dynamics builds on information feedback theory, which provides symbols for mapping business systems in terms of diagrams and equations, and a programming language for making computer simulations (Pugh-Roberts Associates 1986; Richmond et al. 1987). System dynamics also uses behavioral decision theory to specify a model's information flows and decisionmaking processes (Morecroft 1985; Sterman 1987). In system dynamics the firm and its environment are viewed as a collection of decisionmaking players whose decisions and actions are coupled (Morecroft 1988). Each player is represented by a decision function with information inputs and an output that is information or action. The information that a player in the system receives depends on the player's position in the organization and such factors as the goals, rewards, and measurement systems of the organization. The system dynamics approach focuses on how these players interact over time and how policies might be changed to improve the firm's performance.

The theory of dynamical system models is quite intricate and so (just as with microeconomic theory) is unsuitable for direct use by management teams. Instead management teams can use diagrams of policy functions to identify players in a business system and specify their decisionmaking processes, and then later on they use policy maps, computer models, and simulations.

Figure 1-5 is a blank policy function that might be used with a management team. It is made up of six concentric circles that depict the decisionmaking process under review (for example pricing, or customer ordering, or production). A number of curved dotted lines represent information flowing into the decision process. The straight line represents the output of the function in terms of action or information. The five outer circles are filters of information. They are visual reminders of ideas from behavioral decision theory that the information made available to different players is conditioned by the organization (Simon 1976, ch. V; Forrester 1961, ch. 10). Each filter has a label to signify which process of the organization is conditioning information flow—operating goals, measurement systems, organizational structure, or culture and traditions. A management team can have an interesting discussion of policy functions taken one at a time, but the major value of the modeling framework comes from linking many functions to get an overview of operating structure, and from making simulations to trace how structure determines firm performance.

Figure 1-6 shows the symbols that are used to connect many policy functions into a map of the organization. The box on the right is a level that accumulates action. In the center is a composite symbol that represents an action flow (shown as an arrow) and a flow regulator (shown as a "T") that controls the size or volume of

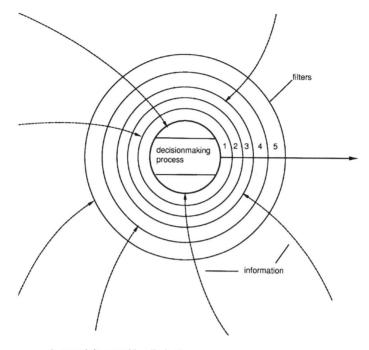

1. people's cognitive limitations
2. operating goals, rewards, and incentives
3. information, measurement, and communication systems
4. organizational and geographical structure
5. tradition, culture, folklore, and leadership

Figure 1-5. A blank policy function

the flow. Finally, on the left is a source (shown as an irregular "blob") that supplies the action flow. There is a simple rule, coming from information feedback theory, for connecting the symbols in Figure 1-6 to a set of already-specified policy functions. The required sequence of connection is: level—information (or influence)—policy function—action—level. This is a feedback representation.

What possibilities does such a set of symbols and connecting rules offer for support in a management team meeting? Here I think there is an important distinction in comparing with the value-chain framework. The value chain provides a *working space* of boxes and labels to categorize facts. The mapping symbols provide *building blocks* to assemble and connect knowledge about the operating policies of a business. Once a map is created and filled in it provides a tangible focus for discussing operating structure. Moreover, maps can be converted into algebra and simulation models. Simulated scenarios can then be used with a management

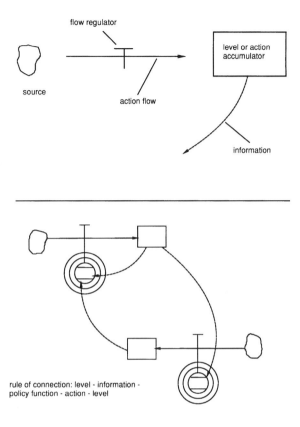

Figure 1-6. Symbols used to connect policy functions

team to debate the implications of policy change, and to link a firm's strategic performance to its operating structure.

Figure 1-7 shows a policy map for the administration of pricing in two competing motor gasoline retailing organizations. List price is set centrally by a pricing committee while pump price is set locally by each dealer. There are two policy functions, one for each dealer's price setting. The functions are surrounded by unlabeled information filters as a visual reminder that dealers know and act on only locally available information. In particular, a dealer considers competitor pump price, his own pump price, volume purchased, and list price when making price adjustments. If a local competitor's pump price goes down, a dealer quickly (often in a matter of hours) matches the change. If volume declines a dealer drops his price. Price changes accumulate in the pump price level and influence volume purchased by the customer.

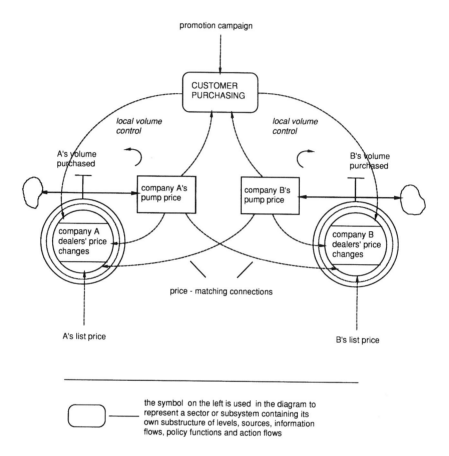

Figure 1-7. The administration of pricing in competing gasoline retailing organizations

This partial model together with simulations can generate interesting discussion in a management team. One might ask for example how a company can gain market share. Let us suppose that company B reduces *list* price in order to gain share and that company A, due to administrative delays, is slow to make a corresponding reduction in list price. Nevertheless, company B is unlikely to gain share because the moment the *list price* drop is converted to a *pump price* drop at B's dealers, then A's dealers match it. Suppose instead that company B uses a promotion campaign to gain share. The campaign is successful (in that B's own customers like the glasses or mugs on offer). Even so, if company B begins to gain new customers then A's dealers will likely retaliate with a price cut because they are losing volume. So increases in market share from B's national promotion campaign are offset by "automatic" (volume-induced) pump price reductions of A's dealers. Suppose a third company C launches a successful promotion campaign instead of B. If C's campaign begins to gain new customers then both A and B's dealers will respond "automatically" with price cuts that could degenerate into a price war.

The interesting strategic feature of the model is that the operating structure, linking dealers' pricing to customer purchasing, leads to tight control of volume at the dealer level and therefore rigid national market share. The model focuses strategic discussion on dealers' pump price setting. It shows that if dealers adjust pump price in response to sales volume then gasoline retailing firms can do little to change market share without invoking a price war.

The policy map shows a management team the structure that results from piecing together their descriptions of individual policies. They can debate the structure, use it to build a shared mental image and shared vocabulary for the business, and, in conjunction with simulations, use it to develop and test strategic scenarios.

Simulations amplify and clarify scenario thinking. The ability to bring a model to life, to see the consequences of structural assumptions, to try out "what-ifs," and to challenge managerial intuition are significant advantages that system dynamics has to offer over purely qualitative mapping frameworks. Reconsider the scenario in which company B launches a promotion campaign to gain share. Imagine a successful campaign, whose impact builds gradually over a 16-week period to a plateau that attracts up to 20 percent of A's customers. Figure 1-8 shows the campaign's effect graphically. The launch takes place in week 5. As the weeks go by, fewer and fewer customers buy from A's stations until week 20 when only 80 percent of customers who would normally buy from A continue to do so. The rest have defected to B. The simulation raises several questions. Does a campaign in fact

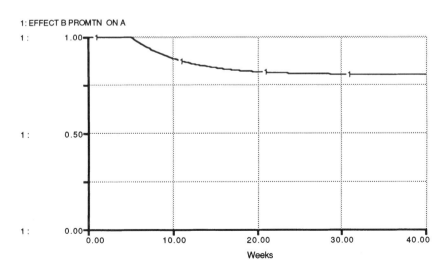

Figure 1-8. Promotion campaign scenario

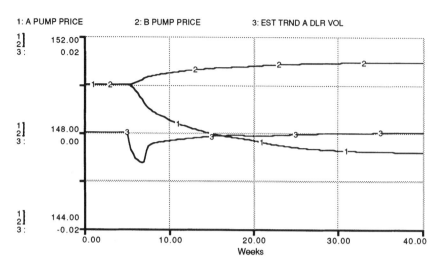

Figure 1-9. Behavior of pump prices

build up in the way assumed? If so, what will be the impact on A's pump price and market share?

Figure 1-9 shows that A's dealers reduce pump price in response to the sharp drop in volume (as shown by line 3 that represents the "estimated trend in A's dealer volume" EST TRND A DLR VOL). Price falls by about 2 percent from 150 to 147 cents per liter, quickly at first and then more gradually, as the price cuts stem further loss of volume. Suprisingly, the simulation suggests that B's pump prices rise slightly—a result that could prompt some discussion about the degree of internal coordination between pricing and promotion campaigns. (If dealers use price to control volume, then how do they factor-in the effect of a successful national promotion campaign? Is it possible that dealers' local pricing undermines national campaigns?)

Figure 1-10 shows that market share remains almost static in response to the combined effect of B's promotion campaign and A's volume induced cut in pump price. The simulation assumes that A and B start with equal market shares of 50 percent. When the promotion campaign is launched in week 5, B's market share begins to rise, but not for long, because A's low price wins back some customers from B. By week 40 the promotion campaign achieves only 2 percent extra share, even though the campaign is assumed to have the potential of increasing B's share by 10 percent (in the absence of pump price cuts by A).

Purely verbal argument gives limited opportunity for teams to consider the consequences of strategic actions and reactions. Words and opinions are fleeting

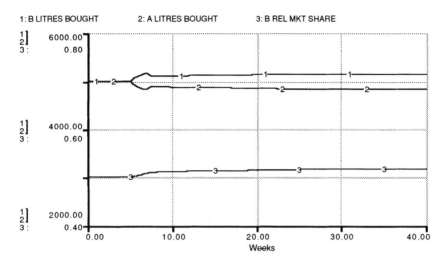

Figure 1-10. Market share

sounds captured selectively by listeners and inadequate as a focus for discussion. By contrast, simulations are much more tangible. They help people to visualize outcomes: to see how a campaign unfolds over time, to trace the movement of prices and market share. They encourage people to understand outcomes: to assess the buildup of a campaign and to explain the pricing actions and reactions of dealers. They help a team to build alternative time paths into the future and to share scenarios.

What skills are required to use system dynamics modeling in management teams? As with the value-chain there is a need for a facilitator who is familiar with the mapping symbols of system dynamics and with some of the behavioral decision theory that lies behind the diagram of the policy function. The role of the facilitator is to translate the operating knowledge of the management team into the labels and connections in the policy map and to be the architect of the model structure. There is also a need for a technically skilled modeling team to convert the policy maps into equations and then to design and conduct simulation experiments. Finally, the facilitator (who might be a member of the technical modeling team, and certainly needs to be "close" to the equations and model vocabulary) is needed to interpret the policy maps and simulations and draw the management team into debate and discussion of structure and scenarios. Just as with the value chain, facilitation skills and expert knowledge of theory and technique are needed to bring the framework constructively into a management team dialogue.

CURRENT RESEARCH THEMES

Once you accept the idea that models are instruments for management team discussion and learning then the scope of enquiry for modelers becomes very broad. You become interested in knowledge elicitation, mapping, the design of meetings, process facilitation, learning, the measurement of learning, and even software development. The articles in this volume are chosen to show readers a cross-section of topics that now interest a group of professional model builders. Almost all the authors have particular expertise in system dynamics modeling coupled to broader academic interests that span areas such as strategic management, group decision support, systems thinking, organizational behavior, behavioral decision theory, management science, and operational research.

The first four chapters (including this one) are all methodological papers about the process of model building. In "Model Building for Group Decision Support," Vennix et al. survey the literature of cognitive psychology and small group processes in search of guidelines for eliciting knowledge from groups. Is it best to develop a model with a team of managers or with individuals? How should one harness the expertise of a management team in the different phases of model building from conceptualization to mapping, equation writing, and simulation? The approach of most practitioners is quite informal and intuitive. Vennix et al. argue that questionnaires, individual interviews, and group workshops should all be used depending on the context—whether the conceptual task is brainstorming, exploring courses of action, or evaluating situations. In addition they argue that, in many modeling situations, the roles of modeler and meeting facilitator should be separated.

In "Policies, Decisions, and Information Sources for Modeling," Forrester reviews the foundations of system dynamics modeling. Using ideas that originated in *Industrial Dynamics* (Forrester 1961) he explains decisions and information feedback, multi-loop decision-making systems, and the nature of the decision process. His early ideas are as relevant today as when they were first written over thirty years ago. He shows how a graphical representation of decisionmaking, action, and information flow can serve as an intermediate step between the knowledge-rich mental models of a management team and an algebraic simulation model. Modern graphical modeling packages capitalize on this strength—seeing relationships is important (Richmond and Peterson 1990). He also comments on the mental data base as a rich source of descriptive information for model building, arguing that the breadth and relevance of this store of mental information far exceeds that of written and numerical sources of information on which much computer modeling still relies.

"Modeling as Learning" by Lane gives a view from inside Shell International Petroleum Company of the experience of introducing interactive modeling to management teams. At the time of writing, the author was working in Shell's internal business consultancy division, leading a variety of successful modeling projects.

He describes a shift in modeling style away from traditional expert consultancy toward modeling as learning. Under the new style, modeling is an integral part of management discussion, consultants provide tools that capture and express the mental models of clients, soft issues are considered, and the models are owned, run, and interpreted by the clients. The paper comments on the goals and benefits of modeling as learning and includes a brief survey of projects.

The next four chapters all come under the heading "Feedback Modeling in Action" and cover in-depth case studies of the model-building process with particular emphasis on representation, conceptualization, elicitation, group processes, and team involvement. "Knowledge Elicitation in Conceptual Model Building" by Vennix and Gubbels covers the very early stage of model conceptualization, when one is seeking agreement on structural links, labels, and vocabulary. The particular case is the Dutch Health Care System. The authors describe how a preliminary Health Care model arose from brainstorming by a small project team comprising two health care planners and two experienced system dynamics modelers. They then go on to describe how a large group of sixty health care professionals were able to participate in model development through creative use of questionnaires, workbooks, and workshops. These varied exercises are called a "policy Delphi." The preliminary model/policy Delphi approach is particularly interesting because it puts basic conceptualization in the control of a small group, yet encourages "ownership" by a large group by inviting them to challenge assumptions and propose modifications. In addition, the policy Delphi matches the various tasks in model building with individual and group work.

"Modeling the Oil Producers" by Morecroft and van der Heijden reports a modeling project with a team of senior managers and planners from Shell. It traces model conceptualization from discussion to algebra. The chapter focuses particular attention on the use of the behavioral decision function as a graphical aid to activate and capture the knowledge of the team. All system dynamics modelers are faced with the challenging task of converting fleeting ideas culled in a meeting into a specific feedback representation, and ultimately algebra. Here the approach of the modeler/facilitator is to shape the discussion by having the team identify major categories of oil producers and then think about the logic of their production decisions. Decision functions drawn on flipcharts stimulate team discussion of factors such as oil quotas, reserve costs, investment criteria, cartel structure, quota allocation—factors about which the team members are knowledgeable. The flipchart drawings activate knowledge but also collect the knowledge in a form that is compatible with a feedback representation.

"A Systematic Approach to Model Creation" by Wolstenholme presents a step-by-step approach to the difficult task of model conceptualization. Here is another procedure to classify and organize the wide range of information from a typical management team meeting. The modeler collects fragments of structure that, to begin with, are just lists of key resources, states, and resource flows. Lists are a good way to capture managers' categories and concepts. These particular lists also generate the raw material for an influence diagram. Wolstenholme's approach gently shapes a discussion first into a list and then into a diagram that eventually shows feedback loops, delays, and organizational boundaries. He illustrates the approach with a model of a fledgling software company specializing in expert systems.

The three examples up to this point deal principally with conceptualization, the process of mapping mental models, and activating team knowledge. In the next chapter, "Systems Thinking and Organizational Learning," Senge and Sterman argue that effective learning processes involve three stages: mapping mental models, challenging mental models to reveal inconsistencies, and finally improving mental models. Management teams must be involved in all three. Mapping by itself generates ownership of the assumptions included in the model. Simulation provides the inference engine to deduce the consequences of the assumptions and thereby challenge mental models. The authors illustrate their arguments about model supported learning with a case study of claims management in a leading American property and liability insurance company. They describe how a small team of modelers and senior managers used STELLA to map the assumptions of current strategy. They then describe the design of a "learning laboratory," a three-day computer workshop, intended to communicate insights from the model to company managers. The approach has some similarities to Vennix's preliminary model and policy Delphi. What is distinctive is the use of a gaming-simulator to package and disseminate systems thinking insights.

Part 3 of the book includes three chapters that deal with the topic of learning from modeling and simulation. I have argued earlier in this article that learning takes place when there are changes in people's mental models. But how do you know whether a computer model is the agent of change? How would you measure the impact that a model or gaming-simulator had on someone's understanding of a business situation? How does model-supported learning compare with more conventional approaches to learning such as the case method used widely in business schools? Are there limits to model-supported learning that come from the way current practitioners build and use their models? The measurement and evaluation of learning is difficult. The three papers describe some of the significant progress that is now being made.

"Model-Supported Case Studies for Management Education" by Graham et al. reports recent developments in combining computer simulation models with conventional case studies to create learning environments for management education. The case method has the advantage of confronting students with real-life detail. Different types of information are mixed together (numbers, descriptions, anecdotes, figures, etc.). The case teacher offers frameworks that guide class discussion and help students organize case information and form opinions. But case studies provide limited opportunities for testing the effects of alternative courses of action. Using the People Express Airlines case and the Intecom telecommunications equipment case, the authors demonstrate how modeling and simulation can be integrated into case teaching. The mapping symbols of system dynamics (feedback loops and policy maps) can be used as a qualitative framework to guide discussion of complex business situations and to identify the physical, organizational, and decisionmaking structure of systems. Gaming-simulators can be used by students in workshops to infer correctly the dynamics of a given structure. The authors conclude with some comments on evaluating the effectiveness of model-supported cases.

"Experimentation in Learning Organizations" by Bakken, Gould, and Kim describes three different experiments to evaluate the learning of groups using models and gaming simulators. The interesting feature of this work is the authors' ability to make inferences about participants' learning when using a gaming simulator. A simulator is a rich laboratory for studying decisionmaking and mental models. It stores a record of participants' decisions and the performance that results. Comparisons of one simulation to another (between groups or across time) can reveal marked differences in performance which the experimenter can trace to people's reasoning and mental models. Obviously, careful design of the gaming protocol is called for, but the paper illustrates the potential for controlled experimentation. The authors use three gaming-simulators representing quite different business situations: the People Express Management Flight Simulator, the Claims Learning Laboratory from the insurance industry, and an oil tanker market simulator. In each case there is a description of the gaming protocol, participants' preparation, workshop design, and briefing materials. The authors draw conclusions about the transfer of learning and changes of mental models in each situation.

"Overcoming Limits to Learning" by Isaacs and Senge strikes a cautionary note on the limits to computer-based learning. Using the theoretical perspective of Action Science developed by Argyris and Schön, the authors comment on individual, group, and organizational counter pressures to learning that can undermine the benefits of modeling and gaming simulation. It is easy enough for modelers to become fascinated with representation schemes, software, the mental models of clients, and cognitive imperfections in dynamic decisionmaking, yet lose sight of individual and group behavior on which models depend for both ideas and legitimacy. Individuals can react adversely to computer-based learning environments by adopting a video-game mentality, treating the computer as an oracle, or using model-based results selectively to reinforce prior views. The authors trace these reactions to individuals' natural learning processes. Groups pose other problems. When team members use a model or gaming simulator they may feel threatened and react defensively by undermining the model's credibility or, worse still, by passively accepting model conclusions without revealing or changing their own assumptions. The authors examine these issues and many others in an attempt to understand how computer-based learning environments interact with the existing "natural" learning systems of individuals and groups. The paper ends with some guidelines for the design of learning environments and suggestions for further research.

The final part of the book contains a collection of short articles on software design. Software has always been important in system dynamics, but in recent years the pace of software development has increased dramatically. What is interesting to note is the different emphasis that developers give to mapping, graphics, documentation, simulation diagnostics, and gaming capabilities. Several developers have written about their software design philosophy and their views on where software tools are likely to move in the future. The articles are written in noncommercial style that allows readers to appreciate broad design principles, architecture, and trends in modeling software. However, to avoid abstract description, they include material that is quite specific about the software and its uses, and that conveys to readers the look and feel of each package.

The final chapter, "Hexagons for Systems Thinking," by Hodgson, is about software, but it is also about representation. The kind of model you build, the knowledge you activate and capture, and the style of group process you can employ all depend on the representation scheme (symbols and media) you use. I have made this point already with the contrast of the value chain and the policy function as mapping symbols. Hodgson's article reinforces the point and stimulates new thinking on representation by presenting a graphical and qualitative modeling approach that is quite different from system dynamics, and deliberately chosen for that reason. Hexagon modeling uses brightly colored hexagons to capture and organize ideas from a management team. As statements come out in conversation, a facilitator captures each distinct idea as a summary headline on a magnetic-backed hexagon which can be placed, initially at random, on a large steel whiteboard. (Alternatively you can work on a computer with screen hexagons.) Ideas can be color coded. They can be moved around, reorganized, and clustered to build a shared map of the team's concerns. The author describes the process in detail and reflects on the value of the approach for stimulating creative thinking and group problem solving. I hope that readers will compare and contrast this approach to more structured modeling approaches. Can methods like this be used for conceptualizing feedback structure? Can other modeling methods stimulate similar creative thinking about business issues and problems?

CONCLUSION

The nature of modeling is changing. The technical barriers that used to prevent people getting their ideas on and off the computer are rapidly crumbling. Simulation models that once appeared on computer screens as sinister skeletons of algebra are now fleshed out with text and clothed in color graphics. Executives who once shied away from computers now attend modeling courses. Managers who have never before built a model enthusiastically spend a day or more with a gaming-simulator to think about business strategy (Sterman 1989; Pugh-Roberts Associates 1988).

In this climate of change, model builders are rethinking their approach to modeling. There is a broader view of what models can do for management teams: They can activate knowledge, focus discussion, challenge mental models, and aid learning. Managers help to build models, so it is important to think about facilitation and groups. Managers work with the computer, so it is important to think about workshop design, gaming protocols, and the learning process. The collection of articles cited in this volume show the scope and diversity of current work. There are some fascinating research challenges. The reward is a powerful union of practical executive knowledge, theory, process, and technology to guide strategic change and accelerate organizational learning.

REFERENCES

Birnbaum-More, P.H., and A.R. Weiss (1990), "Discovering the Basis of Competition in 12 Industries: Computerized Content Analysis of Interview Data from the U.S. and Europe," in A.S. Huff, ed., *Mapping Strategic Thought*, Chichester, U.K.: Wiley, 53-69.

Checkland, P. (1989), "Soft Systems Methodology," in J. Rosenhead, ed., *Rational Analysis for a Problematic World*, Chichester, U.K.: Wiley, 71-100.

Eden, C. (1989), "Using Cognitive Mapping for Strategic Options Development," in J. Rosenhead, ed., *Rational Analysis for a Problematic World*, Chichester, U.K.: Wiley, 21-42.

Eden, C. (1990), "Managing the Environment as a Means to Managing Complexity," in C. Eden and J. Radford, eds., *Tackling Strategic Problems: The Role of Group Decision Support*, London: Sage.

Fiol, C. Marlene (1990), "Explaining Strategic Alliances in the Chemical Industry," in A.S. Huff, ed., *Mapping Strategic Thought*, Chichester, U.K.: Wiley, 227-49

Forrester, Jay W. (1961), *Industrial Dynamics*, Portland, Ore.: Productivity Press.

Forrester, Jay W. (1980), Information Sources for Modeling the National Economy, *Journal of the American Statistical Association* 75, no. 371: 555-74.

de Geus, Arie P. (1988), "Planning as Learning," *Harvard Business Review*, March-April, 70-74.

Hambrick, D.C. (1982), "Environmental Scanning and Organizational Strategy," *Strategic Management Journal* 3: 159-74.

Hax, A.C., and N.S. Majluf (1991), *Strategic Management: An Integrative Perspective*, Englewood Cliffs, N.J.: Prentice-Hall.

Hodgkinson, G. P., and G. Johnson (1994), "Exploring the Mental Models of Competitive Strategists: The Case for a Processual Approach," *Journal of Management Studies* (forthcoming).

Huff, Anne S., ed. (1990), *Mapping Strategic Thought*, Chichester, U.K.: Wiley.

Huff, Anne S. (1982), "Industry Influence on Strategy Reformulation," *Strategic Management Journal* 3: 119-31.

Johnson-Laird, P.N. (1987), *Mental Models*, Cambridge: Cambridge University Press.

Kraemer, K.L., and J.L. King (1988), "Computer-Based Systems for Cooperative Work and Group Decisionmaking," *ACM Computing Surveys* 20, no. 2: 115-46.

Minsky, Marvin (1986), *The Society of Mind*, New York : Simon and Schuster.

Morecroft, John D.W. (1988), "System Dynamics and Microworlds for Policymakers," *European Journal of Operational Research* 35, no. 3: 301-20.

Morecroft, John D.W. (1985), "Rationality in the Analysis of Behavioral Simulation Models," *Management Science* 31, no. 7: 900-16.

Narayanan V.K., and Liam Fahey (1990), "Evolution of Revealed Causal Maps During Decline," in A.S. Huff, ed., *Mapping Strategic Thought*, Chichester, U.K.: Wiley, 109-33.

Norman, Donald A. (1976), *Memory and Attention* (2d ed.), New York: Wiley.

Norman, Donald A. (1990), *The Design of Everyday Things*, New York: Doubleday Currency.

Papert, Seymour (1980), *Mindstorms*, New York: Basic Books.

Phillips, L.D. (1990), "Decision Analysis for Group Decision Support," in C. Eden and J. Radford, eds., *Tackling Strategic Problems: the Role of Group Decision Support*, London: Sage.

Porter, M.E. (1985), *Competitive Advantage*, New York: Free Press.

Prahalad, C.K., and R.A. Bettis (1986), "The Dominant Logic: A New Linkage Between Diversity and Performance," *Strategic Management Journal*, 7: 485-501.

Pugh-Roberts Associates (1988), *The Executive Training System*, Cambridge, Mass.: Pugh-Roberts Associates.

Pugh-Roberts Associates (1986), *Professional DYNAMO Introductory Guide and Tutorial,* and *Professional DYNAMO Reference Manual*, Cambridge, Mass.: Pugh-Roberts Associates.

Richmond, Barry M., and Steven Peterson (1990), *Ithink: The Visual Thinking Tool*, High Performance Systems, 45 Lyme Road, Ste. 300, Hanover NH 03755.

Richmond, Barry M., Peter Vescuso, and Steven Peterson (1987), *STELLA for Business*, High Performance Systems, 45 Lyme Road, Ste. 300, Hanover NH 03755.

Rosenhead, J., ed. (1989), *Rational Analysis for a Problematic World*, Chichester, U.K.: Wiley.

Simon, H.A. (1976), *Administrative Behavior* (3d ed.), New York: Free Press.

Sterman, J.D. (1987), "Testing Behavioral Simulation Models by Direct Experiment," *Management Science* 33, no. 12: 1572-1592.

Sterman, J.D. (1989), *The People Express Management Flight Simulator*, Cambridge: Sloan School of Management, MIT.

University of Virginia Case Services (1980), "The British Motorcycle Industry—Norton Villiers Triumph Ltd." (Case UVA M-2000), Charlottesville: University of Virginia.

Zajac, E.J., and M.H. Bazerman (1991), "Blind Spots in Industry and Competitor Analysis: Implications of Interfirm (Mis)Perceptions for Strategic Decisions," *Academy of Management Review* 16, no. 1: 37-56.

2

MODEL BUILDING FOR GROUP DECISION SUPPORT: ISSUES AND ALTERNATIVES IN KNOWLEDGE ELICITATION

JAC A.M. VENNIX, DAVID F. ANDERSEN,
GEORGE P. RICHARDSON, AND JOHN ROHRBAUGH

ABSTRACT: System dynamics models are often created using multiple streams of information including quantitative data, written records, and information contained in the mental models of both individuals and groups. While qualitative sources of information are widely recognized as important in all stages of the model-building process, little systematic research has been completed on how best to elicit and map this knowledge from groups of experts. In this article, we survey the existing literature on mapping and eliciting knowledge for system dynamics modeling and also explore the literature in the broader fields of cognitive psychology and small group processes. Special attention is paid to new software advances to support these processes. Two case studies illustrate how these knowledge-eliciting techniques can be used to support the construction of computer simulation models.

THE PROBLEM

The topic of Group Decision Support has grown rapidly in interest over the last decade. In the literature several types of Group Support Systems (Nunamaker et al., 1989) are discussed, varying from collaborative writing to computer supported negotiation to decision making (cf. Johansen 1988; Nunamaker 1989; Lee et al. 1988; Reagan-Cirincione and Rohrbaugh [1991]). In this article we will focus on building computer simulation models with client groups as an activity to support decision making in management teams. We take the system dynamics model-building approach as an example, since system dynamics modelers have done modeling with client groups for more than a decade (cf. Roberts 1977; Randers 1977; Stenberg, 1980; Weil 1980,1983; Richmond 1987).

System dynamics modelers typically rely on multiple, diverse streams of information to create and calibrate model structure. Such streams include quantitative data, written records, and information contained within the mental models of key actors in a system. Commonly, the techniques for drawing out germane and accurate information from these mental models are informal and highly intuitive. Accessing the most productive source of information for model building—the minds of experts and actors in the system—is largely an art. Rarely does the academic preparation of modelers include training or exposure to academic literature that helps to build formal skills in eliciting information for model building. But practitioners know that the arts of knowledge elicitation and mapping are subtle, and can be particularly complex when the modeling process calls for drawing information out of groups of people rather than individuals.

In other fields more or less related to modeling and decision support, there already exists considerable literature that casts light on the modeler's information-gathering task. And increasingly, a number of system dynamics practitioners have begun to explore variations on the intuitive model development process described in the literature (Randers 1977; Stenberg 1980; Weil 1980, 1983). This article explores these developments in an effort to push forward our understandings of productive processes for eliciting knowledge for the purpose of model building. We will focus on a number of important issues and present several alternatives involved in eliciting and mapping knowledge for model-building with management teams. After having discussed these issues, we will present two recent cases showing the state of the art in eliciting and mapping knowledge in system dynamics model building. As an organizing framework for our discussion we will first present the steps in the construction of a system dynamics model and show the various kinds of information needed to build a model.

THE MODEL-BUILDING PROCESS: TYPES OF TASKS TO BE SUPPORTED BY CLIENT GROUPS

Richardson and Pugh (1981) define seven stages in building a system dynamics model: problem identification and definition, system conceptualization, model formulation, analysis of model behavior, model evaluation, policy analysis, and model use or implementation. Roberts et al. (1983) use an almost identical set of six stages to organize their pedagogical approach. Table 2-1 summarizes the steps and stages in model-building.

As this table shows, the process of constructing a computer simulation model involves a wide variety of conceptual activities. These range from "brainstorming" variables to be included or excluded from the model's boundary, to determining specific parameter values, to identifying the important feedback loops within a system. Psychologists specializing in cognitive processes, however, have commonly distinguished between three general types of tasks: eliciting information, exploring courses of action, and evaluating situations (Hackman and Morris 1975; Morris 1966; Hackman 1968; Bourne and Battig 1966; Simon 1960). Different phases of the modeling process emphasize different combinations of these three types of psychological tasks. Hence, knowledge-eliciting approaches for one phase may not be appropriate for another.

Table 2-1. Stages and steps in model-building

Stage	Steps
Problem formulation	• define time horizon • identify reference modes • define level of aggregation • define system boundaries
Conceptualization	• establish relevant variables • determine important stocks and flows • map relationships between variables • identify feedback loops • generate dynamic hypotheses
Formulation	• develop mathematical equations • quantify model parameters
Analysis/evaluation	• check model for logical values • conduct sensitivity analyses • validate model
Policy analysis	• conduct policy experiments • evaluate policy experiments

Eliciting Information. The terms "brainstorming" or "divergent thinking" have often been applied to some conceptual behavior of this sort. In the system dynamics model-building process, this type of thinking is often most necessary in the problem definition or model conceptualization phases where an individual or a group is attempting to determine what factors or variables to include or exclude from a system's boundary, or in the model evaluation phase where the group is brainstorming how to design or evaluate a model's performance. In addition, this eliciting process may also be evoked during some phases of the model formulation process where several different formulations need to be considered.

There is considerable evidence that work on elicitation tasks in group settings should be performed by noninteracting, "nominal" groups, rather than with full discussion and exchange of ideas in an open forum (Lamm and Trommsdorf 1973). The quantity and diversity of ideas tend to be greater in nominal groups. The greater interplay of ideas that can occur in discussion groups appears to be outweighed by tendencies of interacting groups to inhibit divergent production.

Exploring Courses of Action.   Solutions to problems are discovered through devising, specifying, or following combinations of procedures that might achieve specific objectives. Problem solving within the context of the system dynamics modeling processes involves tasks such as specifying the feedback paths to be included within a model or devising a specific rate formulation.

Often referred to as a form of "convergent thinking," such group activity is thought to be at its best when organized and highly systematized. However, the paucity of rules specifying what constitutes key information or what is the essential information to be structured typically makes this type of a task most puzzling to organize for a group. Deep knowledge of the system being studied and the nature of the model-building task at hand is necessary to structure appropriate group activities. However, once the task has been structured we have found that a facilitator with generic group facilitation skills is often better at directing the group process than a skilled modeler. Most often, both roles are required to manage properly this class of cognitive tasks.

Evaluating Situations.   The most common modes of evaluation are judgment (assessing individuals, objects, or events one at a time on some scale) and choice (selecting one or more individuals, objects, or events from a set). In the process of building system dynamics models, evaluation includes tasks such as selecting parameters, assessing the validity of model output, assessing the performance of various policies, choosing between alternative structural formulations, or choosing which policies to investigate within the context of model simulations. In both judgment and choice, evaluation is based on the explicit and/or implicit use of one or more cues that inform the group in completing its task. Judgment and choice processes do not necessarily lead to the same conclusions, however. Preferences expressed in one mode may be reversed in the other (Lichtenstein and Slovic 1971, 1973). Hammond et al. (1977) and Rohrbaugh (1981) have proposed using specific techniques such as social judgment analysis to support evaluation tasks. Finally, as discussed in one of the cases below, multiattribute utility theory provides a framework for evaluating competing options, such as outcomes of policy simulations, on multiple criteria.

SOME BASIC RESULTS FROM GROUP PROCESS RESEARCH

While different types of cognitive processes are involved in various stages of the model-building process, Forrester (1980 and Chapter 3 of this work) has noted that a wide variety of sources of knowledge must be incorporated into the model-building process. These sources of knowledge range from quantitative data to written records to the mental models of both individuals and of groups. Our emphasis here is strictly on eliciting knowledge from groups. Richardson et al. (1989) have surveyed qualitative methods for dealing with written documents and individual interviews, questionnaires, and workbooks.

McGraw and Harbison-Briggs (1989) have demonstrated that the type of knowledge and the quality of judgments acquired from experts in a group setting differ from information obtained when they are questioned as individuals. Shaw (1932) found that one advantage of using groups was their ability to recognize and reject incorrect or impossible solutions and suggestions. Steiner (1972) has found that a group of experts may be better able to solve a problem that involves exploring courses of action than individuals working alone; improvement comes from subdividing the task into related tasks and matching the expertise of participants with a particular sub-task. Sniezek (1990) also points out that if group members share relevant information, groups are not superior to individuals.

The effectiveness of groups also seems to be correlated with group size, type of tasks, and structure of the group process. With larger groups, for instance, formal brainstorming techniques in nominal groups have been found to be superior to interacting groups (Lamm and Trommsdorf 1973). Communication among group members decreases as the size of the group increases. Slater (1958) has found that for tasks involving decisions based on evaluation of exchanged information, groups of five or fewer are most effective. Bouchard (1969, 1972) indicates that introducing structure in group sessions drastically improves group performance. Hart et al. (1985) also point out that without structuring of tasks and group processes, participants might become frustrated and group performance rapidly decreases. In addition, in freely interacting groups there is a tendency for strong personality types or high status persons to dominate discussions (Fox 1987). Freely interacting groups also tend to rapidly narrow their focus on a few approaches to the problem and to concentrate on evaluation of ideas. These common defects in group process can usually and easily be overcome by a skilled group facilitator, once again underscoring the need to add generic group facilitation skills to a strong modeling team.

Given what is stated above, it is useful to make a distinction between strongly or weakly structured group sessions or workshops for model building. Less structured group processes and discussions are the approaches used by most system dynamicists working in a consulting mode. Introduction of structure in group sessions can be related to two aspects: the tasks to be performed and the group process itself.

Structuring the tasks in model building can be accomplished either by breaking the modeling process into smaller sequential steps or by presenting the group with a preliminary model that can be discussed systematically one part at a time.

An example of breaking the model-building process into smaller sequential steps is Duke's technique for designing a gaming simulation. The process begins with a brainstorming session in which participants write down on small pieces of paper all kinds of concepts that come to mind when thinking about the policy problem under study. Duke (1981, 64) calls these little pieces of paper *snowcards.* The second step is to organize and classify these concepts into broader categories by removing duplicate concepts, merging similar concepts, and classifying groups of concepts. The third step involves constructing a diagram of system structure using these broad categories. Differing specific small group techniques are used to support each of these small steps within a structured group workshop.

Hart et al. (1985) and Vennix (1988) present examples of structured workshops using the preliminary model approach. In this approach the modeler first designs a preliminary model and then presents it to the client, who can criticize it extensively. The client is encouraged to redesign flawed or inadequate parts of the model. Skill and judgment need to be exercised when engaging in preliminary modeling work. Too much model development without client interaction can suppress the client group's ownership and creativity in the project.

Structuring of group sessions can also relate to the group process itself. For instance, to decrease the dominance of certain participants and to guarantee that all participants have an equal chance to put forward their ideas, one could divide the total group into smaller subgroups during the session. The ideas generated in the subgroups can be presented and discussed with other subgroups in a plenary session.

FACILITATOR VERSUS MODELER

Given that groups will almost always be a part of the model-building process, it is important to consider the issues involved in facilitating groups, a task which diverges considerably from building a system dynamics model. Recently, system dynamics modelers such as Richmond (1987) and Schuman and Richardson (1987) have begun to experiment with the reference group approach (cf. Randers 1977) by using new software products such as STELLA (Richmond, Peterson, and Vescuso 1988) to get groups of decision makers to interact more directly with a model's structure and output as the model is being developed. In his work, described in more detail below,

Richardson had considerable success in separating the role of the professional modeler, who sat in the back of the room and operated a STELLA-based model being projected for review by the group, from that of a professional group facilitator who managed the group. This group facilitator was familiar with system dynamics modeling but brought generic group facilitation skill rather than system dynamics modeling skill to the overall group process.

HARDWARE AND SOFTWARE SUPPORTS FOR KNOWLEDGE ELICITATION

Even as a large literature is beginning to emerge on how individuals and small groups approach problems and structure knowledge for problem solving, a variety of software packages exist for supporting individual or group brainstorming sessions. For example MAXTHINK (IBM compatible) or MORE (Macintosh) provide a set of flexible text processing and sorting utilities that can help both to elicit and organize verbal concepts. When projected in front of a small group, these software programs can be used to support group brainstorming, acting as a sort of infinitely flexible "electronic flipchart."

Shachter (1986) has developed DAVID, a modeling tool that helps to structure influence diagrams and representations of probabilistic and deterministic decisions. DAVID can be used as a software support in the conceptualization or problem definition phases of a modeling project where causal loops are being either generated or discussed by a group. DESIGN on the Macintosh can be used similarly. The potential of these software tools for model conceptualization in groups has, to our knowledge, not yet been tested.

Most system dynamics practitioners are by now familiar with STELLA as developed by Richmond et al. (1988). This very powerful model-building tool allows modelers to create models at a conceptual level very different from what had been previously possible using conventional simulation languages such as DYNAMO and DYSMAP. Using STELLA, analysts work with screen-oriented icons that allow them to construct system flowcharts interactively. While users respond to several prompts and queries at key decision points (usually rates and auxiliaries), the STELLA system writes equations in the background and can then execute a simulation. As the model is simulated, the software can animate on the computer screen the rise and fall of accumulations in the stock-and-flow diagram. Diehl (Chapter 15 of this work) and Richmond and Peterson (1989) have developed gaming interfaces for STELLA. Using these interfaces, modelers may create an animated game-like view of a simulation. Using these animations, users may interact directly with the simulation model, often without having to come to grips with or understand the structure of the system under study. Such a facile ability to interact with a model, of course, has both positive and negative implications.

Modern versions of DYNAMO contain front-end packages that allow users to interact more easily and directly with a simulation model once it has been created. Using a structured and menu-driven series of screens, users respond to a series of queries and the package creates a stream of commands, much like the traditional RERUN streams that create a new model run. Packages such as these are very useful for allowing users to interact with a model once it has been constructed. Expert modeling support is needed to construct the model and to program the front-end package.

The above software tools were designed primarily to support a single terminal or work station. It is important to note, however, that many of these software tools are being used with groups by having output projected for review and discussion by a group as a whole.

Recently, a number of sites have experimented with multiple, linked work stations or terminals designed to support knowledge elicitation. The two most well known are at the decision and planning laboratory at the University of Arizona and at Xerox PARC's COLAB. Arizona has a research facility for studying the impact of automated support for planning and decision making. It is used by executives, managers, and students for planning sessions and to address complex, unstructured decision processes. As described by Nunamaker, Applegate, and Konsynski (1988), the lab has been operational since March 1985 with state-of-the-art computer hardware and software. Two of their software tools are used to support the process of deliberation: electronic brainstorming and stakeholder identification and analysis. Electronic brainstorming permits participants to network using microcomputers to share comments and contributions with other participants. Comments from all participants are consolidated and an analysis support tool is used to identify common issues or categories. This computer-based technique is adapted from manual procedures developed in association with Strategic Assumptions Surfacing and Testing as reported in Mason and Mitroff (1981).

The use of dynamic interactive media at Xerox is part of COLAB. This computer lab's purpose is to increase the effectiveness of meetings and to provide a research environment to investigate the effects of computer tools on meetings. Stefik et al. (1987) report that within COLAB a variety of tools are available to provide participants with a coordinated interface, enabling them to interact cooperatively. COLAB tools support simultaneous action, allowing group members to work in parallel on shared objects. Conflicts (e.g., more than one member attempting to act on the same image) are handled by a busy signal. There are a variety of software tools to extend the uses of COLAB.

Both the Arizona and the Xerox labs can be seen as experimental mechanisms for eliciting the group knowledge useful in model building. However, their effectiveness in designing models is as yet to be assessed, since these facilities have never been used to support the construction of system dynamics models.

GUIDELINES FOR STRUCTURING THE KNOWLEDGE ELICITATION PROCESS

Given that such a wide variety of knowledge elicitation techniques and approaches exist, the key question becomes knowing how to approach the elicitation process and when to use which technique. We have identified five factors that help the modeler to select appropriate knowledge elicitation techniques: the phase in the model-building process and the type of task being performed, the number of persons involved in the process, the purpose of the modeling effort, the time available for participants, and finally the costs involved in using various techniques.

The recommendations that follow are still quite tentative. How to combine these five critical factors in selecting appropriate knowledge elicitation techniques remains more of an art than a science. However, the guidelines do suggest an important checklist of items that always deserve attention in client-oriented modeling.

Phase of the Modeling Process and Type of Task. The phase of the model-building effort interacts subtly with the type of cognitive task being undertaken in determining which type of knowledge elicitation techniques are most appropriate in a given specific situation. Hence in each phase of the modeling process various techniques might have to be employed in combination, depending on the type of task that has to be performed.

From a psychological point of view, eliciting, exploring, and evaluating tasks need to be approached very differently. As a general rule, the eliciting task, requiring divergent thinking, can best be performed by individuals alone or in nominal non-interacting groups. Performing these tasks in the context of well-structured group interactions will actually decrease the quality of group versus individual performance.

Evaluation tasks on the other hand can best be performed in structured group sessions. The literature on evaluation, whether it involves individual or group evaluation of options, events, or alternative formulations, is quite well-developed. Specific techniques such as the Delphi technique (Linstone and Turoff 1975), multiattribute utility theory (Edwards and Newman 1982), social judgment analysis (Hammond et al. 1975), and nominal group techniques (Huseman 1973) have well-developed theoretical underpinnings and have been well-explored in experimental settings.

The exploring (problem solving) task is both most central to the model-building process and least well-developed in the psychological literature. Some evidence suggests that well-trained or knowledgeable individuals can perform as well as or even better than groups. Simply put, a well-trained model builder can do as well as a group of model builders in tasks such as proposing formulations or designing feedback structures. Involving a group may have an apparent purpose of designing model structure, but have as a real purpose developing understanding of the system under study or of the model-building process (see section below on purpose of modeling effort). One way to improve the difficult exploring tasks involved in model-building is to include an experienced group facilitator with significant under-standing of model-building in the project team.

Purpose of the Modeling Effort. The process of eliciting and mapping knowl-edge to build system dynamics models is not a straightforward one. Rather it is iter-ative—through successive cycles of refinement the ultimate model gradually appears. So knowledge elicitation and mapping is not just simply a process of uncovering a fixed body of knowledge and representing it. Model building induces learning in participants as their mental models are reshaped by discussion and inter-action. This iterative view of the knowledge elicitation process has profound impli-cations for the methods and techniques to be used. In addition to written documents and individuals as a source of knowledge, modelers will have to employ methods that allow interaction and discussion in order to improve mental models and to clar-ify a problem. Hence, in modeling policy problems, groups as a source of knowl-edge will almost always have to be included in the modeling process.

Number of People. The number of people involved in the modeling project will dictate the appropriate knowledge elicitation techniques because of two factors. First, the smaller the number of people involved, the more unstructured the tech-niques may be. If a large number of people are involved (as in public policy model-ing), the approaches will have to be more structured to prevent discussions from getting out of hand. Second, as more people become involved in the modeling process, it becomes necessary to use labor-saving techniques such as question-naires, workbooks, and structured workshops (Vennix 1990). Structured workshops are especially valuable because they can be repeated several times and the results from several workshops accumulated over time.

Particularly with larger groups, the use of software support may allow the group to interact more effectively and may speed up the process of model-building.

Time Available for Participant Discussion. A simple but powerful criterion for determining which knowledge elicitation techniques to use is the amount of time the management team or reference group can spend on the task. The less time they have available for active participation in the modeling effort, the more the process will have to be carefully structured and prepared. For example, a group might begin with a preliminary model rather than attempt to develop a model from scratch.

A second critical factor centers on how far along the group is in its thinking about the problem. If they are just starting to address issues, then overstructuring the problem definition may be inappropriate. If the issues are complex, then diver-gent thinking will be best encouraged by a blend of approaches that ask individu-als to brainstorm in isolation, and then to share ideas and contemplate issues in group discussion.

Cost. Finally, the costs associated with the various techniques must be carefully factored into the selection of knowledge elicitation and mapping techniques. Costs include participant costs (usually in terms of time devoted to the modeling process) as well as the costs of time for the modeling team. Usually costs (both monetary and time costs) will be negotiated at the beginning of a project and the modeler's task will be to select the best techniques given cost constraints. Hence cost considerations are most important at the stage where a modeling contract or agreement is being designed.

Overall the conclusion must be that in such complex processes as eliciting knowledge in the model-building process, one cannot rely on the use of one single technique. Rather one will have to employ hybrid techniques (Nutt 1984), i.e., a useful combination of approaches and techniques that will support each of the tasks in each of the stages as optimally as possible.

In the next sections we will present a few examples showing the use of hybrid techniques for knowledge elicitation in model-building. The first example aims at eliciting knowledge for building a conceptual model of the Dutch Health Care system (cf. Vennix et al. 1988). The techniques used to elicit knowledge from relevant participants have been chosen in such a way that they carefully fit the various tasks and stages in eliciting the necessary knowledge. The second example is on model-building in medical malpractice insurance (Schuman and Richardson 1987; Richardson and Senge 1989). Here too, a combination of system dynamics modeling with formal multiattribute utility techniques (Edwards and Newman 1982; Gardiner and Ford 1980) was used to evaluate the effects of a variety of policy runs. Moreover, this case clearly shows the uses of software and the beneficial effects of separating the role of the facilitator and the modeler in working with groups.

EXAMPLE 1: MODELING DUTCH HEALTH CARE: THE POLICY DELPHI APPROACH

The model-building process of Dutch Health Care was conducted to provide more insight into the factors and processes underlying increasing health care costs (cf. Vennix et al. 1988).

The elicitation process is started by a project group that designs a preliminary model of the problem. Next a policy Delphi procedure (Linstone and Turoff 1975) is employed to have a number of experts (60) in the field comment on this preliminary model. The first Delphi cycle consists of a questionnaire, dealing with dyadic relationships in the model, i.e., relationships between two variables. The second cycle builds on the results of the first and takes the process one step further by having experts criticize more complex submodels. Here a so-called workbook is used to elicit knowledge from the expert group. The third cycle consists of a structured workshop, in which a number of experts can thoroughly discuss parts of the conceptual model. The first two Delphi cycles serve a focusing function: They eliminate those elements from the discussion on which there is a great deal of consensus in the expert panel. The sequential stages in the elicitation process are summarized in Figure 2-1.

The preliminary model was designed by the project group, consisting of two persons from the client organization and two system dynamics modelers. The model was based on available literature and insights within this group and was used as the basis for the Delphi cycles. A group of approximately 60 persons (e.g., general practitioners, scientific researchers, financial planners, hospital managers), of which 90 percent responded, was consulted in the first cycle.

The project group for the first cycle subdivided the questionnaire into a number of sections, each dealing with one of the important decisions in the health care system (e.g., prescriptions, consultations). These form the "dependent variable." In each section a number of statements were presented describing a relationship

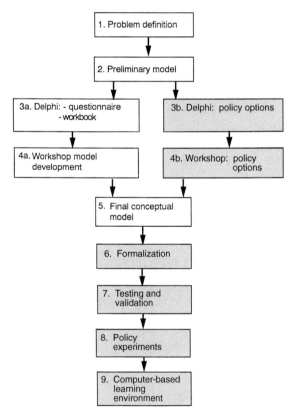

Figure 2-1. Phases in the model-building project

between this "dependent" variable and some independent variable. For instance, in the section "prescriptions by general practitioners" one of the statements is:

The heavier the workload of a general practitioner, the higher his number of prescriptions.

Participants were asked to state whether they "agreed fully," "agreed partially," or "disagreed fully" with the statement. However, the project group was primarily interested in uncovering causal arguments from the participants' mental models, particularly those which were not included in their preliminary model. To extract these causal arguments they asked the respondent after each statement to indicate why one did or did not agree with the statement. Content analysis with regard to the answers to the "why questions" revealed a number of interesting things, for instance, new concepts that might be included in a causal relationship, thereby clarifying it. Each section in the questionnaire, focusing on one "dependent" variable, thus contained a number of these statements together with "why questions." In addition, at the end of each section the respondent was asked to add variables, not yet mentioned, which they perceived to affect the dependent variable. Finally, in each section the respondent was asked to name the three independent variables that he considered to have the largest effect on the dependent variable.

In the second cycle of the Delphi, the project group switched to a workbook which was based on the results of the questionnaire. It enabled the respondent to focus on sets of interrelated variables instead of only dyadic relationships. Second, the workbook was also used as a means to prepare participants for the workshop. A subset of 18 respondents was selected from the 60 respondents who participated in the first cycle.

The workbook contained four submodels. These submodels were designed by the project group, based on the preliminary model and the results of the questionnaire. The submodels were gradually introduced into the workbook using causal diagrams as an aid for the participant. At regular intervals the respondent was asked to comment on the arguments in the workbooks and to indicate in the final diagram of the submodel which parts one did not agree with by circling these parts. The completed workbooks were sent to the project group one week before the workshop. The final step in this approach involved two structured four-hour workshops (with nine participants each) in which participants discussed the submodels in more depth. The entire session was broken down in four stages: introduction (one-half hour), subgroup activities (one hour), plenary session (1 ½ hours), and finally evaluation (one-half hour).

A few aids were used to structure the discussions in the subgroups. First of all, each member of the group was assigned a role. For instance, one person took notes and presented the results in the plenary session, while another person was responsible for time management. Second, diagrams were copied from the workbook and group members used different colors to indicate which person had commented on what parts of the submodel in his workbook. The colored parts of the submodels had to be discussed first during the subgroup meeting. Participants were asked to make changes in the diagrams according to the results of their discussions. To accomplish this task, they were provided with the relevant diagram of the workbook, which was put on the table in the subgroup room. During the discussions they employed this diagram as a kind of scrap paper to make changes according to their discussions, by removing or adding variables and/or relationships between variables.

After having completed their discussions, one person was responsible for integrating the final changes into a large diagram, hanging on the wall in the subgroup room. This large diagram was then put on the wall in the plenary session room to assist the discussion during the plenary session. On the basis of this diagram the spokesperson of a subgroup was given ten minutes to explain the results of the discussions and the changes made in the submodel by the group. During the next twenty minutes the other subgroups were permitted to ask questions and comment on the results. The same procedure was used in discussing the results of the activities in the other two subgroups. The total time for plenary discussion was thus 1 ½ hours. Participants in both the small groups and the plenary sessions were quite involved and there seemed to be consensus on a number of issues.

EXAMPLE 2: THE MEDICAL MALPRACTICE INSURANCE DECISION CONFERENCES

The New York State study began in the fall of 1987 at the request of the State Insurance Department. The Department, headed by the state insurance commissioner appointed by the governor, has overall responsibility for the proper functioning of insurance programs operating in the state. Actuaries in the department check that rate increases requested by insurers are justified, and they monitor the financial health of insurance companies. Both of these duties are intended to serve the public interest: If rates are excessive then the public overpays, and if rates are too low and companies move toward insolvency then the public will not get what it has paid for—insured parties will not be covered and victims will not receive just compensation.

Legislation passed in 1985 regulating doctors' premiums for medical malpractice insurance was due to expire in April 1988. The Legislature asked the State Insurance Department to provide advice to avert an impending crisis. Before the 1985 legislation, premium increases on the order of 40 to 50 percent demanded by the insurance companies were so large that doctors threatened to cut back services. Some mothers-to-be found it almost impossible to find an obstetrician willing to care for them. The crisis was averted when the legislature passed a bill limiting increases in doctors' premiums to 14 percent the first year and 9 percent for each of the next two years. Recognizing that such low increases would not match the increasing costs of the insurance companies, the Legislature also decreed that no insurer would be declared insolvent and be barred from selling malpractice insurance in the state during these years. Indeed, such a provision was necessary: By the Insurance Department's later reckoning, the five New York State medical malpractice insurers were statistically insolvent by 1986 with assets below projected liabilities by more than $2 billion.

Now that the three years were up, the Legislature wanted a more permanent solution. The State Insurance Company contracted with members of the faculty of the Rockefeller College to run three decision conferences designed to develop consensus within the department about more than 40 policy options they were considering. To provide decision support, the Rockefeller College team decided to include the development of a system dynamics model to project the implications of various policy options.

A model reference group was formed (Stenberg 1980) and met three times over a six-week period to discuss model structure and the focus of the modeling effort. The group consisted of actuaries and analysts in the Insurance Department and an outside consultant, and included all of the people who would be involved in writing the final report to the Legislature, under the signature of the Commissioner. In the most productive of these reference group meetings, the roles of group facilitator and model-builder were separated, enabling the modeler to concentrate solely on gathering, interpreting, and reflecting back information for the model-building process.

The decision conferences were designed to evaluate a maze of more than 40 policy options that the Department, its consultants, and the Legislature wanted to consider. The conferences were facilitated by professionals in group process and decision support from the Rockefeller College, and were computer-aided by the use of system dynamics simulations and multiattribute utility analyses projected for all to see and reflect upon.

The initial list of policy options given by the Insurance Department served to focus the modeling effort; the data for reference modes for the dynamic model came part way through the modeling effort. Because of the time constraints leading to the first decision conference at which the system dynamics model would be used, the model was developed to address a small subset of the policy options facing the State Insurance Department. The model (Schuman and Richardson 1987; Richardson and Senge 1989) consisted of about 300 active equations (22 levels).

The initial policy options being considered emphasized financial solutions, so the model was more detailed on the financial side and had only a rudimentary treatment of the processes underlying the dramatic growth in settlement awards. It was, in fact, an outcome of the fall decision conferences that policies that ignore the growth in awards would work only in the short run, if they worked at all. Confidence in the model in the decision conferences was the result of confidence in the model reference group that contributed to its formulation, the close dynamic fit between the model and historical time series, and the fact that participants could give real-system explanations for model behavior in the policy simulations shown.

The most important simulation shown in the first decision conference, at least in terms of its effect on the thinking of the group, was a simulated test of switching the malpractice insurance system to a pay-as-we-go system. The idea was seductively attractive: In the current scheme, the system operates as a true insurance system, in which a stock of assets is required to cover the stock of projected liabilities. In a pay-as-we-go system, the stock of assets would only be required to cover the flow of payments over some number of years (as with social security in the United States). Switching to pay-as-we-go for the malpractice insurance system would immediately and dramatically drop the asset requirement for insurers and cure the insolvency problem. In addition it would allow doctors' premiums on the average to drop significantly. It looked like a win-win policy.

The simulation shown to the group altered that perception. In the simulation, beginning in 1988 the system switched to a policy of assets required to cover a year's flow of malpractice payments, and the requirements of insurance companies were given much greater weight in the premium-setting process. The result is immediate solvency for insurers, which lasts beyond the year 2000 but turns into insolvency and then bankruptcy within five more years. Doctors' premiums actually decrease and stay below their 1987 levels until 1992. The system is still driven, however, by 20 percent annual growth in settlement awards. Trying to come closer to the premiums required to keep insurers solvent results in faster premium growth: The average doctor premium actually exceeds the base run value by 1995. Pressures to hold down the increases accumulate and finally can not be ignored. The system collapses about the same time as it did in the base run.

Seeing that the policy gains only about eight years of premium relief, and hearing the explanations of that result from the actuaries around the table at the decision conference, the state insurance commissioner ruled out the pay-as-we-go policy option. It was not discussed again and was dismissed in the policy recommendations sent on to the Legislature (NYSID 1988, 163-71).

To focus the decision group on the dynamics of their detailed policy options, participants were given graphs of the six time series from 1975 to 1986 and asked to complete them to 2015 for every policy option they considered. Those graphs and the increasingly sophisticated mental models of the participants formed the basis for the detailed multiattribute utility analyses that structured the group's evaluation of policy options. In the multiattribute utility evaluations, the group identified six constituencies and generated more than 40 criteria those constituencies would use to evaluate policy options. Most of the discussion in the decision conferences focused on generating policy options and evaluating them in detail on these criteria. The simulation model was revised as necessary during the conferences and used at the close of each conference to test the favorite policy mix.

One month before their April 1988 report was due, the Insurance Department held a final decision conference to check their recommendations in a structured setting. A revised simulation model was used to predict aggregate impacts of three policy sets, one developed by the Department and two others developed by outside consultants. The policy recommendations were extremely detailed and complex, and the model was able to represent them only approximately. The simulations suggested that only the Department's own proposals were adequate to prevent the insolvency from getting worse. The day-long discussions and policy evaluations, again primarily aided by multiattribute utility analyses, reinforced the Department's thinking and convinced them to go ahead with their proposals to the Legislature.

The Department's subsequent report to the New York State Legislature was a book of more than 240 pages describing the problem and its history, why action was necessary as soon as possible, what options were available and what outcomes they were likely to produce, and an outline of the processes the Department went through to produce its recommendations. The Department's preferred policy option package contained 29 detailed proposals in four categories: Ways to decrease malpractice, Spreading the costs of the system across a wider base, Tort changes, and Procedural changes. The proposals reflected the Department's thinking about the political acceptability of the total package as well as the efficacy of its elements.

Faced with time running out on the 1985 legislation, the complexity of the problem and the recommendations, the observation that none of the insurers were in danger of immediate bankruptcy, and the possibility that further research might suggest a better solution, the legislature passed continuing legislation that simply extended the 1985 law another three years. This potentially disappointing result was probably appropriate: Much work remained to be done to develop deep understandings about the systemic causes of the problems and to identify focused, high-leverage policy options that should be adopted.

SUMMARY AND CONCLUSIONS

A rich body of theoretical and experimental work already exists on how to elicit and map qualitative knowledge that resides in the mental models of individuals and groups. An interesting array of software products is beginning to emerge to support such model-building exercises. Finally, several interesting experiments such as the COLAB at Xerox and the Group Decision Support Laboratory at the University of Arizona are attempting to provide more advanced computer-based support to knowledge elicitation and mapping processes, especially the thorny problems associated with exploring courses of action and problem solving.

Increasingly, this body of research is being integrated into system dynamics practice. A number of researchers have come to realize that the careful structuring of group process to match the type of cognitive task facing the group can greatly enhance the productivity of the group. And since various stages of the model-building process involve quite different psychological processes, various researchers have begun to conclude that group techniques appropriate for one phase of model building and knowledge elicitation may not be appropriate for another phase. We have presented a number of heuristics and rules of thumb for diagnosing which type of group process might be best suited to which model-building task.

However, knowledge elicitation to support model building is still much more of an art than a science. While isolated pockets of best practice have emerged guided by good modeling intuition, these results are not generalizing to the model-building community as a whole. It seems clear that those who write about the system dynamics modeling process are not paying close attention to developments in other fields that hold great promise for improved system dynamics practice. Similarly, those most experienced in the art of modeling appear not to have the time or inclination to write down the lessons that they have learned from years of practice working on knowledge elicitation and mapping.

As a result, the critical phases of problem definition and model conceptualization appear to be arrested at the point where they remain true art forms. Simply put, systematic research is not being conducted that will advance our understanding of how modelers and management teams or reference groups do or ought to interact in the model-building process. This lack is all the more disturbing because psychologists, ethnographers, management scientists, and software engineers working in fields closely related to system dynamics are making progress in precisely these fields. The field of system dynamics needs to begin the work of formulating rigorous research programs that get at general rules helping to make more precise and less artful the process of eliciting and mapping knowledge.

REFERENCES

Bouchard, T. (1969), "Personality, Problem Solving Procedure and Performance in Small Groups," *Journal of Applied Psychology* 53: 1-29.

Bouchard, T. (1972), "A Comparison of Two Group Brainstorming Procedures," *Journal of Applied Psychology* 56: 418-21.

Bourne, L.E., and W.F. Battig (1966), "Complex Processes," in J.B. Sidowski, ed., *Experimental Methods and Instrumentation in Psychology,* New York: McGraw-Hill.

DESIGN. Meta Software, 150 Cambridge Park Drive, Cambridge, MA 02140. Reviewed in *Mac User,* April 1988.

Duke, Richard D. (1981), "A Paradigm for Game Design," in C.S. Greenblat and R.D. Duke, *Principles and Practices of Gaming-Simulation,* Beverly Hills: Sage.

Edwards, W., and J. Robert Newman (1982), *Multi-Attribute Evaluation,* Beverly Hills: Sage.

Forrester, Jay W. (1980), "Information Sources for Modeling the National Economy," *Journal of the American Statistical Association* 75, no. 371: 555-74.

Fox, William M. (1987), *Effective Group Problem Solving,* San Francisco: Jossey-Bass.

Gardiner, P.C., and A. Ford (1980), "Which Policy Run Is Best and Who Says So," *TIMS Studies in the Management Sciences* 14: 241-57 (System Dynamics).

Hackman, J.R. (1968), "Effects of Task Characteristics on Group Products," *Journal of Experimental Social Psychology* 4: 162-87.

Hackman, J.R., and C.G. Morris (1975), "Group Tasks, Group Interaction Process, and Group Performance Effectiveness: A Review and Proposed Integration," in L. Berkowitz, ed., *Advances in Experimental Social Psychology* (Vol. 8), New York: Academic Press.

Hammond, K.R., T.R. Stewart, B. Brehmer, and D.O. Steinmann (1975), "Social Judgment Theory," in M.F. Kaplan and S. Schwartz, eds., *Human Judgment and Decision Processes,* New York: Academic Press.

Hammond, K.R., J. Rohrbaugh, J.L. Mumpower, and L. Adelman (1977), "Social Judgment Theory: Applications in Policy Formation," in M.F. Kaplan and S. Schwartz, eds., *Human Judgment and Decision Processes in Applied Settings,* New York: Academic Press.

Hart, S., M. Boroush, G. Enk, and W. Hornick (1985), "Managing Complexity Through Consensus Mapping: Technology for the Structuring of Group Decisions," *Academy of Management Review* 10, no. 3: 587-600.

Huseman, R. (1973), "The Role of Nominal Groups in Small Group Communication," in R.C. Huseman, D.M. Logue, and D.L. Freshley, eds., *Readings in Interpersonal and Organizational Communication* (2d ed.), Boston: Hollbrook.

Johansen, R. (1988), *Groupware: Computer Support for Business Teams,* New York/London: Free Press.

Lamm, H., and G. Trommsdorf (1973), "Group Versus Individual Performance on Tasks Requiring Ideational Proficiency (Brainstorming): A Review," *European Journal of Social Psychology* 3: 361-88.

Lee, R.M., A.M. McCosh, and P. Migliarese (1988), *Organizational Decision Support Systems,* Amsterdam/New York: North-Holland.

Lichtenstein, S., and P. Slovic (1971), "Reversals of Preference Between Bids and Choices in Gambling Decisions," *Journal of Experimental Psychology* 89: 46-55.

Lichtenstein, S., and P. Slovic (1973), "Response-Induced Reversals of Preference in Gambling: An Extended Replication in Las Vegas," *Journal of Experimental Psychology* 101:16-20.

Linstone, H., and M. Turoff (1975), *The Delphi Method: Techniques and Applications,* Reading, Mass.: Addison-Wesley.

Mason, R., and I. Mitroff (1981), *Challenging Strategic Planning Assumptions,* New York: John Wiley and Sons.

McGraw, K.L, and K. Harbison-Briggs (1989), *Knowledge Acquisition: Principles and Guidelines,* Englewood Cliffs, N.J.: Prentice-Hall.

Morris, C.G. (1966), "Task Effects on Group Interaction," *Journal of Personality and Social Psychology* 4: 545-54.

Nunamaker, J.F., L.M. Applegate, and B.R. Konsynski (1988), "Computer-Aided Deliberation: Model Management and Group Decision Support," *Operations Research* 36, no. 6 (Nov.- Dec.): 826-48.

Nunamaker, J.F. (1989) "Experience with and Future Challenges in GDSS, preface," *Decision Support Systems* 5: 115-18

Nunamaker, J., D. Vogel, and B. Konsynski (1989), "Interaction of Task and Technology to Support Large Groups," *Decision Support Systems* 5: 139-52.

Nutt, P.C. (1984), *Planning Methods, for Health and Related Organizations,* New York: John Wiley.

NYSID (1988), "A Balanced Prescription for Change: Report of the New York State Insurance Department on Medical Malpractice." State of New York Insurance Department, 160 West Broadway, New York, New York 10013.

Randers, Jørgen (1977), *The Potential in Simulation of Macro Social Processes, or How to Be a Useful Builder of Simulation Models,* Oslo: Gruppen for Ressursstudier.

Reagan-Circione, P., and J. Rohrbaugh (1991), "Decision Conferencing: A Unique Approach to the Behavioral Aggregation of Expert Judgment," in G. Wright and F. Bolger, eds., *Expertise and Decision Support,* New York: Plenum.

Richardson, George, and Alexander Pugh (1981), *Introduction to System Dynamics Modeling with DYNAMO,* Portland, Ore.: Productivity Press.

Richardson, G.P., and P.M. Senge (1989), "Corporate and Statewide Perspectives on the Liability Insurance Crisis," in P.M. Milling, E.O.K. Zahn, eds., *Computer-Based Management of Complex Systems. Proceedings of the 1989 International Conference of the System Dynamics Society,* Berlin: Springer-Verlag, 442-57.

Richardson, George P., J.A.M. Vennix, D.F. Andersen, J. Rohrbaugh, and W.A. Wallace (1989), "Eliciting Group Knowledge for Model Building," in P.M. Milling and E.O.K. Zahn, eds., *Computer-Based Management of Complex Systems: Proceedings of the 1989 International Conference of the System Dynamics Society,* Berlin: Springer-Verlag, 343-57.

Richmond, Barry, (1987), *The Strategic Forum,* High Performance Systems, 45 Lyme Road, Ste. 300, Hanover NH 03755.

Richmond, Barry, S. Peterson, and P. Vescuso (1988), *Academic User's Guide to STELLA*, High Performance Systems, 45 Lyme Road, Ste. 300, Hanover NH 03755.

Richmond, Barry, and S. Peterson (1989), *STELLAStack*, High Performance Systems, 45 Lyme Road, Ste. 300, Hanover NH 03755.

Roberts, Edward B. (1977), "Strategies for Effective Implementation of Complex Corporate Models," *Interfaces* 7, no. 5 (November 1977).

Roberts, Nancy, David Andersen, Ralph Deal, Michael Garet, and William Shaffer (1983), *Introduction to Computer Simulation: A System Dynamics Modeling Approach,* Portland, Ore.: Productivity Press.

Rohrbaugh, John (1981), "Improving the Quality of Group Judgment: Social Judgment Analysis and the Nominal Group Technique," *Organizational Behavior and Human Performance* 28: 272-88.

Schuman S., and G.P. Richardson (1987), "Medical Malpractice Insurance: Policy Implications and Evaluations," *New York State Insurance Department Policy Development Conferences: vols. I (Conference Results) & II (Technical Appendices),* Decision Techtronics Group, Rockefeller Institute of Government, 411 State Street, Albany, New York 12203.

Shachter, R.D. (1986), "DAVID: Influence Diagram Processing System for the Macintosh," Working Paper, Department of Engineering-Economic Systems, Stanford University, Palo Alto, Calif.

Shaw, M. (1932), "A Comparison of Individuals and Small Groups in the Rational Solution of Complex Problems," *American Journal of Psychology* 44: 491-504.

Simon, H.A. (1960), *The New Science of Management Decision,* New York: Harper and Row.

Slater, P. (1958), "Contrasting Correlates of Group Size," *Sociometry* 25: 129-39.

Sniezek, J.A. (1990), "A Comparison of Techniques for Judgmental Forecasting by Groups with Common Information," *Group & Organization Studies* 15, no. 1: 5-19.

Stefik, M., G. Foster, D. Bobrow, K. Kahn, S. Lanning, and L. Suchman (1987), "Beyond the Chalkboard: Computer Support for Collaboration and Problem Solving in Meetings," *Communications of the ACM* 30, no. 1: 32-47.

Steiner, I. (1972), *Group Process and Productivity,* New York: Academic Press.

Stenberg L. (1980), "A Modeling Procedure for Public Policy," In J. Randers, *Elements of the System Dynamics Method*, Portland, Ore.: Productivity Press, 290-312.

Vennix, J.A.M., J.W. Gubbels, D. Post, and H.J. Poppen (1988), "A Structured Approach to Knowledge Acquisition in Model Development," in *Proceedings of the 1988 International Conference of the System Dynamics Society* (La Jolla, Calif.), Cambridge, Mass.: The System Dynamics Society.

Vennix, J.A.M. (1990), "Mental Models and Computer Models: Design and Evaluation of a Computer-Based Learning Environment," Ph.D. dissertation, University of Nijmegen.

Weil, Henry B. (1980), "The Evolution of an Approach for Achieving Implemented Results from System Dynamics Projects," In J. Randers, *Elements of the System Dynamics Method,* Portland, Ore.: Productivity Press, 269-89.

Weil, Henry B. (1983), "The Dynamics of Strategy Implementation," *Dynamica* 9, no. 1 (summer): 43-47.

3

POLICIES, DECISIONS, AND INFORMATION SOURCES FOR MODELING

JAY W. FORRESTER

ABSTRACT: A simulation model is based on explicit statements of policies (or rules) that govern decision making in accordance with conditions that may arise within the system being modeled. The decision-making process consists of three parts — the formulation of a set of concepts indicating the conditions that are desired, the observation of what appears to be the actual conditions, and the generation of corrective action to bring apparent conditions toward desired conditions. The model should generate "true" conditions of underlying variables but, in general, these true conditions are not available to people in real systems and should likewise not be used directly for decision making in a model. Distorted and delayed information about actual conditions forms the basis for creating the values of desired and also of apparent conditions. Corrective action will in turn be delayed and distorted by the system before influencing actual and then apparent conditions. In modeling business and economic behavior, and in representing policies and decision making, all kinds of information should be used, not merely numerical data. Rich stores of information about governing policies and economic structure are available from mental data bases built up from experience and observation.*

*This paper is based on Chapter 10 of *Industrial Dynamics* (Forrester 1961). The text of the original chapter has been revised, and new sections of text have been adapted from two previously published articles: Forrester (1980a), "Information Sources for Modeling the National Economy" and Forrester (1980b), "System Dynamics—Future Opportunities." I am indebted to Professors John Morecroft and John Sterman for assistance in developing this paper.

THE FEEDBACK VIEW OF MANAGEMENT AND POLICY

Management is the process of converting information into action. This conversion process we call decision making. Decision making is controlled by various explicit and implicit policies through which available information is interpreted.

As used here, a "policy" is a *rule* that states how day-by-day operating decisions are made. "Decisions" are actions taken at any particular time and result from applying policy rules to particular conditions that prevail at the moment.

If management is the process of converting information into action, then management success depends primarily on what information is chosen and how the conversion is executed. The difference between a good manager and a poor manager lies at this point between information and action. Every person has available a large number of information sources. But each selects and uses only a small fraction of all available information. Even then, we make only incomplete and erratic use of that selected information.

A manager sets the stage for action by choosing which information sources to take seriously and which to ignore. A manager's success depends on both selecting the most relevant information and on using that information effectively. How quickly or slowly is information converted to action? What is the relative weight given to different information sources in light of the desired objectives? How are these desired objectives created from available information?

In system dynamics models we look upon managers as information converters to whom information flows and from whom come streams of decisions that control actions within an organization (Simon 1976). Much human behavior might be properly viewed as the conversion of information into physical action. A manager, however, is not paid a premium salary in recognition of physical effort exerted but instead for converting information into decisions at control points in an organization. A manager receives incoming information flows and combines these into streams of managerial instructions.

Viewing a manager as an information converter shows immediately why we are interested in decision making and information flows. An industrial organization is a complex interlocking network of information channels. Information channels emerge at various points to control physical processes such as hiring of employees, building of factories, and production of goods. Every action point in a system is controlled by a local decision point that depends on information sources in other parts of the organization and the surrounding environment (Cyert and March 1963).

Figure 3-1 shows a decision stream in the simplest framework of an information-feedback system. Information is the input to a decision-making point that controls action yielding new information. The diagram shows the fundamental structural relationship. In each box there are delays. Information about actions is not immediately available. Decisions do not respond instantaneously to available information. Time is required for executing actions indicated by decision streams. Likewise, each box contains amplification which I use here in all of its positive, negative, and nonlinear senses. In other words, the output of a box may be either greater or less than is seemingly indicated by the inputs. Likewise, the output may be noisy or distorted. Amplification, attenuation, and distortion at each point in a system can make the system more sensitive to certain kinds of disturbing influences than to others.

An industrial system is not a simple information-feedback loop as shown in Figure 3-1. Instead, it is a complex multiple-loop and interconnected system, as implied by Figure 3-2 (Beer 1981; Deutsch 1963; Richardson 1991). Decisions are made at multiple points throughout a system. Each resulting action generates information that may be used at several but not at all decision points. This structure of cascaded and interconnected information-feedback loops, when taken together, describes an industrial system. Within a company, decision points extend from the shipping room and the stock clerk to the board of directors. In a national economy, the control loops extend from aggregate decisions of consumers about purchasing automobiles to the discount rate of the Federal Reserve Board.

Figure 3-1.   Decisions and information feedback

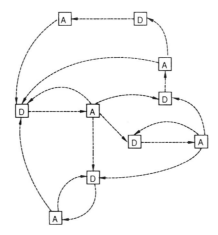

Figure 3-2.   Multi-loop decision-making system

Feedback loops form the central structures that control change in all systems (Richardson 1991; Senge 1990). Likewise, feedback loops are the organizing structure around which system dynamics models are constructed. Although "feedback" has become a word in the public vocabulary, there is little appreciation of its full significance. Most discussion, whether in cocktail parties or corporate board meetings, is organized as in Figure 3-3. A problem is perceived, an action is proposed, a result is expected. But the result often does not occur. The reason lies in the more realistic structure of Figure 3-4, as extended to more complexity in Figure 3-5. Symptom, action, and solution are not isolated in a linear cause-to-effect relationship, but exist in a nest of circular and interlocking structures. In such structures an action can induce not only correction but also fluctuation, counterpressures, and even accentuation of the very forces that produced the original symptoms of distress. All change takes place within the control of feedback loops. Growth, decline, goal-seeking, and oscillation are a consequence of feedback loop dynamics.

NATURE OF THE DECISION PROCESS

We now examine in finer detail the decision process whereby information is converted to action. Figure 3-6 shows a system structure surrounding a decision point. A decision is based on the state of the system, which is here shown by the condition of various levels. Some levels describe the present instantaneous condition of the system and others the presumed knowledge about the system. A level may be an inventory, number of employees, average sales for last month, accomplishment assumed to date in a research project, degree of optimism about the economic future, size of a bank balance, and so forth. These are the inputs to decisions. The output from a decision point controls the rate at which some system level will change.

I am using "decision" here in a very broad sense. Decisions control filling of orders from an existing inventory, placing purchase orders for new replacement goods, authorizing factory construction, hiring research scientists, and budgeting advertising expenditure. But "decisions" also control natural and physical processes like deterioration of equipment, transit of goods through a transportation system, and internal subconscious processes that maintain life. In other words, decisions control all processes of change.

An important concept in this organizational structure specifies the directional relationship between parts shown in Figure 3-6. Levels are the inputs to the flow of decisions. Decisions control flow rates to and from levels. The flow rates cause changes in levels. But flow rates themselves are not inputs to the decisions. Instantaneous present rates of flow are in general unmeasurable and unknown and cannot affect present instantaneous decision making. Only rates resulting from decisions change levels. Only levels control decisions and rates of flow.

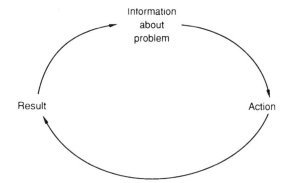

Figure 3-3.   Open-ended perception of decision making

Figure 3-4.   Basic loop structure within which all policies exist

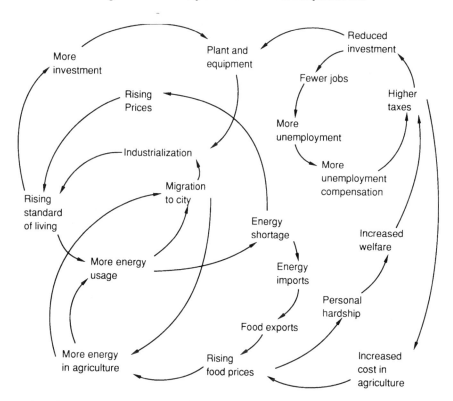

Figure 3-5.   Interconnected loops produce growth, instability, and goal-seeking as policies interact

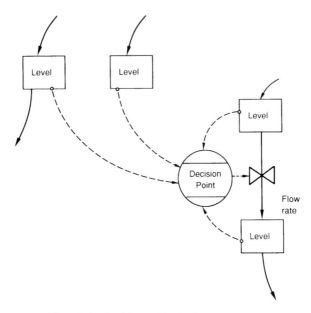

Figure 3-6.   Decision making in the system structure

In an industrial organization a particular person may be responsible for controlling only one flow rate, as for example the replacement orders for the maintenance of an inventory. On the other hand, a particular person may embody several separate decision points controlling several separate flow rates. If so, we should look upon these separate roles as lying within different parts of the information and action network in a system. A system dynamics model represents the decision-making structure, not the structure as seen on a personnel organization chart.

Finer detail in a decision process appears in Figure 3-7. Decisions involve three components. First is creation of a concept of a *desired* state of affairs. What do we want the condition of the system to be? What are we striving for? What are the goals and objectives at this particular decision point? Second is the *apparent* state of *actual* conditions. In other words, available information leads to observations that are believed to represent the present state of a system. These apparent conditions may be either close to or far removed from the actual present state, depending on the information flows that are being used and the amount of time lag and distortion in links from information sources. The third part of a decision process is generation of decisions to control *action* that will be taken in accordance with any discrepancy between the apparent and the desired conditions.

In general, the greater the discrepancy between apparent and desired conditions, the greater the resulting action, although the entire process of forming a concept of desired conditions, detecting actual conditions, and creating from these a course of

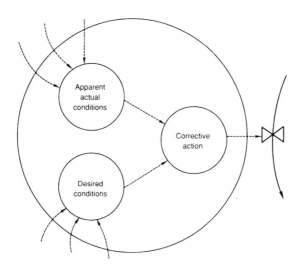

Figure 3-7. The decision process

action is highly nonlinear and noisy. Small discrepancies between apparent and desired conditions may seem of no consequence and create less than proportional action. A mounting discrepancy may lead to rapidly escalating attempts to correct actual conditions toward desired conditions. However, a sufficiently high level of discrepancy can be reached where the maximum possible corrective action is already being exerted, and beyond that point further widening of the gap between desired and actual system states will no longer cause proportionate changes in flow rates.

Decision making is presented here as a continuous process. Decision making is a conversion mechanism for changing continuously varying flows of information into control signals that determine rates of flow in a system. Decision points are continually responding to pressures from the environment to take advantage of new developments as they occur. Decision streams are always adjusting to the state of affairs. Decisions are always attempting to adjust actual conditions toward desired goals. The amount of action depends on the discrepancy between goals and observed system status.

We are here viewing decision processes from a very particular distance. We are not close enough to be concerned with the mechanisms of human thought. We are not even close enough to see each separate decision, but instead observe a modulated stream of decisions. We may not be close enough to care whether one person or a group action creates the decision stream. On the other hand, we are not so far away as to be unaware of the decision point and its place in the system. Choosing the proper distance and perspective from which to view and to model a system is important. We are not as close as a psychologist delving into the nature and sources of cognition, personality, and motivation. On the other hand, we are not as remote as a public stockholder who is so far from the corporation as to be unaware of the internal structure, social pressures, and decision points.

Our viewpoint is more like that of the managerial superior of a particular person who is charged with certain responsibilities. The superior is close enough to know how desired goals are established and is in a position to observe and probably provide the information sources to be used by the subordinate to determine assumptions about actual conditions. The superior knows in general the guiding policies and the manner in which the subordinate decision maker would respond to various kinds of circumstances.

POLICY

So, the focus is on policies. The word "policy" is used here as a broad term to describe how decision processes convert information into action. What actions will result from certain information inputs? What conversion process lies between information sources and a resulting decision stream?

We first define policy and later consider whether or not such policies exist and whether or not their forms can be determined.

A policy is a formal statement giving the relationship between information inputs and resulting decision flows. Policies are often referred to in the literature as decision rules. In physical systems, particularly in the field of servomechanisms, the corresponding term is "transfer function." A transfer function tells how outputs of a particular box depend on its inputs. A transfer function need not deal with the particular physical way whereby the conversion is accomplished, if the transfer function adequately describes the action resulting from present and past inputs to the box.

Much management and social science literature deals with what is here called policy. How will individuals and groups respond to various circumstances and pressures? If conditions change in a certain direction, what will be the direction of the response? In industrial organizations, some policies are very formal and reduced to writing for the guidance of subordinates. But most guiding policies are informal, although fully as influential. Informal policy results from habit, conformity, social pressures, ingrained concepts of goals, awareness of power centers within the organization, and personal interest.

Decision making might be divided into two levels of abstraction. At the first level are unrationalized intuitive reactions, which in fact result from the available flows of information but where there is no comprehension by the participant about the structure and the basis for actions. This first level represents the actions of lower animals where there are reasons for their actions, but without their being aware of a logical process determining action. At the second level of abstraction lies an awareness of the formal reasons for decisions. Not only are decisions made, but people have self-awareness of reasons for decisions, and are able to anticipate with some reliability the kinds of reactions that others will exhibit in response to changes in their environments.

Awareness of the formal bases for decisions, which I am here calling the guiding policies, certainly goes back as far as the written record of civilization. Humans are most conspicuously separated from lower animals by self-awareness of reasons for action. In other words, history and literature discuss the reasons, or policies, that cause human decision makers to react in certain ways. When we discuss reasons for action, we are describing policies whereby information is converted to action.

DETECTING GUIDING POLICIES

Now consider whether or not one can hope to detect the nature of guiding policies with sufficient accuracy to understand better the behavior of industrial and social systems. Clearly, people are of two minds on this question. Most literature on decision making implies great difficulty and subtlety. Social scientists make simple experiments with individuals or small groups, in an effort to determine how decisions are made. On understanding the human decision-making processes, social scientists will often assert that not even a good beginning has yet been made. Yet historians, novelists, managers, and all of us in our everyday lives are much bolder. We readily discuss why "so-and-so" acted in a particular way, by which we are discussing guiding policy and how a person did or should have responded to available information.

The dichotomy in views about detecting policies is illustrated by encounters with two different colleagues. One flatly stated that it was impossible to introduce actions of the Federal Reserve Board into a formal model of national economic behavior because we do not know the process by which such decisions are reached. He reasoned that such decisions are subtle, subjective, intuitive decisions for which we cannot know the guiding policy. The other incident took place in a doctoral oral examination. Another colleague, as a routine matter, casually asked the candidate to describe the factors that would lead the Federal Reserve Board to make adjustments in various directions in its discount rate and open-market policies. In other words, the doctoral candidate was expected to know the essential nature of the policy that would guide the stream of Federal Reserve Board decisions. To be sure, there may be a high noise content that can cause timing variations and uncertainty in the extent of a response. However, the broad underlying outlines of guiding policy were expected to be within the understanding and comprehension of a student.

Contradictory opinions about decision making are similar to differences in thinking about the process of invention. There is argument and little agreement about how invention and research results are achieved. Yet almost complete agreement acknowledges that more intelligent and experienced people, greater expenditure, more motivation, and higher need for results will all enhance the probability of a successful outcome. This agreement on the nature of the conversion function that couples financial and manpower inputs to scientific output is the basis for congressional action and military department appropriations.

In short, civilization is founded not only on the presumption that a basis exists for the guidance of human action but also on the conviction that we know a great deal about the specific nature and extent of guiding policies.

Many people believe that a sharp break exists between automatic decisions that are completely formal, like computing a payroll, and other levels of management decisions. Such persons reject any possibility of defining formal policies to describe major aspects of management. There is a revealing contradiction in the attitudes of many managers toward the formal basis for decisions.

Any manager must of necessity admit the existence of the region of automatic accounting decisions, because these are common practice. The majority of managers argue that their intuitive-judgment decisions are so subtle that they cannot be captured in formal decision rules.

Yet those same managers, when faced with decisions lying beyond the capabilities of their intuitive judgment, fall back on formal decision-making procedures. I here refer to the whole field of sales, market, and economic forecasting when done on the basis of statistical analysis of past data. Forecasting is essentially a decision-making process. It consists of converting past and presently available information into results that indicate a course of action. I am not a supporter of the wisdom and validity of the majority of forecasting procedures, but simply point out the contradiction in attitudes.

There are those who relegate simple decisions to automatic procedures and rely on formal statistical decision procedures with respect to the most subtle and difficult decisions, but reserve the middle ground as a region for judgment, which they assert is untouchable by formal decision rules.

There is now ample evidence that this middle region of decision making is not as obscure as has so often been pictured (Forrester 1975b). People are not good calculators of the dynamic behavior of complicated systems. The number of variables they can in fact properly relate to one another is very limited. The intuitive judgment of even a skilled investigator is quite unreliable in anticipating the dynamic behavior of a simple information-feedback system of perhaps five or six variables. Such failure to anticipate behavior is true even when the complete structure and all parameters of a system are fully known (Sterman 1989a; Sterman 1989b; Sterman 1989c). The mental models used to explain behavior of industrial and economic systems usually do not rank in complexity beyond a fourth-order differential equation. People think they give consideration to a much larger number of variables, but I doubt that these are properly related to one another in groups larger than a few at a time. In dealing with the dynamics of information-feedback systems, humans are not subtle and powerful problem solvers (Simon 1976).

Many reasons have delayed fully effective use of policies in simulation models. These confusions might be classified into three categories.

The first category of confusion about decision-making policies relates to the matter of perspective, or viewing distance mentioned earlier. Social scientists have tended to look at individuals with emphasis on psychology and motivation. Many laboratory experiments, done with small groups in artificial environments for brief periods of time, lack the strong social and organizational forces of precedent, conformity, incentives, goals, and pressures to behave as a superior might wish. Studies of individuals, especially over short periods of time in artificial environments, have tended to accentuate the belief that decisions are capricious, infrequent, disconnected, and isolated. Such studies in the past have not been organized within feedback structures that cause past decisions to exert influence on current decisions (Hogarth 1987). More recent work has included feedback dynamics in laboratory decision-making experiments (Brehmer 1989; Kleinmuntz 1985; Sterman 1989b).

At the other extreme, economists have viewed corporations from too great a distance. An entrepreneur is seen as a person who maximizes profit, without asking whether or not there is available information and mental computing capacity to find a maximum. Such viewing from too great a distance tends to over-stress the importance of top management decisions compared to those made in lower and middle levels of a corporation. A directive from top management does not change the prejudices, habits, and self-interest objectives of middle-level decision makers. For example, the public press has well documented the futility felt by successive Secretaries of Defense who have tried to change the character, attitudes, and practices of military departments. It is a slow process. Various "upheaval" incidents are misleading. A proxy fight followed by a complete change of top management and the firing of half of the middle-management structure will indeed change attitudes and traditions of an organization. But such drastic surgery is not common.

To understand a corporate information-feedback system, one should look neither at isolated individuals nor at the exterior of a system. It is from the intermediate viewpoint of seeing individuals and groups in their working environments that we can capture the true character of a business operation.

The second category of confusion about decision-making policies has arisen from assuming the process is more subtle and skillful than it actually is. Consideration of decision making has been too heavily influenced by the long and difficult history of trying to make computers play chess as well as a grand master. Chess is not a relevant example. In chess, full and exact information is available. Chess requires visualizing spatial relationships, which a person does well but machines do poorly. There are other situations, such as generating scenarios of business performance, where a computer can determine in seconds what the consequences of a set of policies will be and for which people could argue inconclusively for days about what follows from a given set of assumptions.

In a dynamic information-feedback system, human decision makers have access to much less than the total existing information. Furthermore, much less than the information available is actually being used. In general, actions arising from any given decision point will usually be conditioned by less than ten information inputs. What a person does with these few information sources is apt to be rather stereotyped. System dynamics accepts the "bounded rationality" interpretation of policy in which decisions are based on limited information and action is directed toward local goals (Morecroft 1983; Simon 1979; Simon 1982).

Some information inputs are used to create a concept of desired objectives, others serve to form impressions of the true state of affairs. From the difference between desired and observed conditions, reasonably straightforward and obvious actions will result. But what seems obvious may not be best. Some of the biggest improvements in social systems come from policies opposite to those that traditions and folklore indicate. Understanding of the dynamics of complicated information-feedback systems is so inadequate that intuitive judgment should not be trusted to reveal even whether improvement or degradation will result from a given direction of policy change (Forrester 1969).

The third category of confusion about decision-making policies arises from skipping the second level in the hierarchy of decision-making abstraction mentioned above. At the first level, actions are rational but there is no self-awareness of what the governing policies might be. At the second level, people throughout recorded history have described policies, that is reasons, for individual decisions. Such discussion of reasons for action is already a major step toward the ability to formulate explicit, quantitative, policy-governed decisions. At this second level, art and intuitive judgment are applied to development of a better understanding of policy rather than to day-by-day making of decisions.

Art, judgment, and intuition at this second level are no longer applied to individual separate decisions but to the definition of policies to govern streams of decisions. This process of looking at a social system and seeing governing policies rather than individual decisions is the level of abstraction most relevant to model building. Numerous successes have been achieved, but there is not general agreement on method. There is not yet an adequate literature on what constitutes the practice of identifying decision-making policy.

In spite of shortcomings in the art that exists at the policy-detection level, some social scientists are skipping to a still higher level in the hierarchy of abstraction. They are attempting to develop formal methods to be routinely applied to extract governing policies from quantitative data gathered from a system. Here intuitive art and judgment are applied to setting up rigid rules whereby the formal decision policies can be derived. I feel we are not yet ready for this last level of abstraction until we have demonstrated teachable methods for applying art and intuition to the extraction of decision policies themselves. After detection of policies is well understood, it may then be possible to reduce the process to a rigid and orderly procedure. We should move through the levels of abstraction one at a time. At each level, art and judgment are devoted to establishing the rules whereby the lower levels can be automatized.

An example of moving to successively higher levels of a conceptual hierarchy is found in the history of computer programming. In the 1950s one wrote specific machine code for solving a particular problem. The second level of abstraction was to write a program of logical instructions to tell the machine how to create its own running program for a specific problem. The hierarchy of abstraction in computer programming is now much deeper. At the next level, people develop concepts that allow computers to formulate specific statements of problems, which another computer program converts into machine language. This is similar to the above hierarchy of rules related to decision making.

To deal with the dynamic characteristics of social systems, we must represent the essential policy skeleton governing decisions. Such requires an approximate controlling policy at each significant decision point in a system. This understanding of policy can be accomplished if:

We have the proper concept of what a decision is and of the difference between policies and decisions.

We use the proper structure relating system states to the policies that govern actions.

We realize that the self-correcting behavior of feedback loops removes the need for high accuracy in describing policies.

We use to best advantage the extensive body of operating experience in people's heads wherein lies most of the available information about system structure and policies.

We realize that a formal quantitative statement of policy carries no implication regarding absolute accuracy. We can make a formal quantitative statement corresponding to any statement that can be made in descriptive English. Lack of accuracy does not prevent quantifying ideas about policies. Assigning a number does not alter the accuracy of the original statement, but it does create a much more explicit basis for communication. The common belief that one cannot quantify decision rules because of lack of accuracy is confusing accuracy and precision. One can precisely make an inaccurate statement. We can quantify regardless of accuracy. After achieving precision of statement and communication, one can then deal with the question of what is sufficient accuracy.

All these steps have been repeatedly demonstrated. We now have many examples of policy structures applied to industrial, social, and economic systems (Forrester 1961; Forrester 1969; Forrester 1971b; Meadows 1970; E. Roberts 1964; E. Roberts 1978).[1]

Policies in a company or an economy encompass much more than formal policies set down in executive memoranda or in national laws. "Effective policy" is the

---

[1] See also issues of the *System Dynamics Review.*

framework for reaching decisions. Policies are established by sources of available information, success measures and rewards, mores of the society, and prejudices and habits impressed by past experience. When decisions are examined in the light of such a broad framework, they emerge as far more predictable than are usually supposed. Even for a particular individual, one can assume a certain degree of consistency and can meaningfully discuss probable effects of various pressures. For a class of persons in similar environments, the likely average response to changes in surrounding forces can be observed with even higher confidence.

A principal use of a dynamic model is to study the influence of alternative policies on system behavior. In formulating a model, we must extend the concept of policy beyond its usual meaning. All decisions in a model come under the complete control of policies. Policies control flows at all points in a system. We are forced to explore policies in depth to see how decisions are generated from the various circumstances that can arise. The concept of policies governing decisions goes well beyond that of human, managerial decisions. A model must also make "decisions" that are of a physical nature—for example, the number of unfilled orders that can be filled depending on the state of inventories.

OVERT AND IMPLICIT DECISIONS

It is sometimes helpful to divide decisions and their governing policies into two categories, depending on whether they represent ordinarily conscious, "free" human decisions or whether they arise inexorably from the physical condition of a system. The dividing line is not sharp. *Overt decisions* are here defined as the conscious decisions by people as part of management and economic processes. Overt decisions include executive decisions and consumer purchase decisions. *Implicit decisions* are the unavoidable result of the state of a system. Included here are usually (1) present ability to deliver, depending on the present state of inventories, (2) the output rate (goods delivered) from a transportation system, resulting from the input rates, the goods in transit, and the transport delays, and (3) taxes due as a result of profits. Also, "decision" processes in biology and nature are implicit and result from the system feedbacks without overt human intervention.

Factory production serves to emphasize the distinction between overt and implicit decisions. Actual, present production rate is usually the result of an *implicit* decision function that shows how production rate is a consequence of employment, available equipment, and materials. It is not usually an overt decision; it is not possible to decide arbitrarily on a production rate and thereby have that rate exist immediately and with certainty. The accompanying *overt* managerial decisions are the decisions to *attempt* to hire people and to *order* equipment and materials. Whether or not people are in fact hired as a result of an overt decision depends on the implicit decision functions within the "physical" state of the system which recognize such factors as the supply of workers, the wages being offered, and attractiveness of the job. Whether or not materials and equipment result from orders depends on the available supplies.

Overt and implicit decisions are not handled differently in a model, but thinking of them separately helps to avoid omission of important steps in the flows of information and the resulting decisions and actions. Including both overt and implicit decisions makes it possible, in the model, to deal with the *wish* as well as the *actuality.* Conditions lead to a *desire* for a change; the desire interacts with the state and resources of the system to determine what, if anything, is to happen.

Introducing the concepts of both overt and implicit decisions is one step in eliminating the necessity for simultaneous equations that arise in some models, such as in making production decisions continuously equal to consumption decisions. Production and consumption decisions are actually made separately and independently and are eventually coupled through inventories, prices, and various information flows. The overt decisions to *want* or to *attempt* are a result of *information* available to the decision maker. The implicit decisions, which create the actions, recognize the existing true state of the system as well as the desires.

INPUTS TO POLICIES

In formulating policies (the rate equations in a model), decisions must be generated only from variables that would actually be available at the decision point. In general, information available for overt decisions is not identical to actual variables represented by the information. The information may be late, biased, and noisy. Here again, a distinction between implicit and overt decisions may arise. Overt decisions are usually based on information (which may be perturbed) *about* the primary variables. The more mechanistic implicit decisions control routine flows that depend on actual system states and therefore on true values of the variables in a model.

The distinction between the *true* value of a variable and the value of information *about* the variable can be illustrated by an inventory. Ability to deliver an item from an inventory, being dependent on whether or not the item is present, can usually be thought of as an implicit decision controlled by the actual, present, true state of inventory. This present, true inventory should be one of the variables in a model. The overt policy that controls reordering of material for inventory may depend on *information about* the inventory, such information being subject to delay and inaccuracy. What the inventory is *believed* to be may, in some models for some purposes, need to be included separately as a second and different variable. In addition, "desired inventory," which is different from either true or presumed inventory, would become a third variable with a still different value relating to the same inventory.

As a second example, a model of an economic system would continuously generate actual, instantaneous, gross national production rate; but this rate should not be available as an input to any overt decisions (such as planning plant expansions). The information about actual conditions in a model should be delayed and should have various kinds of errors introduced to represent the real-life processes of gathering and interpreting information.

A model, like the real world, must often generate both "true" values of variables and also associated corrupted values that are available for decision making.

DETERMINING THE FORM OF A POLICY STATEMENT

A model for simulating dynamic system behavior requires formal policy descriptions to specify how decisions are to be made. Flows of information are continuously converted into decisions and action. No plea about the inadequacy of our understanding of the decision-making processes can excuse us from estimating decision-making criteria. To omit a decision point is to deny its presence—a mistake of far greater magnitude than any errors in our best estimate of the process.

Can estimated decision functions be good enough to be useful? In general, it appears that they can be. Perceptive observation, searching discussions with persons making the decisions, study of already existing data, and examination of specific examples of decisions and actions all illuminate factors that influence decisions. In considering a factor influencing a decision, we progress through four states:

- What factors are significant enough to include?

- What is the direction of effect?

- What is the magnitude of effect?

- What nonlinearities should be recognized?

Inputs to Include

In deciding how to formulate a particular decision function (policy) in a model, the first step is to list those inputs that are important influences on the decision. The answer may be obscure. What at first may appear to be a most significant factor will sometimes be found to have little influence on model behavior or on the actual system. A factor that is ordinarily overlooked in everyday management practice may turn out to hold the key to important characteristics of the total system.

Choosing factors that affect a decision must depend on characteristics of the encompassing information-feedback system. No one has reliable intuitive judgment about such systems. Working with system models helps develop insights about closed-loop behavior. The decisive test for significance of an input to a policy in a model is to observe model performance with and without the input. In this way the model itself can be used to help determine what it should contain.

The degree of influence of an input on a decision is not the only consideration. We must also consider the degree of repercussion of the decision back onto the input entering into a decision, and the timing of such feedback. Relatively slight influences on decisions can be important in "positive feedback" conditions, where the input influences a decision and the decision affects the input to create still more change in the decision. Such amplification is found in many places. For example, when customers order further ahead in response to increasing delay in delivery of goods, the increased ordering rate increases the backlog of unfilled orders; in turn, the rising backlog means that each new order is delayed even more than those before it, and the increasing delay leads to still more advance ordering (Forrester 1961, chs. 17 and 18).[2]

Direction of Effect

There will usually be little doubt about the direction in which a decision will be influenced by changes in a particular input. However, we must be alert to represent properly the "worse-before-better" sequences that often arise. The short-term and long-term influences on a decision by a particular input are often in opposite directions, and the dynamic behavior of a model can be seriously affected if only the long-range effects are included.

Several examples will illustrate the kinds of inputs that can have short-term effects (often overlooked) that are opposite to the long-term effects that are ordinarily considered:

It is commonly assumed that higher prices are an incentive to greater output of a product, but in the short run this sometimes will not be true. In the production of beef, the first step in increasing production is to withhold cattle from market to build up breeding herds, thus reducing sales for two or three years. Also, rising prices mean an appreciation in value of live "inventory," which results in lengthening the fattening interval in the feed lot and also reduces sales rates for a period of several months.

In some types of mining a rise in prices makes it economically feasible to process lower-grade ore; fixed-tonnage-rate equipment is then applied to a lower-yielding raw material, a procedure that can result in reduced total output until marginal mines that were not previously operating are opened.

In an expanding research activity more people may be needed to accelerate the completion of a project, but the first effect may be reduced progress while these people are trained and absorbed into the organization.

In a full-employment national economy, the demand for more goods may require diverting workers from producing goods into the manufacture of additional factories and machinery; the first step to achieve more long-term output tends initially to reduce production (this effect may of course be counterbalanced by other factors such as a longer work week).

---

[2] Another example is where a cumulative cycle of sales causes increases in advertising and advertising causes increases in sales until some other effect (depletion of the prospective-customer pool) limits the regenerative process. See Forrester 1961, ch. 16.

Magnitudes of Effects in Policies

The dynamic behavior of information-feedback systems is determined by the way in which *changes* in one variable cause *changes* in another. This might lead one to expect a high system sensitivity to the exact values of parameters in the decision functions, but such will usually not be true (Ogata 1970, 190).[3]

If a model is properly constructed to represent the actual information-feedback structure of a social system, the model will have the same self-correcting adaptability that exists in real-life situations. Any policy parameters that must be estimated act on one or more input levels to determine the rate of flow controlled by that decision. The source levels are in turn adjusted by the resulting decision. An inaccurate parameter in a policy can then lead to compensating readjustments of levels in the model until the rates of flow are properly related to one another.

Some examples illustrate this internal readjustment to compensate for changes in parameter values:

> In estimating a parameter determining the *delay* in repaying accounts receivable, one might choose too high a value; this would cause the level of accounts receivable to run slightly high, but repayment *rate* is still equal to the *rate* at which new obligations are being incurred.

> Or too high a labor mobility in describing a labor market could produce levels of unemployment that run lower in the model than in the actual economy, while still retaining the proper effects of policy changes on model dynamics. The model would readjust or warp internally, as does the real economy, so that a closer approach to the limit of full employment would counterbalance any built-in tendencies to create excessive employment rates.

> In a model, too low a consumer propensity to buy automobiles would cause the consumer stock of automobiles to decline and progressively decrease transportation service until the automobile purchase rate reaches a balance point. Changes in the level of consumer stocks of automobiles will help to compensate for an inaccurate purchase-rate decision function, while still leaving the dynamics of purchase-rate *changes* qualitatively correct with respect to other variables in the model.

We should be more concerned with what the model tells us about the factors that will cause *changes* in the rates and levels than about the absolute magnitudes of system levels.

A properly constructed model is often surprisingly unaffected by mis-specification over any plausible range in most parameter values—even sometimes changes of several-fold. In a model, the sensitivity to values of parameters should be no greater than the sensitivity of the real system to the corresponding factors. It seems obvious that our actual industrial and economic activities must not be highly sensitive to their fundamental parameters and that these parameters do not change rapidly. This must be true because the significant *characteristics* of organizations persist for long times. A successful company tends to remain so for extended periods—a

---

[3] A parameter is a constant for a given model run whose value has been assigned in constructing the model. It can of course be changed between one simulation run and another.

success that is founded in basic organization and policies (including the essential aspects of its leadership). National economies have exhibited surprisingly similar economic business cycles throughout industrial history, in spite of great changes in technology, monetary structure, transportation and communication speed, relative importance of industry and agriculture, and magnitude of government activity.

Nonlinear Policies

Nonlinear relationships occur in a model within the policies that determine rates of flow (Forrester 1987b). Nonlinearities are essential to the proper representation of corporate and economic behavior. Some examples may help.

The first form of nonlinearity occurs when the influence of an input to a policy is not simply proportional to the input. For example, the available stock of goods for sale affects the delivery rate of goods. When stocks are low, unavailability of goods reduces the ability to deliver; but, in the range of "normal" inventories, delivery rate will be very little affected by inventory changes. We can expect that most variable inputs to policies will be nonlinear and show increasing or decreasing importance as the ranges of the inputs change.

The second source of nonlinearity in policies occurs when decisions are not independently responsive to two or more causative input variables but to a product or other inter-relationship of the variables. In the previous example, the delivery of goods is not independently and separately responsive to the stocks of goods and to the unfilled orders that have been received for goods. We may not simply add the two separate contributions. If there are no orders, stocks are immaterial in determining delivery; if there are no stocks to deliver from, orders cannot produce delivery.

Various types of nonlinearity will often occur in combinations. Consider production rate capability of a factory as it depends on present employment level and on available capital equipment. Figure 3-8 shows how production rate might rise as employees are added. At first, as employees are added, each can have access to any equipment needed, labor productivity is high, and total production rises steeply and in proportion to labor. As the maximum capacity of equipment is approached, additional production per worker decreases. Still more employees finally result in the maximum possible production from the equipment. Beyond this level of employment, additional people would create only congestion and confusion and loss of total production. For a fixed amount of equipment, production is not proportional to employment and is a nonlinear relationship. Furthermore, the contribution to production of any given change of employment depends on the amount of equipment, so that the two inputs interact on one another. At low employment levels, it is unimportant where the amount of equipment might be in the range of K to 2K. At higher levels of employment, the contribution of additional workers is increasingly affected by whether or not equipment is added.

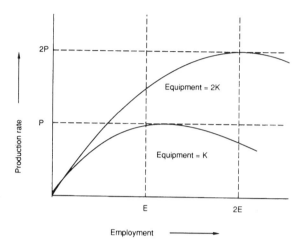

Figure 3-8.   Production rate as a function of employment and equipment

Linear approximations to these nonlinear relationships are usually not satisfacto-ry. Normal operations will vary over ranges wide enough that the nonlinearities are highly significant. Very often, the *approach* to one limit becomes the input signal to some compensating action (in the above example, the lowering man-hour efficiency caused by crowding is one of the inputs to the decision to order more equipment).

Policies should be valid over wide ranges of inputs for several reasons. We will want to use a model to explore wide ranges of conditions. We may not know how far some variables will be called upon to move. A model should be useful outside the operating ranges that have already been encountered by the real system because the design of new policies implies operation outside of historical practice.

In building a model, all pertinent information should be used about the system that is being represented. An indispensable class of information is knowledge of what to expect under extreme conditions of operation. Very often more is known about extreme limiting conditions of a relationship between variables than about the normal range of operation. Very often we know the value or the slope that a curve relating two variables must assume as the input variable approaches zero or some absurdly high value. If such extreme limiting conditions are reflected in a model, they help to define and make more reliable the normal operating range. By selecting functional relationships that match all our bits of knowledge, we enhance our chances of obtaining a model that acts properly.

Most actual limiting conditions exert their influence in a progressive way as the limit is approached. It is poor practice to approximate such functions by a linear section that is "clipped" to stop its travel suddenly.

Correctly shaped functional relationships facilitate internal self-adjustment wherein a model seeks values that balance one another. Realistic behavior is easier to achieve in a nonlinear than in a linear model because nonlinear models lead more quickly to the factors on which actual system behavior depends.

NOISE IN DECISION STREAMS

Policies in a model necessarily incorporate only the more important of the factors that influence decisions. Beyond these will be a host of minor influences that will unavoidably be omitted. The omissions can represent two quite different categories.

In the first category of omissions are slight influences from variables that are a part of the actual system but not represented in the model. Such omissions actually eliminate some of the feedback paths among model variables. These omissions happen because of necessity for simplification. However, omitting a variable from a policy in a model is the omission of an input that may be correlated in time with decisions created by the policy. We cannot substitute for this type of omission by random variables incorporated into decision processes of a model.

A second class of omissions from policies has a very different character. These missing inputs are not themselves affected by each other or by other variables in a model. Their source is outside of and independent of the real system being represented. An example is uncertain influence of weather—not only its obvious influence on agriculture but also its effect on Easter sales, sports equipment, and day-by-day department store business. Also we might classify as random the incidents of local, national, and international political news that may not be completely independent of business and economic affairs but that are often sufficiently loosely related to be looked upon as uncorrelated happenings. Here also would be a purchasing agent's vacation or production manager's illness and the effect they have on the smooth flow of business. This flood of unpredictable "noise" adds its contribution to all decision points in actual social systems. Such random noise variation can be included in policies of a model.

The theoretical treatment of noise inputs and how to design them comprise a complex subject to be taken up elsewhere. The practical question of what noise characteristics should be included in a model will, like many other inputs, be decided primarily by knowledge of the system being represented.[4]

Noise inputs to policies can be used to represent the second class of omissions from a model where the omitted factors are unrelated to the system being modeled. Noise cannot substitute for the first class of omissions, which constitute omissions of parts of the information-feedback structure of a system.

---

[4] It should be noted that neither the "random numbers" of statistics nor the "white noise" of the engineer can be employed without modification. Due regard must be given to sampling interval, the high and low cutoff frequencies contained in the noise sequence, and the way the noise is inserted at the decision point with respect to the closed-loop channels of which it becomes a part. See Richardson and Pugh (1981) for an elementary treatment.

SOURCES OF INFORMATION

Information for modeling is available from many different sources (Forrester 1980a). Figure 3-9 suggests three kinds of data bases: mental, written, and numerical. I use the term *data bases* in an extended sense. Those working with statistics may think of data as always coming in measured, numerical form. But *Webster's Third Unabridged Dictionary* gives no hint that data are restricted to numerical information. Webster's defines *data* as "something that is given from being experientially encountered," and "material serving as a basis for discussion, inference, or determination of policy," and "detailed information of any kind." This broad definition must include data stored mentally in people's heads, data stored descriptively in writing, and data available numerically.

As suggested by the figure, the amount of available information declines, probably by many orders of magnitude, in going from mental to written information and again by another similar large factor in going from written to numerical information. Furthermore, the character of information content changes as one moves from mental to written to numerical information. In moving down the diagram, there is a progressively smaller proportion of information about structure and policies. Each kind of information can fill a different role in modeling a business or social system.

Mental Data

Human affairs are conducted primarily from the mental data base. Information in people's heads is far more extensive than other stores of information. Anyone

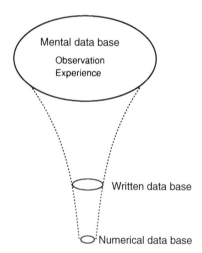

Figure 3-9.   Mental data base and decreasing content of written and numerical data bases

who doubts the dominant scope of remembered information should imagine what would happen to an industrial society if it were deprived of all knowledge in people's heads and if actions were guided only by written policies and numerical information. There is no written description adequate for building an automobile, or managing a family, or governing a country. I am putting special stress in this paper on the mental data base because that information is not adequately appreciated in the management and social sciences.

If the mental data base is so important to conduct of human systems, then I believe a model of such systems must reflect knowledge of policies and structure that resides only in the mental data. Effective model building must draw on the mental data base.

Written Data

The written data base contributes to a dynamic model at several stages. Part of the written store of information is simply a recording of information from the mental store. Another part of the written record contains concepts and abstractions that interpret other information sources.

Published material makes information more widely available than if it remains in the mental stores from which the written record can be drawn. In its totality, the written record is an excellent source of information about system structure and the reasons for decisions. I refer here primarily to the daily and weekly, public and business press, in which current pressures surrounding decisions are revealed.

The temporal nature of a decision sharply restricts the kind of literature in which actual operating policy will be revealed. Decisions control actions. Decisions are fleeting. There is only a single instant in time when one can act. That time is now. Action must take place in the present moment that separates history from the future. One cannot act in the past or in the future but only in the present.

The ever-advancing present moment in decision making is the manager's and politician's world of action. It is the world of placing orders, hiring people, buying capital equipment, borrowing money, changing wages, shipping goods, setting interest rates, and extending credit. These actions are continuously modulated by changes that occur in system states such as backlogs, inventories, plant capacity, debt, liquidity, and number of employees.

As a consequence of the fleeting life of a decision, it is primarily the literature of the present in which decisions are discussed in terms of goals, threats, limited information, and restraints on action. In business and economic activity that literature of the present means such publications as the *Wall Street Journal, Business Week, Fortune,* and the daily newspapers. The multifaceted conflicting pressures of real decision making are almost absent from economics textbooks and journals. The professional literature emphasizes how decisions should be made rather than how they are made and how equilibrium is determined rather than how dynamic behavior arises.

But the current business literature is not easy to use for model building. No single issue of a publication is meaningful by itself. The business and economic world keeps changing. At any one time, only a subset of possible inputs is important to a particular decision point. At one time, it may be high and rising inventories, at another time falling liquidity, and at still another time the need for more production capacity. Comprehensive policies, suitable for a model that will operate properly over a wide range of conditions, must embody all the considerations that can occur. To be useful, the literature must be pieced together, decisions must be interpreted into policies, and policies and structure must be perceived as causing modes of behavior that may extend over years or decades. One must read between the lines and round out each picture with information from other times and places. It may be that such interpretation of the current business literature cannot be effectively done without first-hand knowledge of the mental data base used by operators in business and politics. Such first-hand knowledge can be obtained only by living and working where the decisions are made and by watching and talking with those who act in social systems.

The written record has two major shortcomings compared with the mental data from which the written data were taken. As a first weakness, the written record usually cannot be queried. Unlike the mental data base, the written record is not responsive to probing by the analyst in search of a fit between structure, policy, and behavior. As a second deficiency, in being transformed from the mental store to writing, information has already been filtered through the perceptions and purposes of the writer. The writer's purpose may have been very different from that of a person seeking the internal causes of a particular dynamic behavior.

Part of the written data base deals with abstractions about structure. An example is the Cobb-Douglas production function as used by microeconomists. Closely related is the concept of marginal productivity of the factors of production. Such concepts are seldom explicitly recognized by practicing management and would not emerge from discussions with those who make economic decisions. The fact that such important concepts are hidden from the practitioner leads to a fundamental issue in designing a system dynamics model.

There are processes that one believes important in real life but that do not enter explicitly into practical decision making. Such processes play a role that is not directly visible. How are such hidden concepts to be handled in a dynamic model? Such hidden processes should be included in a model because they are believed to be real, but they should be veiled from the decision points of the model just as they are obscured in real life. For example, it is generally accepted that marginal productivities do exist for each factor of production. But managers have no way of determining quickly and reliably the values of marginal productivities. Management does not know with assurance whether money would most effectively be spent for a production worker, a lathe, more raw inventory, a vice president, advertising, or another pilot for the executive jet. Yet if marginal productivities are seriously out of balance, the underlying truth will gradually be perceived. It emerges from conflicting pleas, crises, and repetition of minor bits of evidence. The hidden true marginal productivities are the source of the signals that eventually diffuse into management awareness.

This example of handling marginal productivity illustrates how a modeler must play a dual role in dealing with underlying fundamental concepts in constructing a model. On the one hand the model builder must act as an omniscient observer who puts into the model what must exist in real life. But on the other hand, the modeler must degrade information about "true" conditions within the model before it is used in decision making by the model, so as to approximate the distortion that occurs in the actual system.

Numerical Data

The numerical data base is of narrower scope than either the written or mental data bases. Missing from numerical data is direct evidence of the structure and policies that created the data. Numerical data do not reveal the cause-to-effect direction between variables. From numerical data one can make statistical analyses to determine which data series correlate with one another, but that leaves unanswered the question of internal causality.

The numerical data base contains at least two bodies of information that are useful in modeling:

> First, specific numerical information is available on some parameter values. For example, average delivery delay for filling orders exists in corporate records and summaries of business information. Estimates of labor and machine productivity can be found. Many normal values, around which variation occurs, are available, such as money balances, inventory coverage, and time to fill job vacancies.

> Second, numerical information contains time-series data. In system dynamics modeling, time-series data are used much less as the basis for determining parameter values than in econometric models. But in system dynamics, the simulation model itself generates synthetic output time-series data that can be compared in a variety of ways with the real time-series data. I believe this independent use of time-series data for validating model behavior is less vulnerable to errors in the data than is the econometric use of data for trying to derive meaningful parameters (Graham 1980; Senge 1977; Senge 1978).

RELIABILITY OF INFORMATION

For modeling purposes, mental information can be classified three ways, as shown in Figure 3-10. The categories differ in reliability and in their role in modeling.

The first category includes observations about structure and policies and deals with why people act as they do and how the parts of a social system are interconnected. The mental data base contains extensive information about policies and structures, the very things one wants to know to build a system dynamics model.

The mental data base is rich in structural detail; it contains knowledge of what information is available at various decision-making points, where people and goods move, and what decisions are made. The mental data base is especially concerned with policy, that is, why people respond as they do, what each decision-making center is trying to accomplish, what are the perceived penalties and rewards in the specific social system, and where self-interest clashes with institutional objectives.

The first category of mental information—information about policy and structure—can be directly tapped for transfer into a system dynamics model. In general, the mental data base relating to policy and structure is reliable. Of course, it must be cross-checked. Exaggerations and oversimplifications can exist and must be corrected. Interviewees must be pressed beyond quick first responses. Interrogation must be guided by a knowledge of what different structures imply for dynamic behavior. But from the mental data base, a consensus emerges that is useful and sufficiently correct.

But the second category of mental information is not reliable. Expectations about system behavior are mental simulations that presumably represent dynamic consequences of detailed information in the first category. The second category—the expectations about behavior—represents intuitive solutions to the nonlinear, high-order systems of integral equations implied by the structure and policies in the first category. Such intuitive solutions to complicated dynamic systems are usually wrong. For example, Congress may pass a law intended to relieve the social and economic distress of cities (Forrester 1969). The law belongs to the first category in the figure; the law is a statement of policy; that policy is explicit and known. But the expectation that the law will relieve urban distress belongs to the second category, and such intuitive simulations about consequences are too often incorrect (Brehmer 1989; Kleinmuntz 1985; Sterman 1989b).

The third category of mental information is useful. It is information about observed past behavior of actual systems. From past behavior come symptoms of

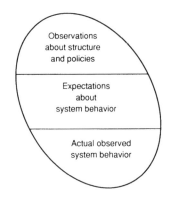

Figure 3-10.   Content of the mental data base as related to components and behavior of a social system

difficulty that provide motivation for a dynamic study and for a model. After a model is operating, behavior of the model can be partially evaluated against knowledge of past behavioral characteristics of the real system.

USE OF INFORMATION IN THE MODELING PROCESS

The preceding discussion of information and methodology leads to the modeling process shown in Figure 3-11. From the mental and written data bases comes the purpose of a model. Motivation for a model usually arises from troublesome behavior of the real system. In a corporation, perhaps market share has been falling, or employment has been fluctuating more widely than for other companies in the same industry.

During model construction, central focus is on information available from mental and written sources and numerical information other than time-series data. Such other numerical data include, for example, average delays in filling orders, typical

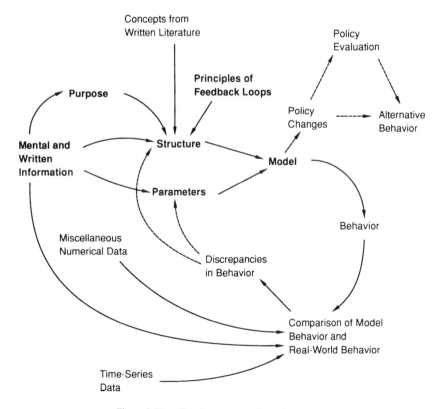

Figure 3-11.   Creating a system dynamics model

ratios of inventory to sales rate, relative costs of production inputs, and lead times for ordering materials and equipment.

The full range of information and the purpose, along with appropriate modeling concepts, are interpreted through principles from feedback-loop theory to yield a model structure.

Parameters are also usually derived directly and individually from mental, written, and numerical data bases. I believe that in the social sciences too sharp a distinction is drawn between structure and parameters. The distinction is fluid. For a simple model to be used over a short time span, certain quantities can be considered constants that for a model dealing with a longer time horizon should be converted into variables. Those new variables would in turn depend on more enduring parameters. For example, a policy for reordering goods for inventory might in the short run suffice if it sought to maintain a specified number of units in inventory. But for a model intended to be valid over a longer time, sales might change substantially, and a constant inventory would no longer be appropriate. The policy for managing inventory might instead be cast in terms of a variable target inventory that would try to maintain inventory equal to a specified number of weeks of average sales. Weeks of sales covered by inventory is a more enduring parameter than an absolute level of desired inventory. In creating a structure of variables and the associated parameters, one must continuously decide what will be considered a variable and what a parameter.

In a system dynamics model, every parameter should have meaning in the real-life setting. Its numerical value should be discussible with operating people in that part of the real system to which the parameter applies. Some parameters can be estimated from time-series data, but structures and parameters should not be excluded from a model merely because measured values are unavailable. Then, simulation tests can help to refine a parameter value within its plausible range. A particular parameter is likely to influence primarily a single dynamic mode of a system and some specific behavior within that mode. Because two parameters seldom have the same effect on system behavior, a change in one parameter will not often substitute for a change in another parameter. Sensitivity testing, with results interpreted against a wide array of real-life data, tend to converge toward a rather well-defined set of parameters. Further sensitivity testing will usually show that a choice between policy alternatives is not likely to be affected by reasonable changes in parameters.

A determination of structure, policies, and parameters yields a model. But, as suggested in the figure, an initial model formulation is only the beginning of the system dynamics process. Model behavior is generated in the form of time-series data for as many of the model variables as one chooses to plot. The diversity of variables makes possible a multitude of comparisons between the model and the real system (Bell and Senge 1980; Forrester and Senge 1980).

Model behavior can be compared with many kinds of information from real life. Available information even includes knowledge of logical possibilities that have not been experienced in the real system. For example, real inventories do not go negative even though model inventories often do in dynamic models with inadequate shipping functions. When such a finding is traced back to its cause in the model, a weakness is revealed, or an intended shortcut in model construction is shown to be unacceptable.

Time-series data are used primarily in comparing time-series output of a model with time series from real life. Because of the way randomness in decision making influences both the real world and a model of that real world, one does not expect model output and historical data to match on a point-by-point basis. Instead, one looks at behavioral characteristics of time-series data from the model and compares them with the corresponding characteristics of real data. For example, one can compare typical time lags among variables in business cycles of a system dynamics economic model with historical information.

The comparison of real-world behavior with model behavior will reveal discrepancies. Each discrepancy must be evaluated to judge whether it justifies the time and effort to make a correction. Discrepancies become the sign posts that lead back through the prior stages of model formulation. Discrepancies create a new perspective from which to reevaluate the mental, written, and numerical data bases, to test parameters for their effect on behavior, and to modify structure so its behavior aligns better with the real system.

After a model has been judged satisfactory for its particular purpose, the model can then be used for policy analysis. A policy is changed, usually by a parameter change in a policy statement, and a new simulation run obtained. Behavior from the new policy is compared with behavior from the old policy to evaluate relative desirabilities of the policies.

OVERVIEW

System dynamics has now developed into a profession. It is a profession that integrates knowledge about the real world with concepts of how feedback structures cause all change through time, and with computer simulation for dealing with systems that are too complex for mathematical analysis. System dynamics is a practical profession that starts from important problems, comes to understand the structures that produce undesirable symptoms, and moves on to finding changes in structure and policies that will make a system behave better. It is a profession that can lead to an improved framework for understanding complexity. It is a profession that can unify the diverse aspects of society and nature by combining the interactions between science, psychology, politics, biology, environment, economics, and management.

By contrast, some people still see system dynamics as nothing more than use of one of the special system dynamics software packages (High Performance Systems 1990; Pugh 1986). Often a person claims to understand system dynamics after using a particular modeling software. This is like saying one is a qualified surgeon because of having used a knife. Well-developed and widely available tools often usurp center stage and divert attention away from the philosophy, insights, information sources, understanding of dynamics, and ability to conceive relevant model structures that together form the profession of system dynamics (Forrester 1975a; Forrester 1976; Randers 1980).

I use "profession" here in the sense applied to engineering, law, and medicine. A profession should be activist, meaning that it deals with challenges and problems of the real world. It should seek solutions that can be realized in practice. It interacts with society. Its success is measured by the good it can do for human activity. It integrates hard facts with intangibles. It is learned through many channels—reading, theory, laboratory work, internship, and practice. It is useful in small doses (as a first-aid course can be a useful acquisition of medical knowledge) but it continues in depth to the frontier of knowledge (like the unending medical search for better treatments and improved surgical procedures).

System dynamics is being taught in an expanding number of universities, business schools, and colleges. Many of the leading business schools in North America and Europe have begun to integrate model-supported case studies into management education. More companies are applying system dynamics, and some have introduced in-house company training programs (Forrester 1961; Lyneis 1980; Morecroft, Lane, and Viita 1991; E. Roberts 1978; Wolstenholme 1990). Governments in many countries are using system dynamics to understand social and economic change. System dynamics deals with change. Understanding and managing change are central tasks in both technological and social systems.

Well-known and widely debated system dynamics models have illustrated the social and business forces in growth and stagnation of cities (Alfeld and Graham 1976; Forrester 1969; Mass 1974; Schroeder, Sweeney, and Alfeld 1975).

System dynamics studies of growth in population, industrialization and pollution captured attention around the world (Forrester 1971a; Forrester 1971b; Meadows, Meadows, Randers, and Behrens 1972; Meadows and Meadows 1973). *The Limits to Growth* book has reportedly sold over three million copies and been translated into more than 30 languages.

System dynamics promises to show how government and business policies interact to create economic behavior (N. Forrester 1982; Low 1980; Mass 1975). Other models have demonstrated the basis for the economic long wave or Kondratieff cycle (Forrester 1977; Sterman 1985; Sterman 1986). The System Dynamics National Model program at MIT is probably the most extensive application to economic behavior (Forrester 1979; Forrester 1980a; Forrester 1985; Forrester 1987a).

To me, the most exciting frontier for system dynamics lies in its use as a foundation for a far more effective pre-college education. Nancy Roberts pioneered the first work (N. Roberts 1975; N. Roberts 1978). Since then, educational programs based on system dynamics are well advanced in some 30 junior and senior high schools in the United States and some activity has started in 300 more (Forrester 1990; Forrester 1991).

Results show that a dynamic foundation can be created at the pre-college level that underlies mathematics, physics, social studies, economics, history, the students' own life experience, and even literature. With a framework into which facts can be placed, learning becomes more relevant and meaningful.

A joint program among the Scandinavian countries is advancing system dynamics for education of younger students. Germany has developed a program for using system dynamics and the STELLA software for teaching elementary physics (Schecker 1993).

But the field still lacks adequate educational materials. The traditional introductory books have been widely used (Forrester 1968; Goodman 1974; Richardson and Pugh 1981; N. Roberts, Andersen, Deal, Garet, and Shaffer 1983). However, none of these are fully developed textbooks supported by assignments, study plans, workbooks, and special readings. Although much material exists in course outlines and informal memoranda, almost nothing is published and widely available for advanced study in system dynamics.

Rather than being a mature field after 35 years of development, system dynamics is now on the threshold of its greatest expansion with rapidly diversifying opportunities in business, society, and education.

REFERENCES

Alfeld, Louis Edward, and Alan K. Graham (1976), *Introduction to Urban Dynamics,* Portland, Ore.: Productivity Press.

Beer, Stafford (1981), *The Brain of the Firm* (2d ed.), Chichester, England: John Wiley.

Bell, James A., and Peter M. Senge (1980), "Methods for Enhancing Refutability in System Dynamics Modeling," in A.A. Legasto, Jr., ed., *System Dynamics,* TIMS Studies in the Management Sciences, New York: North-Holland, 61-73.

Brehmer, B. (1989), "Feedback Delays and Control in Complex Dynamic Systems," in P. Milling and E. Zahn, eds., *Computer-Based Management of Complex Systems,* Berlin: Springer-Verlag, 189-96.

Cyert, R., and J. March (1963), *A Behavioral Theory of the Firm,* Englewood Cliffs, N.J.: Prentice Hall.

Deutsch, Karl W. (1963), *The Nerves of Government,* London: Collier-MacMillan.

Forrester, Jay W. (1961), *Industrial Dynamics,* Portland, Ore.: Productivity Press.

Forrester, Jay W. (1968), *Principles of Systems* (2d ed.), Portland, Ore.: Productivity Press.

Forrester, Jay W. (1969), *Urban Dynamics,* Portland, Ore.: Productivity Press.

Forrester, Jay W. (1971a), "Counterintuitive Behavior of Social Systems," *Technology Review* 73, no. 3: 53-68.

Forrester, Jay W. (1971b), *World Dynamics.* (1973 second ed.), Portland, Ore.: Productivity Press.

Forrester, Jay W. (1975a), *Collected Papers of Jay W. Forrester.* Portland, Ore.: Productivity Press.

Forrester, Jay W. (1975b), "Market Growth as Influenced by Capital Investment," in *Collected Papers of Jay W. Forrester,* Portland, Ore.: Productivity Press, 111-32.

Forrester, Jay W. (1976), "Educational Implications of Responses to System Dynamics Models," in C. West Churchman and Richard O. Mason, eds., *World Modeling: A Dialogue,* Amsterdam: North-Holland, 27-35.

Forrester, Jay W. (1977), "Growth Cycles,"*De Economist* 125, no. 4: 525-43.

Forrester, Jay W. (1979), "An Alternative Approach to Economic Policy: Macrobehavior from Microstructure," in Nake M. Kamrany and Richard H. Day, eds., *Economic Issues of the Eighties,* Baltimore: Johns Hopkins University Press, 80-108.

Forrester, Jay W. (1980a), "Information Sources for Modeling the National Economy," *Journal of the American Statistical Association* 75, no. 371: 555-74.

Forrester, Jay W. (1980b), "System Dynamics: Future Opportunities," in A.A. Legasto, Jr., ed., *System Dynamics,* TIMS Studies in the Managaement Sciences, New York: North-Holland, 7-21.

Forrester, Jay W. (1985), "Economic Conditions Ahead: Understanding the Kondratieff Wave," *The Futurist* XIX, no. 3: 16-20.

Forrester, Jay W. (1987a), *Comparison of the 1920s and 1980s,* Working paper D-3890, System Dynamics Group, Sloan School of Management, MIT, Cambridge, Mass.

Forrester, Jay W. (1987b), "Nonlinearity in High-Order Models of Social Systems," *European Journal of Operational Research* 30, no. 2: 104-109.

Forrester, Jay W. (1990), "System Dynamics as a Foundation for Pre-College Education," in David F. Anderson, George P. Richardson, and John D. Sterman, eds., *Volume 1: System Dynamics '90,* Lincoln, Mass.: System Dynamics Society, 367-80.

Forrester, Jay W. (1991), "System Dynamics—Adding Structure and Relevance to Pre-College Education," in Kenneth R. Manning, ed., *Shaping the Future,* Cambridge: MIT Press.

Forrester, Jay W., and Peter M. Senge (1980), "Tests for Building Confidence in System Dynamics Models," in A.A. Legasto, Jr. , J.W. Forrester, and J.M. Lyneis, eds., *System Dynamics,* TIMS Studies in the Management Sciences, New York: North-Holland, 209-28.

Forrester, Nathan B. (1982), *A Dynamic Synthesis of Basic Macroeconomic Theory: Implications for Stabilization Policy Analysis,* Ph.D. thesis, Sloan School of Management, Massachusetts Institute of Technology, Cambridge, Mass.

Goodman, Michael R. (1974), *Study Notes in System Dynamics*, Portland, Ore.: Productivity Press.

Graham, Alan K. (1980), "Parameter Estimation in System Dynamics Modeling," in Jørgen Randers, ed., *Elements of the System Dynamics Method,* Portland, Ore.: Productivity Press, 143-61.

High Performance Systems (1990), *STELLA II Users Guide,* High Performance Systems, 45 Lyme Road, Ste. 300, Hanover NH 03755.

Hogarth, R.M. (1987), *Judgment and Choice: The Psychology of Decision* (2d ed.), New York: Wiley.

Kleinmuntz, D. (1985), "Cognitive Heuristics and Feedback in a Dynamic Decision Environment," *Management Science* 31: 680-702.

Low, Gilbert W. (1980), "The Multiplier-Accelerator Model of Business Cycles Interpreted from a System Dynamics Perspective," in Jørgen Randers, ed., *Elements of the System Dynamics Method,* Portland, Ore.: Productivity Press, 76-94.

Lyneis, James M. (1980), *Corporate Planning and Policy Design: A System Dynamics Approach,* Cambridge, Mass.: Pugh-Roberts Associates.

Mass, Nathaniel J., ed. (1974), *Readings in Urban Dynamics: Volume 1*, Portland, Ore.: Productivity Press.

Mass, Nathaniel J. (1975), *Economic Cycles: An Analysis of Underlying Causes*, Portland, Ore.: Productivity Press.

Meadows, Donella H., Dennis L. Meadows, Jørgen Randers, and William W. Behrens III (1972), *The Limits to Growth,* New York: Universe Books.

Meadows, Dennis L. (1970), *Dynamics of Commodity Production Cycles*. Portland, Ore.: Productivity Press.

Meadows, Dennis L., and Donella H. Meadows, eds. (1973), *Toward Global Equilibrium: Collected Papers*, Portland, Ore.: Productivity Press.

Morecroft, John D. W. (1983), "System Dynamics: Portraying Bounded Rationality," *Omega* 11, no. 2: 131-42.

Morecroft, John D.W., D.C. Lane, and P.S. Viita (1991), "Modelling Growth Strategy in a Biotechnology Startup Firm," *System Dynamics Review* 7, no. 2: 93-116.

Ogata, K. (1970), *Modern Control Engineering,* Englewood Cliffs, N.J.: Prentice-Hall.

Pugh, Alexander L., III (1986), *Professional DYNAMO Plus Reference Manual*, Software manual, desktop PC computers, Pugh-Roberts Associates, 41 William Linskey Way, Cambridge MA 02142.

Randers, Jørgen, ed., (1980), *Elements of the System Dynamics Method*, Portland, Ore.: Productivity Press.

Richardson, George P. (1991), *Feedback Thought in Social Science and Systems Theory,* Philadelphia: University of Pennsylvania Press.

Richardson, George P., and Alexander L. Pugh III (1981), *Introduction to System Dynamics Modeling with DYNAMO,* Portland, Ore.: Productivity Press.

Roberts, Edward B. (1964), *The Dynamics of Research and Development,* New York: Harper and Row.

Roberts, Edward B. (1978), *Managerial Applications of System Dynamics*, Portland, Ore.: Productivity Press.

Roberts, Nancy (1975), *A Dynamic Feedback Approach to Elementary Social Studies: A Prototype Gaming Unit,* Ph.D. thesis, Boston University, Boston, Mass.; available from University Microfilms, Ann Arbor, Mich.

Roberts, Nancy. (1978), "Teaching Dynamic Feedback Systems Thinking: An Elementary View," *Management Science* 24, no. 8: 836-43.

Roberts, Nancy, David Andersen, Ralph Deal, Michael Garet, and William Shaffer (1983), *Introduction to Computer Simulation: A System Dynamics Modeling Approach,* Portland, Ore.: Productivity Press.

Schecker, Horst P. (1993), "The Didactic Potential of Computer Aided Modeling for Physics Education," in D.L. Ferguson, ed., *Advanced Educational Technologies for Mathematics and Science,* Berlin: Springer-Verlag.

Schroeder, Walter W., III, Robert E. Sweeney, and Louis Edward Alfeld, eds. (1975), *Readings in Urban Dynamics: Volume 2*, Portland, Ore.: Productivity Press.

Senge, Peter M. (1977), "Statistical Estimation of Feedback Models," *Simulation* 28, no. 6, 177-84.

Senge, Peter M. (1978), *The System Dynamics National Model Investment Function: A Comparison to the Neoclassical Investment Function,* Ph.D. thesis, Sloan School of Management, MIT, Cambridge, Mass.

Senge, Peter M. (1990), *The Fifth Discipline,* New York: Doubleday.

Simon, Herbert A. (1976), *Administrative Behavior*, New York: Free Press.

Simon, Herbert A. (1979), "Rational Decision Making in Business Organizations," *American Economic Review* 69, no. 4: 493-513.

Simon, Herbert A. (1982), *Models of Bounded Rationality (two volumes),* Cambridge: MIT Press.

Sterman, John D. (1985), "A Behavioral Model of the Economic Long Wave," *Journal of Economic Behavior and Organization* 6: 17-53.

Sterman, John D. (1986), "The Economic Long Wave: Theory and Evidence," *System Dynamics Review* 2, no. 2: 87-125.

Sterman, John D. (1989a), "Misperceptions of Feedback in Dynamic Decision Making," *Organizational Behavior and Human Decision Processes* 43, no. 3: 301-35.

Sterman, John D. (1989b), "Modeling Managerial Behavior: Misperceptions of Feedback in a Dynamic Decision Making Experiment," *Management Science* 35, no. 3: 321-39.

Sterman, John D. (1989c), *The People Express Management Flight Simulator*, available from the author, Sloan School of Management, MIT, Cambridge MA 02142.

Wolstenholme, Eric F. (1990), *System Enquiry: A System Dynamics Approach,* Chichester, England: John Wiley & Sons.

4

MODELING AS LEARNING: A CONSULTANCY METHODOLOGY FOR ENHANCING LEARNING IN MANAGEMENT TEAMS

DAVID C. LANE

ABSTRACT: This article reviews the experiences of a practicing business consultancy division. It discusses the reasons for the failure of the traditional, expert consultancy approach and states the requirements for a more suitable consultancy methodology. An approach called "Modeling as Learning" is introduced, its three defining aspects being: client ownership of all analytical work performed, consultant acting as facilitator, and sensitivity to soft issues within and surrounding a problem. The goal of such an approach is set as the acceleration of the client's learning about the business. The tools that are used within this methodological framework are discussed and some case studies of the methodology are presented. It is argued that a learning experience was necessary before arriving at the new methodology but that it is now a valuable and significant component of the division's work.*

*This is an updated and expanded version of a paper which was originally presented at the Third European Simulation Congress, Edinburgh, 1989, at which time the author was working with Shell International Petroleum Co. Ltd. in London.

My particular thanks go to Elke Husemann for her contribution to the design of Figures 4-1 and 4-4 and many other encouragements. I would also like to thank Graham Galer, James Gibb, and Chris Booth for giving me the opportunity to record these ideas, and to thank the clients whose cases are presented here.

INTRODUCTION

"Modeling as Learning" is a consultancy methodology or philosophy that is currently being used by my colleagues and myself in the Business Consultancy department of Shell International Petroleum. It has arisen out of the recognition of the limits of traditional O.R. analysis, combined with the continued need to provide management support. It brings together ideas and experiences from various sources but its chief influence is the company's Group Planning department. By marrying together these ideas with our own experience of business needs, we have created a methodology that brings the power of simulation and analysis into the heart of business discussions so that it can have practical benefits to the company. Here the term modeling is used in a very broad sense, from a highly quantitative, simulation-style representation of the problem to a soft form of analysis that helps to address less well-defined issues.

However, most of our successes have derived from our use of the ideas of system dynamics. Along with de Geus (1988), debts for the formulation of our methodology are therefore owed to Forrester (1961). Both the ideas of system analysis and facilitation consultancy (qv.) are to be found in this work and we frequently find ourselves in the position of trying to apply to our business ideas that exist already in the literature. We are aware that many of the comments made and ideas espoused are not new. However, we offer them here as a record of this particular department's experience in wrestling with the shortcomings of the traditional approach and slowly synthesizing a new means of conducting its work.

In the following sections we discuss the traditional method of consultancy and share the experiences of its failings and limitations. We discuss the needs of a management team and then present the new consultancy methodology that tries to address them. We touch briefly upon some of the tools that our department uses and then close with some examples of the approach and discuss the improvements made to the business in consequence.

LIMITS TO EXPERT CONSULTANCY

Because Modeling as Learning has evolved from the standard consultancy approach used previously by ourselves and by all too many other analytical groups, it is valuable to compare and contrast it with that approach, referred to here as "expert consultancy."

The Methodology

Let us consider a management team with responsibility for an area of a business. Since the business environment is always changing, new issues and problems are continually appearing and the team is required to take effective action. The process may then be illustrated by Figure 4-1. The left side shows the activities of the management, designated by the white background. When no outside intervention occurs, the process advances along the two arrows—discussion takes place between the responsible parties and from this a decision is made and the appropriate actions taken. However, the management team may feel that, in order to complete the decision-making process, some form of modeling is appropriate. In this case another group of participants, the consultants, are invited to listen in on the discussion so that they are in a position to bring their expertise to bear. In the figure they are indicated by the black background.

It is important to clarify the purpose of this step, since it defines the expectations and the roles of all parties concerned. In the example here, it is assumed that the management team accepts that the consultants are expert in techniques that will allow them to perform an analysis of the problem for the clients. An example of this from the oil industry is the standard use of linear programming by those managing the product mix of a refinery (see Uhlmann 1988). Here, the technique has credibility with those who are not themselves expert in it. The management of a refinery simply request that an O.R. department use the algorithm on their problem in order to supply the right, or optimal, answer.

The consultants withdraw and conceptualize the problem so as to apply a suitable analytical technique and then deliver the results of this analysis back to the client team. The nature of the deliverable is important. It may be a model, or the results of a model, or an interpretation of results back into the business context. However, it will generally be presented, implicitly or explicitly, as the "right answer" to the problem. In the representation of Figure 4-1, it is shown as the missing piece that completes the process.

Management

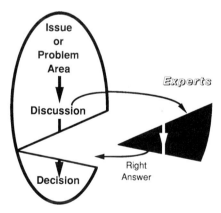

Figure 4-1. A representation of the expert consultancy methodology: The decision-making process of the management (white background) is completed when they are supplied with the analysis, or missing piece, of the expert consultants (black).

Simplified though this description may seem, it does capture the essence of the approach. The expertise that is brought to bear can vary widely. For technical questions, it may be the ability to simulate complex problems accurately, or to use any of the other tools of traditional O.R. Examples are the refinery analysis mentioned above or advanced techniques of oil reservoir simulation. More business-centered problems would require expertise in methods such as the value chain or Porter's five competitive forces (1980). Wherever in this spectrum of tools a particular piece of work may be located, it will have the same essential properties: the existence of a technique that captures and/or optimizes the functioning of a system, the implicit trust in that technique by the client, and the expertise in that technique by a team of consultants.

When Expert Consultancy Fails

Expert consultancy has a long and distinguished pedigree and its wide-ranging use bears witness to the validity of the approach. It is used widely by more analytically oriented groups both inside Shell and in other companies, as the author has himself observed. Why, then, when it comes to the senior executives of a company or even a government, are decisions made about problems of great complexity without recourse to any form of technical support? Such people simply reject the ability of any form of modeling to help them in their day-to-day business because all too often this approach fails to effect any real change in the business. The rejection is expressed in a variety of forms and serves to prevent the consultants' work from being useful to the client. Such rejections are characterized by the quotations in Figure 4-2. Objections such as these arise for three related reasons listed below:

- Analysis/results not client-owned
- "Expert" role rejected
- "Hard" modeling inappropriate

Lack of Ownership. The first problem arises because the consultants operate as a separate group. It is then natural for their work to be done behind closed doors and thus easy for the techniques used to run ahead of the client. The consultants spend long periods operating in their own world of abstractions in order to understand the problem. Of course, this can be very fruitful, but it does mean that any results or insights produced are hard to deliver back to the client in terms that can be understood. Any reader who has derived an important business result from examining, say, a three-dimensional phase space and then been asked to explain such an abstract idea to a nontechnical client will recognize this difficulty. Kathawala's (1988) evidence is consistent with our experience when observing that many analytical techniques are not fully understood by managers. In such cases it is easy for a client to feel that the whole modeling process has moved away from tackling the

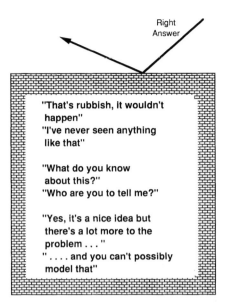

Figure 4-2. Typical comments rejecting the expert consultancy methodology

real issue and become too involved in some technical or abstract modeling details, even when this is not actually the case.

Expert Role Rejected. The second problem with expert consultancy arises because of the roles that both consultant and client frequently fall into playing. Unless considerable care is taken, the consultants may inadvertently present themselves in the role of "teacher," someone who has superior knowledge that should be listened to and accepted on faith even if not fully understood. The other side of this unfortunate scenario requires that the client be willing to act as the willing pupil to this pedagogue, lapping up the pearls of wisdom that are produced! We as consultants should be sufficiently objective to note the sheer pleasure felt by some experts in having a client dependent on one's advice. However, there are clearly good reasons why the giving of such expert advice is a fundamental part of the role of a Business Consultancy department. For example, such a group can act as a focal point for technical know-how which would be unmanageably burdensome—in financial and manpower terms—for all parts of an organization to possess.

When an expert consultant sends the message, "I am an expert in techniques that will teach you about your business," they may be setting up a relationship with a client that will be accepted and prove very fruitful. However, they may find that the client resents and rejects the power positions of such a project. Rightly or wrongly, the client may not accept that the "experts" are actually expert in their business.

Hard Modeling Does Not Address the Problem. The third difficulty that confronts an expert consultant is that the issue being analyzed is not soluble by traditional analytic means. The tendency of O.R. to concentrate on the "objective facts" of an issue and ignore the people involved has been criticized before by Ackoff (1979a). Stephen Watson of Cambridge (1988) has said that:

> The time is long passed when we can make a significant contribution to our subject [O.R.] without considering the subjectivity of our work.

Yet the error persists. We still imagine that an optimal solution will be executed by the empowered parties simply because it shines with self-evident truth. The reality is that any problem is embedded in a network of political, cultural and power relationships. It is naive and futile to imagine that these can all be cut through because a solution is known to be mathematically optimal. Any solution that requires action to be taken will need to address the relationships of those involved, account for them, and take time to organize their re-configuration. In his story "Slow Sculpture," Theodore Sturgeon (1990) describes this problem vividly using the metaphor of a Bonsai tree: The grower's planned design can be very beautiful but it takes many years to redirect gently the tree's branches so that they form the desired pattern.

The above discussion assumes that a hard O.R. solution exists. Yet many expert consultancy projects fail, not because the implementation of the solution has failed to consider the full organizational or "political" complexity of the problem context, but because the real problem is itself "political" in nature. Eden, Jones, and Sims (1983) warn against attempts to filter out the "noise" of the personalities involved, in order to get to the "real" problem. They are clearly correct in saying that sometimes the real problem *is* the political one. A problem may have arisen, for example, because of a conflict between two personalities, or because two interest groups concerned have widely divergent goals, or because the parties involved do not have a common language or means of expressing their views. Although O.R. has increasingly begun to tackle these sorts of questions, it is a fact that the bulk of knowledge referred to as O.R. and the majority of papers published in the journals concern methods to solve well-posed, quantifiable problems. It is not surprising, then, that just these sorts of methods are most frequently used by expert consultants and that, for the reasons discussed here, they often fail. The client is then correct in feeling that the process did not tackle the real issue but just managed to isolate—or even create—a small part of it, the part upon which analytical work can be done.

In concluding this section, we might draw together the discussion on why expert consultancy fails by using a caricature called "letter-box" consultancy. Aspects of it will seem all too familiar to many analysts. The client outlines a problem and writes it down on a piece of paper, which is then posted through the door of the consultants' room. Here the consultants isolate a strand of the problem that is amenable to analysis in traditional terms. They operate their computers, perform their analysis, and generally weave their own special magic. The results appear as a thick report, which is, somehow, pushed back out under that same door into the hands of the client. The report has on its title page, "Here is your answer, now get on with it." The consequence is that the old adage holds: A manager will not enact a solution that he/she does not understand, whose proponent does not have his/her confidence, or that does not solve the real problem. The report is tossed into a cupboard and ignored. Nothing is gained by the client. The business is not improved. Money is wasted. The world turns.

ASSEMBLING A NEW METHODOLOGY

In the section titled "Limits to Expert Consultancy," we discussed our views on why the traditional, or expert, approach to consultancy can and does fail. And yet it was also clear to us that in many cases just this methodology continues to be highly successful. What did these two types of experience tell us? That modeling could be used only to analyze tangible physical processes? That it could be used only by technical experts whose views are implicitly trusted? That it had no place amongst senior decision makers? Our belief was that we could give a firm "No" to all of these questions. Modeling, and other forms of problem analysis, could have a role among decision makers if we examined their needs and used a modeling philosophy that avoided or overcame the three problems discussed above in a way that addressed those needs. In this section we recount the way in which we began to assemble an idea of the sort of methodology that is required by a management team.

Creating Ownership

Why is ownership an issue? To demonstrate, let us consider a team that is confronted with a complex problem and ask what utility or value some form of analysis might have. We can think of the value of such a process as being dependent on the size of the model used or the functionality of the modeling tool employed. The logic of traditional, expert, consultancy says that the bigger a model is, the more ideas and effects it captures, and the greater its functionality, the better it is. The utility curve for this logic is shown in Figure 4-3a.

It is possible to quibble about the exact form of this relationship; we all know that large models are hard to maintain, run, and interpret, and therefore hard to get value from. However, we would argue that this curve is monotonic increasing for the majority of cases. This curve, then, helps to represent the logic behind the many successful expert consultancy projects that occur. They work because the model builders have credibility as experts and because the output of such models is implicitly trusted. Again, oil reservoir simulation is a fine example of this logic

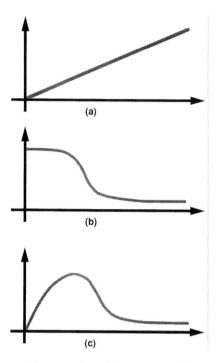

Figure 4-3. Three measures of the utility of a modeling or analytical process. Horizontal axis is size, or functionality of modeling process. Vertical axis is utility of process to client (a) for expert consultancy logic, (b) from chance of clients changing behavior after process, and (c) a combination of the two.

in successful action. With such a logic, movement to the right—increasing complexity—adds to the utility of the exercise.

There is another measure of the value of a modeling process, one derived from the probability that a manager will truly grasp the results of a piece of analysis and act on it. For the majority of members of any organization this relationship is very different (see Figure 4-3b). The justification for this shape is simply that the output from big models is usually harder to explain and that managers will very seldom look at a piece of code (try getting your client to look through a FORTRAN printout with you). Although a model contains ideas, they are usually expressed in a way that is unusual and unreadable for most clients. This is true whether the ideas in a model are only those of the client (the ideal) or include those of the model builder (the reality). By this measure, a model *falls* in value the more complex it becomes.

We can think of these two curves also as the ability of a model to take knowledge *in* (Figure 4-3a) and to pass knowledge *out* (4-3b). By using a utility measure that says, quite reasonably, that both of these are important, we get a third curve (Figure 4-3c). The message this gives is that there is a tradeoff between model complexity and the delivery of the value of that model, a compromise between functionality and transparency. This indicates that there is value in using tools that capture ideas and allow analysis of them, but that can be seen clearly to contain those ideas in a readily understandable form. In other words, we come to the conclusion that

Clients' ideas must not just be in a model,
they must be seen to be in a model.

The Role of the Consultant

In tackling the issue of ownership, we have already begun to address the problem of a consultant in an expert role. It is the complexity of the analytical techniques used that tends to turn a consultant into a "technical high priest," a guardian of a large model that is, at best, incompletely understood by the client. It is by making the analytical tools themselves more transparent that it becomes possible to change the role of the consultant. It is possible for a consultant to bring the method of analysis right into the heart of the management debate of Figure 4-1 and quickly and clearly capture the ideas of the team. If the tools that are used to do this are simple and easy to understand, then it will be easy for the clients to view and amend the representation of their ideas. It thus becomes possible for the consultant constantly to return to the client and ask again for the client's comment and correction on the model of an idea of the business.

The means of sustaining an expert role is now clear: Don't. Rather than attempting to take the position, "I am an expert in techniques that will teach you about your business," the consultant should offer a process in which the ideas of the team are brought out and examined in a clear and logical way. The knowledge that is generated derives from the discussion of the team's ideas. The consultant's role is then to provide a set of tools for representing clearly the ideas of the team members. It is this activity in which the consultant is an expert. His or her role with respect to the clients may be characterized as, "I accept that you are the experts in your business but I have an approach and a set of tools that will help you use that knowledge more effectively." We recognize one of the originators of these ideas by using Schein's (1969) term and describe this role as "facilitation consultant," since the consultant facilitates or organizes the process by which the ideas of the team are brought out and examined.

Coping with "Soft" Problems

We have discussed our understanding of the complexities that can surround the application of a "hard" O.R. solution and said that the actual problem may not be amenable to such analysis. Perhaps the main point to make here is that the majority of problems that confront management are of this type. A cold, clear solution to an abstraction of the problem would not constitute the solution because of the personalities concerned. What was required was a means of encompassing these dimensions of the problem. We needed tools that helped people to clarify their own and others' positions. These could at least help managers realize exactly what it was that they were arguing about. We needed processes that ensured that the ideas of all team members were surfaced and considered on an equal footing. We needed to have the basic consultancy skills of drawing information out of clients and confirming our understanding of it. We needed to use exciting ways of studying problems so that managers were persuaded to make time to study an issue and not be driven by fire-fighting everyday events. We also needed to represent the presence of real individuals in our models, not the hypothetical "rational economic man."

MODELING AS LEARNING

"Modeling as Learning" is the name that I have given to the approach that I have been evolving over the last three years and that is employed by my colleagues and myself in the Business Consultancy department at Shell. The name indicates the debt owed to the Group Planning department. In response to the general questioning in business circles of the role of corporate planning departments, Shell evolved a notion of planning as facilitating learning, or "Planning as Learning" (de Geus 1988). Our Business Consultancy department has been fortunate in being exposed to these concepts and in playing a major part in their implementation. We have re-molded these ideas and substantially added to them to match them to the needs of our department, our motivation being to overcome the problems discussed in "Limits to Expert Consultancy" and to fulfill the requirements considered in "Assembling a New Methodology."

In this section we discuss the process, its benefits, and its goals. Because these factors are mutually dependent and so not best suited to a linear exposition, it is useful to orient this section with a brief statement of what is meant by this term.

> "Modeling as Learning" is a consultancy methodology for decision support that involves the use of analytical tools in close association with the clients. The consultants act as facilitators of the group process. They provide an interactive framework for capturing clients' ideas and assumptions in a form that is both straightforward to understand and amenable to the application of suitable analytical tools. The resulting models give the clients the ability to check the coherence of their ideas by considering consistency and consequence. They also provide a representation of a business system on which experiments with strategy can be performed. The goal of the process is to enhance the clients' understanding of the appropriate business issues, to focus discussion, and to generate new options and ideas which therefore improve decision making.

In this section we try to draw out the common features of such a project and discuss them in general terms. Specific examples may be found in the section below titled "Examples of Modeling as Learning Projects." Further discussion of the theory of the approach may be found in Lane (1994a and b).

Key Aspects of the Process

Listed below are the main aspects of the Modeling as Learning process, followed by a more detailed discussion of each.

- Modeling is an integral part of the management discussion

- Consultants provide tools that capture and express the mental models of the clients

- Soft issues are considered

- The models are owned by the clients

- The models are run/used and interpreted by the clients

Integral Part of the Discussion. In order to achieve the first element of the above list it is vital to get access to the decision makers. This is a central requirement of the approach. One of the main goals is to prevent the separation of analysis and discussion illustrated in Figure 4-1. It is vital that managers be persuaded to give to such a project the time that is necessary to get the full value out of it. The clients must be persuaded to be part of a process of model building and not just send the consultants off to fix a model detail. This is partly a question of handling the expectations of the clients from the start. Our experience has shown that letting clients see very quickly that there are benefits to be gained by participating is an effective way of coaxing time out of them. Delivering a harangue and demanding that the client contract into the whole process from the start is neither appropriate nor successful. In the successful projects, getting time and access with clients has ceased to be a major problem. Indeed, there have been cases of clients asking to spend more time with a model.

Capturing Mental Models. When we speak of capturing and expressing a manager's mental models we are essentially saying that we want to find out how the client thinks a situation works. Our models of how things work are what enable us to make sense of the world. They allow us to add structure to everyday events. They allow us to understand why something has happened and what its ramifications are. We have such models for almost every situation that we come across. When clients use phrases like, "That's not possible," "I don't think it works like that," or "No, he wouldn't have done that," they are appealing to their mental models of a system or person. Without mental models our lives would seem capricious, random, and meaningless. Models supply structure to a stream of events. The reason mental models are important is that they are what people use to make decisions. Thus, to help a manager react to a problem, it is necessary to examine their mental model of how that problem works and, if necessary, help them to change it. This requires an array of tools and we will discuss these in more detail in the section below titled "Modeling as Learning Tools." The role of the consultant is simply to encourage clients to put forward their ideas, to clarify them if necessary, and to record them in a form that is both permanent and transferable. We use the term "articulated model."

In formulating and constructing such models we should not take the expert consultancy view and try to model with high accuracy the functioning of a whole system. There are many reasons for this, some rather abstract, some very practical. Special relativity and quantum mechanics tell us that it is impossible to capture the full behavior of a system, and the theory of chaos tells us that even supposedly deterministic systems can be effectively unpredictable because of sensitivity to initial conditions. On a different level, we should not try to model a system since there is no end to the effects that should be included in order to capture what is "really" happening.[1] So, in order to put a boundary on the effects to be included and to prevent the exercise from bogging down in the question of what effects are "really" known, we model only one issue. We place the issue in the context of a system and then include only those aspects of the system that the *client* considers to be important or that they wish to concentrate their study on. There is no *a priori* requirement of certainty regarding quantification, or even cause and effect. The very discussions that take place around such points are part of the process, part of the deliverable. This viewpoint has much in common with the distinctions drawn between frequentist and subjective probability and the way that these two approaches are used in practice (see French 1988).

Soft Issues Considered. To cope with the problem that most management-level issues are not amenable to "hard" solutions we use a mixture of two approaches. To discuss systems that have in them the arbitrary behavior of real people, it is necessary to capture the idea that systems are not controlled by omniscient optimizers, hypothetical "rational economic men" capable of sifting all incoming information and processing it accurately to configure an optimal policy decision in consequence. We need to capture the idea that, when human decisions are made, there are information and cognitive limitations. This is expressed well by Simon (1957):

> The capacity of the human mind for formulating and solving complex problems is very small compared with the size of the problems whose solution is required. . .

---

[1] The University of Bristol physicist Michael Berry gives an excellent example of this in Wolpert and Richards (1988). He says that even if you had an ideal gas in an isolated, closed container and even if, despite Heisenberg, you could know the initial position and momentum of every particle (which you cannot), then by as few as 50 collisions into the future you could not tell which way a given molecule would bounce if you ignored the effect of the gravitational attraction of a single electron at the observable limit of the Universe!

The recognition of this fact, the "Principle of Bounded Rationality," must be included if we are not to drift off once more into models of abstracted and unreal systems. It is important therefore to look beyond the physical processes of a system. Every system has a complex flow of information running around it and it is important to include the effects of this intangible information network. We must be able to capture these intangibles, the flows of information, the policies that are embedded in a system, and the associated decision.

It is more difficult to handle the other reasons that can make a "hard" approach fail, that is, the characters of those taking part in the project. It is inappropriate to repeat the discussions of this here, except to say that the ability to assess the characters of clients, to see the relationships between them, and to foresee and handle any problems that might arise in consequence are by no means secondary requirements of a consultant. They are quite central to the successful implementation of any form of analysis.

Model Ownership. If the correct approach and tools are used and enough access to the management team is possible, then model ownership by the team should follow. This means that a model is unequivocally seen by the clients to be a statement of their ideas of the way the world works. These ideas do not have to be exhaustive or perfectly accurate but they must be expressed. It is by doing this that we avoid clients rejecting the messages of a model. If a team or an individual can be truly facilitated to construct a model or representation of their ideas, rejecting the message that that model then produces becomes a rejection of their own ideas.

Models Interpreted by Clients. The final point of our list concerns the process of getting information out of a model. It is important that it does not fall to the consultant to make a model work. Whether a model be a representation on paper or a piece of computer code, it is important that the clients be helped to read and interpret it themselves. This implies that the client must be helped to learn whichever techniques are used in a project. In consequence, the consultant has a duty to provide tools that are easy to pick up and that express powerful ideas simply. The tools must be simple to operate, not requiring esoteric tricks to get them to work. Software must have an interface that encourages exploration.

Goals and Benefits of Modeling as Learning

The initial goals of a piece of work and the benefits that consequently flow from it are closely linked and so we discuss them together here. For a Modeling as Learning project we list some of the goals and benefits, starting with the most important:

- Change mental models; improve business.
- Create learning and intuition.
- Allow risk-free experimentation.
- Express ideas in an explicit, logical way.
- Reveal systemic complexity.

Improving the Business. If mental models are altered then ideas are structured and shared, intuition is enhanced, new paths are explored, new ideas are generated, and commitment to a course of action is made. This is the way in which a business is improved and, in the context of our understanding of the wide nature of the stake-holding group in a business such as ours, this must always be the primary goal of our projects.

Creating Learning. The idea of learning and intuition building as the goal of a modeling process is, in practice, new to business. A powerful exponent of the fundamental idea is Papert (1980), who describes an alternative means of enabling children to understand mathematical ideas. Rather than use the classic teaching method of drumming facts into children (cf. expert consultancy), he created the computer language LOGO, which introduced children to concepts of shape by encouraging them to do their own very simple programming, which they could see "acted out" by a small robot carrying a pen. In attempting to make the robot draw shapes using instructions that they had themselves created, the children could take charge of their own learning and discover in their own way some of the fundamental ideas of geometry. Similarly, Ackoff (1979b) speaks of the role of O.R. not as being a predictor of the future but rather as a process of investigating systems so that they can be steered by their owners towards a desired and chosen future. The application of these ideas to business is described by de Geus (1988) from the perspective of a planning department and is central to the Modeling as Learning approach. It is, in fact, expressed succinctly by Galileo's comment that "One cannot teach a man anything. One can only enable him to learn from within himself." Let us consider a decision maker in Shell, or in any other large company or organization. Such an individual will never grasp the full complexity of the company and its business environment, simply because there are limits to any person's cognitive abilities. Yet over a period of time successful managers acquire a "feel" for the functioning of a business' most important parts that allows them to move the business in a chosen direction. This intuition comes through experience and through trial and error. When thinking of the cost and lead time of this learning we see a role for a method of accelerating this process. That method is to provide a different learning environment for managers.

The idea of using models to promote learning requires many changes to our standard view of modeling. Central to this is the question of the "deliverable" of the exercise, that is, the thing that is summoned up as a consequence of doing a piece of analysis. In the case of expert consultancy, the deliverable is a model or some results. We must emphasize very strongly that this is not the case with Modeling as Learning. The deliverable is a process, a process that produces enhanced learning in the minds of those involved. In close parallel with the approach of Richmond (1987), the deliverable is the creation of an effective learning environment in which managers can "play" with representations of their business and so enhance their intuition for how it works. My department has been one of a number to discover that Papert's ideas can be applied to managers: that learning is accelerated if we use "transitional objects," models that allow users to feed in their own assumptions and have played back to them the consequences of those assumptions.

The key question is then: What is learning? At its most abstract level, I would define learning as either the *addition of information* to a participant's mental model, or an *increase in the coherence* of such a model. The first idea tallies with our basic understanding of learning as being about the accumulation of facts. In the second idea, I use "coherent" in the sense that Rescher (1970) does, asserting that a set of beliefs and actions can only be considered to be coherent if they are rational, logically consistent with each other, and have no mutual contradictions. This definition clearly has much in common with the systems perspective of Forrester (1961), which encourages the link between events, behavior, and systems structure. However, I would wish to place further emphasis on the need for holism. To be considered coherent, I would propose that a belief set must include the interactions between the system's components and the higher level effects that are built up. Checkland (1981) uses the term "emergent properties" to label properties that are consequences of a whole system, not of any of its parts. Learning should include an understanding of these if it is to be truly effective.

The operationalization of these principles is of more immediate interest to business. In this context, "learning" can mean an understanding that different departments are pursuing incompatible goals. Or that the solution that produces quick relief ("hire more staff") makes the problem worse in the long term ("the training burden has increased"). Or the insight that cause and effect can be well separated in time and/or space ("reducing hiring will solve my staff glut—but what effect will it have on the reputation of my recruiters on college campuses?"). In the case studies of the section below titled "Examples of Modeling as Learning Projects," the learning points are clearly stated. Senge (1990) provides similar examples of systems thinking and how it may be put into practice as well as a powerful endorsement of the importance of organizational learning. In all cases, "learning"—an increase in the coherence of mental models—leads to decisions much more likely to produce the desired outcome.

Risk-Free Experimentation. If we use the above philosophy to create some model or representation of a set of ideas, then we can experiment by changing some parts of the model and seeing the effect of that change. The change can be a parameter or a policy. If the model is indeed a representation of a client's ideas on how the world functions, then this microcosm, or microworld, is the transitional object upon which the experimentation is performed. The user gains what Eden and Sims (1981) have called "computerized vicarious experience" of the world. The difference is that in this microworld the risks of making a poor decision are virtually nil. Highly unconventional policies can be tested that would never be tried in the real world. This is important because, as de Geus (1988) would have it, "Fear fences in imagination." By experimenting in such a way the user can gain an understanding for the way the system operates and which parameters are important and should be considered. Sterman (1989) provides an excellent example of the value of this with a production system that most experienced people would claim to understand but which, in the majority of cases, in fact proves uncontrollable because a vital piece of information is not considered when making decisions. Experience with this model can encourage people to look for the useful pieces of information in real life situations.

Expressing Ideas. In order to capture ideas as they emerge and so produce models that represent client's mental models, we must express those ideas in a clear and logical way. Expressing ideas in a simple language has many advantages. It helps individuals clarify their own thinking—how many problems have you only really understood after you had to explain them to someone else? It can also mean that a person can use more of the facts that they have in their mind. There is a limit to the number of factors that any person can take into account. Someone may in principle have a very large and complex mental model of a given situation but be able to access only a small part of it to make a decision. By expressing such a mental model in some external form, we can help a client use effectively a much greater proportion of the knowledge that they possess. We describe this process as

> Helping people to know better what they know already.

The most widely used reasons for creating an external representation of mental models is the great benefit that can be gained by structuring and sharing information. There are many reasons why it can be hard to transfer information from one person to another, but one of them is certainly that it can be hard to express ideas in a form that can be understood. Modeling as Learning uses tools that convey ideas simply and clearly and yet can contain complex notions.

Revealing Systemic Complexity. Whether working with a team or an individual, a clear expression of ideas has many advantages. It can allow clients to view the complexity of a given situation when perhaps they had only viewed parts of it. As

T.S. Eliot expresses very clearly, "I know that history at all times draws / The strangest consequence from remotest cause," but it is frequently hard for people to imagine the consequences of an action after it has worked through a very complex system. Various sources comment on the general lack of systemic thinking; for example, Meadows (1989) describes her difficulties and frustrations when trying to convey systemically complex ideas in articles for the U.S. press. As humans create a world of increasingly complex systems, it becomes more important that we be able to formulate views on their operation that are coherent (and holistic). A tool that allows a client to grapple with some of his/her ideas can lead, for example, to the discovery that goals that seemed reasonable when only part of the system was viewed are inconsistent or impossible in the context of the whole system. Another benefit comes when a model reveals how a high-level result, opinion, or consequence has been built up by small components. It is particularly interesting and useful to take two opposing positions and look at their component assumptions to isolate the exact point of disagreement. This is an excellent process for beginning to resolve such conflicts of opinion.

As regards the sharing or creation of knowledge amongst the participating clients, we should comment that it is frequently a subtle task to get people to recognize what they have gained from such a project. If the process is truly a success, then the new knowledge is so deeply embedded in the clients' mental model that it can be hard for them to remember their not knowing it! It then requires some skill and patience to get the client to see the process for what it was (and hence think that the consultants gave value for money!).

To contrast this approach with that of expert consultancy, we use the representation shown in Figure 4-4 for the Modeling as Learning process. There are no longer two separate areas of activity; rather, the contribution of the consultants (black) supports all of the management activity (white) and the two form a single, rounded whole. Starting with the problem issue, the consultants facilitate a discussion. This is frequently highly divergent, raising many issues, and may lack clarity, but a great deal of information on the mental models of the participants can be elicited. The consultants work with the clients to represent their mental models in some clearly articulated and represented form. This may be a causal-loop diagram, a STELLA model, or some other tool. The use of some means of clearly representing ideas does much to promote the discussion as it raises new lines of inquiry and questioning. We therefore show a loop back from the articulation stage to the discussion stage. This iterative process may take place across a number of meetings or within a single one. The purpose of eliciting and representing the mental models of a management team is to enable the clients to make their views coherent. This can mean that they are helped to take a holistic view of a problem or are brought to a realization that they have an inconsistent set of opinions. Such knowledge internalization, or learning, can then mean that the process itself ends and the managers are

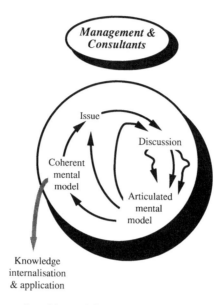

Figure 4-4. A representation of the Modeling as Learning consultancy methodology. The process is a joint one in which the consultants support the various stages indicated by the arrows. The process is frequently iterative but on completion results in a decision of some sort.

able to apply that learning, perhaps by making a specific decision. However, there are other possibilities that involve further iterations through the process. The key one is the recognition by a team that they have been focusing on the wrong issue. This can come either from their considering the consequences of a coherent mental model, or may arise earlier during the discussion phase when a new and more important issue is uncovered. An example of such a turn of events is given in the subsection below titled "Future Developments of a Natural Gas Market." The distinction between these two possibilities is sometimes hard to observe and both are represented in Figure 4-4.

We might offer here a brief comparison with other approaches. This process has most in common with Richmond (1987) in that it provides a context within which decision makers can generate greater insight into, and greater commitment to, an effective strategy by sharing and challenging their mental models via a STELLA representation. An interesting contrast is the work of Vennix et al. (1990), with whom there has been considerable cross-fertilization of ideas. Their three-stage process of preliminary conceptual model, Delphic workbook, and structured workshop is tailored particularly for larger groups requiring a more consensus-based course of action. With this in mind, there are still great similarities between their stages 1 and 3 and the model described above—we are certainly able to confirm their observation that as models are revisited, variables are seldom dropped, it being far more likely that intermediate variables are added to clarify the nature of the causality. Generally, though, pressure of time has required that our processes be more intense and involve far fewer people.

MODELING AS LEARNING TOOLS

The tools that are used in our department's projects are spread across a wide spectrum. We may group them into four headings, although there is considerable overlap:

- Basic consultant's skills

- Conceptual frameworks

- Qualitative modeling tools

- Quantitative modeling tools

All of these tools are useful in externalizing and representing mental models and helping to change them, and we discuss our experiences in each of them below. For a description of further tools and of the philosophical linkages between them, see Lane (1994a and b).

Basic Consultant's Skills

There are certain minimum requirements for anyone wishing to be successful in a consultancy role. They must have the courage and skill to establish early on with a client a contract, or statement of the role that the consultant is required to play and hence which duties he or she is required to perform. They must be prepared to listen and have the interpersonal skills necessary to coax information out of a client. They must be a clear and rapid thinker so as to pick up connections and gaps in anything that a client says. They must have the courage and objectivity to probe a client's fundamental assumptions. And they must be an intelligent mirror to a client's comments, a good person to bounce ideas off. A good consultant can help a client clarify their thinking with careful and well-chosen questioning or can offer a re-formulation of a client's ideas in a way that improves their power. If a consultant hears the client say, "So I suppose that what I am really saying is," or " Yes, that's what I really mean," then he or she is on the right track. Other types of intervention skills are required; for example, the expression of comments in another form so as to avoid misunderstanding, and reminding clients of earlier comments, perhaps now forgotten, whose relevance has since emerged.

Conceptual Frameworks

Conceptual frameworks are specific verbal or written devices that help clients extend their understanding of their ideas to broader or more abstract examples or help clients connect together various ideas. They are simply devices which help to trigger thinking and support creativity.

Verbal examples are analogies and metaphors: "This is like the U.S. railway industry," or "This is the snowball effect." Similarly, it is important to establish which type of discussion framework will suit the client best. For clients who wish to generate more ideas it is suitable to work in a divergent discussion framework, that is, prompt the client with questions that facilitate brainstorming and provide a means of recording the resulting material. For clients wishing to move to agreement, a consultant should work in a convergent framework, trying to match ideas, find common ground and nurture consensus and commitment. Clearly these two processes are different, and it is important that a consultant know which approach to use at any given moment.

In order to check on the consistency of ideas we use "scenarios." These are coherent and consistent views of the future and are another product of the work in the Group Planning division at Shell (see Wack 1985). They help a client see which facts are most closely associated. An example might be a "$10 oil price" scenario. The consultant would take this crude price as a basic assumption and then talk through its ramifications. What would be the consequences for renewable energy source development? What would happen to new investment? This process produces not a forecast but a picture of how this particular world state would operate, what its driving forces would be, and what its internal logic would be. A scenario can be supported by the methods discussed below; indeed, the use of scenarios is very important to the Modeling as Learning approach since it is a powerful conceptualization tool for computer-based learning environments. We discuss it here because we have found it useful in its own right at the verbal stage of problem definition.

There is a long list of tools that spark off ideas, most of them very well known. The other ones that we consider useful include SWOT analysis (strengths, weaknesses, opportunities, threats), Porter's five competitive forces (1980), and standard value-chain analysis.

Qualitative Modeling Tools

The boundary between this subsection and the previous one is not clearly defined. Generally, we refer here to means of displaying the boundary of a system or the associations between concepts using some form of structuring technique. Usually this involves the representation of the problem on paper or a computer, using standard symbols or checklists.

From Checkland's (1981 and 1990) work we have found VOCATE analysis very helpful. We have used this as a stand-alone tool, where it can be used as a variation of stakeholder analysis, or as a precursor to a more formal model.

We have found the tools of system dynamics to be of great help. They are not a panacea, since they require that a problem have a time evolution quality. We have used causal-loop diagrams extensively, however, to reveal the dynamics and complexity of systems, using the ideas of Forrester (1968a). The combination of graphical simplicity with analytic power makes this a tool that can be applied widely and with considerable effectiveness. The language can handle both "hard" and "soft" ideas, for example, order backlog and customer confidence. This makes it very valuable for use within the context of ideas discussed in the sections titled "Assembling a New Methodology" and "Modeling as Learning."

We use causal-loop diagrams during interviews in a similar way to that in which Eden et al. (1983) draw COPE-maps with clients. We have found that an experienced consultant can conduct a session with up to six clients in which a causal-loop diagram is constructed on a central whiteboard. The language is so simple that, without exception, such sessions result in the clients' moving to the board to add to or change the diagram. Such sessions usually last two to three hours and are very useful for encouraging information from clients and structuring it.

Although we also use causal-loop diagrams to conceptualize quantitative models (see the next subsection) we should emphasize that we do not consider them to be such precursors only; we have found that they can give and provoke insights as a tool in their own right.

The final qualitative tool that should be mentioned is the "magnetic hexagon" technique. This consists of a large number of magnetized, plastic hexagons on which ideas can be written. The objects are then fixed on a large board where they can be moved around to represent accepted connections or to experiment with possible new ones. It is a very simple idea that can be very powerful. Having the related tools in both group and individual magnetic board form, I have experimented with their use as conceptualization and idea-structuring devices. As a method of displaying associations we have found it useful, and have used photographs of completed diagrams as OHP slides during presentations. We are beginning to experiment with using the tool during divergent, brainstorming processes in order to capture ideas. Further discussion of this technique may be found in Hodgson (1992 and Chapter 18 of this work) and an example of its use in the elicitation of ideas that resulted in a system dynamics model can be found in Lane (1993b).

Quantitative Modeling Tools

The tools discussed here are more akin to standard simulation techniques than the devices of the previous sections. However, we should revisit Figure 4-3c and affirm again that the consultancy approach that we use with these tools means that we seek the maximum of this curve by trading off functionality for transparency. To some extent it has become generally easier to use quantitative tools during the last few years. For example, the modern spreadsheet packages bring a reasonable amount of power to anyone's PC, in a form that can be understood without huge time investment. (We can interpret this as the curve in Figure 4-3b having the decline deferred somewhat and so happening over to the right a little more.)

To conceptualize our quantitative models we employ causal-loop diagrams and, less often, the policy structure diagrams and ideas of Morecroft (1982) and (1983). However, we should note that we have also found causal-loop diagrams useful in illuminating a model that has already been created (see the example subsection below titled "Commodity Production and Training"). We have thus found value in the approaches of both Goodman (1974) and Forrester (1968a).

The principle quantitative tool used for Modeling as Learning by Business Consultancy at Shell International is STELLA, a package produced by Richmond et al. (1987). Our experience is that this package can be used very easily to capture mental models from clients. Ideas on both tangible and intangible concepts can be expressed. Using bounded rationality ideas, the package can be useful for capturing and exploring logics and policies. We have observed that the symbols are easy to understand. It is always possible to explain a model to a client and slowly build it with them, and frequently clients will formulate their ideas in STELLA symbols.[2] We have found that the icon-driven nature of this package makes it interesting and exciting for consultants and clients alike. The interface is fun to use, which we consider to be an important factor in its success with clients. With this package it really is possible to perform analysis *in* meetings *with* clients.

The caveat to be issued regarding STELLA models is that we found it very easy for clients to over-interpret the numerical output. With such models we encourage clients to put numbers to effects that are hard to quantify, just so the consequences of the chosen number could be seen. It then becomes inconsistent to look for detailed information in the numbers that are produced. Despite this, it is an error that we frequently move to avoid. Our main counter is to use scenarios again, since this encourages clients to note the *differences* between runs with different parameter or policy settings and not analyze inappropriately the results of a single run.

The huge volume of work in Forrester (1961) and Lyneis (1980), for example, is readily converted to the new symbology. This means that there is a library of structures with some generic features that can be applied to different cases. However, we must stress that we do not suddenly produce these large structures and give them to clients; this would be against the whole philosophy of the approach. Instead we read around the client's problem to check whether there are any useful structures in existence and, if so, slowly introduce helpful pieces to the client during the process of model building. This approach may not be as fast as just conjuring up a large model, but it does ensure ownership and the benefits that flow from it.

---

[2] As with any kind of idea-structuring technique this can limit, rather than channel, thought but we have found that generally the constructive aspect of directing ideas using STELLA symbols easily outweighs the restriction that this discipline imposes.

EXAMPLES OF MODELING AS LEARNING PROJECTS

This section contains four examples of the application of the Modeling as Learning approach to consultancy projects. For confidentiality purposes, some of the specific details of these have been altered, but the features relevant to this paper are accurate. For each example, we state briefly the business problem or issue studied, give an account of the method that was used in the project, and discuss the value gained by the client in consequence.

Product Launch and Competitive Response Study

For this study, the clients wanted some fresh insight into the myriad of factors surrounding the launch of a new hydro-carbon product, in order to share and confirm ideas. The factors fell broadly into two areas. The first concerned the management of customer base build-up so as to match supply to demand. The second concerned the appearance of a substitute product from a rival and how the Shell company would react. The main measure of success for the product launch was the net present value (NPV) of the whole project.

From these two areas many more detailed issues arose. The team wished to discuss the initial sales force required and the rate at which it should be expanded. They wanted to think about when to build their pilot production plant and when the full-scale plant would be needed. They wished to consider what signals from their own production would attract a competitor. Would the signal be price? Demand? Backlog? Which might be the stronger? Also, the team wanted to discuss the best response to competitor entry. Should they cut price to preserve market share? Or invest in product quality and charge a premium? How robust were any strategies to changes in the timing or strength of competitor response?

Causal-loop diagrams were elicited from the various parties during discussions and were collected to form a single diagram, a collective mental model in clearly articulated form. This diagram, shown in Figure 4-5, was large and complex, containing many intermediate variables. However, it was possible to pick out loops similar to those of Forrester's market growth model (1968b) and so identify the main feedback effects. There were two reinforcing loops and four balancing loops. The first reinforcing loop (R1) involved the generation of more customer confidence as more sales were made and the second (R2) expressed the ability of orders to provide income that could be used to expand the sales force still further. The first balancing loop (B1) concerned the suppressing effect on orders of backlogs. The other three loops concerned the entrance of a competitor, which is attracted by the observed demand for the product (Orders) and by the inability of the Shell company to fill those orders (Backlog). The first (B2) indicates that customers are attracted away to the competitor, the second (B3) expresses the suppression effects on NPV of a price war, while the third (B4) shows that a competitor may trigger

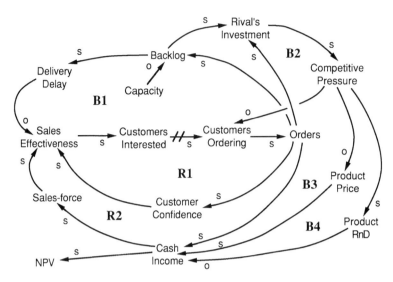

Figure 4-5. Articulated mental model elicited from the clients
during the product launch and competitive response study

response in which the Shell company invests in value-added, quality aspects of the
product, again reducing NPV.

Complex as this diagram was, we were able to work with it by using color-cod-
ing and carefully talking the clients around each of the key feedback loops so that
they themselves understood the feedback consequences of their own structure.

After this extensive discussion of the causal loop diagram, the project team
moved to the construction of a 70-equation STELLA model. Inputs included sales
force expansion policy, plant completion time, and various responses to competition. Additional feedback effects were elicited from the clients in order to express
the relative attractiveness of the two competing products, judged by price and non-
financial attributes. These links therefore contained the advantageous effects of cutting price or investing in value-added qualities. Graphical outputs included NPV,
sales (Shell and competitor), backlog, price, etc. At first, the model was set to
express the assumptions and ideas that the clients had at the start of the process.

Motivated by the complexity of structure in this model, we built it so that it was
possible to switch individual loops on and off. In this way the clients were able to
build up the complexity of the full model loop by loop, pausing at each addition to
ensure that they understood the resulting dynamic output. This also enabled the
clients to observe the relative strengths of the feedback loops and the robustness of
results to changes in variable values.

With its wide range of inputs and its complex structure, the model proved to be
a rich source of scenarios and ideas. It was useful to the clients for experimenting
with ways of matching product supply to demand by varying plant completion

date and sales force policy. This is a frequently occurring dynamic problem involving feedback and delays; just the sort of system that a client needs to play with in order to get a feel for its behavior, to be able to take a coherent view of the feedback. On the question of response to competition, the model replayed to the clients the consequences of investing in price cuts, other product attributes, or both. This output was controversial and, although it cannot be discussed in any more detail here, led the clients to rethink the assumptions that they had had on this subject before the project began. In general terms then, the learning from the process consisted of enhanced understanding of how the different aspects of the launch strategy interacted and which parameters would be important in determining the behavior of the system.

Future Developments of a Natural Gas Market

Here the requirement of the clients was twofold. The prime goal was to assist in the clients' discussion of the influences that shaped the gas market, with particular reference to the energy demand arising from electrical power generation. In addition to this, some key members of staff were leaving the department in question and, as there was a need to get their successors up to speed as soon as possible, it was hoped that a modeling process might aid this.

The process itself consisted of a number of brainstorming sessions. In these the clients first discussed their knowledge of the business and the consultants made causal loop diagram representations of the knowledge to assist the debate. The STELLA symbols were then introduced by presenting a STELLA diagram equivalent of the causal loops. After this the computer package itself was used live in meetings to capture mental models and the clients were able to share and develop ideas. A fully functioning model of some 60 equations was built with the clients. This contained what they felt to be the key influences in the market and it led in turn to further discussions.

This project produced a good demonstration of how a modeling process can be useful, even though it does not claim to forecast. Put in simple terms, the gas demand of this market is supplied in two ways. The first is the standard, contracted supply from gas projects in the neighboring geographical area. Any additional demand is fulfilled by taking advantage of the slack in the system; for example, it is possible to speed up the carriage of the natural gas if the additional cost of transport fuel is defrayed by the increased selling price. These supply sources are shown in Figure 4-6. By building into a model the best ideas on how the system would evolve, it was demonstrated that much more additional supply would be needed since, as demand rose more rapidly than standard supply, the amount of additional supply, implied by keeping demand and supply matched, widened greatly. The clients considered this scenario to be highly unrealistic as a possible future. Yet this meant to them that the model did contain a message: The market logic operating

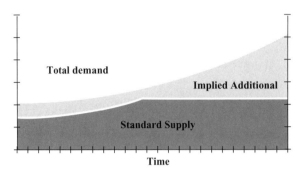

Figure 4-6. Evolution of natural gas supply sources and demand as indicated by model scenario

now, and that had been captured in the model, would have to change in the next few decades. In other words, if the slack in the system would not cover future demand, then either a more flexible supply system would be necessary, or new gas sources would have to be found. The inconsistency of their views was the main learning point that the clients obtained from the process. It was also an interesting example of model output being "wrong" but still useful. At present, the issue of meeting the demand/supply gap is the subject of further study.

We close with a discussion of the other benefits gained by the clients from the project. Using the model based on the clients' assumptions, it was found that one of the extrema for demand quoted in the literature was impossible to obtain under any reasonable set of parameters. This focused the clients' discussions on the assumptions that lay behind that original estimate from the literature. Generally, the clients found that the process had been useful in helping them to capture and structure some of their knowledge (although they commented that STELLA was not suitable for storing large amounts of data and that alternative means would have to be found for that). The tool was found to be useful for analyzing ideas and generating insight into the functioning of the market. One of the team members, who was due to depart, commented that the discussions had allowed him to produce much information that might otherwise not have been captured in such an organized form. As a result, he believed, the team would be able to use its shared understanding of the market much more effectively as they had a common language in which to describe it. One of the new staff members on the client team said that as a result of the project her learning curve had certainly been shortened.

Study of a High Technology Start-Up Company

This project involved the three most senior managers of a high technology start-up firm. The goal was twofold: to help the team study the company that they had only recently been given charge of and to aid in the creation of strategies which would cope with the rapid growth in sales that they firmly believed would occur.

This work is published as Morecroft, Lane, and Viita (1991) in which more detail may be found.

After a full day of very broad discussion and copious note-taking with the clients, it was decided that the most fruitful areas to study were the production side of the business and the customer base. We went straight to the iconography of STELLA, using the symbols as a form of policy structure diagram to articulate ideas about the business. Having gotten the clients to amend and then approve the diagram while in paper form, we progressed to three STELLA representations, two of some 50 equations and a third that combined these two. These were worked on in detail by one consultant and the commercial director of the company in order to ensure credibility with and ownership by the whole team. A visit to the company's factory and discussion with its manager helped in the creation of one of the models. Having supplied the necessary algebra and reviewed the structure, the models were then brought back to the full management team and their formulation explained and amended until they were felt to be satisfactory and clear. The models were then used in discussions with the three clients, to create scenarios and stimulate ideas.

This project was valuable in the three areas for which models were built. Manufacturing involved a complex interplay of parameters, so complex in fact that it was difficult to specify the production capacity to a greater tolerance than one order of magnitude. A model for the factory allowed the clients to come to grips with the parameters, and it was found that if small improvements could be made to certain variables, this would yield large changes in the way orders could be filled. The production manager reported that he had used this insight to motivate his research staff who were currently investigating means of optimizing production. He also said that the projects had been "a useful discipline" for getting the team together to share ideas, since it was all too easy for them to concentrate on their own areas only, especially since one of the three was based in another country.

A model for the customer base, part of which is shown in Figure 4-7, indicated that the growth of sales that the clients had hoped for would not be possible. Although marketing time was spent on recruiting new customers, it also had to be spent on the maintenance of the existing customer base or those customers would slowly be lost. Thus, marketing resources constituted a limit to growth when used in the maintenance role too. Although this insight was revealed using the STELLA model, it then proved easier to explain using a causal-loop diagram, an application of Forrester's view of their use (1968a). This is an example of the use of a modeling process to form a bridge between the assumed behavior of a system and its detailed structure. The clients had begun the project with the firm view that the behavior mode of their company would be rapid growth. However, when encouraged to enunciate the structure of their business, they had learned that the assumed structure did not support such behavior. Various ways around this were explored by considering the key pieces of the STELLA model and discussing how they might

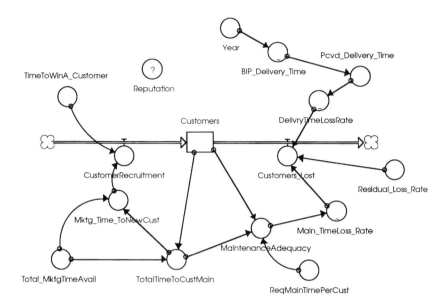

Figure 4-7. Part of the STELLA model created for the high technology start-up company study. The central rectangle represents the accumulation of customers. Customers flow out of this stock at loss rates caused by high delivery time (exogenously generated here), inadequate maintenance (internally generated), and a residual rate caused by the turnover of store managers who have been persuaded to take up the product. Note the division of the total marketing time available between time spent on recruiting new customers and the total time spent on customer maintenance. The "?" in the circle records the clients' inability to add structure to their initial assumption of rapid growth.

be changed to improve performance. This then provided a demonstration of how a process such as this, even if it does not explicitly find a ready solution, helps the clients search for one simply by indicating clearly what the present problems are. It is also an example where the original issue in a study (managing growth) is revealed to be less important than one that is discovered during the study (rapid growth is structurally impossible).

A model that linked orders to production was of particular interest to the managing director. Using the fundamental idea of Forrester (1968b), this revealed a classic systems problem of how to match growth of orders with capacity expansion so as to manage growth. Sensitivity to delivery delays was seen to be a key parameter, and one practical benefit of the project was the sending out of a questionnaire to all of the marketers to try to quantify this further. A particularly striking moment occurred when the MD was running the model and tried a new policy scenario. With the encouragement of a consultant, he predicted the outcome, but on seeing the output graphs he commented, "Yes, but that means that I can . . ." and proceeded to interpret the results back into his business, producing a very new idea for policy. This was a very satisfying example of how a modeling exercise can study certain issues with benefit and still act as a catalyst for ideas in other areas.

Commodity Production and Trading

This project (see also Lane 1993a) centered on a disagreement between two parties regarding the effects on revenues of a maintenance shut-down on production capacity. The commodity in question was produced locally but could also be traded in via a market that itself drew on another neighboring source of production. The producing department felt that during the maintenance period the company's revenues would not fall too badly, while it was the opinion of the trading department that the revenue drop would be about the same proportionally as the production reduction. In this description the local market will be referred to as "western" and the neighboring one as "eastern," though these terms are used only for the purposes of clarity.

Members of the two departments concerned in this project began meeting to find the key factors that made them hold their respective positions. Causal-loop diagrams were used for this and again proved to be very flexible and comprehensible as a means for representing ideas during discussions. After this, a sub-systems overview was created to show the different areas of concern and the nature of the information that was passed between them (see Figure 4-8). Having produced these structures for the main dynamic effects with the support of both parties, we moved to STELLA to try to express the relative strengths. A model of some 45 equations revealed that the producers predominantly based their opinion on the assertion that competitors in the local market would have difficulty in expanding their capacity to fill the supply gap resulting from the maintenance. Hence, although the company volume would fall, the effects on revenues would be partially mitigated by the price moving up. The traders held the view that small price changes would result in the traded market responding by shipping in more volume of the commodity from an

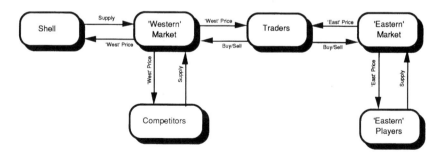

Figure 4-8. Subsystems overview of the model used in the commodity production and trading case. Note how it was possible to define distinct parts of the model, which were then created in detail by specialists in the respective area. They were then linked together by appropriate information flows.

"eastern" market, thus taking advantage of the increased margin. This fact would severely limit any upward price movement, resulting in a fall of company revenues that would be almost proportional to the production reduction while the maintenance took place.

The added value in this case resulted from the disentangling of high-level hypotheses of behavior to find the basic assumptions. This meant that a discussion that was in danger of becoming a "Yes it will/No it won't" event was steered into a constructive discussion about the two specific relationships mentioned in the previous paragraph. In addition, the traders accepted the detailed understanding of the competitors' position implied by the producers, but maintained that, because of the economic characteristics of the "eastern" market, increases in traded imports would occur very rapidly. The producers eventually agreed, on the grounds that they had not accounted for the fact that the trading effect would be so large. The learning thus consisted of the realization that both sides shared predominantly the same mental model of the problem and, for the producers, that the response time for trading was less than they had thought.

Interestingly, having accepted this last fact, the producers did not feel the need to go back to the STELLA model; they were able to build the new assumption on the traders reaction into their mental model of the market and interrogate it to produce the same view on revenues as the traders. Curiosity led the consultants to confirm this using the STELLA model!

CONCLUSIONS

The experience of our department is that there is a difference between the creation of an idea of a consultancy style and its practical application. There are departments that have not responded at a fundamental level to Ackoff's claim that O.R. is dead and his penetrating diagnosis of the ailment (1979a). In our case we perhaps experienced, in microcosm, proof of the Modeling as Learning axiom that people learn more readily from experience than from teaching! We were aware of the ideas of facilitation consultancy and "soft" O.R. (an unhappy term, since it carries a nuance of ease and longueur rather than expressing the ferocious difficulty of such work). Despite this it was necessary for us to view for ourselves the limitations of expert consultancy and to draw out the common strands of its problems, in order to see how it might be improved. We have had to experiment with new ideas, absorbing some from the literature and looking to the experience of our own company for others. We have slowly crafted our own approach, the goal being adapted from that of de Geus (1988), the consultant's role being embellished by Schein (1969) and others, our most commonly used tools originating from Forrester (1961). We are still discovering how flexible the approach can be; each project has its own facets that teach us more about what we can do.[3] If the ideas are not all new, we console ourselves with the thought that this matters little as long as our work improves the business, and we remember Dr. Johnson's comment that "Men more often need to be reminded than informed." In order to arrive at the position that we now hold, we suspect that it was necessary to travel the difficult path of error, self-examination, reconstruction and experimentation that is described here. For us, there was no Royal Road to the new techniques of consultancy. But now that we have a workable philosophy we are able to assess new ideas in the light of it. Although so far system dynamics has provided our most frequently used tool, we can use the check list of client ownership, consultant as facilitator, and sensitivity to soft issues to test whether new ideas can be of value to us. In this way we are slowly extending our portfolio of tools.

We are still employing the tools and approach of traditional O.R. because they are still in demand and have value for our clients. By using Modeling as Learning, however, we now see ourselves tackling problems and working with clients that would have been beyond our reach had we not expanded into this new area. When we add to this the thought that the ability to learn faster than your competitors may be the only sustainable competitive advantage, we see that a driving goal of advancing the company is also achieved using the package of ideas that constitutes Modeling as Learning, and that this confirms Senge's (1990) view on the vital need for an organization to inculcate a culture that supports its own innovation. This is why we believe that this is the way for the future of a significant proportion of the work done by our Business Consultancy department and of the value generated for our clients and the business.

---

[3] When sufficient experience has been gained, an obvious next step would be to do careful, quantified research into how the group process works, how effective it is, and which features help it to be so. With process consultation in general, technological and methodological practices have advanced ahead of scientific inquiry. Kaplan (1979) comments that although the notion that process consultation has practical value has certainly not been disproved, there is insufficient scientific evidence to demonstrate this value clearly. We would therefore need to measure the specific benefits to the client and to isolate the style of process consultation as being a causal factor. At present we can only offer the anecdotal viewpoint that our clients almost always comment that the process enhanced participation, that the computer modeling element (when present) added value, and that the results of the process justified the investment. However, it is interesting to note that these observations have, so far, much in common with the study by McCartt and Rohrbaugh (1989) of a group of decision conferences.

REFERENCES

Ackoff, R.L. (1979a), "The Future of Operational Research Is Past," *Journal of the Operational Research Society* 30, no. 2: 93-104.

Ackoff, R.L. (1979b), "Resurrecting the Future of Operational Research," *Journal of the Operational Research Society* 30, no. 3: 189-99.

Checkland, P. (1981), *Systems Thinking, Systems Practice*, Chichester, U.K.: John Wiley & Sons Ltd.

Checkland, P., and J. Scholes (1990), *Soft Systems Methodology in Action*, Chichester, U.K.: John Wiley & Sons Ltd.

Eden, C., and D. Sims (1981), "Computerized Vicarious Experience: The Future for Management Induction?" *Personnel Review* 10, no. 1: 22-25.

Eden, C., S. Jones, and D. Sims (1983), *Messing About in Problems*, Oxford: Pergamon Press.

Forrester, J.W. (1961), *Industrial Dynamics*, Portland, Ore.: Productivity Press.

Forrester, J.W. (1968a), *Principles of Systems*, Portland, Ore.: Productivity Press..

Forrester, J.W. (1968b), "Market Growth as Influenced by Capital Investment," *Sloan Management Review* 9, no. 2: 83-105.

French, S. (1988), *Decision Theory*, Chichester, U.K.: Ellis Horwood Ltd.

de Geus, A. (1988), "Planning as Learning," *Harvard Business Review,* March-April: 70-74.

Goodman, M.R. (1974), *Study Notes in System Dynamics*, Portland, Ore.: Productivity Press.

Hodgson, T. (1992), "Hexagons for Systems Thinking," *European Journal of Operational Research* 59, no. 1: 220-30, and Chapter 18 of this volume.

Kaplan, R.E. (1979), "The Conspicuous Absence of Evidence That Process Consultation Enhances Task Performance," *Journal of Applied Behavioral Science* 15: 346-60.

Kathawala, Y. (1988), "Applications of Quantitative Techniques in Large and Small Organizations in the United States: An Empirical Analysis," *Journal of the Operational Research Society* 39, no. 11: 981-89.

Lane, D.C. (1993a), "From Discussion to Dialogue: How an Interactive Modeling Process Was Used with Managers to Resolve Conflict and Generate Meaning," in E. Zepeda and J.A.D. Machuca, eds., *System Dynamics 1993* , Boston: System Dynamics Society, 231-34.

Lane, D.C. (1993b), "The Road Not Taken: Observing a Process of Issue Selection and Model Conceptualisation," *System Dynamics Review`* 9, no. 3: 239-64.

Lane, D.C. (1994a), "With a Little Help from Our Friends: How System Dynamics and Soft OR Can Learn from Each Other," *System Dynamics Review 1*0, no. 2-3 (forthcoming).

Lane, D.C. (1994b), "System Dynamics Practice: A Comment on 'A Case Study in Community Care Using Systems Thinking,'" *Journal of the Operational Research Society* 4, no. 3: 361-63.

Lyneis, J.M. (1980), *Corporate Planning and Policy Design*, Cambridge, Mass.: Pugh-Roberts Associates, Inc.

McCartt, A.T., and J. Rohrbaugh (1989), "Evaluating Group Decision Support System Effectiveness: A Performance Study of Decision Conferencing," *Decision Support Systems* 5: 243-53.

Meadows, D.H. (1989), "System Dynamics Meets the Press," *System Dynamics. Review* 5, no. 1: 69-80.

Morecroft, J.D.W. (1982), "A Critical Review of Diagramming Tools for Conceptualising Feedback System Models," *Dynamica* 8, Part I, (Summer): 20-29.

Morecroft, J. (1983), "System Dynamics: Portraying Bounded Rationality," *Omega* 11: 131- 42.

Morecroft, J.D.W., D.C. Lane, and P. Viita (1991), "Modeling a Biotechnology Start-up Firm," *System Dynamics Review* 7, no. 2: 93-116.

Papert, S. (1980), *Mindstorms*, Brighton, U.K.: Harvester Press Ltd.

Porter, M.E. (1980), *Competitive Strategy*, New York: Free Press.

Richmond, B. (1987), "The Strategic Forum," High Performance Systems, 45 Lyme Road, Ste. 300, Hanover NH 03755.

Richmond, B.M., P. Vescuso, and S. Peterson (1987), *STELLA for Business,* High Performance Systems, 45 Lyme Road, Ste. 300, Hanover NH 03755.

Rescher, N. (1970), *The Coherence Theory of Truth*, Oxford: Oxford University Press.

Schein, E.H. (1969), *Process Consultation: Its Role in Organizational Development*, Reading, Mass.: Addison-Wesley.

Senge, P.M. (1990), *The Fifth Discipline: The Art and Practice of the Learning Organization,* New York: Doubleday/Currency.

Simon, H.A. (1957), *Models of Man*, New York: John Wiley.

Sterman, J.D. (1989), "Modeling Managerial Behavior: Misperceptions of Feedback in a Dynamic Decision Making Experiment," *Management Science* 35, no. 3: 321-39.

Sturgeon, T. (1990), "Slow Sculpture," in B. Bova, ed., *The Best of the Nebulas,* London: Robert Hale, 383-98.

Uhlmann, A. (1988), "Linear Programming on a Micro Computer: An Application in Refinery Modeling," *European Journal of Operational Research* 35: 321-27.

Vennix, J.A.M., J.W. Gubbels, D. Post, and H.J. Poppen (1990), "A Structured Approach to Knowledge Elicitation in Conceptual Model Building," *System Dynamics Review* 6, no. 2: 194-208.

Wack, P. (1985), "Scenarios: Uncharted Waters Ahead," *Harvard Business Review*, September-October: 72-89.

Watson, S. (1988), personal communication.

Wolpert, L., and A. Richards (1988), *A Passion for Science*, Oxford: Oxford University Press.

5

KNOWLEDGE ELICITATION IN CONCEPTUAL MODEL BUILDING: A CASE STUDY IN MODELING A REGIONAL DUTCH HEALTH CARE SYSTEM

JAC A.M. VENNIX AND
JAN W. GUBBELS

ABSTRACT: Client-oriented model building entails eliciting relevant knowledge from the mental models of participants. System dynamicists commonly employ interviews with individuals followed by one or more discussions in freely interacting groups to capture knowledge from a client group. At least two problems arise as a result of this approach. First, it usually demands a high time investment from the client group. Second, freely interacting groups have several drawbacks and are often outperformed by individuals when it comes to generating relevant knowledge. To overcome these difficulties a combination of different techniques for knowledge elicitation is proposed, based on useful elements from existing group process methods. The approach consists of three stages with intermediate feedback to participants and can be considered a variant of the "Estimate-Feedback-Talk (EFT)" approach. Its use is illustrated with a case study of model building in Dutch health care.*

*The authors wish to thank Doeke Post and Henk Poppen for their participation in the project and Loes Builtjes, Jan Faber, George Richardson, and Wim Scheper for valuable comments on earlier versions of this article.

Introduction

Studies evaluating the impact of computer models to support policy-making processes in organizations have indicated that client involvement in the model-building process is often a prerequisite for effective model building. One important reason is that the process of model building is frequently more important than the resulting model. Model building itself is largely a learning process about the problem. Most insights about the characteristics of an ill-structured problem are gained during the iterative process of designing a computer model, rather than after the model is finished (House 1982; Meadows and Robinson 1985; de Geus 1988; Vennix 1990). Another important reason is that most information in an organization resides in the mental models of organizational members (Forrester 1987, 1992 and Chapter 3 of this volume). Or as Mintzberg puts it: "Thus the strategic data bank of the organization is not in the memory of its computers but in the minds of its managers" (Mintzberg 1990, 166). To support policy making in organizations it is this knowledge which needs to be captured and represented in the model. An important topic in client-oriented or interactive model building thus becomes the elicitation of relevant knowledge contained in the mental models of participants.

Two important problems arise with regard to interactive model building. The first is related to the time investment of the client group. In general the process of model building takes a considerable amount of time. And among policy makers and managers, time is a scarce resource. The question then becomes how to structure the model-building process in such a way that time investment is kept as low as is reasonably possible.

The second problem is related to the sources of knowledge and the techniques to elicit relevant knowledge. System dynamics modelers have primarily relied on interviews with key persons and discussions in interacting groups to capture knowledge from the mental models of participants (Morecroft et al. 1991; Randers 1977; Richmond 1987; Richardson and Senge 1989; Stenberg 1980; Weil 1980). Freely interacting groups, however, exhibit several characteristics inhibiting group performance. Among these are the tendency of high-status persons to dominate discussions, inequality of participation, and focusing on a single train of thought (Delbecq et al. 1975). Various group process techniques have emerged aimed at improving group performance. Two of the best-known are Delphi (Linstone and Turoff 1975) and NGT: Nominal Group Technique (Delbecq et al. 1975). Although these techniques contain useful elements, their application to interactive model building is not straightforward. Hence, it is worthwhile to create alternative procedures particularly aimed at knowledge elicitation in system dynamics model building. To guide the design process of such procedures, useful elements of existing group process techniques could be used as a basis. In this article we will focus on the design and the implementation of such an alternative procedure. The emphasis is on the design of the procedure and its feasibility. Although we will indicate criteria with which to evaluate the procedure described in this article, we will not primarily be concerned with its evaluation. This will be the topic of future research efforts.

In the following section we first review the literature on relevant group process techniques and outline the design of our procedure. In the section titled "The Policy Problem," we will briefly present the policy problem that is being modeled. In the following sections we discuss each of the stages in our approach in more detail. In a previous article (Vennix et al. 1990) we have given an overall description of this procedure for eliciting knowledge in conceptual model building. In later sections of this chapter, we will concentrate in more detail on the central elements in the procedure, i.e. the preliminary model, the questionnaires and the workbooks. These sections are meant to provide the interested reader with enough information to apply the procedure in an interactive model-building setting. In a final section we discuss the main results of this study.

GROUP PROCESS TECHNIQUES FOR CAPTURING KNOWLEDGE

A procedure for interactive modeling and knowledge elicitation will have to meet several requirements. First, the process must be tailored to the iterative character of model building. Second, as compared to approaches including interviews and interacting groups, the process should significantly reduce the participants' time investment. Third, it must allow structured debate on participants' (tacit) assumptions about reality. This is of importance, since most learning takes place during these discussions, because participants share the knowledge contained in their mental models. And finally, the model resulting from this process should not become overly complex. Particularly when the number of participants is large this latter requirement becomes necessary.

With these demands in mind let us take a look at some well-known and relevant group process techniques, i.e., Delphi, Nominal Group Technique (NGT) and Social Judgment Analysis (SJA), in order to establish their utility for interactive model building.

Delphi was originally designed to reduce the inhibiting effects of interacting groups while at the same time preserving the power of pooled knowledge from a group of experts (Dalkey 1969). This is accomplished by an anonymous procedure employing a series of mailed questionnaires. Results of one iteration are fed back to the panel in the next iteration. The number of cycles is limited by a predetermined criterion, e.g., the level of consensus in the panel or stability in the response patterns. Delphi has been employed numerous times, in particular in studies dealing with technological forecasting. Since the 1970s a number of alternatives emerged. The most well-known of these is the Policy Delphi, which focuses on policy issues rather than on forecasting per se (Linstone and Turoff 1975).

From the perspective of interactive model building, one advantage of the Delphi method is that time investment for participants is relatively low. Delbecq et al. (1975, 29) found that the number of working hours for participants in a Delphi was one half to one third of those participating in a Nominal Group Technique session or in an interacting group. On the other hand, time and cost for the administrators of the Delphi was about twice as much as compared to the other techniques. Another advantage of Delphi is its iterative nature. In terms of elements distinguished by Gustafson et al. (1973) Delphi can be characterized as an iterative Estimate - Feedback - Estimate (EFE) process, without face-to-face interaction (i.e., Talk). However, Delphi also has some disadvantages. The conventional Delphi has been harshly criticized by Sackman (1975) because of, among other things, methodological deficiencies in questionnaire design, the disproportionate emphasis on consensus, and the sloppy execution of most Delphi studies. In addition several empirical studies have revealed that Delphi or EFE processes do not outperform interacting groups (Gustafson et al. 1973; Fischer 1981; Stewart 1987; Sniezek 1990). We have to point out, however, that these studies are primarily concerned with estimation and prediction tasks. When it comes to idea generation Van de Ven and Delbecq (1974) found that Delphi significantly outperformed interacting groups and performed almost as well as the Nominal Group Technique. On the other hand, with regard to satisfaction of participants with the procedure, NGT clearly scored better than both Delphi and the interacting group. One reason the authors suggest for the lower level of participant satisfaction is the lack of opportunity for clarification of ideas in a Delphi (see also Nelms and Porter 1985; Van Dijk 1990). Given our third requirement (the need for discussion in interactive modeling), the lack of interaction and discussion between participants makes a traditional Delphi less suited for our purposes.

In contrast to Delphi, clarification of ideas and interaction between participants is at the heart of both NGT and SJA. NGT is a procedure to generate and evaluate a number of ideas on an issue with a group of people joining together in a session. When it comes to generating information (as opposed to evaluating information) numerous laboratory experiments conducted over the last few decades have shown that nominal groups usually outperform interacting groups (Bouchard 1969, 1972; Lamm and Trommsdorf 1973; Diehl and Stroebe 1987). Hence, in NGT the stage of idea generation is strictly separated from the evaluation of ideas. The process consists of the following steps (Delbecq et al. 1975):

- Individuals silently write down ideas.

- Ideas are listed in a round-robin fashion on a flipchart.

- Each idea on the list is discussed for clarification and evaluation.

- Individuals rank-order or rate ideas. The group decision is mathematically derived from this voting procedure.

As can be seen from the above sequence, NGT basically is an Estimate-Feedback-Talk-Estimate (EFTE) process. Empirical studies have shown that NGT groups (and in general EFTE approaches) outperform interacting and Delphi groups (Gustafson et al. 1973; Van de Ven and Delbecq 1974; Reagan-Cirincione 1991), and would thus be useful in interactive model building to improve group performance. In addition, the idea of rank-ordering and voting on ideas can be usefully applied to identify the most important variables to be included in the model. This will prevent the model from becoming too complex. However, as was the case with Delphi, the application of NGT to conceptual model building is not straightforward. NGT primarily focuses on the listing and evaluation of ideas. Although this is an important aspect, the primary emphasis in model building is on structuring ideas. In this sense, reflecting on NGT, Hart et al. (1985, 588) call idea structuring the neglected component in group decision making.

In contrast to NGT, which primarily relies on a voting procedure to arrive at a group decision, SJA participants are encouraged to explore the differences in "the logic of their underlying judgment policies" (Rohrbaugh 1979, 77). Rather than concentrating on participants' overt opinions the approach focuses on the underlying models participants use to arrive at a decision. This is accomplished by an Estimate - Feedback - Talk (EFT) approach (Reagan-Cirincione 1991). After making an initial individual estimate, participants receive cognitive feedback on the relative weights and function forms each individual applies. Next, differences between individuals in weights and function forms are discussed in an unrestricted manner and the group decision is consensually derived. In two separate studies Rohrbaugh compared Social Judgment Analysis (SJA) with both Delphi and NGT on cognitive conflict tasks of considerable intentional depth (Rohrbaugh 1979, 1981). In both studies Rohrbaugh found that SJA outperformed Delphi and NGT respectively with regard to individual learning, the reduction of disagreement in the group, and the level of satisfaction with the process. For interactive model building the EFT approach as applied in SJA could be extremely useful particularly because it focuses on the systematic discussion of assumptions underlying decisions. An obvious disadvantage is that an iterative EFT procedure would be very time consuming in a complex task like model building.

Summarizing we come to the conclusion that an EFT approach as applied in SJA is useful for interactive model building. Applying this approach to model building would result in a Conceptualize - Feedback - Talk process with one or more iterations, to meet the first requirement. In such a sequence, reduction of the time investment for participants, our second requirement, could be achieved in two ways. First, rather than starting from scratch, by constructing a preliminary model (Hart et al. 1985) that can be adapted by the client group. Second, by including elements from Delphi, which reduces working hours for participants (as we have seen). In addition, mailed questionnaires, in comparison with interviews, might also reduce the time investment for the modeler. To satisfy the third demand, one or more group sessions will have to be organized, in which participants can discuss their opinions and ideas. For this purpose, in SJA function forms are graphically displayed for discussion. In contrast, we primarily rely on causal diagrams to aid and structure discussions. Finally, to meet the fourth requirement (preventing the model from becoming too large) rank-ordering procedures as in NGT could be incorporated in the process.

The approach employed in this case study is based on the above ideas and consists of several stages. After a preliminary definition of the policy problem in the first stage, a small project group constructs a preliminary conceptual model based on a review of the relevant literature and insights within the project group (see also Hart et al. 1985). This preliminary model is used as a basis for the second stage in which the actual participation of the client takes place. In the first cycle of this second stage we employ a questionnaire. The questionnaire aims at eliciting comments from the participants about the significance of concepts and relationships employed in the preliminary model. The questionnaire is followed by a so-called workbook (Underwood 1984) in the second cycle. This workbook provides feedback about the results of the questionnaire. In addition, it invites participants to comment on more complex submodels constructed by the project group on the basis of the information generated in the questionnaires. Both the questionnaire and the workbook are filled out by participants working individually at home. In the third cycle we employ a structured workshop. In this workshop participants discuss their comments on the workbook's submodels in more detail. In this sense the first two cycles serve a focusing function: They identify those elements in the preliminary model on which participants do not agree. In sum the three cycles lead to considerable adaptation of the preliminary model, which results in a final conceptual model. The above mentioned stages are visualized in Figure 5-1.

Before discussing each of the stages in more detail we will first briefly introduce the policy problem.

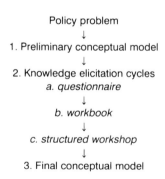

Figure 5-1. Stages in knowledge elicitation

THE POLICY PROBLEM

The model is designed for the Health Care Insurance Organization (HCIO) at Zwolle in the Netherlands. The project group consists of two HCIO health care planners and two experienced system dynamics modelers. In addition, five HCIO staff members assisted in assessing the preliminary model, the questionnaire, the workbook, and the workshops.

The policy problem that is modeled is related to the gradual but persistent rise in health care costs. From 1968 to 1985 total health care costs in the Netherlands increased from about 6 percent of the net National Product to about 10 percent. Studies explaining this rise in health care costs have in general primarily focused on exogenous factors (Grünwald 1987). Little attention has been given to processes within the health care system that might contribute to rising health care costs. Particularly these endogenous factors, however, might provide policy makers and planners with clues on how to control health care costs in the future. This latter perspective forms the basis for this project. The problem definition for the model-building project consists of three related questions:

1. What factors have been responsible for the increase in health care costs in the past?

2. How will health care costs develop in the future?

3. What are the potential effects of several policy options to reduce these costs?

The above three questions guided the design of the preliminary model by the project group.

THE PRELIMINARY MODEL

The process of designing the preliminary model was started by a two hour brainstorming session within the project group in which a flow diagram of the system was constructed. The diagram is shown in Figure 5-2.

Persons with health complaints initially consult their general practitioner (g.p.), who decides whether a patient

- has to return (order a patient back)

- will be referred to a medical specialist

- will be discharged.

The medical specialist, in turn, decides whether his patients

- have to return (order back)

- will be discharged

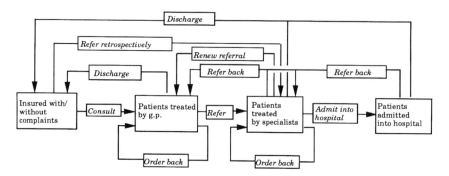

Figure 5-2. Patients' flow in the health care system

- will get a renewed referral from the general practitioner (which is necessary after one year of treatment by a medical specialist)

- will be admitted into the hospital and when they will be discharged from the hospital.

Health care costs for the general practitioner are in general generated by his decision to perform certain required medical treatments or to prescribe one or more drugs. With regard to medical specialists, health care costs are generated by a decision to (re)examine a patient, apply medical surgery (medical transactions) and/or prescribe a drug. Most of these decisions have a quantity and a cost component. For instance: the number of prescriptions by a general practitioner or a specialist (quantity) and the price of the drug prescribed (cost).

The next step is to identify a number of factors that affect the decisions discussed above and to include these in the flow model of Figure 5-2 to form a hybrid diagram as suggested by Richardson and Pugh (1981). A literature search was carried out to find relevant factors which could be used in developing the preliminary model. Table 5-1 summarizes the results.

Interestingly, as can be seen from the table, most studies concentrate on the "forward" flow process, i.e., consultations, referrals, and admissions into the hospital. Almost no research was found on factors affecting flow processes in the opposite direction, i.e., discharges from the general practitioner, the medical specialist and from the hospital. Hence, we decided to first concentrate on this "forward" flow process in the construction of the preliminary model. Most of the variables in Table 5-1 were used in this construction process. Variables that could not be causally related to the decisions of the actors in the system were left out (e.g., urbanization), which is not to say that these could never be incorporated in the model. As we will see in the next section, participants are invited to add factors to the preliminary model that they consider important. In this respect it is important to point out that no effort was made by the project group to make this preliminary model perfect,

Table 5-1. Potential factors affecting decisions in patients' flow model

consultation	order back g.p.	refer to specialist	order back specialist
• patient's age • % of women • (perceived) severity of complaint • duration of complaint • g.p.'s view of job • g.p.'s view of patients urbanization	• patient's age • checking patients • chronic disease • g.p.'s workload	• patient's age • % women • chron. disease • patient's pressure to be referred	• specialist's workload
admit into hospital	# of prescr. by g.p./spec.	# of medical transactions by spec.	cost of medical transactions
• patient's age • specialist's view of job • # of beds	• patient's age • workload	• spec. view of job • patient's age	• patient's age

(Source: adapted from Poppen 1987)

since it primarily serves a "trigger" function to start the knowledge elicitation process. It was argued that a "perfect" preliminary model would hardly be motivating for participants and would most probably not give them a feeling of "ownership" over the conceptual model. The preliminary model is shown in Figure 5-3.

The model shown in Figure 5-3 served as a basis for the first step in the knowledge elicitation process: the questionnaire.

THE QUESTIONNAIRE

In any interactive model building process one has to decide on at least two issues, i.e., the selection of participants and the method to elicit relevant knowledge. To avoid receiving one-sided, biased information, we incorporated a variety of persons with different backgrounds. Our participants belonged to various organizations in three fields, i.e., the actual care system (e.g., general practitioners, medical specialists), the policy-making field (e.g., planning institutions), and the social behavioral research field (e.g., university health care research units). Participants were selected in a two-step procedure. First, relevant organizations were listed. Next, within these organizations we identified some sixty potential participants, fairly well spread over the three fields.

We took several precautions to avoid low response. For example, we enclosed with the questionnaire an abstract of an article written on the construction of the

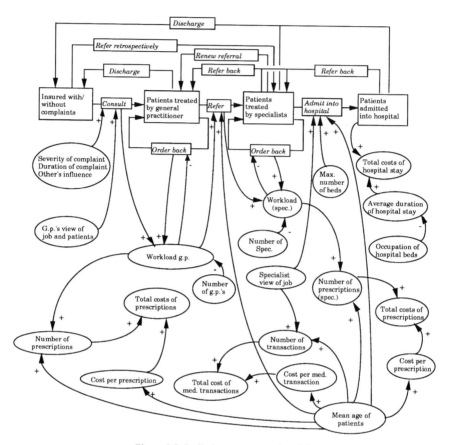

Figure 5-3. Preliminary conceptual model

preliminary model. In addition we pointed out to the respondents that we needed their expert opinion in order to be able to improve the preliminary model. These precautions paid off. The response rate exceeded 95 percent, which is very high for a mailed questionnaire.

The second issue is the questionnaire design. In order to elicit causal arguments we took as our point of departure the dyadic relationships in the preliminary model and translated these into verbal statements. For instance, in Figure 5-3 the accompanying verbal statement for the arrow running from "mean age of patients" to "refer" is: "Older patients are referred more often to a medical specialist than younger patients."

First we asked participants whether they agreed, partially agreed, or disagreed with the statement and second, we invited them to indicate why they agreed or disagreed. Naturally, from the point of view of knowledge elicitation this second part of the question is the most interesting, since it provokes causal arguments from the respondent's mental model. For example, most respondents agree with the above statement presenting explanations like:

- older patients have more and more serious complaints

- they have more pathology

- the chances of serious pathology are much bigger

- more polypathology

- polypathology, more complex diagnosis, more complex therapy etc.

The task of the project group is twofold. First, if possible to combine concepts employed in these arguments into a smaller number of categories. Second, to derive a causal structure from these arguments. In order to accomplish this a couple of persons from the project group conducted a qualitative content analysis and made initial suggestions, which were in turn checked by the other two persons from the project group. Discussions in the project group then led to a final decision for each of the statements. From the arguments presented on the above statement, for instance, the project group derived the following causal argument: "Older patients frequently have more polypathology. This impedes a correct diagnosis, hence a specialist's opinion is needed, which causes older patients to be referred more often." Rather than the two original variables (average age and number of referrals), one now has four variables related into a causal chain: average age, polypathology, complexity of diagnosis and number of referrals. In the second cycle (workbook), this elaborated argument is reported back to the participants and they are invited to indicate whether they agree with this formulation or not.

The example presented above is clear and one of the most straightforward examples of eliciting causal arguments from the participants' mental models. This does not happen in all cases, of course. Sometimes no arguments are presented or the statement itself is considered obvious.

However, causal arguments are not the only type of interesting information that can be derived from the questionnaire. Other interesting conclusions from the "why" part of the questions were related to the concepts themselves. Take for instance the following statement: "The higher a general practitioner's workload the higher the number of prescriptions." Approximately half of the respondents (partially) agreed while the other half did not. This outcome is of course quite confusing. To resolve this apparent contradiction the project group made two lists: one containing the arguments of those who agreed and one containing the arguments of those who did not agree. Careful content analysis and comparison of arguments provided by advocates and opponents revealed that the two groups did not use the same concept. One group obviously had the temporary rush during the consulting hour in mind (for instance caused by an epidemic of influenza). The other group presented arguments related to structural workload. Interpretations like these made by the project group were also reported back in the workbook and participants were asked to comment on them. A similar example on the concept "general practitioners view of his job" will be discussed in the section below when we show a sample of part of the workbook.

The questionnaire was divided in a number of sections each dealing with one "dependent" variable, e.g., number of referrals or number of prescriptions by general practitioners. Each of these sections thus contained a number of statements together with "why questions." At the end of each section we asked respondents to add variables (affecting the dependent variable) that were not included in the preliminary model. As will be clear, this results in quite a number of factors, which cannot all be included in the model. Hence, the last question in each section solicits the three most important factors. A sample of the questionnaire is presented in Figure 5-4.

From the last question in each section, we calculated frequency distributions and the three factors mentioned most frequently as important were used to develop submodels around a dependent variable, in order to carry the conceptual model-building process one step forward.

THE WORKBOOK

To be able to develop more complex submodels and have these criticized by the participants, we employed a so-called workbook in the second cycle. The workbook consisted of about 30 pages (including diagrams and space for comments). It is a kind of questionnaire with a particular format. In the workbooks we explained in more detail the process of model-building and the diagramming tools, we fed back the results of the questionnaire and we again invited participants to comment on the submodels developed in the workbook.

The workbook was also meant to prepare the participants for the third stage in knowledge elicitation: the structured workshop. Two subsets of 9 respondents (from the original 60) were selected to fill out the workbooks and to participate in one of two workshops. We selected 18 participants spread over the three fields mentioned above (i.e., actual care system, policy-making organizations, research institutions) who presented us with the most detailed comments and arguments in the questionnaires. All 18 filled out the same workbook. The workbooks and the two workshops both covered that part of the model which is related to the first echelon (general practitioners), since a number of medical specialists (the second echelon) refused to cooperate because of a conflict between their interest group and the central government. The workbook contained four submodels, centered around four important "dependent" variables in the preliminary model, i.e., consultation by

Introduction and explanation.
....
....
....
Section 1: consulting the general practitioner
....
....
....
Section 2: ordering patients back by general practitioners

A. Statements

1. The higher a general practitioner's workload the more patients he will refer to a specialist

   O agree
   O partially agree
   O disagree

   because..
   ....

2. The broader a general practitioner's view of his job, the more patients he will order back

   O agree
   O partially agree
   O disagree

   because..
   ....

3. etc.

B. Considering the number of referrals by general practitioners do you think there are any other
   factors, apart from the ones mentioned above, which affect the number of referrals ?
   ....
   ....
   ....

C. Which three of the above mentioned factors (including the ones you added in the previous
   question) do you consider most important in explaining the number of referrals ? Please indicate
   the most important first etc.

   1...
   2...
   3...

Section 3: referrals by general practitioners
....
....
....
Section 4: prescriptions by general practitioners
....
....
....

Figure 5-4. Sample questionnaire

patients on the one hand, and prescriptions of drugs, referrals, and "back orders" by general practitioners on the other. These four submodels were developed by the project group using the preliminary model and the results of the questionnaires. This does not mean, however, that the design of the submodels was straightforward. Although the questionnaires provided us with the three most important variables affecting each of the above "dependent" variables and with intermediary links between two variables, this information was not always sufficient to produce a submodel. Hence, the project group frequently had to fill in "causal gaps" between these dependent and independent variables where the questionnaires did not provide that information. Again research literature was consulted and discussed within the project group to generate the necessary information.

In order to simplify matters for the participants the submodels are built up gradually in the course of the workbook. This was accomplished by first linking the most important independent variable (mentioned in the questionnaire) to the dependent variable. Next, variables were identified that could explain this independent variable and so on until a network of causal relationships was constructed. The verbal explanations were summarized by means of a causal diagram, in which the participant could indicate his comments and suggestions for adaptations. The same procedure was followed with regard to the second and third most important variable. In order to illustrate the procedure used in the workbooks, we have reproduced part of the workbook (on the phenomenon of ordering patients back) in Figure 5-5.

Once a submodel was complete, the respondent was invited to summarize his comments by indicating his disagreements with the submodel as shown in Figure 5-6. He then had to continue with the next submodel.

The completed workbooks were sent to the project group one week before the workshop. They were used to determine the topics for discussion and to organize the subgroups.

THE STRUCTURED WORKSHOP

For the actual design of the workshop we relied on our experience with previous workshops and guidelines found in the literature (e.g., Duke 1980; Hart et al. 1985; Mason and Mitroff 1981; Vennix and Geurts 1987). In addition, we employed a few conclusions from the research literature on small groups. One is that the introduction of structure in group activities drastically improves group performance (Bouchard 1969). Another is that participation can be improved by using small task groups (Eden 1985; Hart et al. 1985) and a group facilitator to structure plenary discussions.

1. Consultations by patients

....

....

2. Backorders by the general practitioner

In the previous section we focused on the decisions of patients to consult their general practitioner. In this and the next two sections we discuss three decisions of general practitioners: order patients back, prescribe drugs, refer to a medical specialist or combinations of these. In this section we focus on factors affecting the process of ordering patients back.

2.1 Results of the questionnaire

From the the questionnaire we conclude that with regard to the number of patients ordered back by a general practitioner the uncertainty of the general practitioner is considered the most important factor. About 90 % of the respondents agree with the statement that more uncertainty leads to more patients being ordered back. From the arguments presented with the statements, however, it turns out that the statement cannot be maintained in its current form. We will refer back to this in section 2.2 of this workbook. The second most important factor is the general practitioner's view of his job (about 75% agree with this statement). This statement too will have to be elaborated as we will see in section 2.3 of this workbook. The third most important factor is the general practitioner's workload. We will discuss this in section 2.4.

2.2 A general practitioner's uncertainty

Most respondents indicate that uncertainty leads to more control behavior, which in turn increases the number of patients ordered back. There is a problem however. A number of respondents state that more uncertainty can also lead to more *referrals* to medical specialists. In our opinion this depends on the aspect about which a general practitioner is uncertain. We distinguish three kinds of uncertainty, i.e., uncertainty with regard to:
- the diagnosis
- the expected progress of the disease
- the potential effect of the therapy
In our opinion the first kind of uncertainty will lead to either more referrals or more prescriptions or both. We will come back to that in chapters 3 and 4 of this workbook. The second and the third kind of uncertainty of a general practitioner will lead to more patients being ordered back. We formulate the following statements:

1. The more often a general practitioner is uncertain about the expected progress of the disease, the more often he will order patients back.
2. The more often the general practitioner is uncertain with regard to the effects of the therapy, the more often he will order patients back.

A number of respondents point out that the uncertainty of the general practitioner will decrease with his number of years of experience. Some assume that this is, among others, related to the fact that he will know more about his patients. Hence:

3. The more experienced a general practitioner is in his profession, the better he is informed about the history/background of his patients and the less uncertain he will be.

Figure 5-5. Sample of the workbook used in knowledge elicitation

Using a causal diagram the above statements can be visualized as in the following figure:

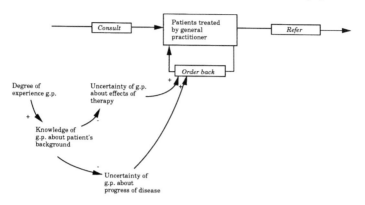

2.3 The general practitioner's view of his job

Task 1:   Please indicate in this diagram with which parts you do not agree by
          crossing these out. Please write down any comments in the space below.

The general practitioner's view of his job also leads to some differences of opinion between respon-dents. Most probably this is due to a difference in the interpretation of the concept of 'view of his job' (as was the case above with uncertainty). Those respondents agreeing with the statement that a broad view of the job will lead to more patients being ordered back argue that a general practitioner with a broad view will carry out more therapeutic and diagnostic transactions and will check more patients himself (rather than refer to a specialist) and hence will order back more patients. These general practitioners will also refer less in those respondents' opinion. Those respondents who do not agree with the statement point out that a general practitioner with a broad view will provide better and more specific aid to his patients, which will lead to less patients being ordered back.

This contradiction between the two groups can in our opinion be explained from the fact that different persons interpret the concept 'view of job' in different ways. One group considers 'view of job' as the number of tasks that a general practitioner considers to be part of his job. The other group seems to interpret the concept as the way a general practitioner handles his patients. From here on we will define 'view of job' as the number of tasks the general practitioner considers to be part of his job. The way a general practitioner handles his patients will be denoted by the concept 'g.p.-patient relationship'. Below we will first focus on the g.p.-patient relationship.

From the comments in the questionnaires we can derive a few factors that are considered important in this respect, i.e. the quality of the communication during consultation and a patient's confidence in his general practitioner. We formulate the following statements about the 'g.p.-patient relationship':

4. The more susceptible the general practitioner is to the patient's complaint, the higher the quality of the discussion during consultation.
5. If the quality of the discussion during consultation increases the patient will get more confidence in his general practitioner.
6. The more confidence a patient has in his general practitioner, the more information (quantitatively and qualitatively) he will provide about his complaint to the general practitioner.
7. The more information a patient provides, the higher the quality of the discussion during consultation.
8. The higher the quality of the consultation discussion, the less a general practitioner will order patients back.

Adding these factors to the previous figure results in the following figure:

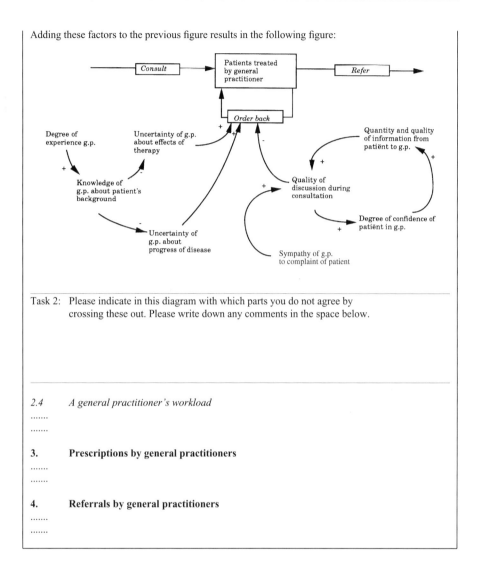

Task 2: Please indicate in this diagram with which parts you do not agree by crossing these out. Please write down any comments in the space below.

2.4   *A general practitioner's workload*
....
....

3.   **Prescriptions by general practitioners**
....
....

4.   **Referrals by general practitioners**
....
....

There were also some impediments that we had to take into account. For example, since general practitioners participated in the workshops these could not be held during daytime. Hence we started at 4 p.m. and had to be finished by 9 p.m.

In order to use the available time as efficiently as possible and to improve participation in the discussions we formed three task groups of three persons to allow in-depth discussions of different submodels during the workshop. Task groups were composed of persons with similar comments on the submodels. Each of the three task groups discussed one of the submodels. From the four submodels in the workbook we selected the three that received most criticism in the workbooks. The program for the workshop was as follows:

4:00–4:15 p.m.	Welcome to participants
4:15–5:00	Introduction and explanation
5:00–6:00	Task group discussions
6:00–7:30	Plenary session
7:30–8:15	Dinner
8:15–9:00	Discussion on feedback loops
9:00–9:15	Evaluation and conclusion

In order to facilitate work in the subgroups each was assisted by one member of the project team. To structure subgroup activities we used a few aids. First, each group member was assigned a role with accompanying responsibilities. For instance, one person was responsible for time management, another for presentation of the results of the subgroup discussions in the plenary session. Second, to feed back the results from the workbook and as a potential starting point for discussion we provided each group with a copy of the submodel diagram. On these diagrams we indicated by means of different colors which person had criticized what part of the submodel (see also Figure 5-6). The diagrams provided to the participants were used as a kind of scrap paper during discussion about the submodels. The diagrams could be modified by participants as they saw fit. In addition we returned the workbooks to participants as an aid in the discussion.

At the end of the task group session, one person recorded the final changes in a large-format diagram that was put on the wall in the plenary session room. The spokesperson of the first task group was then given ten minutes to explain the changes in the submodel. After answering any clarifying questions, there was a 20-minute plenary discussion about the submodel. This procedure was repeated for the other two submodels. After the dinner break there was a discussion on the notion of feedback loops that could be identified within the model.

Participants were quite involved in the discussions and were very satisfied that there was a clear timetable, which was followed quite strictly. Although there was consensus on many issues, it also became clear that several processes in health care are poorly understood. Here the knowledge elicitation process was arrested at the point where there were only vague conjectures. This was for instance true with regard to the number of "back orders" by a general practitioner. Lack of knowledge on general practitioners' back orders is largely due to disinterest of the insurance companies (as far as mandatory insurance is concerned, a change in the number of back orders does not affect the number of payments to general practitioners).

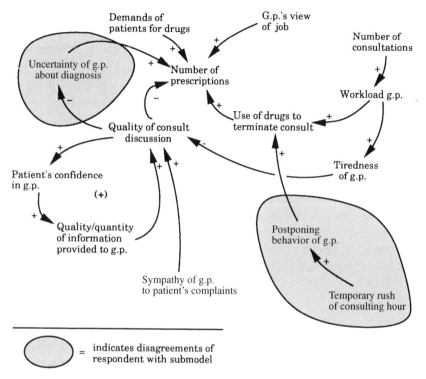

Figure 5-6. Conceptual submodel on "number of prescriptions" from workbook

RESULTS

One important goal of building a simulation model is to enable the modeler to conduct "what if" policy experiments with the computer model. Many modelers consider this as the only useful objective. As various authors have pointed out, however, building a conceptual model often generates very useful policy relevant information (Eden et al. 1983; Meadows 1989; Wolstenholme 1982; Wolstenholme and Coyle 1983).

In our case several tangible results materialized from this conceptual model-building stage. These are related to the quality of the conceptual model, the definition of the policy problem, and the structuring of future research efforts in health care processes.

In our view, the quality of the conceptual model was increased drastically on a number of aspects, first, with regard to the number of variables included in the model. This number increased considerably during the knowledge elicitation stage. Our preliminary model contained about 40 variables and the final model contains more than 80. Although a larger conceptual model is not necessarily better, the increase was primarily caused by refinement of the concepts and relationships in the preliminary model. We consider that as an important improvement of the quality of the model. We have presented several examples in this article indicating that concepts used in the research literature and in discussions about health care are frequently too ambiguous. Concepts like workload, general practitioner's view of his job, and uncertainty of a general practitioner were refined considerably. We have also presented examples of refinement of relationships, sometimes identifying new feedback loops, during the process of knowledge elicitation (see also Vennix et al. 1990).

The model-building process also had an impact on the definition of the policy problem of cost reduction. Before starting the model-building process, various persons were quite convinced that the best way to cut health care costs would be to reduce the number of referrals by general practitioners. This seems obvious since transactions by medical specialists are much more expensive than those by general practitioners, particularly if patients are admitted into the hospital. During the model-building process it became clear that there are feedback processes that might counteract the cost reduction effect from the reduction of referrals; for instance, through an increase in the number of transactions by medical specialists to compensate for the loss of new patients. To gain more insight in these feedback processes the conceptual model was formalized. Preliminary analyses, however, seem to indicate that cost reduction effects do occur when reducing the number of referrals (Verburgh et al. 1990). Future analyses with a more elaborated model will have to provide a more final answer to this question.

A third result that materialized relates to further empirical research into health care processes. As we have stated, the discussions in the workshop showed that various parts of the system are ill-understood. As a result, a research project has been started aimed at filling in the gaps in knowledge of the factors determining back orders by general practitioners.

SUMMARY AND DISCUSSION

In this article we have concentrated on a structured approach to knowledge elicitation for conceptual model-building. The approach basically employs an iterative sequence of Conceptualize - Feedback - Talk. We suggested that a three-step approach, using different kinds of data collection methods, is an appropriate way to structure the knowledge elicitation process. A questionnaire was used to have a number of experts (60) comment on dyadic relationships of a preliminary model designed by the project group. Next a workbook was employed to have a subset (18) of the first group of experts criticize a number of more complex submodels. Finally, in a structured workshop participants were put in a position to discuss these submodels in more detail.

At the beginning of this article we indicated that our primary aim was to develop and implement an alternative procedure for knowledge elicitation in conceptual model building. We did not explicitly aim at systematically and objectively evaluating this procedure. As stated, this is the subject for future research efforts. One obvious way to evaluate it would be to compare it to the "traditional" system dynamics approach to knowledge elicitation, i.e., interviews and group discussions. Without trying to be exhaustive one might think of the following criteria for evaluation:

- the quality of the resulting conceptual model;

- time investment of the participants;

- satisfaction of participants with the process;

- model acceptance and reduction of disagreement;

- the degree to which it improves insight into the problem and generates new solutions.

Although we did not carry out an objective evaluation of this kind, we have indications that the procedure did score well on some of the above criteria. One of these is the time investment. The main reason to use a preliminary model and this approach was to cut the time investment of participants. In sum it took participants in this procedure about 8 to 10 hours to complete the questionnaires, to fill out the workbook, and to participate in the workshop. This seems lower than in most cases where one starts from scratch. Morecroft et al. (1989, 3), for instance, report an average time investment by the client of 2 1/2 days. On the other hand it might well be the case that by using a preliminary model the project group has a great deal of influence on the design of the conceptual model. This might for instance decrease the feeling of ownership over the model for the client. This in turn could affect model acceptance and the actual use of the model in the organization once the model builders have left. Clearly this is one of the topics that needs to be studied more carefully in the future.

Another reason to use this approach was to match the various tasks in model-building with individual and group work. Apart from lower time investment, the procedure allows participants to do several tasks individually at home and to join together once it is clear what the exact topics are which need to be discussed. In that sense the procedure proved to be very valuable, particularly in our case, where there were general practitioners in our sample who lack time to attend meetings of this sort.

As indicated, the quality of the conceptual model clearly increased and the client seems to be rather satisfied with the whole project. This conclusion can be deduced from the fact that the client organization provided additional financial support to write a book on the project. Moreover, the client supports our continuing efforts to formalize the model and to design a flexible computer-based learning environment in which health care planners and workers can conduct policy experiments with the model themselves.

Positive reactions on the project were also obtained during a conference attended by almost 200 persons from the health care field (e.g., general practitioners, scientists, health care planners, modelers). During this conference we had a number of presentations on the project and a panel discussion. At the end of the conference participants filled out a questionnaire. Two-thirds considered the subjects that were presented interesting to very interesting on a five-point scale ranging from very uninteresting to very interesting. Some 24 people were very interested and 35 interested (again on a five-point scale) in talking to the project group about the applicability of this model-building approach for their own organization. As a result, one new model-building project on the organization of home care in the future has been started. This project will use a procedure similar to the one described in this article.

In sum, the whole project, including a similar approach to identify feasible policy options and formalize part of the conceptual model, took several years to complete (Vennix et al. 1990). Calendar time for the procedure described in this article took a little over one year. This was caused by two factors. First, the project group had to design and test various novel procedures (e.g. questionnaire, workbook). Second, the project group did not work full-time. We estimate that, given our experience with this approach, it should be possible to finish a conceptual modeling phase using this approach in about three to six months.

At the moment we have already formalized and quantified part of the model, i.e the patient flow model and the costs involved. Our efforts are now aimed at including a number of influencing factors on this patient flow model. In addition we have designed a computer-based learning environment in which health care policy makers can conduct a number of policy experiments with the computer model (1) to increase their systemic thinking about the subject, (2) to improve communication about health care cost reduction, and (3) to stimulate their insight into potential effects of options aiming at cost reduction.

REFERENCES

Bouchard, T. (1969), "Personality, Problem Solving Procedure and Performance in Small Groups," *Journal of Applied Psychology* 53: 1-29.

Bouchard, T. (1972), "A Comparison of Two Group Brainstorming Procedures," *Journal of Applied Psychology* 56: 418-21.

Dalkey, N. (1969), "An Experimental Study of Group Opinion: The Delphi Method," *Futures* 1: 408-26.

Delbecq, A.L., A.H. Van de Ven, and D.H. Gustafson (1975), *Group Techniques for Program Planning: A Guide to Nominal Group and Delphi Processes*, Glenview, Ill.: Scott, Foresman and Co.

Diehl, M., and W. Stroebe (1987), "Productivity Loss in Brainstorming Groups: Toward the Solution of a Riddle," *Journal of Personality and Social Psychology* 53: 497-509.

van Dijk, J.A.G.M. (1990), "Delphi Questionnaires versus Individual and Group Interviews: A Comparison Case," *Technological Forecasting and Social Change* 37: 293-304.

Duke, R.D. (1980), "A Paradigm for Game Design," in C.S. Greenblat and R.D. Duke, eds., *Principles and Practices of Gaming-Simulation*, Beverly Hills/London: Sage, 63-72.

Eden, C. (1985), "Perish the Thought," *Journal of the Operational Research Society* 36: 809-19.

Eden, C., S. Jones, and D. Sims (1983), *Messing about in Problems: An Informal Structured Approach to Their Identification and Management*, Oxford/New York: Pergamon Press.

Fischer, G.W. (1981), "When Oracles Fail: A Comparison of Four Procedures for Aggregating Subjective Probability Forecasts," *Organizational Behavior and Human Performance* 28: 96-110.

Forrester, J.W. (1987), "Lessons from System Dynamics Modeling," *System Dynamics Review* 3: 136-49.

Forrester, J.W. (1992), "Policies, Decisions, and Information Sources for Modeling," *European Journal of Operational Research* 59, no. 1: 42-63; also Chapter 3 of this volume.

de Geus, A. (1988), "Planning as Learning," *Harvard Business Review*, March/April: 70-74.

Grünwald, C.A. (1987), *Beheersing van de gezondheidszorg*, Den Haag: VUGA.

Gustafson, D.H., R.K. Shukla, A. Delbecq, and G.W. Walster (1973), "A Comparative Study of Differences in Subjective Likelihood Estimates Made by Individuals, Interacting Groups, Delphi Groups and Nominal Groups," *Organizational Behavior and Human Performance* 9: 280-91.

Hart, S.L., M. Boroush, G. Enk, and W. Hornick (1985), "Managing, Complexity Through Consensus Mapping: Technology for the Structuring of Group Decisions," *Academy of Management Review* 10: 587-600.

House, P.W. (1982), *The Art of Public Policy Analysis: The Arena of Regulations and Resources* (2d printing), Beverly Hills/London: Sage.

Lamm, H., and G. Trommsdorf (1973), "Group versus Individual Performance on Tasks Requiring Ideational Proficiency (Brainstorming): A Review," *European Journal of Social Psychology* 3: 361-88.

Linstone, H., and M. Turoff (1975), *The Delphi Method: Techniques and Applications*, New York: John Wiley.

Mason, O.M., and I.I. Mitroff (1981), *Challenging Strategic Planning Assumptions, Theory, Cases and Techniques*, New York: John Wiley.

Meadows, D.H. (1989), "System Dynamics Meets the Press," *System Dynamics Review* 5: 69-80.

Meadows, D.H., and J.M. Robinson (1985), *The Electronic Oracle: Computer Models and Social Decisions*, Chichester, U.K.: John Wiley and Sons.

Mintzberg, H. (1990), "The Manager's Job: Folklore and Fact," *Harvard Business Review*, March/April: 163-76.

Morecroft, J.D.W., D.C. Lane, and P.S. Viita (1991), "Modeling Growth Strategy in a Biotechnology Startup Firm," *System Dynamics Review* 7, no. 2: 93-116.

Nelms, K.R., and A.L. Porter (1985), "EFTE: An Interactive Delphi Method," *Technological Forecasting and Social Change* 28: 43-61.

Poppen, H.J. (1987), "In den eersten lijn gemeeten, een systeemdynamische benadering van de huisartsgeneeskunde," M. Sc. thesis, State University of Groningen.

Randers, J. (1977), "The Potential in Simulation of Macro Social Processes: Or How to Be a Useful Builder of Simulation Models," Oslo: Grupper for Ressursstudier.

Reagan-Cirincione, P. (1991), *Improving the Accuracy of Forecasts: A Process Intervention Combining Social Judgment Analysis and Group Facilitation*, Ph.D. dissertation, Rockefeller College of Public Affairs and Policy, State University of New York at Albany.

Richardson, G.P. and Pugh, A.L. (1981), *Introduction to System Dynamics Modeling with DYNAMO*, Portland, Ore.: Productivity Press.

Richardson, G.P., and Senge, P.M. (1989), "Corporate and Statewide Perspectives on the Liability Insurance Crisis," in P.M. Milling and E.O. Zahn, eds., *Computer-Based Management of Complex Systems*, Proceedings of the 1989 International Conference of the System Dynamics Society, Berlin: Springer-Verlag, 442-57.

Richmond, B. (1987), "The Strategic Forum: from Vision to Strategy to Operating Policies and Back Again," High Performance Systems, 45 Lyme Road, Ste. 300, Hanover NH 03755.

Rohrbaugh, J. (1979), "Improving the Quality of Group Judgment: Social Judgment Analysis and the Delphi technique," *Organizational Behavior and Human Performance* 24: 73-92.

Rohrbaugh, J. (1981), "Improving the Quality of Group Judgment: Social Judgment Analysis and the Nominal Group Technique," *Organizational Behavior and Human Performance* 28: 272-88.

Sackman, H. (1975), *Delphi Critique: Expert Opinion, Forecasting and Group Process*, Lexington, Mass.: D.C. Heath and Co.

Sniezek, J.A. (1990), A Comparison of Techniques for Judgmental Forecasting by Groups with Common Information, *Group & Organization Studies* 15: 5-19.

Stenberg, L. (1980), "A Modeling Procedure for Public Policy," in J. Randers, ed., *Elements of the System Dynamics Method*, Portland, Ore.: Productivity Press, 292-312.

Stewart, T. R. (1987), "The Delphi Technique and Judgmental Forecasting," *Climatic Change* 11: 97-113.

Underwood, S.E. (1984), "An Evaluation of a Participative Technique for Strategic Planning," unpublished paper, University of Michigan, Ann Arbor.

Van de Ven, A.H., and A.L. Delbecq (1974), "The Effectiveness of Nominal, Delphi and Interacting Group Decision Making Processes," *Academy of Management Journal* 17: 605-21.

Vennix, J.A.M. (1990), *Mental Models and Computer Models: Design and Evaluation of a Computer-Based Learning Environment for Policy Making*, Ph.D. dissertation, University of Nijmegen.

Vennix, J.A.M., and J.L.A. Geurts (1987), "Communicating Insights from Complex Simulation Models: A Gaming Approach," *Simulation and Games* 18: 321-43.

Vennix, J.A.M., J.W. Gubbels, D. Post, and H.J. Poppen (1990), "A Structured Approach to Knowledge Elicitation in Conceptual Model-Building," *System Dynamics Review* 6: 194-208.

Verburgh, L.H., J.W. Gubbels, J.A.M. Vennix, and D. Post (1990), "Model-Based Analyses of the Dutch Health Care System," in D.F. Andersen, G.P. Richardson, and J.D. Sterman, eds., *Proceedings of the 1990 International System Dynamics Conference,* Chestnut Hill, Mass. (July 10-13, 1990): 1211-1225.

Weil, H.B. (1980), "The Evolution of an Approach for Achieving Implemented Results from System Dynamics Projects," in J. Randers, ed., *Elements of the System Dynamics Method*, Portland, Ore.: Productivity Press, 271-91.

Wolstenholme, E.F. (1982), "System Dynamics in Perspective," *Journal of the Operational Research Society* 33: 547-56.

Wolstenholme, E.F., and R.G. Coyle (1983), "The Development of System Dynamics as a Methodology for System Description and Qualitative Analysis," *Journal of the Operational Research Society* 34: 569-81.

6

MODELING THE OIL PRODUCERS: CAPTURING OIL INDUSTRY KNOWLEDGE IN A BEHAVIORAL SIMULATION MODEL

JOHN D.W. MORECROFT AND
KEES A.J.M. VAN DER HEIJDEN

ABSTRACT: A group of senior managers and planners from a major oil company met to discuss the changing structure of the oil industry with the purpose of improving group understanding of oil market behavior for use in global scenarios. This broad ranging discussion led to a system dynamics simulation model of the oil producers. The model produced new insights into the power and stability of OPEC (the major oil producers' organization), the dynamics of oil prices, and the investment opportunities of non-OPEC producers.

The paper traces the model development process, starting from group discussions and leading to working simulation models. Particular attention is paid to the methods used to capture team knowledge and to ensure that the computer models reflected opinions and ideas from the meetings. The paper describes how flipchart diagrams were used to collect ideas about the logic of the principal producers' production decisions. A subgroup of the project team developed and tested an algebraic model. The paper shows partial model simulations used to build confidence and a sense of ownership in the algebraic formulations. Further simulations show how the full model can stimulate thinking about producers' behavior and oil prices. The paper concludes with comments on the model-building process.*

*Before joining Strathclyde Graduate Business School, Kees van der Heijden was head of Scenario Planning for the Royal Dutch/Shell Group of Companies, Shell Centre, London.

The authors would like to acknowledge the assistance of Andrew Davis in Shell's Business Consultancy Division for his contributions to building and calibrating the model described in the paper. Also, Ged Davis, a senior member of Group Planning, made many thoughtful suggestions during the model's conceptualization and adapted the model creatively for use in the 1989 scenario publication (Group Planning 1989). The authors are grateful to John Sterman and two anonymous referees for their helpful and perceptive criticisms on an earlier draft of the paper.

INTRODUCTION

The dramatic movements of oil price over the past 20 years have led to economic depression, inflation, huge concentrations of wealth in the oil-rich nations and to booms and busts in the exploration and production industry. As many know well, the 1970s began with low and stable oil prices of around $6 to $7 per barrel (all prices in the paper are in 1985 $). The year 1973 saw prices rocket to more than $20 per barrel as OPEC exercised its newly discovered power. The trajectory of oil prices then stabilized for five years at around $19 per barrel, only to shoot upwards once more in 1978 to hit a peak of $36 per barrel during 1981. The mid-1980s witnessed a dramatic reversal of the trajectory, as prices tumbled to less than $10 per barrel in 1985—back to the low levels of the early 1970s. In recent years, the price has been low and erratic in the $10 to $20 per barrel range (Jennings 1988), until the 1990 Gulf crisis led to a speculative doubling of price in only two months, followed by a decline to the pre-crisis level.

Why and how do such disruptive price movements occur? Is it possible for producing nations and firms to orchestrate a more stable price profile that ensures predictable revenue flows and wreaks less havoc in economic, commercial, and social conditions? What range of oil prices is likely during, say, the next 20 years? (Jennings 1988; Fossli and Wilkinson 1986; Wilkinson 1988; Goldstein 1990). What are the economic prospects for exploration and production in new oil fields? The Oil Producers' model allows oil company managers to explore these questions in depth for themselves. By representing both the political pressures inside the oil producers' organization (OPEC), and the commercial logic of non-OPEC producers, the model has generated new insight into long-term oil market dynamics.

BACKGROUND TO THE PROJECT AND SCENARIO PLANNING

The Oil Producers' model grew out of an ambitious scenario exercise to explore the strategic implications of changes in the structure of the energy industry. In Shell, scenario planning is viewed as a way to discover new concepts and language that enable the organization to become more agile in recognizing significant industry trends, defining emerging business problems, and preparing the minds of senior managers to deal with such problems (de Geus 1988; Wack 1985a and 1985b). Scenario planning is *not* a way of forecasting or predicting the future (as many outsiders seem to think). It works by the development of consistent stories about *alternative futures,* as the basis for what-if thinking in the organization. A consistent story traces a time path into the future that forces managers and planners to think, "What would I do, within my area of business responsibility, if this future were to unfold?" The internal consistency of the stories, creating credibility and persuasiveness, is an important factor in evaluating the usefulness of scenarios—much more important than the ex-post accuracy of the time paths. Scenarios are selected for their ability to make the organization a skillful observer of the business environment. As such they do not have to describe the "most likely" future, but the reasoning behind the scenarios must be plausible.

Models that "fit" scenario planning do not have to be accurate predictive models. But they should have the capability to stimulate novel thinking about future business options. Moreover, models that are used to construct consistent stories need to be understood by the "story writers" (often senior planners) in order to be communicated effectively to the story readers (corporate executives and business unit managers). A black-box predictor will not lead to the desired result, even if it has a good record of predictive power.

These criteria of scenario planning and scenario models help explain the style of modeling adopted—the need for a comparatively simple model, the relatively closed process (the project did not make direct use of other world oil market models or enlist the aid of world oil market experts as consultants), and the intense participation of senior planners in model conceptualization. The project was not intended as an exercise in developing another general model of the oil trade to forecast better. The project team wanted to model *their understanding* of the oil market. Within the group there was an enormous amount of experience, reflecting knowledge about the actors in the oil market and observations about market behavior. But the knowledge was scattered and anecdotal, and therefore not very operational. The group also recognized that the interlinkages in the system were complex. The desire of the group was to engage in a joint process through which their knowledge could be pooled and put into a framework through which real events could be interpreted. This framework could then be used to develop internally consistent scenarios. Most of the group members were not professional modelers. Other existing energy models to them were nontransparent black boxes, useful as a reflection of others' views, but quite unsuitable for framing their own knowledge.

THE STARTING POINT AND PREPARATION OF THE PROJECT TEAM

Scenario planners initially conceived of industry change in terms of broad themes which they described in phrases such as:

> The structural evolution of the oil industry; the oil/energy producers and their position on the industry cost curve; the economic, commercial and political pressures on OPEC countries; the evolving role of the nation state; changes in market structure by geographical region (e.g., North America, the USSR, Eastern Europe, the Far East, etc.), and by business segment (e.g., the gas business, the power business, government).

From these wide-ranging themes emerged a behavioral simulation model of oil market dynamics. But how? The paper traces the process of model conceptualization from discussion to algebra. The first step was to assemble an experienced team of planners and managers (ten people in all) and to use their knowledge of the oil industry as the basis for a conceptual model. The team met three times for working sessions lasting three hours each. The meetings were facilitated by an experienced system dynamics modeler. One member of the team kept detailed minutes of the meetings (including copies of flipchart notes and diagrams) in order to preserve a permanent trace of the model's conceptualization. A subgroup of the project team met separately to develop and test a full-blown algebraic model.

Extracts from the original brief used to organize the meetings are quoted below to indicate how the facilitator intended to use modeling (and more specifically a qualitative decision-making and feedback perspective) to shape the team's thinking and discussion.

> To examine industry structure, the planning department should convene a forum to discuss the main players in the industry, their decision-making processes, motivations, resources, internal needs, external needs, culture, etc.

> The forum will consist of a series of meetings of a project team comprising experienced managers invited by the planning department.

> The project team should prepare for the forum by reading selected papers that indicate the desired qualitative and participative style of modeling based on system dynamics (e.g., de Geus 1988; Morecroft 1985; Richmond 1987; Kalff 1989; Morecroft 1990; Vennix and Geurts 1987; Management Brief 1989).

> In addition the team should participate in a preliminary meeting to set the ground rules for future working meetings and to clarify the modeling/problem-structuring framework by reviewing the mapping symbols and in particular the behavioral decision function (Morecroft 1992 and 1988) as a graphical aid to capturing team knowledge and mapping feedback structure.

> The forum should aim to produce a map showing the main players and information flows which make up the industry structure. The map will be accompanied by explanatory text and possibly, though not definitely, some small simulation models based on fragments of the map.

The key point here is the preparation of the team. The facilitator wanted a wide-ranging discussion that activates the knowledge of the team members and allows them to feel involved in the model-building process. At the same time the facilitator needed to converge on a behavioral simulation model. The seeming conflict between divergent discussion and convergent modeling was eased with readings and a preliminary meeting that explained the mapping symbols, the behavioral decision function, information flows, and feedback loops—in short, the representation scheme to be adopted. This preparation or "conditioning" of the project team helps to activate knowledge that is appropriate for model conceptualization—but without imposing a rigid structure on the discussion.

The procedure for mapping builds on the two-phase modeling approach described in Morecroft (1985). Phase 1 is a descriptive and qualitative survey of decision making that characterizes the bounded rationality of actors in the system, their limited information sources, their goals and motives, standard procedures, rules of thumb, political pressures, and cultural biases. This descriptive and anecdotal information, collected in the form of maps, is used in Phase 2 as the basis for an algebraic model to produce simulated scenarios.

EARLY CONCEPTUALIZATION

Figure 6-1 is the team's own framework (exactly as recorded during the first working meeting) for representing oil industry structure. The oil producers are divided into three categories: swing producer, supporters, and other producers. The swing producer together with the supporters make up the oil producers' organization (OPEC). An intermediate market stands between the producers and consumers. The market adjusts price according to the supply-demand imbalance. Demand comes from consumers who, in the figure, are regarded as anything downstream of the crude oil market. The figure uses the label "U/S" to denote the upstream part of the oil industry—crude-oil exploration and production as opposed to downstream refining, distribution, and retailing. The dotted-line boxes labeled "D/S" denote downstream, as a visual reminder of downstream activities featured in the team's early discussion of industry structure, even though the downstream was absent from later model development.

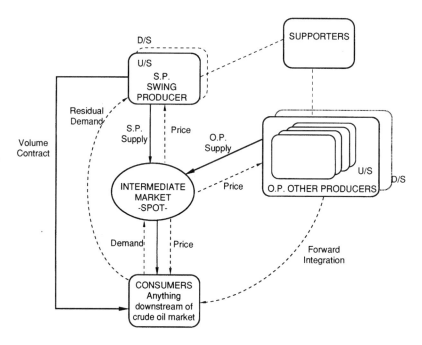

Figure 6-1. The team's initial framework for oil industry structure

The diagram is far from a fully specified algebraic model, yet it is clearly much more focused than the scenario planners' initial list of themes about energy industry structure. How did this focus arise? The minutes of the first working meeting reveal prolonged discussion of the issues, objectives, and scope of the project. The talk was divergent—people were proposing alternative ways to view industry structure, based on brief verbal descriptions. The fascinating process of knowledge activation was at work. One member of the team suggested that the scope for the exercise should be the entire oil chain, from the upstream sector down to the ultimate consumer, on a global geographical basis, encompassing everything connected with the use of liquid fuel (easy to say—but imagine the model!). Another member proposed four different "cuts" at industry structure:

1. corporate: who owns what;

2. analytical: integration versus disintegration—where are the rents in the oil chain?

3. technical: skillpools organized into lobbies;

4. geopolitical: power blocks searching for control of a strategic commodity.

These preliminary ideas prompted a convergent thought: The purpose of the project should be to assess different plausible and sustainable structures that have accompanied periods of stability in oil markets. (Note that the group's shared understanding of concepts like "sustainable structure" and "periods of stability" was initially quite vague, but became clearer as the meeting progressed.)

Undoubtedly this convergent thought shaped the subsequent discussion and ultimately the form and content of the model. Attention shifted to the historical structure of the oil industry and in particular those periods during which, with the benefit of hindsight, the structure seemed particularly stable. Here structure implicitly meant the key producers and the means by which they coordinated production. Stability was associated with the stable identity, number, and relative power of the key producers, but it was also loosely associated with periods of price stability. For example one member of the team stated that "the most important factor in the stability of the pre-1972 industry structure was day-to-day balancing of supply and demand by the major oil companies (who at that time controlled production) with each player sticking to his own territory, not trying to increase sales at the expense of someone else."

The participants began to attach a specific and limited meaning to structure (unconsciously at first) in terms of the relationships and coordinating mechanisms between crude-oil producers. The theme of the discussion became: Let's understand more about the existing crude-oil producers, the means by which they set quotas and production rates, the influence they have on price-setting, and the industry conditions that could force the coalition to break down. This focus was later justified and rationalized on the grounds that better understanding of volatility and uncertainty in crude-oil production and prices would provide greater insight into the reasons for industry-wide structural change.

The facilitator, sensing an opportunity to steer the discussion in the direction of a feedback model, asked the team to think about the relationship between price behavior and industry structure. A senior planner outlined three different "views" of price behavior:

1. "Industry cost curve," where there is perfect competition and price is determined by the cost of the marginal producer;

2. "Total vertical/horizontal integration," the situation prevailing in the post-war period prior to the 1970s when the major oil companies controlled the majority of crude oil production as well as refining, distribution and retailing;

3. "Horizontal integration/swing producer," the situation prevailing in the 1970s when OPEC accounted for 60 percent of crude oil production and used a swing producer to exercise price control.

Notice that these three views are far from polished descriptions of structure and price behavior. They are labels and phrases, fragments of mental models—typical raw material for model building from the mental data base.

With the conversation now centered on structure and price behavior, the facilitator asked the team to think more carefully about the players one would need to include in a full description of 1980s-style "horizontal integration." The facilitator also took the opportunity to remind participants of the representation scheme: players as information processors and decision makers in a feedback system. Each player is represented as a node of decision making, gathering and selecting information about the state of the system, deciding, and acting. The players are linked in a feedback network that interconnects crude-oil production, price-setting, and consumption.

In the subsequent discussion (facilitated with flipchart notes) the participants first considered ways to categorize producers. They quickly recognized that it was neither feasible nor desirable to include each and every producer they could name. They began with the label "swing producer," the producer (or group of producers) with the capability to adjust production to ensure that total crude-oil supply equals demand. In the late 1970s to early 1980s Saudi Arabia fit the label, but the team was aware that the role of swing producer had shifted historically and might shift again in the future. (For example, one member identified the Texas Railroad Commission as the swing producer in the 1930s, and another talked about Petromin. The point to note here is that experienced people often have in their minds robust categories that remain valid even as details change—ideal material for the model builder.) Next, a division of the other producers was suggested, based on three categories: supporters, opportunists, and independents. Supporters and oppor-tunists were described as "those producers or countries, somewhat related to the swing producer, such as the other OPEC members, or outsiders like Egypt or Norway, prepared to commit themselves to some sort of production restraint." The label "supporter" denoted producers with a record of supporting the swing producer by adhering strictly to production quota. The label "opportunist" denoted producers with a record of exceeding quota. Independents were regarded as those producers who control production levels on economics alone, rather than responding to politi-cal or cartel pressures.

With producer categories identified, the team quickly agreed to the schematic in Figure 6-1: a system comprising producers linked through an intermediate market to consumers. There was very little discussion (at this stage) of the market or con-sumers, just a recognition that these two components were necessary to close the model in order to explore the interaction of the different producer groups.

From a process point of view it is significant to note that a meeting comprising mostly free-flowing project team discussion yielded a broad-brush conceptual model. It was the team's own model. Clearly, the facilitator played an important role in the final outcome, by steering the discussion at appropriate moments. But the participants were not put in a conceptual straitjacket—their concepts, categories and knowledge were incorporated in Figure 6-1. It is also significant to note that, although the content of the model became more precisely defined in later meetings, its architecture could always be recognizably traced to Figure 6-1.

PROCESS FOR MAPPING DECISION FUNCTIONS

The second half of the meeting (and much of the next meeting) concentrated on qualitative mapping of decision functions. No computers were present in the meet-ing room, and the maps that were used to guide and capture team discussion were all drawn on flipcharts. By avoiding the early introduction into the meeting of very structured modeling (e.g., STELLA or detailed system dynamics diagramming) it was possible to generate a free flow of discussion and therefore to sustain active participation by the project team.

Figure 6-2 shows just the major components (without interconnections) of a refined conceptual model. By comparison with Figure 6-1 there are numerous addi-tions to content and one important architectural change—the explicit inclusion of OPEC quota. Underneath each producer category there is the name of the decision function being modeled and then a list of decision factors. For example, underneath "swing producer" the production decision is modeled. This involves factors such as quota, price control, and punitive production. Underneath "independents" the capacity expansion decision is modeled. This involves factors such as project prof-itability, development cost, technology, and expected oil price.

Figure 6-2. Producers and the market — components of a conceptual model

The need for an explicit representation of OPEC quota setting only became clear late in the first working meeting as participants described how the swing producer decides how much to produce—it must depend in part on the swing producer's own quota, which in turn comes from quota setting.

Imagine now the team discussion at the point where participants have identified the producer categories. To progress towards a behavioral simulation model, the facilitator needs much more information about producers' decisions: How much does each produce, how (if at all) do they coordinate production, which factors influence their decision-making processes, how important is cost or price, where and how do political factors enter? An experienced team has answers to all these questions and many more—the challenge is to ask the "right" questions, to reach into the participants' knowledge base, record the knowledge, and in the process activate still more knowledge. It's surprising how much people know if only you have an interactive way to represent, record and display the fragments of verbal, numerical and graphical information they typically provide.

In this case the facilitator began by sketching a large circle on a blank flipchart and labeling it "swing producer's production." He then drew several curved lines with arrow heads, each line starting near the edge of the paper and ending on the circle. The curved lines represent information flows—in this case the information the swing producer uses to make production decisions. Using the symbols together with background knowledge of behavioral decision theory (Morecroft 1983; Sterman 1987 and 1989), an experienced modeler can pose many "leading questions" such as: What information does the swing producer need to make production decisions, where does the information come from, how can the swing producer know whether there is a supply/demand balance, what does the swing producer know about total demand and price (or about output of the other producers), how accurately is supply/demand information known, how important is production cost in the decision to produce, which person or group of people are responsible for the production decision, what motivates them, what are their goals and incentives, how does the swing producer's logic compare with say the independents, what are the differences in their information sources, why? And so on. In this way, using flipchart-plus-symbols, the facilitator can conduct an in-depth 30 to 60 minute team discussion of "producer logic."[1]

A similar process of facilitated team discussion took place for each of the other producers and for the box representing the market. How does OPEC decide on a production quota; how is the quota allocated; what motivates the independents to change production; how does the production logic of the independents differ from the opportunists or swing producer; what information does the market use to measure supply-demand imbalances; how rapidly does price adjust to a supply shortage of say 1 million barrels per day; which anchors and cues shape the consumers' demand decisions?

The meeting yielded about 20 flipchart pages showing graphically the information flows entering the producers' and consumers' behavioral decision functions, with text notation to indicate the team's opinions on how the information is processed. Additional text pages captured the team's judgments on factual information such as production rates, operating capacity, surplus capacity, producers' market share, current price, price profiles, and demand.

THE SWING PRODUCER

This section and the next show sample diagrams similar to the flipchart drawings from the team meetings. The intention here is to show the kind of information collected during qualitative mapping—*not* to provide a complete description

---

[1] Qualitative graphical mapping software or magnetics (CTI Publications 1990 and Creativity Software 1990) might be used in place of flipcharts.

of the model structure or to compare the model with other world oil market models in the literature.[2]

The diagrams use symbols for policy maps (Morecroft 1982 and 1992). A large circle with horizontal bars represents a behavioral decision making process. Labeled, curved lines with an arrowhead represent a flow of information—information that is used in the decision-making process in question. Straight lines in bold represent the output of a decision-making process such as the swing producer's production. Labels in bold represent important policy levers (not present in the original conceptual model but added later as simulator controls). The diagrams are best understood by putting yourself in the position of the decision makers—imagine being a swing producer, or sitting in on a capacity expansion meeting of an independent producer.

The role of the swing producer is to produce just enough to defend the intended price, known in the industry as the marker price. A producer taking on this role must have both the physical and economic capacity to increase or decrease production quickly, by as much as 2 million barrels per day or more, in order to absorb unexpected variations in demand (due, say, to an unusually mild winter) or to compensate for cuts in the output of other producers. (Few producers are capable of

---

[2] A full description of the Oil Producers' model is beyond the scope of this paper, whose focus is on the process of capturing and structuring oil industry knowledge. Future papers by the authors will describe in detail the algebraic formulations and feedback structures used to represent the decision making logic of oil producers, cartel quota setting and oil demand. These papers will also put the model in context with other world oil market models. However, energy modelers might be interested in a few comments on the model's relationship to the literature. It should be clear that the "closed" process of conceptualization (using the knowledge of an in-house team of experienced oil industry planners and managers) has led to a model that is independent of other models in the academic literature. This independence is not absolute (for example, team members during meetings often used microeconomic concepts such as perfect competition, industry structure and rents) but will nevertheless make for interesting future comparisons.

Powell (1990) has provided a useful summary of existing world oil market models which helps position the Oil Producers' model. In his view, most models (such as those described in the Energy Modeling Forum summary report [1982] and in Griffin and Teece [1982]) can be classified as either intertemporal optimization models or behavioral simulation models. The optimization models usually assume economically rational behavior on the part of the actors in the market, whereas behavioral models portray decision makers as highly constrained by limited information, limited computational ability, rules of thumb, and limited decision-making sophistication. The Oil Producers' model clearly belongs in the class of behavioral simulation models. However, it differs in significant ways from what Powell describes as the dominant behavioral model—the so-called Target Capacity Utilization model, variants of which appear in the Energy Modeling Forum's 1982 study, and more recently in Gately (1983 and 1986), and Sweeney and Boskin (1985). The Target Capacity Utilization model portrays OPEC as a unitary swing producer, supplying the difference between world oil demand and non-OPEC supply (the call on OPEC), and also setting oil prices. The assumed decision rule for pricing is a behavioral rule of thumb based on the gap between OPEC's current capacity utilization and a target level of capacity utilization. By contrast, the Oil Producers' model disaggregates OPEC into a swing producer and group of opportunists. The model explicitly represents a behavioral decision rule for OPEC quota setting (that allows OPEC the option to set quotas either above or below the call on OPEC) and a political bargaining process of quota allocation based on the ratio of swing producer to opportunists' production capacity (as a surrogate for bargaining power). Price is set in the market by the balance of supply and demand and cannot be set directly by OPEC, though the swing producer can influence price by withholding production when the market price is lower than OPEC's intended marker price (or vice-versa). The Oil Producers' model also represents the political and socioeconomic pressures that cause opportunist producers to exceed quota. Capacity is determined endogenously through capacity expansion policies for both opportunists and independents.

handling such variability of output and revenue.) But how does the swing producer decide how much to produce? Figure 6-3 shows the range of factors entering the decision-making process.

The swing producer operates in two modes—"normal swing mode" and "punitive mode." In swing mode, the swing producer sets a production rate that is equal to the swing quota, unless the oil price deviates from the intended price—meaning posted price or marker price for long-term contracts. When a price deviation is detected, he quickly increases or decreases production of crude in order to regulate the price. In swing mode, the swing producer can influence market price by making production adjustments, the size of which depend on the price he is trying to defend. In the model, price control is exercised through the policy lever *oil price bias,* shown on the left of the diagram. A value for oil price bias of "0" is neutral, meaning that the swing producer is defending a price equal to the average market oil price. A positive value of, say, ".1" means that the swing producer is defending

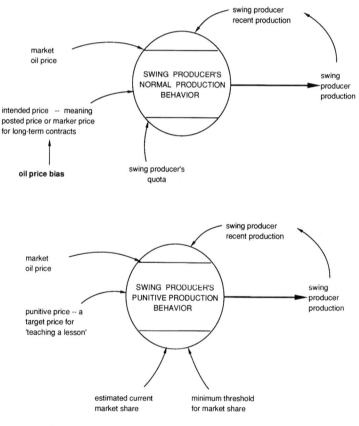

Figure 6-3. The logic of the swing producer — two modes. Normal swing mode is shown at the top and punitive mode at the bottom

a price that is 10 percent higher than the average market oil price and so is trying to edge market prices up. Conversely, a negative value for the bias means the swing producer is trying to edge prices down.

In punitive mode, the swing producer feels that his production is inadequate—he is not getting a fair share of the market—and so decides to reestablish his position by punishing the other producers.[3] In the model, the swing producer has a minimum threshold below which he is unwilling to allow market share to fall. When market share reaches the threshold, the swing producer increases the volume of production in order to flood the market and quickly lower the price. The team spent some time discussing the details of punitive behavior. For example, how does the swing producer decide on the volume of punitive production, and when does he switch back to swing mode? The proposal was to include a punitive price, a very low target price, for teaching a lesson to the other producers. Punitive production continues to expand until market oil price reaches the punitive price, or until the swing producer regains an acceptable market share (which is the signal to return to swing mode). The switch to punitive mode can send a powerful price signal to discipline the other producers, but it is an act of last resort, because in this mode the swing producer has abandoned the role of price regulator—essentially the market is no longer managed.

STELLA Map for the Swing Producer

Figure 6-4 shows a STELLA map (Richmond et al. 1987) of the swing producer. The map was constructed by a four-person modeling team which was a subgroup of the full project team, starting from the flipchart drawings and meeting notes. (The modeling team included two experienced managers, an external consultant acting as facilitator and model designer, and a model builder.)

The figure traces how the swing producer's production responds to quota and to market oil price. The principal logic of changes in production is shown in the top left-hand branch of the figure. Indicated swing production (towards which production adjusts) depends on the swing quota and production pressure from the marker price. In the absence of price pressure, the swing producer produces at quota. But when the market oil price falls below the intended marker price (the price that OPEC is defending) the swing producer reduces production to compensate, and vice-versa. The intended marker price is shown as a function—actually a two-year average—of the market oil price, modified by the oil price bias (an exogenous para-

---

[3] The team members debated whether market share or revenue should be the principal variable driving the swing producer in and out of punitive mode. In the end they selected market share. The reason is that share is a power element. A swing producer can only operate from a position of power. His production level must be large enough to allow swings to take place, without affecting too much his internal economic conditions. A swing producer requires a minimum share of the market in order to be effective. The swing volume required to stabilize the market is proportional to the size of the market, just as required stock levels in manufacturing are related to days throughput. This requirement for swing volume is more important to the swing producer than his revenue position. As soon as he becomes driven by revenue he has to give up the role of swing producer. For further background the reader is referred to Hargreaves (1991).

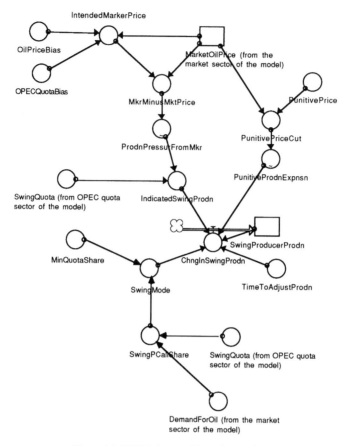

Figure 6-4. STELLA map of the swing producer

meter representing the swing producer's tendency to edge oil price up or down) and the "OPEC quota bias" (another exogenous parameter which represents the degree to which OPEC intends to under-produce or over-produce).

The right-hand branch of the figure shows the logic of punitive production. When the swing producer switches into punitive mode he ignores quota and price control and instead engages in punitive production expansion dictated by a punitive price cut. The size of the price cut depends on the difference between market oil price and a "punitive price," representing the low target price for disciplining the cartel and also the rock-bottom price that the swing producer is prepared to tolerate.

The switch between swing mode and punitive mode is shown in the bottom section of the diagram. Swing mode is switched on whenever the swing producer's call share (SwingPCallShare) exceeds the minimum quota share (MinQuotaShare). But when call share falls below the minimum quota share, swing mode is switched off and punitive production begins. The swing producer's call share is modeled as the ratio of swing quota (a variable whose value is computed in the OPEC Quota sector of the model) to demand for oil (which is computed in the market sector of the model). Note that in drawing the STELLA map, the modelers refined the original concept of market share to the more specific concept of call share which measures the swing producer's market influence as set by quota negotiations.

In order to help team members trace the connection between the STELLA model and the original conceptual model, the modelers made sure that STELLA maps were always displayed alongside policy functions. Briefing documents used in the second working meeting of the project team juxtaposed pictures and text of producer logic to show the connection between verbal comments of participants and the model's relationships. Briefing documents prepared for the model-building team went one step further by juxtaposing pictures, text, STELLA maps, and the algebra of producer logic.

THE INDEPENDENTS

The independents are all those producers—state-owned oil companies, the majors, and other private producers—that are not part of OPEC. The independents are assumed to produce at economic capacity all the time. So unlike the OPEC members, they do not operate with economic capacity surplus. Their production rate is therefore dictated by their capacity expansion decisions, and the speed at which they can change production is limited by the long time lag in constructing new capacity and in depleting existing fields.

The rationale for capacity expansion is dominated by commercial factors as shown in Figure 6-5. The independents will expand capacity (and therefore production) when they judge that it is profitable to do so. If the investment climate is unfavorable (as during a period of low oil prices) then no new upstream capacity is added, resulting in a net loss of output as the production of established fields peaks and then declines.

The model replicates the major inputs to upstream investment decisions in order to calculate the average profitability of potential projects. The independents obviously have to take a view of the development costs of new fields and the expected future oil price over the lifetime of the field. Knowing future cost, price, the likely size of a new field, and the tax regime, one can calculate the future profit stream and apply a hurdle rate to identify "acceptable projects." In reality, each project undergoes a thorough and detailed screening, using well-tried upstream investment appraisal methods. The model treats project appraisal at the level of broad industry averages and computes a "recommended fractional increase in capacity." For example, if, at a specific hurdle rate, average industry project profitability is say 24 percent, then the recommended fractional increase of capacity as computed by the

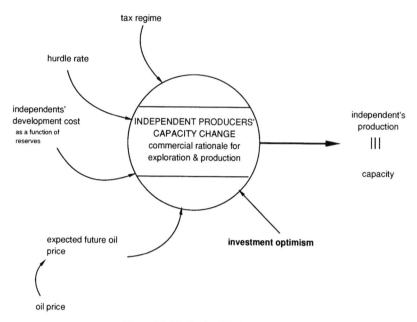

Figure 6-5. The logic of the independents

model is 20 percent per year. Executive control over the recommended expansion is exercised through the policy lever *investment optimism.* A value of 1 is neutral, meaning that approved expansion is equal to recommended expansion. A value greater than 1 means that oil company executives are bullish about the investment climate and approve faster expansion than recommended—for example 50 percent faster than the recommended rate if optimism is set at 1.5. A value less than 1 represents pessimism.

Development costs in the model are estimates of *industry marginal costs* starting in 1988. The independents begin with a large pool of undeveloped reserves.[4] The development cost profile for these reserves (assuming no cost improvements from technology) is, broadly speaking, a curve that rises as reserves are depleted. A small quantity of low-cost reserves is assumed. Once low-cost reserves are exhausted the cost profile rises quite sharply and then levels out to a gently-rising

---

[4] The estimation of fossil fuel reserves is a major topic in its own right that has received the attention of system dynamics modelers (Sterman, Richardson, and Davidsen 1988; Sterman and Richardson 1985). Their work has shown that reserve estimation is essentially a behavioral, judgmental decision making process, despite the seeming "hard" scientific and geological inputs to the process. The search for oil, its discovery, and ultimate production take place in a feedback system that supplies the economic incentives for exploration and production through oil price. When commonly-used estimation algorithms are embedded in such a feedback system they show a tendency to exaggerate the size of recoverable reserves, especially during the mid-to-late stages of the depletion life cycle. The 1988 starting value of independents' crude oil reserves used in the Oil Producers' model is a global aggregate (excluding reserves of Eastern Block countries) compiled from the best estimates of corporate planners.

plateau. Finally, the cost profile rises steeply as known industry reserves approach zero—in other words, there is a finite supply of commercially viable oil. The precise industry cost profile used in the model is confidential.

Technology can undoubtedly be expected to lower costs as more efficient production and recovery methods are devised. The model's technology profile assumes a significant improvement over the next ten years. Thereafter the effect of technology is assumed to remain constant. Again, the precise profile used in the model is confidential.

PARTIAL MODEL SIMULATIONS—OWNERSHIP AND A SYSTEMS PERSPECTIVE

To build confidence and a sense of ownership in the algebraic model, the facilitator designed a number of partial model simulations to demonstrate the "algebra in action." Two partial model simulations are shown below, similar to the ones used in the team meetings (though based on a more polished version of the algebraic model). Needless to say, the following simulations *are not predictions* of oil supply, price, and demand for the next 25 years. They are scenarios, initially used to raise questions about the model and later to stimulate thinking about oil market behavior.

Figure 6-6 is a simulation isolating the effect of the swing producer's price control when acting in swing mode. The simulation represents a "thought experiment" in which the oil market starts in a supply-demand equilibrium of 50 million barrels per day in 1988, and is disturbed by a 5 percent exogenous decrease in oil demand

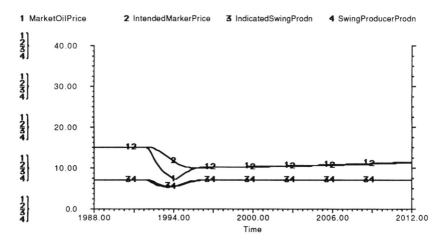

MarketOilPrice and IntendedMarkerPrice are on a vertical scale from 0 to 40 dollars per barrel
IndicatedSwingProduction and SwingProducerProduction are on a vertical scale from 0 to 40 million barrels per day

Figure 6-6. Swing producer price control

in 1992, followed by a 5 percent increase in 1994. The experiment assumes that only the swing producer is able to change production (the output of the other producers is held constant at a value of 43 million barrels per day, a condition that implicitly assumes the independents have fixed marginal development costs of just over $9 per barrel). Price adjusts to the supply-demand imbalance, but has no feedback effect on demand in this run. The swing producer withholds production in an attempt to hold market price at the target value set by the marker price. The marker price itself adapts with a two-year delay toward the market price. The experiment isolates the dynamic behavior of the swing producer's price control loops shown in the top half of Figure 6-7. The major balancing loop regulates market oil price through swing production. If the intended marker price is greater than the market

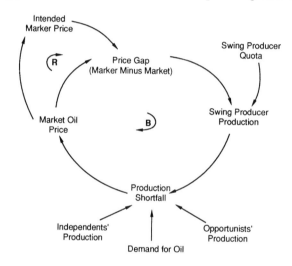

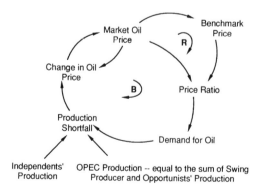

Figure 6-7. Feedback loops controlling market oil price

oil price then the resulting price gap creates pressure to reduce production below the swing quota. As a result a production shortfall develops that causes the market price to rise. In addition, the partial model contains a floating goal for intended marker price. The floating goal is responsible for the drift in market oil price seen in the simulation.

The simulation of this (artificial) situation shows the oil market in equilibrium from 1988 to 1992. In 1992 the 5 percent step decrease in demand generates excess supply of 2.5 million barrels a day, which sends price plummeting from $15 per barrel to about $7 per barrel by 1994. In response the swing producer cuts back production from 7 million to 5 million barrels per day. The production cutback limits the price decline, but does not restore price to the original level of $15 per barrel. The price drift is a result of prolonged oversupply that causes the intended marker price to decline gradually from $15 per barrel to about $12 per barrel in 1994. Then, demand (not shown) steps back up by 5 percent. Quickly, a new market equilibrium is established in which price settles at $10 per barrel, and the swing producer expands production back to 7 million barrels per day.

Figure 6-8 is a simulation showing the change in dynamic behavior that occurs when realism is increased somewhat by activating an endogenous influence on demand from price. The conditions of the experiment are identical to those used in Figure 6-6, with the exception that demand rises as price falls, and vice-versa. The market starts in equilibrium. The same profile of demand is used, a 5 percent decrease, sustained for two years. The difference is that the 5 percent demand shift is applied to a "base demand" that is itself evolving. Only the swing producer can

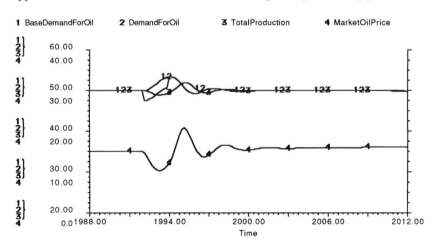

MarketOilPrice is on a vertical scale from 0 to 40 dollars per barrel
BaseDemandforOil, DemandforOil, and TotalProduction are on a vertical scale from 20 to 60 million barrels per day

Figure 6-8. Interaction of the price control and demand-price loops

change production in this run. The experiment isolates the dynamic interaction of the swing producer's price control loop and the newly formed price-demand loop that links the variables shown in the bottom half of Figure 6-7.

Demand and production start out in balance at 50 million barrels per day, and price is steady at $15 per barrel. In 1992, demand for oil falls by 5 percent. Market oil price begins to fall. Unlike the previous run, falling price stimulates additional demand. As a result, base demand for oil (the volume of demand computed before taking out the exogenous step decrease) actually begins to rise and peaks at about 53 million barrels per day. Demand for oil mirrors the upward trend in base demand, and returns to 50 million barrels per day by 1993. Price bottoms out at $10 per barrel and begins to increase again during 1993. In 1994, demand steps back up, causing a price spike that peaks at just over $20 per barrel during late 1995. Gradually a new equilibrium is established (after mild price and production fluctuations). Market oil price settles at $16 per barrel, and swing producer production returns to 7 million barrels per day.

The partial model simulations increased the modeling team's confidence in the algebraic model by showing results that were intuitively plausible. The "stories" of dynamic behavior made sense and details of the simulated trajectories often matched people's expectations. When minor surprises occurred (such as oil price drift) the simulations provided the basis for a plausible explanation. Of course one can argue that qualitative opinions about simulations of thought experiments do not validate the model—but they do build ownership and insight. The model is not a black box.

SELECTED SIMULATIONS OF THE FULL MODEL

The full STELLA model contains 99 equations (including constants and graph functions). Separate pages of the STELLA map are devoted to the opportunists, the swing producer, OPEC quota setting, the independents, demand and price, and revenue calculations.

The model is capable of generating a very wide range of oil industry scenarios over a period of 25 years. To illustrate the model's output, a selection of simulations is presented below, taken from an "OPEC supply squeeze scenario" for the period 1988 to 2012. A supply squeeze is created starting in 1994 by causing OPEC to set quotas that are 10 percent lower than the call from the market (the call is OPEC's estimate of the difference between total demand and independents' production). The quota restriction is maintained from 1994 to the end of the simulation in 2012. The opportunists are assumed to produce at quota, so there is no cheating on quota by OPEC members. External pressures on demand from the economy, technology, and the environment are assumed to be neutral. In other words, in the absence of price changes, demand stays constant at 50 million barrels per day. The independents are assumed to adopt a neutral capex policy, meaning that they expand capacity at exactly the rate recommended by project appraisal methods, rather than being optimistic or pessimistic. (The reader should bear in mind, once again, that the simulations associated with this scenario are *not forecasts* that either the project team or the company believe will happen in the oil market in the period to 2012. They are thought provokers, the basis for internally consistent "what-if" stories.)

Figure 6-9 shows the demand profile for the supply squeeze scenario. Demand begins at 50 million barrels per day in 1988 and rises gently to a peak of almost 52 million barrels per day (mbd) in 1994, which is the year OPEC's supply squeeze begins. The immediate effect of the squeeze can be seen as the trajectory for total production (line 2) falls noticeably below demand (line 1) throughout 1994. Demand begins to fall and continues its decline for almost a decade until 2003. The decline is a result of OPEC's sustained policy of quota restriction. By 2004 demand has leveled out at 43 million barrels a day. Suddenly, in early 2004, total production begins to rise sharply (for reasons explained below), peaks at 48 million barrels per day after only 6 months, and then falls back again to 43 mbd by late 1995. Three similar spikes of production occur in the interval between 2006 and 2012. These marked variations in supply induce lagged variations in demand.

The behavior of demand can best be understood by examining the trajectory of market oil price shown in Figure 6-10. Price begins at $15 per barrel in 1988 and falls until 1991 due to a supply excess (shown in the figure by the slight difference between DemandMinusProduction and the reference zero, RefZero, line). The sup-

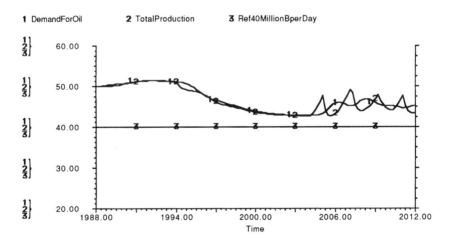

DemandForOil and TotalProduction are shown on a vertical scale
from 20 to 60 million barrels per day

Figure 6-9. Demand profile for OPEC supply squeeze scenario. OPEC's quota is set 10 percent lower than the call on OPEC, starting in 1994

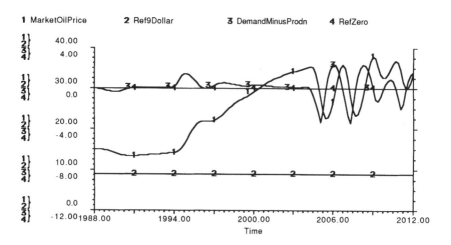

1 MarketOilPrice   **2** Ref9Dollar   **3** DemandMinusProdn   **4** RefZero

MarketOilPrice is shown on a vertical scale from 0 to 40 dollars per barrel
The production shortfall, called DemandMinusProduction, is shown on a vertical scale
from minus 12 million to 4 million barrels per day

Figure 6-10. Oil price and the supply-demand balance for OPEC supply squeeze scenario

ply excess arises from a surge of independents' new production capacity, already in the construction pipeline in 1988, that comes onstream during the period 1988 to 1991. Supply and demand remain in almost perfect balance during the period 1991 to 1994 with the result that price remains static at $13 per barrel. In 1994 price begins to rise sharply as a result of OPEC's supply squeeze. The squeeze results in excess demand that peaks at 1.5 million barrels a day in mid-1994. Meanwhile, price rockets to $22 per barrel. The price surge causes a noticeable reduction of demand as consumers take short-term measures to reduce energy use (lowering thermostats in winter, raising them in summer, driving slowly, making fewer and shorter trips). As a result, demand and supply equilibrate briefly during 1995, leading to a price plateau at $22 per barrel that lasts for more than a year. (This tendency of price to settle at a plateau is an example of oil price drift seen in the earlier partial model simulations.) But the market balance is short-lived. OPEC continues to set quotas 10 percent lower than the call, so a demand excess appears once more. Oil price shows a steady increase to $35 per barrel by 2003. Starting in 2004, oil price becomes quite unstable, fluctuating between peaks as high as $40 per barrel and troughs as low as $23 per barrel.

The production profile of the three producer groups is shown in Figure 6-11. In 1988 the independents are the dominant producers with an output volume of 26 mbd. The opportunists' volume is 17 mbd and the swing producer's is 7 mbd. Up to 1994 production shares remain steady, with the independents showing a slight increase at the expense of the OPEC producers. In 1994 the opportunists' produc-

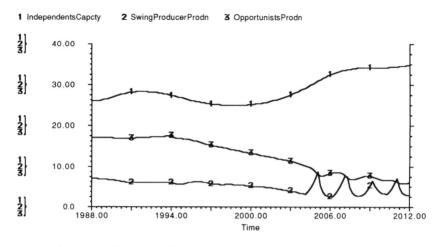

IndependentsCapacity, SwingProducerProduction, and OpportunistsProduction
are shown on a vertical scale from 0 to 40 million barrels per day

Figure 6-11. Production profiles of the three producer groups for OPEC supply squeeze scenario

tion begins a steady decline which reflects the implementation of the supply squeeze. The decline continues until 2004 by which time the opportunists' volume has fallen to 10 mbd. Meanwhile, the independents' production declines slowly but steadily until about 1998, when it reaches a minimum of 25 mbd. Production then begins to rise, reaching a plateau of 33 mbd by 2008 which stretches to the end of the simulation. It is interesting that independent production declines between 1994 and 1998, despite the significant price rise. This lack of response to improving price occurs in part because independents' development costs are rising quickly and in part because of the long time lags in exploration and production.

The swing producer's volume is on a downward trend from 1994 to 2004, like the opportunists. But, despite the OPEC supply squeeze, production recovers temporarily in 1995 and 1996. This recovery occurs because the swing producer must compensate for the decline in independents' production. But in 1997, the downward trend resumes, reaching a minimum of 3.7 mbd in 2004. By this time, ten years after the introduction of the supply squeeze, OPEC's market power is much weakened. The swing producer's market share falls to the threshold, causing a surge of production as the swing producer switches to punitive mode. Between 2004 and 2012 the swing producer's volume fluctuates between 3 mbd and 9 mbd as he switches back and forth between punitive and swing mode in an unsuccessful attempt to discipline a now powerless cartel. By the end of the scenario, the independents are the dominant producers with an output volume of 35 mbd, at a price of $33 per barrel. OPEC (as a result of its sustained supply squeeze) is reduced to a combined volume of about 9 mbd, shared between the opportunists at 6 mbd and the swing producer at 3 mbd.

USES OF THE MODEL AND REFLECTIONS ON THE MODELING PROCESS

To date, the model's main use has been as an input to scenario planning.[5] A somewhat elaborated version of the model (containing extra detail about independent producers and their reserves) generated simulations that were published in the company's scenario planning book, *Group Planning* (1989).[6] This modified model was used repeatedly to explore the effect on oil price and production of alternative OPEC strategies. For example, scenarios similar to the supply squeeze were created by simulating the effect of quota restrictions, ranging from 10 percent down to 0 percent. The supply scenario was extended by simulating the effect of OPEC quota surpluses, also ranging from 0 to 10 percent. New scenarios were created by varying other parameters that control producer behavior such as the degree of quota cheating in the cartel or the optimism of the independents' investment decisions. A graphical compilation of the simulations revealed a "geography" of future price profiles. The geography showed three distinct areas, which were labeled "mountains, plains, and plateau," depending on whether oil price fluctuates, or is stable at a low or higher price level.

The scenario planners felt that the model's characterization of OPEC in terms of three behavioral decision making components—swing producer, opportunists, and quota setting—made possible a wider range of industry scenarios than the conventional models they knew of, which represent OPEC as a unitary swing producer and price setter (see Energy Modeling Forum [1982] and Powell [1990] for a review of published models in the field). Moreover, because the planners had themselves been involved in conceptualizing and building the model they felt comfortable interpreting model simulations, writing scenario stories, and integrating the simulations and stories into the overall scenario book.

It is too early to say at this stage whether there are clear normative lessons about the design of the modeling process to be derived from this project. However, there was a well-defined procedure for involving the team members, capturing their

[5] Recently the model has been converted into a gaming simulator and computer-based learning environment using the Microworlds software (see Diehl [1992] and Chapter 15 in this work). Game players (who need not be familiar with system dynamics) can take the role of the oil producers and create their own scenarios. The gaming simulator is currently used in Shell's internal management development programs.

[6] The elaborated model, which was known as the "Industry Structure model," represented OPEC in terms of a swing producer, opportunists, and quota setting, the same as the smaller Oil Producers' model on which it was based. Extra detail was added to the portrayal of independents' reserves, exploration decisions, and upstream capacity expansion decisions. Some of these more detailed formulations were borrowed from a much larger Upstream Investment model. In addition, the independents were disaggregated to show explicit producing countries.

knowledge, mapping structure, and generating ownership. Some comments on this procedure may add to the wisdom and experience that is accumulating on model building with management teams, as reported in this volume and elsewhere in the system dynamics and group decision support literature.

The procedure comprises two distinct phases that separate qualitative modeling from algebraic modeling and simulation. The first phase involves issue conceptualization (choosing which issue to model) and the mapping of major sectors and decision functions. Because the first phase is qualitative it is easy to involve team members in the discussion—even people who have little or no experience of computer modeling The representation scheme is deliberately rather loose—boxes to represent sectors, and circles (with information flows entering and leaving) to represent system actors. Using simple and familiar media like flipcharts and whiteboards, a facilitator can quite easily capture a wide range of comments by drawing boxes and circles, and by writing text.

The facilitator plays a key role in shaping the discussion. It appears to be very helpful for the facilitator to have in mind a framework to guide the meeting and to formulate questions. The more flexible the framework the better—one does not want to impose an "answer" on the group. Obviously the framework here is based on system dynamics and systems thinking, because the objective is to elicit knowledge and information that are suitable for constructing a feedback model. However, several options are available that reflect different styles of model conceptualization. In this case we derived the architecture of the model by mapping system components and behavioral decision functions. The approach appears to work well because it accesses participants' detailed structural knowledge of the oil markets: in this case the motives of the different players, the information sources used in production and capacity expansion decisions. Another approach (which is gaining in popularity) is to organize model conceptualization around archetypes or generic feedback structures. The archetypes (eloquently described in Senge [1990], chs. 5–7) are commonly occurring feedback loops, like a balancing loop with a delay, that generate characteristic dynamic behavior such as fluctuations. The archetypes are qualitative and can be used in a group to focus discussion and as the seed around which to crystallize a new model. (An example is reported in Morecroft, Lane, and Viita [1991] where the "growth and underinvestment archetype," derived from Forrester's [1968] Market Growth Model, is used as the basis for a model of a biotechnology startup firm.) Yet another option is Wolstenholme's (1992) modular approach, described in Chapter 7).

Whichever option is used, it is helpful to prepare the team in advance for the representation scheme to be adopted. For example, if using archetypes, one might ask participants to read chapters from Senge's book. In our case the participants read de Geus (1988) and Morecroft (1985). The reason for this preparation is to condition people, just gently, to think in terms of behavioral decision making, archetypes, or causal diagrams (whatever the particular approach emphasizes). When the participants know something about the representation scheme it is much easier for the facilitator to activate and filter team knowledge that is relevant for a feedback model.

Phase two of the project involved algebraic modeling and simulation. A small team, four out of the full team of ten, took part in this phase. It is difficult to imagine how one would have engaged the full team in this more detailed work. Nevertheless, since it is our view (widely shared in the literature) that important learning takes place during equation writing and simulation, we took steps to ensure that this learning would not be lost or restricted to the technical modeling experts. First the modeling team included two experienced scenario planners, who would be using the model and interpreting simulations. Second, deliberate efforts were made to retain a clear linkage from the original conceptual model to the later STELLA maps and the algebra. For example, STELLA maps were organized so that each page represented a particular producer and were shown (in presentations and reports) side by side with the corresponding map of producer logic. Third, partial model simulations were designed to help all members of the modeling team understand how the model worked. These three steps were quite time consuming, but the investment was judged by the team to be worthwhile.

In retrospect there is room for improvement in our two-phase approach. Most particularly, the critical stage of issue conceptualization (at the start of phase one) was rather haphazard. The way the team came to focus on the upstream oil industry (after a period of creative and divergent discussion about the changing structure of the energy industry as a whole, including upstream, downstream, oil, gas, and nuclear) seemed as much by chance as by design. Our view now is that issue conceptualization should become the first phase of a three-phase approach and should make use of tools like hexagon modeling (Hodgson [1992] and Chapter 18 of this work) to manage the vital and creative step of selecting a topic. Then systems thinking and mapping tools can help structure participants' knowledge of the issue.

Obviously there are still many challenges remaining in the quest to hand over systems thinking and modeling tools to busy executives and planners. But, as this paper and others in the volume show, there is growing expertise and understanding in the design of group processes that can capture knowledge for model building and accelerate team learning.

REFERENCES

CTI Publications (1990), *Thinking with Hexagons,* company publication, Idon Ltd., Edradour House, Pitlochry, Perthshire, Scotland, PH16 5JW.

Creativity Software (1990), *CK Modeller,* company publication, Idon Ltd., Edradour House, Pitlochry, Perthshire, Scotland, PH16 5JW.

Diehl, E. (1992) "Managerial Microworlds as Learning Support Tools," *European Journal of Operational Research* 59, no. 1: 210-15; also Chapter 15 in this work.

Energy Modeling Forum (1982), *World Oil: Summary Report,* Terman Engineering Center, Stanford University, Stanford, Calif.

Forrester, J.W. (1968), "Market Growth as Influenced by Capital Investment," *Sloan Management Review* 9, no. 2: 83-105; also in *Collected Papers of Jay W. Forrester,* Portland, Ore.: Productivity Press (1975), 111-32.

Fossli, K., and M. Wilkinson (1986), "Subroto Warns of Oil Price Collapse," *Financial Times,* May 4, 1986.

Gately, D. (1983), "OPEC: Retrospective and Prospects 1973-1990," *European Economic Review* 21: 313-31.

Gately, D. (1986), "Lessons from the 1986 Oil Price Collapse," *Brookings Papers on Economic Activity* 2: 237-84.

de Geus, A.P. (1988), "Planning as Learning," *Harvard Business Review,* March-April: 70-74.

Goldstein, W. (1990), "The Supply and Demand for Oil in the 1990s," *Energy Policy,* September: 593-95.

Griffin, J.M., and D.J. Teece (1982), *OPEC Behavior and World Oil Prices,* London: George Allen & Unwin.

Group Planning (1989), "1989 Scenarios, Challenge and Response," *Group Planning Publication* (confidential), PL 89 S12, Shell International Petroleum Company, London.

Hargreaves, D. (1991), "Saudis Back in Control," *Financial Times,* March 14, 1991, p. 18.

Hodgson, T. (1992), "Hexagons for Systems Thinking," *European Journal of Operational Research* 59, no. 1: 220-30; also Chapter 18 in this work.

Jennings, J.S. (1988), "The Oil and Gas Industry in the 1990s," an address to the Third Annual North Sea Conference of the British Institute of Energy Economics, London, June 27, 1988, Shell Publications, Public Affairs, Shell International Petroleum Company, London, U.K.

Kalff, D. (1989), "Strategic Decision Making and Simulation in Shell Companies," *Strategic Planning in Shell* ("blue guide to planning") no 8, Shell International Petroleum Company, Group Planning, Shell Centre, London U.K.

Management Brief (1989), "Decisions, Decisions," *The Economist,* July 22, 1989, pp. 76-77.

Morecroft, J.D.W. (1982), "A Critical Review of Diagramming Tools for Conceptualizing Feedback System Models, *Dynamica* 8, no. 1: 20-29.

Morecroft, J.D.W. (1983), "System Dynamics: Portraying Bounded Rationality," *Omega,* 11, no. 2: 131-42.

Morecroft, J.D.W. (1985), "The Feedback View of Business Policy and Strategy," *System Dynamics Review* 1, no. 1: 4-19.

Morecroft, J.D.W. (1988), "System Dynamics and Microworlds for Policymakers," *European Journal of Operational Research* 35: 301-20.

Morecroft, J.D.W. (1990), "Strategy Support Models," in Robert G. Dyson, ed., *Strategic Planning: Models and Analytical Techniques,* Chichester, U.K.: Wiley; originally published in *Strategic Management Journal* 5, no. 3: 215-29 (1984).

Morecroft, J.D.W. (1992), "Executive Knowledge, Models, and Learning," *European Journal of Operational Research* 59, no. 1: 9-27; also Chapter 1 in this work.

Morecroft, J.D.W., D.C. Lane, and P.S. Viita (1991), "Modeling Growth Strategy in a Biotechnology Startup Firm," *System Dynamics Review* 6, no. 2: 97-118.

Powell, S.G. (1990), "An Evaluation of Behavioral Simulation Models of OPEC," *Proceedings of the 1990 International System Dynamics Conference,* Chestnut Hill, Mass., July 1990, 878-92 (copies available from The System Dynamics Society, Massachusetts Institute of Technology, Cambridge MA 02142).

Richmond, B.M. (1987), "The Strategic Forum: From Vision to Operating Policies and Back Again," High Performance Systems, 45 Lyme Road, Ste. 300, Hanover NH 03755.

Richmond, B.M., P. Vescuso, and S. Peterson (1987), *STELLA for Business,* High Performance Systems, 45 Lyme Road, Ste. 300, Hanover NH 03755.

Senge, P.M. (1990), *The Fifth Discipline,* New York: Doubleday Currency.

Sterman, J.D. (1987), "Testing Behavioral Simulation Models by Direct Experiment," *Management Science* 33, no. 12, 1572-1592.

Sterman, J.D. (1989), "Misperceptions of Feedback in Dynamic Decision Making," *Organizational Behavior and Human Decision Processes* 43: 301-55.

Sterman, J.D. and G.P. Richardson (1985), "An Experiment to Evaluate Methods for Estimating Fossil Fuel Resources," *Journal of Forecasting* 4: 197-226.

Sterman, J.D., G.P. Richardson, and P.I. Davidsen (1988), "Modeling the Estimation of Petroleum Resources in the United States," *Technological Forecasting and Social Change* 33: 219-49.

Sweeney, J.L., and J.M. Boskin (1985), "Analysing Impacts of Potential Tax Policy Changes on U.S. Oil Security," *The Energy Journal* 6: 89-108.

Vennix, J.A.M., and J.L.A. Geurts (1987), "Communicating Insights from Complex Simulation Models," *Simulation and Games* 18, no. 3: 321-43.

Wack, P. (1985a), "Scenarios: Shooting the Rapids," *Harvard Business Review,* November-December: 139-48.

Wack, P. (1985b), "Scenarios: Uncharted Waters Ahead," *Harvard Business Review,* September-October: 72-80.

Wilkinson, M. (1988), "Opec's Dangerous Market Game," *Financial Times,* September 27, 1988.

Wolstenholme, E.F. (1992), "The Definition and Application of a Stepwise Approach to Model Conceptualisation and Analysis," *European Journal of Operational Research* 59, no. 1: 123-36; also Chapter 7 in this work.

7

A SYSTEMATIC APPROACH TO MODEL CREATION

Eric F. Wolstenholme

ABSTRACT: This paper addresses the difficult task of creating system dynamics models and developing a starting point for model analysis. It suggests the adoption of a clear, standardized, stepwise approach. The thinking behind this approach and its application in a case study are presented.

INTRODUCTION

The process by which system dynamics models are created and developed for problem solving has received much attention in recent system dynamics research and a number of approaches are reported in this volume and elsewhere (Vennix et al. 1990; Richmond et al. 1987; Morecroft et al. 1989; Senge and Sterman 1992).

The purpose of this paper is to assist these activities by providing some clear, standardized guidelines for model construction and analysis and to demonstrate their use in a business case study.

The guidelines are presented in the form of a stepwise methodology intended to be used directly by analysts and system owners to create simulation models that are a reflection of their mental models. The perceptions of individual managers concerning their organizations differ widely and a key activity in creating models is to generate a forum for managers to share and reach a consensus view of the way in which their company is structured and organized. Only in this interactive way can understanding be created and appropriate, lasting change implemented.

Such a stepwise approach to model creation has much in common with the soft system problem-solving methodologies currently being developed as alternatives to quantitative approaches (Checkland 1983; Rosenhead 1989; Bryant 1989; Eden 1979).

In describing the case study which applied the methodology, emphasis is placed on how it can be used to explore the problem domain and lead towards a model capable of promoting holistic understanding and change within the organization concerned. The method was applied in this case study through a set of meetings with senior managers from the company, which took place in four phases.

The end point was a diagrammatic model on which qualitative analysis was performed. This was not a quantified and calibrated simulation model. The modeling process was stopped at this point as the management concerned were happy that they had gained sufficient insight from this qualitative study to change the way in which the company operated.

MODEL CONSTRUCTION

Any system dynamics study should clearly be based on a defined cause for concern. Ideally, the concern should be specified in terms of existing, undesirable system behavior and such a mode of system behavior is often labeled as a reference mode of behavior for the system. The definition of the concern is of great importance, since it dictates the shape and boundaries of the model.

In practice, System Dynamics models have tended to be constructed in two basic ways (Wolstenholme 1982, 1983, and 1990), which are often used together. They can proceed by identifying feedback structures (or loops) responsible for the reference mode behavior of the system (the feedback loop approach), or by identifying specific examples of the underlying components of system dynamics; that is, examples of process, information, delay, strategy, or organizational boundaries associated with the cause for concern. This method is referred to here as a modular approach. These two approaches will now be explained in more detail.

The Feedback Loop Approach to Model Construction

Consider first the identification of feedback structure. It is well known in system dynamics that certain types of simple feedback loops create certain types of system behavior. It follows, therefore, that if the existing reference mode of behavior of a system is known, then it should be possible to infer the types of loops of which it is composed (Forrester 1961 and 1968; Lyneis 1980; Richmond et al. 1987; Coyle 1981).

For example, if a system exhibits slow growth it is possible that there is a dominant positive loop present, but that this is being inhibited or constrained by a negative one. Similarly, a system which is declining slowly might be construed as being dominated by a positive degenerate loop, whose effect is moderated by the imposition of a number of negative loop control policies.

Alternatively, a stair-step or sigmoidal type of growth pattern might be indicative of a positive loop that is dominant most of the time, but that is occasionally overwhelmed by a negative influence. Similarly, an S-shaped growth might indicate a shift in dominance from an initial positive growth loop to a negative control loop.

This method of model construction evolves by identifying loops and linking them together. The skeleton loops are then fleshed out by identifying intermediate variables and classifying the variables into rates, levels, and auxiliaries. This can be a difficult task, but it assists with differentiating between physical and information flows, which is a necessary step in moving towards a quantitative model.

The Modular Approach to Model Construction

The second method of model construction is almost the opposite of the one described above. Here it is necessary to start with one or two key variables associated with the cause for concern and to try to relate examples of process, information, delay, strategy, or organization to these.

Which of the components is used as the starting point in the modular approach depends on the purpose of the investigation and the type of system. For example, in a study originating from a reorganization of managerial responsibility, it would be logical to start with the new organizational boundaries and to study how the underlying processes of the organization will be affected; when studying the effects of a new information system, it would be useful to start with the information flows; when examining bottlenecks in flows it might be appropriate to examine the physical processes of the system; when given a number of alternative strategies or policies it might be sensible to start with the variables that these are aimed at controlling.

Finally, if the reference mode highlights extreme examples of a variable being out of phase, delays within processes might provide the key starting point.

Each of these components of the system dynamics method will now be considered separately as a background to aid understanding of the modular approach.

Process Structure

The processes within a system are not easily visible, and in order to create a sound process perspective of a system it is usually necessary to stand back from the system and view it over a sufficient time frame and at an appropriate level of aggregation. For example, if the concern is provision of homes for elderly people, it is important not to focus too finely on the needs of the individuals or on the national total of elderly, but to view the total number of people in homes in one accounting unit, say a city, and the weekly or monthly flow into and out of these.

The system dynamics approach to creating the process structure of systems is to recognize that the fundamental process in any natural or managed system is that of converting resources between states. The word *resource* here should be treated in its widest sense and could include material, people, cash, orders, goods, knowledge, etc. A state of a resource can then be defined as any accumulation of the resource that is relevant to the concern and, hence, purpose of the model. The states are alternatively known as system *levels* or *stocks*. They are the measurable quantities of any resource in a system at any point in time, and their dimensions are usually in resource units. If a photograph or static view is taken of the system, then its resource states will still be present and this technique provides a good way of identifying such variables. Figure 7-1 gives some examples of resources and their states.

Resource	State 1	State 2	State 3	State 4	etc.
Land	Wild	Cultivated			
Minerals	Undiscovered	Discovered	Exploited	Refined stock	
Productive plant	Under construction	New, Efficient plant	Old, obsolete plant	Scrap metal	
Hospital patients	Waiting for treatment	In hospital	Recuperating at home	Back at work	
Scientists	University based	Working on research	Senior staff	Retired	
Labor	Untrained	Trainees	Trained		
Orders	Backlog	In production	Satisfied		
Money	Bills collectible	Cash in hand			

Figure 7-1. Examples of resources and their states

The rate at which resources are converted between states is represented in system dynamics by *rate* variables. Rate variables are control variables that directly increase or deplete resource levels, and their dimensions are usually in units per period of time. That is, they control flows into and out of stocks. Rates can be considered as taking place instantaneously and therefore are not directly measurable.

The process structure of systems, as represented by resource flows made up of levels and rates, can be described by two types of diagrams. These will be referred to here as pipe diagrams and influence diagrams (alternatively known as causal-loop diagrams). The alternative name for a "pipe" diagram is a "flow" diagram. Influence diagrams only will be considered here since these can later be used to form a framework for model analysis.

Figure 7-2 shows an influence diagram for a resource flow, representing patients flowing into hospitals and out into the community. Here, the resource is the people and the states chosen are patients in the hospital and ex-patients in the community.

The "influences" of the rates on the level are specified using arrows and the sources. Further, the polarity of the influences is specified and, in the convention used in this paper, the levels are boxed.

To use influence diagrams comprehensively it is vital to have a thorough understanding of the concept of polarity. In general, if a change in the magnitude of the tail variable of an influence arrow causes a change in the magnitude of the head variable in the same direction, then the link is a positive one. Conversely, if a change in the magnitude of the tail variable of an influence arrow causes a change in the magnitude of the head variable in the opposite direction, then the link is a negative one.

For example in Figure 7-2, an *increase* in the hospital *admission* rate would result in *more* patients in hospital and a *decrease* would result in *fewer.* Hence, the direction of the influence is designated as positive. Conversely, an *increase* in the hospital *discharge* rate would result in *fewer* patients in hospital and a *decrease* would result in *more.* Therefore the direction of the influence is designated as negative.

The polarity attached to links in influence diagrams is important and facilitates analysis of composite models as will be seen in the later case study.

In Figure 7-2 it is important to realize that the direction of the resource flows is from left to right even though some of the influence links point from right to left.

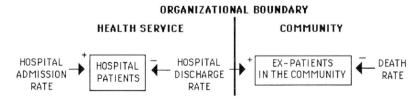

Figure 7-2. Influence diagram for a resource flow

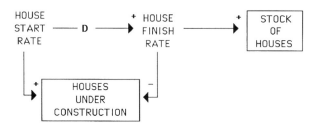

Figure 7-3. Influence diagram of a delayed resource flow

Delays

One of the major factors contributing to system behavior over time is that of delays. It is frequently the case that there is a lag between the start and finish of a resource conversion rate and this can be represented in an influence diagram by a letter "D" linking the start and finish rates as shown in Figure 7-3.

In general, in resource flows, levels can only depend on rates. Levels should never depend on other levels and, with the exception of delays, rates should never depend on other rates. The reason for the exception is that a delay is actually a hidden level, where the resource is held up and the quantity of resource that is delayed can be measured as shown in Figure 7-3.

Organizational Boundaries

Once the process structure of a system has been drawn, it is useful and important to superimpose any relevant organizational boundaries that exist within and between each resource flow. For example, in Figure 7-2 the resource of people flows through two different organizations; these are the health service and the community. The main purpose of marking such boundaries on the diagrams is to try to clarify which organizations or people control each rate variable in the process. In the example it is clear that the health service controls the hospital admission and discharge rates and that the community has no control over the numbers of ex-patients discharged into it.

Further, it may be necessary to draw any relevant departmental boundaries that exist within each organization. If, for example, different departments or people within the health service control the admission and discharge rates, it is important to recognize this.

One of the most common reasons for problems encountered in lengthy processes in large systems is the number of different organizations controlling different parts of the process. If organizations do not integrate their control strategies with adjacent organizations, the processes will not flow smoothly.

Information Structure and Strategy

It will be appreciated from the previous section that the magnitude of resource flows are controlled by the rate variables. In Figure 7-2 these variables have not yet been defined, in the sense that no causality has been specified for them and no arrows lead into them. In fact, the diagram of Figure 7-2 can be described as an open loop model. Creating information structure will convert this into a closed loop model.

Two pieces of knowledge are required before the rates can be specified. The first piece of knowledge is which system states will be defined to have a causal effect on the rate. The second is what rule will be defined to specify the type of effect.

In managed systems the first piece of knowledge is the information chosen by the system owners and the second is the strategy by which to use the information. For this reason rate variables in managed systems are usually referred to as policy, strategy, or decision variables.

Often the setting of rate variables involves defining targets (desired or objective states) for levels and implementing strategies to eliminate any discrepancies between the target and actual values of the levels.

A composite influence diagram containing both resource and information flows and target states is shown in Figure 7-4. The strategy represented in both diagrams is to fill the hospital capacity. That is, at any time the hospital admission or discharge rate will be changed to remove any discrepancy that exists between the capacity (target number of beds) available for patients and the actual number of beds filled.

The important idea in closed loop models is that information flows link knowledge about levels to rates and specify how the rates are to change in the future to change the quantities of the resources in the levels. In Figure 7-4 it is implied that as the number of patients in hospital increases (towards the hospital capacity), the admissions rate must be reduced and/or the discharge rate increased.

In natural systems rates change over time even though they are not directly influenced by managerial action. They are affected by natural laws, which often change in proportion to the magnitude of system levels.

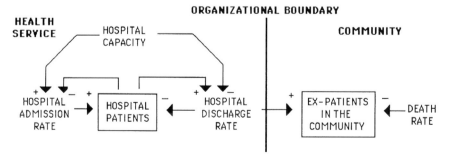

Figure 7-4. Influence diagram for a combined resource and information flow

Hence, although they are not strictly information flows they can be depicted in a similar way. Such flows are referred to as behavioral flows.

A Composite Stepwise Approach to Model Construction

The stepwise methodology to model construction is based on a combination of the feedback loop and modular approaches. It begins by identifying, wherever possible, a reference mode of behavior for the system under study. (In the absence of a reference mode, it is suggested that a clear cause for concern should be defined.) An attempt is then made to hypothesize the feedback loops responsible for this behavior. These loops should be drawn in skeleton form and their polarity defined.

The method proceeds by trying to flesh out these feedback loops using the modular approach. The steps are first, to identify key variables in the loops; second, to identify system resources associated with the key variables; third, to identify some initial states of each resource; and fourth, to construct resource flows for each resource, containing relevant resource states and their associated rates of conversion.

Each resource flow should contain at least one resource state and one rate. If, as in Figures 7-2 and 7-4 more than one state of a resource is involved the resource flows should be cascaded together to produce a chain of resource conversion.

Delays in processes and organizational boundaries should be identified and superimposed on the diagram at this stage.

The information structure within a resource flow is then created by identifying which information is used in determining each rate variable.

In a practical model, the procedure of creating process and information structure would be carried out for a number of resources in turn. In addition to the information/behavioral links created between levels and rates within each resource flow, similar links should be identified that exist between different resource flows.

This linking of resource flows should recreate any feedback loops identified in Step 1. Alternatively, where no loops were identified in Step 1, these should now emerge.

In general, once started the stepwise approach to model construction can be developed to explore the system and its environment. It is often useful to begin the process of diagram conceptualization using one or two loops and resources and a small number of levels at a high degree of aggregation and with a clear time horizon (that is, the time scale of change of the concern) in mind. Even at this stage it helps to think about the order of magnitude of the variables involved. For example, it would be foolish to consider levels in the same model that had absurdly different magnitudes or rates that ranged from microseconds to years.

As the model develops by the superimposition of information/behavioral links on process structure, new resources or states relevant to the concern can often be identified or existing resources or states eliminated. When adding new resources or states it is necessary to reiterate the whole process to investigate how the new elements intermesh with the old.

The stepwise approach to model creation is iterative and geared to focusing attention on the best compromise between the degree of resolution of the model and its size. This usually involves expanding the boundaries of the model initially and then progressively contracting them.

The ideal outcome of the conceptualization process is a model that captures all the salient features of factors affecting the cause for concern in the simplest and most compact way.

The whole procedure can be described as exploring the system and its environment diagrammatically, and a summary of the steps in the modular approach to model creation and development is presented in Table 7-1.

Table 7-1. Summary of the stepwise approach to system dynamics model creation and development

1. If possible, identify a reference mode of behavior for the system under study and sketch skeleton feedback loops responsible for this mode. Try to identify the polarity of such loops. If a reference mode is not available, define a cause for concern as clearly as possible in words.

2. Identify the key variables associated with the skeleton feedback loops or with the perceived cause for concern.

3. Identify some of the initial system resources associated with the key variables.

4. Identify some of the initial states (levels) of each resource. These initial states should be defined at a reasonably high level of aggregation.

5. Construct resource flows for each resource, containing the identified states and their associated rates of conversion. Include any significant process delays in the resource flows. (A resource flow must contain at least one resource state and one rate.)

6. If more than one state of each resource is involved cascade the resource flows together to produce a chain of resource conversion or transfer, alternating the levels and rates.

7. Within each resource flow identify organizational boundaries, behavioral/information flows, and strategies by which the levels influence the rates. Include any significant delays in the information flows.

8. Identify similar organizational boundaries, behavioral/information flows, and strategies between different resource flows. This linking of resource flows should recreate any feedback loops identified in Step 1. Alternatively, where no loops were identified in Step 1, these should now emerge. The resultant diagram should be the simplest representation possible, consistent with relating the key variables of the investigation.

9. As the diagrammatic model develops, identify any new feedback loops and repeat Steps 2 to 8.

10. Reiterate as necessary for each feedback loop identified in Step 1.

MODEL ANALYSIS

Once finalized, there is no mandatory need to convert the diagrammatic model into a computer simulation model. Premature development of a computer model with its complexity and software requirements often loses the attention of the system owner, and the power of the diagram alone to provide a framework for thinking should not be underestimated.

System dynamics diagrams can be used to provide a range of insights into system performance. One of these is to provide a clear description of the processes at work in the system. This may seem to be trivial, but is not, as perceptions of most human activity systems (that is, those constructed and operated by people) tend to center on spheres of managerial responsibility and compartments of activity, rather than on the processes for which the system exists.

The primary use of a system dynamics model is, of course, to infer the behavior of the system from the system structure and the reasons for it (that is, understanding "what is"). This can then lead logically to system redesign (that is, designing "what should be").

Behavior of the model over time can be qualitatively assessed. This is achieved by identifying major information feedback loops and by tracing out the effects of changes to specific rate variables round the variables of the loops. The behavior can then be compared with the reference mode of behavior of the system to provide some degree of confidence in the validity of the model.

It is then possible, by manipulating information links and hence strategies within a system, to change its feedback structure and hence its behavior. The type of manipulation to be undertaken depends on the objectives defined for behavior. For example, if fast growth is the aim, then it is important to promote positive feedback effects. However, if arresting a decline is the target, then it is important to promote negative feedback loop control.

An important issue in moving towards improved control is to identify specific variables that are performing in an unsatisfactory way. If these lie within the boundary of an organization, then scope to control them exists. This may seem rather obvious but, all too often, organizations spend too much time responding to or trying to influence external variables and too little time on controlling internal variables.

One way of implementing control is to define desired states for internal variables. Simple control strategies can then be introduced to eliminate discrepancies between the desired and actual states. In some circumstances, it may be necessary to introduce additional resource flows to implement control (controlling resources), for example, recruitment of additional categories of employees.

The underlying concept behind system dynamics analysis is that only by understanding with system actors how the elements of a system combine holistically to create its performance can sensible and lasting change be made. It is often the case in practice that actions taken to improve system performance are piecemeal, and restricted only to affecting the obvious symptoms of problems. Such change can at best be of only temporary advantage and at worst is detrimental.

Table 7-2. Summary of the stepwise approach to model analysis

1 Identify the major feedback loops in the model, whether arising intuitively or from the modular approach to model construction.

2. Assess the general mode of behavior of the individual loops and the whole model over time arising from the strategies contained with them. This can be achieved in simple cases by determining the polarity of each feedback loop or in more complex cases, by tracing round each loop the effect of a change in one of its constituent rate variables. Check if this mode of behavior is consistent with any reference mode available for the system.

3. Identify the rate variables within each loop that are available to be controlled. That is, those that are within the boundaries of the organization trying to implement the system control.

4. Identify possible ways to control these variables, for example, by defining target states for them or by linking them to information sources (levels) elsewhere in the model and specifying appropriate strategies by which to use the information.

5. Assess, as in Step 2, the general model of behavior of the model arising from any new feedback loops created in Step 4.

6. Reiterate from Step 3, if necessary.

A summary of the steps involved in applying a stepwise approach to model analysis is given in Table 7-2. An expanded list of these steps can be found elsewhere (Wolstenholme 1990). An example will now be presented to demonstrate the full use of the approach for developing a model, for using it to provide a comprehensive hypothesis of a perceived problem, and for identifying appropriate solutions.

A CASE STUDY IN MODEL CONSTRUCTION AND ANALYSIS—THE ESS CASE

The Problem as Described by the Company

This business problem concerned a small company (ESS) specializing in expert system software. Its initial product (Bradsoft) on which it was founded sold well on a worldwide basis with income from both sales and long-term after sales support contracts. These contracts covered client training, problem solving and assistance with integrating the product into the client organization. This success encouraged the company to invest profits into developing other similar products.

However, sales and profits of Bradsoft began to fall after two years and many customers ceased to use the product. Further, the turnover of staff at ESS increased, resulting in training problems.

The company intended to invest more heavily in expanding the product range by taking on additional product development staff. Their intention was to develop more frontier products to stay ahead of the field and to spread the risk.

The Modeling Process

This process consisted of a series of meetings with the Managing Director and senior departmental heads of the company to explore the areas of concern referred to in the initial problem statement. Initial meetings had the objective of assembling individual views on the problem. All, obviously, shared the view that the trend in falling profits had to be reversed. However, views varied on the reasons for this trend and the corrections necessary.

The product development manager was very much of the opinion that the problems that had arisen were as a result of external factors. The loss of customers he put down to the poor quality of client's staff and their inability to absorb new technology. The loss of sales he saw as due to the actions of competitors and as a function of the product being ahead of its time for a large section of the potential market. The loss of staff was seen as inevitable for a market leader.

The product support manager was equally adamant in his opinion that this department was under-resourced and unable to devote sufficient time and effort to the purchasers of Bradsoft. The personnel manager supported this view, and his feedback from staff who left was that the major reason was burnout, rather than the need for more money.

From a modeling point of view the initial meetings clearly identified a clash between the product development and support managers with each trying to justify their own resource needs. In other words a conflict between these two sectors of the organization was identified as a major issue inhibiting the smooth running of the resource flows of the company.

What was also captured in this conflict was a divergence of view regarding the influence of external factors on the company. The product development manager clearly believed that there was little wrong internally and that outside factors were unfavorable. What is emphasized in system dynamics is that focus should equally be placed on the internal workings of the company. It is these workings that can be directly controlled, and the initial hypothesis in this subject is always that a large proportion of problems are self-inflicted. In other words it is important to explore the internal interactions between process, organization, and strategy that might lead the company to shoot itself in the foot.

Application of the Stepwise Approach to Model Construction

The model construction will now be described using the steps outlined in Table 7-1. It was recognized very early that a clear reference mode of behavior for profit existed. This was of an initial rise followed by a fall and this mode was kept in mind during the model construction phase. It was anticipated that positive feedback loops might be responsible for this early growth in profit, but that these might later be dominated by negative loops. Figure 7-5 suggests a possible skeleton feedback loop based on the opinions of the product support manager, which

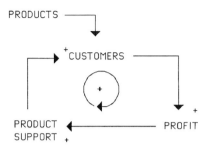

Figure 7-5. Initial skeleton feedback loop

might explain the initial rise in profit. Here, products lead to customers and profit, which is used to create product support and to reinforce growth by maintaining the base of customers.

This loop was used as a starting point for the model construction (Steps 1 and 2). The resources underpinning the variables of Figure 7-5 are listed in Figure 7-6 (Step 3). The thinking behind the construction of Figure 7-6 will now be discussed.

Four resources of interest to the problem were identified from Figure 7-6. The first of these was products, which played a significant part in the company's intended development strategy. The second was money, which was both the key cause for concern and, potentially through investment, the road to salvation. The third was people, or more specifically staff, who are necessary for both product support and development. The fourth was customers.

A number of states associated with each resource were then identified and resource flows created for these (Steps 4, 5, and 6).

Two relevant states for the resource "products" were those "under development" and "at market," and a resource flow linking these is constructed in Figure 7-6. Products must be developed over a period of time before attaining the salable state of being "at market." Those in the development pipeline can be considered as "under development."

An initial relevant state for the resource of money was that of profit. This is increased by revenue and depleted by sales and investment, as shown in the resource flow in Figure 7-6.

Two states were identified for the resource of staff. These were product support and product development staff. Two structurally equivalent resource flows are shown for these states in Figure 7-6. Both involve recruitment rates, training rates, training delays, and leaving rates.

Finally, for the resource customers, the company was chiefly concerned with those in the state of "active customers." A resource flow for this centers around the ideas of generating customers by sales and maintaining them as active by minimizing the customer loss rate.

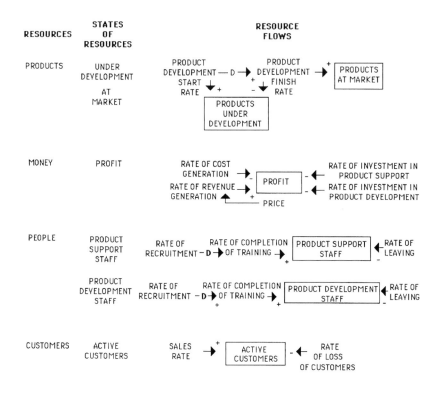

Figure 7-6. Resources, states, and resource flows for the ESS case

Figure 7-6 was acceptable to all management at the company, since it placed no weight on the interactions between resources and, hence, between departments within the organization.

Having developed the ideas in Figure 7-6, the next step was to try to link the individual resource flows together into a composite structure, which would start to explain the behavior of the company's profit.

A start was made in a second series of meetings with the same staff by constructing the processes and strategies within the company, that combined to promote the initial growth of the company.

An Initial Composite Model

Figure 7-7 shows a composite influence diagram, which links together the resource flows of Figure 7-6 (Steps 7 and 8). The sales rate of the single product (Bradsoft) adds to the number of active customers using the product. The revenue generation rate, which cumulates into profit, is created both from sales and from active customers paying maintenance contracts.

The early strategy of the company was to use profits to recruit and train product support staff whose activities reinforced the growth rate by maintaining the base of active customers. This is similar to the explanation given to Figure 7-5. The main difference here is to clarify that product support staff are necessary for product support and that their purpose is to prevent customers being lost. The development of Figure 7-7 strengthens the positive feedback loop shown in Figure 7-5.

Figure 7-7 also raises the possibility of other additional interactions. Decisions were made in the second phase of meetings as to whether these should be incorporated into the model or assumptions made to exclude them. For example, product support staff will introduce additional costs to offset the revenue that they generate from reducing the loss of customers. Further, it might also be argued that both sales and the rate of loss of customers are a function of price. The management of ESS were in agreement that price was not a significant factor and could be treated exogenously to the qualitative model. Additionally, while accepting that product support staff directly affect costs, they were of the view that this effect was small relative to the contribution of these staff to revenue creation.

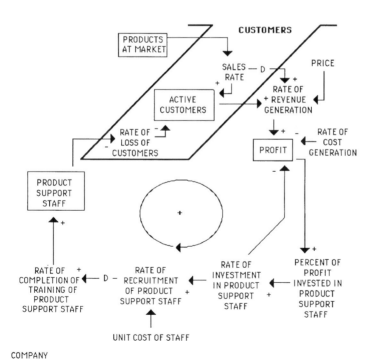

Figure 7-7. ESS — influence diagram 1

A Second Composite Model

A third series of meetings was then initiated to expand the influence diagram to capture the more recent strategy of ESS, which was to try to expand its product line. The expansion was achieved by investing strongly in product development via the recruiting of product development staff. As shown in Figure 7-8, increasing the rate of investment of profits in product development creates a positive product development loop (A) similar to the product support loop. The product development feedback loop was identified at this stage (Step 9). The loop was developed by repeating Steps 2 to 8 of the methodology.

Investment in product development, however, decreases the rate of investment in supporting the current product. The polarity of the product support loop (B) is, consequently, changed from positive to negative. The new product support loop is highlighted in Figure 7-8 by the sequence of thick influence arrows. (Note that this loop contains three negative links and its net effect is, hence, negative.)

It should also be noted that the diagram and the associated dialogue can now begin to address the problem of departmental conflict outlined in earlier meetings.

At this point, the methodology for model construction tends to merge with the methodology for model analysis. As will be described in the following paragraphs,

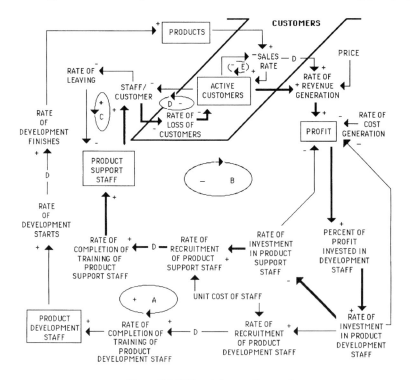

Figure 7-8. ESS — influence diagram 2

further feedback loops emerged and the effects of each of these on the behavior of the company was assessed using Steps 1 and 2 of Table 7-2.

As more product development takes place the number of staff supporting each customer of Bradsoft is reduced. The ratio of product development staff to customers is defined as a new variable in Figure 7-8. It is a ratio of two levels and is added to the product support loop in Figure 7-8 as a useful representation of the quality of product support. As the customer load of each product support person increases, it is likely that there will be an increase in the leaving rate of these staff via the positive feedback loop (C) and further deterioration in product support will take place.

The reduction in product support is likely to be masked initially by individual staff increasing their effort and workload, but eventually lower support will contribute to customers being dissatisfied with the length of time it takes to install and operate the complex piece of software. Some may, in fact, abandon the product, which will ease the product support problem temporarily, via the negative feedback loop (D). As fewer customers successfully integrate the software, sales may well fall, via the negative loop (E).

These effects are all contained in Figure 7-8. If and when the next product reaches the market, there will be a very welcome surge in sales and profits, but in the longer term the existing effects will be drastically compounded.

It should be apparent from the above that it would be disastrous for ESS to undertake further product development at this stage, since it is incapable of supporting its existing product, has less money to invest due to falling profit, and has a lengthy product development delay.

What is apparent from the above analysis is that the company has no internal control. It is purely reacting to the revenue generated from its customers and even then employing this revenue stream badly.

In system dynamics terms the lack of control is strongly indicated in Figure 7-8 by the absence of any feedback loops that lie wholly within the organizational boundaries of the company. All the feedback loops discussed pass through the customer boundary and depend on variables such as "sales rate," which is not directly under the control of ESS. Such an observation highlights the purpose of superimposing organizational boundaries on diagrams.

The diagram of Figure 7-8 represents a hypothesis of how the organizational structure of ESS and its departmental objectives and policies interact with each other. Further, since the diagram evolved from joint discussions with the departmental managers, an overall understanding of how current views might lead to an undesirable total outcome for the company was established.

Redesign of Strategies

By providing an understanding of the problem faced by ESS, system dynamics can provide a basis for designing appropriate changes or controls. A number of points emerge from the above analysis via a fourth series of meetings, which could be used to define controls.

First, the analysis indicated that customers are effectively the integration or accumulation of the sales rate; hence, to maintain a given ratio of product support staff to customers, the number of product support staff must be increased in proportion to the cumulative sales.

There is an interesting analogy here between the number of product support staff in ESS and the number of spare parts required to be produced by many large manufacturing organizations. It is often not realized in the latter type of company that spare parts must be produced in proportion to sales of new machinery and, indeed, stocked for the estimated period of life of those machines.

Second, a control mechanism should be devised to control the allocation of investment between product support and product development.

In general, as previously illustrated, the design of control for a system requires the identification of variables that are performing badly and the creation of measures to improve the control of these (Steps 3 and 4 in Table 7-2). In the case here, from a project support point of view, such a variable is the ratio of product support staff to customers, for no apparent control yet exists for this variable. Control could be introduced by defining a desired state for it, perhaps at a value that might prevent customer loss. In order to implement the control, new information structure must be superimposed on the model and, eventually, on the company. This is shown in bold type in Figure 7-9 and will now be described.

A knowledge of the actual number of customers and the desired support staff per customer enables calculation of the desired number of support staff needed. A comparison of this with the actual number of support staff then enables (in conjunction with an appropriate strategy) the calculation of a desired rate of recruitment of support staff and the calculation of the desired percentage of available investment required for support staff. This will, in turn, regulate the actual percentage of profit invested in development and product support, which is one of the existing model variables.

This control introduces a negative feedback loop within the boundary of ESS, which is highlighted by the sequence of thick influence arrows in Figure 7-9. The control will ensure that an adequate level of product support is always maintained (Step 5, Table 7-2). The consequence should be a more stable customer base and an improvement in sales, revenue, and future product development, while ensuring a lower turnover of product support staff.

What emerged from the analysis was that the product support and development functions should have a better appreciation of each other's role in achieving a planned growth of the company, and that a periodic review of their competing demands should be carried out based on the control ideas described. In other words, a compromise or tradeoff position should be regularly negotiated between the

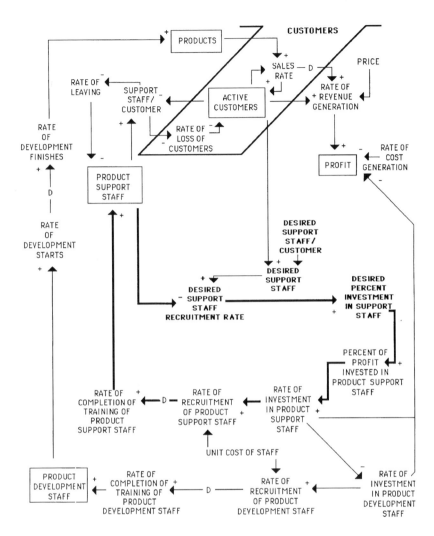

Figure 7-9. ESS — influence diagram 3

departments, with the Managing Director arbitrating as necessary. Both departments conceded the need for improved communication.

CONCLUSIONS

This paper has suggested a stepwise approach to model construction and analysis for use in system dynamics. This is based on a combination of identifying information feedback loops and a modular approach.

By involving the underlying components of quantitative system dynamics and simulation modeling throughout its application, the modular approach creates a tool by which problems can be explained and appropriate actions for change decided jointly by the owners of a problem. The rigor of the approach assists the understanding of the system and draws thinking towards the identification of alternative structures and strategies for the system from the beginning of the study.

REFERENCES

Bryant, J. (1989), *Problem Management, A Guide for Producers and Players,* New York: Wiley.

Checkland, P.B. (1983), "O.R. and the Systems Movement: Mappings and Conflicts," *Journal of the Operational Research Society* 34: 661-75.

Coyle, R.G. (1981), *Management System Dynamics,* New York: Wiley.

Eden, C., S. Jones, and D. Sims (1979), *Thinking in Organisations,* London: Macmillan.

Forrester, J.W. (1961), *Industrial Dynamics,* Portland, Ore.: Productivity Press.

Forrester, J.W. (1968), *Principles of Systems,* Portland, Ore.: Productivity Press.

Lyneis, J.M. (1980), *Corporate Planning and Policy Design: A System Dynamics Approach,* Cambridge, Mass.: Pugh-Roberts Associates.

Morecroft, John D.W., David C. Lane, and Paul S. Viita (1989), "Modelling Growth Strategy in a Biotechnology Startup Firm," *System Dynamics Review* 7, no. 2: 93-116.

Richmond, B., S. Peterson, and P. Vescuso (1987), *An Academic User's Guide to STELLA,* High Performance Systems, 45 Lyme Road, Ste. 300, Hanover NH 03755.

Rosenhead, J., ed. (1989), *Rational Analysis for a Problematic World, Problem Structuring Methods for Complexity, Uncertainty and Conflict,* New York: Wiley.

Senge, P., and J.D. Sterman (1992). "Systems Thinking and Organizational Learning: Acting Locally and Thinking Globally in the Organization of the Future," *European Journal of Operational Research* 59, no. 1: 137-50, and Chapter 8 of this volume.

Vennix, J.A.M., L.D. Verburgh, J.W. Gubbels, and Doeke Post (1990), "Eliciting Group Knowledge in a Computer-Based Learning Environment," in Andersen, Richardson, and Sterman, eds., *Proceedings of the 1990 International System Dynamics Conference,* 1187-1198.

Wolstenholme, E.F. (1990), *System Enquiry—A System Dynamics Approach,* New York: Wiley.

Wolstenholme, E.F. (1982), "System Dynamics in Perspective," *Journal of the Operational Research Society* 33: 547-56.

Wolstenholme, E.F., and R.G. Coyle (1983), "The Development of System Dynamics as a Methodology for System Description and Qualitative Analysis," *Journal of the Operational Research Society* 34,

8

SYSTEMS THINKING AND ORGANIZATIONAL LEARNING: ACTING LOCALLY AND THINKING GLOBALLY IN THE ORGANIZATION OF THE FUTURE

PETER M. SENGE AND JOHN D. STERMAN

ABSTRACT: To learn more rapidly and increase flexibility in a world of growing complexity and change, firms are experimenting with new modes of organization, new reward systems, and less authoritarian values—for example, reducing hierarchy, increasing local decision-making responsibility and individual incentives, and rewarding innovation. But local decision making and individual autonomy lead to management anarchy unless managers account for the interconnections and long-term side-effects of their local decisions. Laudable goals such as "empowering" and "enabling" individuals often prove counterproductive unless managers can act locally and think globally. Managers must become "systems thinkers" as well as better learners. This paper reports on one approach to these issues: forming collaborative action research partnerships with corporations to (1) develop new tools to accelerate learning, and (2) test those tools in real organizations where managers face pressing issues. We argue that simulation is an important element of successful learning laboratories to develop systems thinking and promote organizational learning. A case study focused on improving quality and total cost performance in the insurance industry is presented to illustrate how these tools can both produce insight and focus change.

THE "NEW WORK" OF MANAGERS

Eroding competitiveness, declining productivity growth, and explosive techno-logical, political, and environmental change form the familiar litany of problems that threaten traditional organizations and management practices. Organizations stressed by these pressures have worked to clarify their missions, visions, and val-ues. Many seek to reorganize into leaner, more locally controlled and market-responsive structures. Yet all too often the core operating (as opposed to espoused) policies guiding organizational behavior remain unchanged. Efforts to improve strategic management often founder because new strategies and structures threaten traditional habits, norms, and assumptions. The problem lies, in part, with failing to recognize the importance of prevailing mental models. New strategies are the out-growth of new worldviews. The more profound the change in strategy, the deeper must be the change in thinking. Indeed, many argue that improving the mental models of managers is the fundamental task of strategic management:

> The choice of individual courses of action is only part of the manager's or policy-maker's need. More important is the need to achieve insight into the nature of the complexity being addressed and to formulate concepts and world views for coping with it (Mason and Mitroff 1981, 16).

> Strategies are the product of a worldview... the basis for success or failure is the microcosm of the decision makers: their inner model of reality, their set of assumptions that structure their understanding of the unfolding business environment and the factors critical to success... When the world changes, managers need to share some common view of the new world. Otherwise, decentralized strategic decisions will lead to management anarchy (Wack 1985, 89, 150).

In response, managers and academics alike have identified organizational learn-ing, the process whereby shared understandings change, as a key to flexibility and competitive advantage in the 1990s. In a recent study of the beleaguered manufac-turing industries, Hayes, Wheelwright, and Clark (1988) conclude, "There is one common denominator in high-performance plants: an ability to learn—to achieve sustained improvement in performance over a long period of time. When assessing a manufacturing organization, learning is the bottom line." Analog Devices' CEO Ray Stata (1989) argues that "the rate at which individuals and organizations learn may become the only sustainable competitive advantage." Arie de Geus (1988), former chief of planning at Royal Dutch/Shell, observes that an organization's abil-ity to survive depends on "institutional learning, which is the process whereby management teams change their shared mental models of their company, their mar-kets, and their competitors. For this reason, we think of planning as learning, and of corporate planning as institutional learning."

All agree that learning organizations will require profound shifts in the nature of managerial work. William O'Brien, CEO of Hanover Insurance Companies, notes, "The dogma of the traditional hierarchical organization was planning, managing, and controlling. The 'dogma' of the learning organization of the future will be vision, values, and mental models" (Senge 1990a). Similarly, the "quality of organizational learning," in Don Schön's view (1983a), is determined by the quality of the "organizational inquiry that mediates the restructuring of organizational theory-in-use."

Organizational learning processes are more effective when they help managers develop a more systemic and dynamic perspective. Organization development professionals have long advocated a systems perspective for effective change (Beckhard and Harris 1987; Katz and Kahn 1978; Schein 1985; Weick 1979). A recent strategic management text begins by citing the views of Bruce Henderson, a "senior statesman" of the strategy field, who criticized

> the essentially static nature of…earlier work…[which neglected] time, second order effects and feedback loops…the ingredients for the insightful analysis that was needed to move the field of strategy its next step forward (Lorange, Scott Morton, and Ghoshal 1986, xviii).

The challenge is how to move from generalizations about accelerating learning and systems thinking to tools and processes that help managers reconceptualize complex issues, design better operating policies, and guide organization-wide learning.

One new approach involves "learning laboratories" or "microworlds"— microcosms of real business settings where managers play roles in a simulated organization. As an aircraft flight simulator allows pilots to try new maneuvers and experience extreme conditions without risk, so too a learning laboratory provides a flight simulator for managers. A microworld compresses time and space, allowing managers to experience the long-term, system-wide consequences of decisions (Sterman 1988a; Graham, Morecroft, Senge, and Sterman 1992 and Chapter 9 of this volume). But an effective learning laboratory is much more than just computer simulation. It trains managers and teams in the full learning cycle, as originally conceived by John Dewey: Discover—Invent—Produce—Reflect. Learning laboratories help managers see through superficial symptoms to the underlying causes, reorganize perceptions into a clearer, more coherent picture of business dynamics that can be effectively communicated, and create tools that can accelerate the learning of others. We do not claim that the learning laboratory approach is essential or even useful in addressing all important issues in corporate strategy or organizational learning. However, we argue here that it is helpful in overcoming some of the persistent difficulties facing managers in complex organizations, difficulties growing more severe in the rapidly changing global environment.

SYSTEMS THINKING: NEW INSIGHTS, NEW PERSPECTIVES

The research draws on the system dynamics methodology developed originally at MIT (Forrester 1961, 1969; Roberts 1978). For systems theorists, the source of poor performance and organizational failure is often to be found in the limited cognitive skills and capabilities of individuals compared to the complexity of the systems they are called upon to manage (Simon 1979, 1982; Perrow 1984; Forrester 1961). A vast body of experimental work demonstrates that individuals make significant, systematic errors in diverse problems of judgment and choice (Kahneman, Slovic, and Tversky 1982; Hogarth 1987). Dynamic decision making is particularly difficult, especially when decisions have indirect, delayed, nonlinear, and multiple feedback effects (Sterman 1989a, 1989b; Kleinmuntz 1985; Dörner 1989; Kluwe, Misiak, and Haider 1989). Yet these are precisely the situations in which managers must act. Systematic dysfunctional performance due to misperceptions of feedback has been documented in a wide range of systems:

- Managers in a simple production-distribution system generate costly fluctuations, even when consumer demand is constant (Sterman 1989b; MacNeil/Lehrer 1989);

- Managers of simulated consumer product markets generate the boom and bust, price war, shake-out, and bankruptcy characteristic of industries from video games to chain saws (Paich and Sterman 1993);

- In a simulation of People Express Airlines, students and executives alike frequently bankrupt the company, just as the real management did (Sterman 1988a);

- In a publishing industry simulation, people often bankrupt their magazines even as circulation reaches all-time highs, just as did a number of real publications (Hall 1976, 1989);

- In a forest fire simulation, many people allow their headquarters to burn down despite their best efforts to put out the fire (Brehmer 1989);

- In a medical setting, subjects playing the role of doctors order more tests while the (simulated) patients sicken and die (Kleinmuntz 1985).

These studies all show that performance deteriorates markedly as the time delays grow longer and the feedbacks more powerful (Diehl and Sterman 1993). Market mechanisms and financial incentives do not eliminate the errors (Camerer 1987; Smith, Suchanek, and Williams 1988). Experience and training do not solve the problem: Professional economists create depressions in simple economic models (Sterman 1989a); in simulations of real estate and shipping, a majority of managers tested go bankrupt at least once before learning how to survive, despite experience in these industries (Bakken 1990); government officials playing an economic development game often impoverish their simulated nations through foreign debt, poison their environments, and starve the population (Meadows 1989).

These findings have significant implications for learning. In the past simulation models were often constructed by expert consultants who then explained the results to policy makers. The "traditional consulting" approach has produced many notable successes and use of system dynamics in a variety of industries is growing (Morecroft 1988; Weil 1980; Cooper 1980; Roberts 1978). Nevertheless, while models developed and interpreted by outside experts may change what managers think about a particular issue, they rarely change the way managers think about future issues. In contrast, the model builder often acquires enduring insight. Why? Model development creates a laboratory microworld in which hypotheses must be tested, evaluated, and revised. Model builders probe the substantive issues deeply and develop skills in scientific method and critical thought.

LEARNING LABORATORIES

Our research attempts to develop learning processes aimed at (1) improving managers' shared mental models so that they become more systemic and more dynamic, and (2) developing managers' abilities to view new situations systemically and dynamically. In our view, this can only be achieved if managers themselves become the modelers to a far greater extent than in most prior work. Researchers in system dynamics and other systems traditions have experimented with many processes to catalyze systems thinking in management teams. While effective learning processes are iterative and flexible, for purposes of exposition they can be divided into three stages:

- *Mapping mental models*—explicating and structuring assumptions via systems models;

- *Challenging mental models*—revealing inconsistencies in assumptions;

- *Improving mental models*—continually extending and testing mental models.

Mapping mental models involves the explication and sharing of the managers' assumptions. These mental models are typically quite poor maps of the terrain. Axelrod's (1976) study of the cognitive maps of elites painted a

> ...picture of the decision maker...[as] one who has more beliefs than he can handle, who employs a simplified image of the policy environment that is structurally easy to operate with, and who then acts rationally within the context of his simplified image.

But flaws in mental models cannot be corrected until mental models become more explicit. Forrester (1971) argues:

> The mental model is fuzzy. It is incomplete. It is imprecisely stated. Furthermore, within one individual, a mental model changes with time and even during the flow of a single conversation. The human mind assembles a few relationships to fit the context of a discussion. As the subject shifts so does the model...Each participant in a conversation employs a different

mental model to interpret the subject. Fundamental assumptions differ but are never brought into the open.

Many cognitive mapping tools have been developed to elicit and portray the mental models of individuals and groups (Morecroft 1988; Richardson and Pugh 1981; Eden, Jones, and Sims 1983; Checkland 1981; Hall 1984, 1989). Mapping tools serve many purposes. They assist in generating issues, capturing and framing knowledge, sharing concepts, focusing discussion, and reaching consensus. Good mapping tools for our purposes should also help people capture the time delays, long-term effects, and multiple impacts of decisions—the characteristics that cause the most serious misjudgments in dynamic decision making. The more effective tools, increasingly computer-based, also facilitate group input and rapid revision (Richmond 1987; Morecroft 1988, 1982). In the mapping stage there is no attempt to converge upon a single, integrative model. The most important result of the mapping stage is to uncover critical assumptions and set the stage for challenging them.

Challenging mental models is testing for internal and external validity. Once team members have gone public with their mental models they can begin to discover internal inconsistencies and contradictions with data and others' knowledge. Experienced managers frequently have accurate perceptions of causal structure and decision-making process but draw erroneous conclusions about what happens when different parts of a system interact. Challenging models thus requires an inference engine to deduce the consequences of interactions among the elements of the map. Simulation provides that engine. For simulation to be effective in challenging the managers' mental map, the team members must have a high level of ownership of the simulation models. Managers should be able to construct the models themselves in a short period of time. Managers must understand the software without computer expertise or technical training. We have used STELLA, software for graphical construction of dynamic simulation models on microcomputers (Richmond, Peterson, and Vescuso 1987). STELLA is widely used in the natural sciences, and applications in management and economics are growing rapidly (Milling and Zahn 1989; Nyhart and Samarasan 1989; Nyhart 1988; HealthCare Forum 1990; Solomon 1989). STELLA is designed to be used first as a mapping technology. The simulation model is then built directly from the cognitive map. Managers frequently can learn the mechanics of STELLA in an hour.

The "reality check" models developed at this stage are designed to uncover overlooked dynamics that bear on the success of the team's strategy. A good reality check model is simple. It should be a straightforward translation of the team's strategy map, and will typically be built up from pieces that are well understood and agreed upon in the mapping stage.

Challenging mental models is delicate. Managers' beliefs are called into question. Inconsistencies are revealed. If trust and openness are not well established, individuals may be threatened and react defensively. It has often proven useful to work with the team members on developing inquiry skills and recognizing defensive routines. A number of approaches to team development have been used successfully in conjunction with mapping technology, including Ed Schein's process consulting (Schein 1969, 1987) and the action science approach of Chris Argyris and colleagues (Argyris and Schön 1978; Argyris 1982; Argyris, Putnam, and Smith 1986; Argyris 1985) among others (e.g., Dyer 1987; Schön 1983b).

Improving mental models is the open-ended process of explicating, testing, and revising managerial assumptions. Now the team expands the simple reality check models to include potentially important feedback dynamics. Assumptions about exogenous factors are questioned. Factors excluded from the initial maps are brought inside the boundary of the model. Linkages with other functions in the organization, and with other organizations in the environment, are considered.

The key to the process is the discipline imposed by the modeling tools. Ideas for improvement must be translated into specific changes in policy and structure. There is no guarantee the models will predict what would occur if a new policy were implemented. But the assumptions behind new initiatives will be explicit and subject to continued testing and improvement. The managers become experimentalists practicing scientific method to improve the structure and functioning of their organization.

The full benefits of the learning process may accrue over a considerable period of time, in some cases several years. New conceptual perspectives are assimilated gradually, stimulated by ongoing processes of dialogue and debate (Levitt and March 1988). Eventually, new perspectives lead to new perceptions. The formal process is best viewed as catalyzing a larger, more diverse organizational learning process, gently nudging managers toward a more systemic and dynamic view of their world.

A CASE STUDY: THE INSURANCE CRISIS

A number of learning laboratories and management microworlds have been developed. We discuss here a learning lab developed for a leading American property and liability insurance company to address the runaway costs that threaten the entire liability insurance industry: The tort system in the United States consumes more than 2.5 percent of GNP, the highest in the world. Premiums on auto insurance doubled from 1983 to 1988. Between 1979 and 1985, the number of product liability cases increased 150 percent. The average size of jury verdicts increased five-fold from 1973 to 1985. Public backlash against escalating insurance premiums is growing: Outraged Californians recently passed ballot referenda rolling back automobile insurance premiums. In New York state, rate caps have left all five providers of medical malpractice coverage technically bankrupt (Richardson and Senge 1989).

Commonly cited causes of the crisis include the high number of lawyers in the United States, increasing litigiousness of society, juries which side with victims rather than uncaring big business, and the growing technological complexity of society (Huber 1987). Notably absent from such accounts are explanations relating to the management practices of insurers themselves. Why are there so many tort lawyers and lawsuits? Why are insurers perceived to be uncaring? Some of the top managers at Hanover Insurance, of Worcester, Massachusetts, were asking the same questions. These managers intuitively felt that their own management practices had contributed significantly to the problem. They distrusted easy explanations that fix the blame on outsiders. Blaming greedy lawyers, juries, and policyholders is psychologically safe, absolving insurers from responsibility. While not denying the role of these factors, they also saw that blaming the problem on external forces prevented the company from contributing to constructive solutions.

Hanover Insurance is a medium-sized firm specializing in property and casualty (Table 8-1). In 1989 Hanover earned $83 million on premium income of about $1.5 billion. Assets were $3 billion. Founded in 1852, Hanover went through a dramatic transition in the last twenty years. In the mid-1960s the company was at the bottom of the industry. In 1969 State Mutual purchased a 50 percent interest in Hanover, injecting much-needed reserves and installing a new president, Jack Adam.[1] With his marketing vice president and eventual successor, Bill O'Brien, Adam began to reorient the company around a new set of guiding principles designed to address deeply rooted problems in Hanover's traditional authoritarian management style:

1. *Purpose:* an antidote to a weak sense of common direction;

2. *Merit:* an antidote to rampant politics and bureaucracy;

3. *Openness:* an antidote to widespread game playing through hoarding information or operating from private agendas;

4. *Localness:* an antidote to institutional blocks to strong morale and decision making by front line units;

5. *Vision:* an antidote to low self-image and difficulties in communicating the scale of the firm's aspirations.

The new culture did not quickly take root. Personnel and structural changes accompanied the internalization of the new philosophical foundation. Many of Hanover's original managers were unprepared for the organization Adam and O'Brien envisioned. During the early 1970s management turnover was high. A level of regional management was eliminated to encourage local autonomy and authority. Later, internal boards of directors were established to further strengthen the autonomy of local business units.

---

[1] Since this article was written, Hanover was acquired by State Mutual.

Table 8-1. Hanover Insurance Financial Highlights, 1989 (Source: 1989 Annual Report)

Revenues:	Net premiums earned	1421
	Net investment income	154
	Other income	48
	Total revenues	**1622**
Expenses:	Losses and loss expenses	1,076
	Other expenses	463
	Total expenses	**1539**
Net Income:	**Net income**	**83**
Other:	Total assets	2,955
	Shareholders' equity	741
	Combined ratio	105.9 percent
	(Industry average	110.7 percent)

* Totals may not add due to rounding.

By the mid-1980s Hanover emerged as a leader in the property and liability industry. Hanover's combined ratio, the ratio of operating expenses to premium income (a measure of the profitability of the insurance side of the business), has bettered the industry average in each of the past eleven years. During the same period Hanover grew 50 percent faster than the industry as a whole. There is a widespread belief in the organization that the company's business success is linked to its guiding principles (Bergin and Prusko 1990).

After some exploration with managers throughout the firm, claims management emerged as a candidate for a systems thinking experiment. The problem is highly dynamic: Hanover's growth placed ever greater demands on the claims operation. There were more complex claims and increasing numbers of claims requiring litigation or subrogation (recovering costs from other insurers). The problem cut across all levels of management, corporate functions, and regions. Most importantly, the claims managers knew they faced difficult issues and were open to a new approach.

The project proceeded in three stages. First, a team of top managers worked with MIT researchers to develop shared models of the problem. Next, a simulation model developed in phase one was converted into an interactive "Management Flight Simulator." The Hanover team designed a three-day workshop, the Claims Learning Laboratory, using the flight simulator. Over one hundred managers have now participated in the CLL. In the third stage, now underway, a second workshop is under development to help in managing change, systems thinking tools are being introduced throughout the firm, and the effectiveness of the approach is being evaluated through longitudinal studies.

The first stage involved a management team consisting of the senior vice-president for claims and two of his direct reporters. The team met every two weeks for about a year with the MIT researchers. The group appeared to have a high level of openness and mutual trust, reflecting several years of working together in Hanover's culture. At the first meeting the team developed an initial statement of objectives, strategies, and problems. The team's vision statement expressed their intent to be preeminent among claims organizations in the insurance industry, to provide "fair, fast, and friendly" service. Their image of the ideal claims adjuster soon emerged: a person capable of conducting thorough professional investigations, possessing excellent communication and negotiation skills, keeping accurate and complete records, and able to educate claimants regarding the fair value of their claims, while spotting those with the slightest fraudulent inclinations. They enumerated ten measures of performance and a dozen strategies to achieve them.

When asked to discuss the problems they faced, the claims VP talked about having too many "balls in the air," the challenge of simultaneously keeping many performance standards on target, like a juggler. Whenever Hanover worked to improve performance on a particular objective, such as controlling settlement costs, there was backsliding on others, such as prompt settlement of claims. Typically, the team's vision statement expressed high aspirations but was unconnected to the current situation or how to get there from here. They had created a laundry list of disjoint problems and solutions. Interconnections were expressed through operationally vague metaphors such as the juggler with too many balls in the air.

The process of mapping, challenging, and improving mental models began in the first meeting. STELLA was used to map assumptions of the current strategy. Simple reality check models quickly showed a mismatch between the anticipated growth in underwriting volume and the resources allocated for claims settlement. The team was soon developing and testing their own models (Senge 1990b provides a detailed description). The final model, though more complex than the original map, was comparatively simple. It had been thoroughly tested. The model contains numerous nonlinear response functions, e.g., how do adjuster productivity and turnover respond to chronic pressure to settle more claims per person? Many of the critical relationships involve such "soft variables' for which there are few quantitative data. These were estimated with quantitative data where available, supplemented by expert judgment (the roles of soft variables in and criteria for validation of simulation models discussed in Sterman 1988b.) Most important, it was the team's model. They had built it. They knew what was assumed and why. The laundry list had been transformed into a sophisticated theory of the problem dynamics. Moreover, the team's model carried potentially significant implications for long-standing management practices.

The analysis suggested rising settlement costs are largely caused by systematic, long-term underinvestment in claims adjusting capacity. Hanover simply has too few adjusters, with inadequate skills, experience, motivation, and incentives, to provide the quality of investigation and personal attention to the customer required to be fair, fast, and friendly. Figure 8-1 shows the feedback structure that underlies the drift to low performance Hanover, and the industry, has experienced. We stress that this diagram was developed after the project. While such causal diagrams are excellent aids to conceptualization and communication, simulation was essential in the iterative process of formulating and testing the theory described below.

Individual adjusters in a claims organization constantly adjust the pace of work to control the backlog of pending claims. A high pending pool means more dissatisfied customers as claimants find themselves waiting longer. Claims processing centers carefully monitor the pending pool, regularly reporting various measures of work flow. An increase in incoming claims causes the pending pool to rise, intensi-

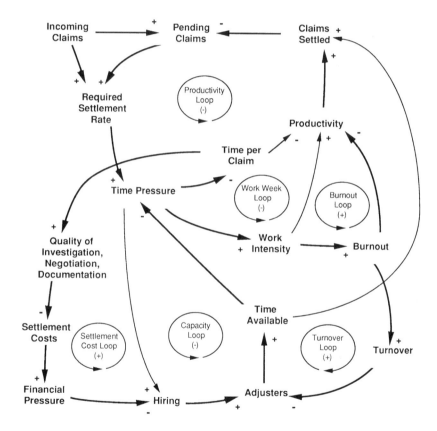

Figure 8-1. Feedback loops controlling claims settlement, with processes causing self-reinforcing erosion of quality and increasing settlement costs. Arrows indicate the direction of causality. Signs ("+" or "-") at arrow heads indicate the polarity of relationships: a "+" denotes that an increase in the independent variable causes the dependent variable to increase, ceteris paribus (and a decrease causes a decrease). Similarly, "-" indicates that an increase in the independent variable causes the dependent variable to decrease. Positive loop polarity (denoted by [+] in the loop identifier) indicates a self-reinforcing (positive feedback) process. Negative (-) loop polarity indicates a self-regulating (negative feedback) process. See Richardson and Pugh 1981.

fying the time pressure on each adjuster. Time pressure measures the adequacy of the adjuster staff and skills available to handle the current case load. There are only three ways in which high time pressure can be relieved:

- devote less time to each claim

- increase work intensity

- add adjuster capacity

Each option forms a balancing feedback process that seeks to restore time pressure to normal. However, the three channels for controlling the work flow involve very different time delays, costs, and side effects.

- Adding adjuster capacity means hiring additional adjusters, improving training, and reducing turnover, thereby increasing time available and settlements, reducing the pending pool, and relieving time pressure (the Capacity loop in Figure 8-1). But building adjuster capacity takes time. New adjusters must be found, hired, and trained. Adjusting is a highly skilled profession, and the ability to handle complex claims effectively requires years of experience. Building capacity is also expensive and requires top-management authorization. Adding adjuster capacity was therefore the last resort in the organization.

- Increasing work intensity means longer workweeks, fewer breaks, and less time spent in "non-productive" activities such as talking with colleagues or training new hires, thereby increasing the time spent settling claims and draining the pending pool (the Work Week loop). Overtime is frequently used to control the pending pool. However, sustained high work intensity produces stress, low morale, and burnout, thereby lowering productivity and increasing turnover. These delayed side-effects form reinforcing feedbacks, vicious cycles, which can actually worsen time pressure (the Burnout and Turnover loops in Figure 8-1).

- By far the easiest and quickest way to control time pressure is to settle each claim faster. Individual adjusters have a high degree of control over the time they spend on a claim. They decide how aggressively to pursue investigation, whether to visit the claimant or handle the claim by "telephone adjusting," how long to negotiate with the claimant, how much time to spend keeping records. When time pressure rises adjusters cut back on all of these activities, quickly cutting the pending pool and easing time pressure.

However, spending less time on each claim inevitably erodes the quality of the settlements.

- Inadequate attention to documentation means the firm is less successful in litigation and subrogation, increasing settlement costs. Effort is wasted trying to locate and reconstruct evidence improperly recorded at the time of the loss, increasing the time required to settle and further intensifying time pressure in a vicious cycle.

- Less investigation and negotiation means settlements are likely to be inflated. Settlement costs increase as adjusters under time pressure tend to agree to a claimant's initial request, up to the amount they are authorized to pay without a supervisor's approval: "Hello, Mr. Smith? Your basement was flooded? How much was your loss? Fine. The check will be in the mail tomorrow."

- Telephone adjusting and limited customer contact reduce customer satisfaction. Experienced adjusters report that customer satisfaction arises more from procedural fairness rather than objective results—more from listening to a customer, empathizing with them over their loss, and negotiating a settlement value that the customer understands rather than the dollar amount of the settlement. After hanging up the phone, Mr. Smith's first reaction is likely to be "They gave me what I asked for - it must have been worth more!" Spending less time on each claim creates a paradox: costs increase *and* quality falls. Worse, the unhappy policyholders, having had little opportunity to develop personal relationships with company representatives, are more likely to litigate or attempt fraud, further increasing the burden on the adjusters and legal staff. The result is higher settlements and increased financial pressure to control costs, making it even harder to increase adjuster capacity—another vicious cycle (the Settlement Cost loop).

These feedbacks describe a system biased towards quality erosion and gradual escalation of settlement costs. Whenever pending claims increase, management exerts strong pressure to increase the rate of settlements. Given the costs and delays in building adjuster capacity, adjusters are driven to process ever more claims per week. To the individual adjuster, lowering standards is the easiest way to relieve the time pressure. In the short run spending less time on claims appears to increase productivity. But in the long run customer dissatisfaction, inadequate investigation, and poor documentation cause settlement costs to rise. The financial burden created by higher losses creates organization-wide campaigns for cost reductions and further reductions in capacity, intensifying time pressure and forcing quality standards even lower.

Counterpressures to the erosion of quality are weak. Management focuses on the tangible, measurable aspects of performance: settling claims, controlling the pending pool, and controlling expenses. Quality, in contrast, is hard to assess. It is multidimensional. Customer feedback about quality is delayed, diffuse, and often distorted by customers' desires to influence their settlements—and by management's suspicions about customer motives. The claims VP called these intangible aspects of quality "the fuzzies," saying, "in this business there are lots of ways to look good without being good." Feedback from poor quality is not only delayed, it manifests in other areas such as increased litigation, market share erosion, and pressure for government regulation. By the time low quality is apparent, rising settlement costs, increasing turnover, low morale, and high stress may prevent the organization from increasing quality. Periodic campaigns to increase quality fail because they increase time pressure, causing powerful compensating pressures to settle claims more rapidly.

The culture of the claims organization changes as quality erodes. Adjusters who reduce quality to handle a backlog crisis quickly learn that lower standards are not only acceptable but even rewarded since they allow the adjuster to excel on the salient measures of production. Because turnover is high, new adjusters enter a culture that increasingly focuses on processing claims swiftly, and are neither trained in nor asked to perform to the old standards. The firm's response to high turnover is to routinize the adjuster's job to reduce training costs and minimize the skill level and salary requirements of recruits. Bob Bergin, senior manager for property claims at Hanover, notes:

> In my thirty years in the business, I have seen a steady decline in the pay and status of insurance adjusting. Once it was a respected profession. Today, most adjusters are young college graduates with no aspirations to a career in adjusting. Our management practices both react to and reinforce this attitude.

The insidious aspect of these dynamics is the gradual shift in the burden of controlling the workload from capacity expansion to quality erosion. The erosion in quality standards becomes self-reinforcing: Once time pressure is relieved, so are the signals that more capacity is needed. In the short run, slipping quality standards works. Pending claims drop. Time pressure is relieved. Management will not authorize an increase in adjuster head count since there is no apparent problem. In fact, management attention shifts to other problems, for example, what appears to be an inadequate legal staff to handle a growing volume of litigation—litigation brought on, in many cases, by insufficient adjuster capacity.

There are several implications of the feedback processes revealed by the model. First, the adequacy of capacity cannot be assessed through comparisons to competitors. The claims vice president wondered aloud if perhaps "We may have half the adjusting capacity that we actually need for our current case load, from the standpoint of high service quality and low total costs." One of us (Senge) responded that it seemed quite possible. The VP said, "You don't understand what a crazy thing I am saying. We already have a lower case load per adjuster than almost all of our competitors." When all firms suffer similar quality erosion none serve as role models to demonstrate the potential leverage of increased adjuster capacity. Entire industries can thus experience eroding quality standards, as exemplified by many U.S. firms in the 1960s and 70s.

A second implication is that simply increasing the adjuster head count will not solve the problem. Low quality standards have been institutionalized. Adjuster skill levels are constantly depleted by high turnover. Ambitious and talented people avoid claims and seek careers in underwriting, finance, or marketing. Increases in resources will be effective only in concert with changes in the prevailing mental models throughout the organization.

Yet the potential impact of increased investment in adjuster capacity is substantial. The model, consistent with the judgment of the project team, suggests reductions in settlement costs of 5 to 20 percent may be realized by increasing investigation and negotiation quality (Moissis 1989). Since settlements comprise about two-thirds of all expenses, a reduction of ten percent would more than double net income.

THE CLAIMS LEARNING LABORATORY

After working for a year with the claims managers, the MIT team felt that the model captured the causes of important dynamics. The managers had been intimately involved in conceptualizing and analyzing the model. They could articulate the policy implications of the model with clarity and conviction. A traditional consulting project might have ended here with high confidence of implementation. In fact, the results of the model were virtually unimplementable. The model suggested a need for investment in adjuster capacity at a time when the firm, and the entire industry, is under intense pressure to cut costs. Moreover, the model implied that responsibility for the insurance crisis rests in part with established management practices, when most within the firm regard the problem as externally caused. Specifically, the model suggested that established policies had produced declining quality and increasing settlement size—precisely the opposite of the organization's lofty vision and espoused policies.

The problem now facing the team was how to develop shared understanding throughout the organization. The managers who went through the intense learning process could not expect those who had not to agree with its "counterintuitive" implications. At Hanover, and increasingly in other firms, decision-making responsibility is widely distributed. There are hundreds of individuals who implement new policies and may easily thwart new initiatives. For significantly new policies to come into practice, each person must go through their own personal learning process.

The team decided to develop a workshop for claims managers to stimulate rethinking of established policies and practices. The workshop had to compress into a few days the process of mapping, challenging, and improving mental models the team itself went through in the previous year. The resulting Claims Learning Laboratory (CLL) is a three-day workshop attended by groups of about fifteen managers. It was impractical in a workshop format to have each group of managers build their own model from scratch. Instead of STELLA, the CLL employs a computer simulation game or Management Flight Simulator embodying the model. The game uses easily learned software to simulate a claims processing center together with the decisions, data, pressures, and constraints characteristic of the real organization. Significantly, the Hanover team developed and delivers the CLL without substantial assistance from the MIT modelers (Bergin and Prusko 1990; Moissis 1989; Kim 1989).

The CLL has now been in operation for about two years. Almost all claims managers, and a surprising number of managers from other functional areas, have attended. Bob Bergin and Gerry Prusko, two of the managers who deliver the workshop, report:

> The results of the learning laboratory have been positive. It has been credited with:
>
> 1. Shortening the learning curve for new managers
>
> 2. Improving communication skills
>
> 3. Creating an atmosphere for organizational learning
>
> 4. Clarifying and testing assumptions
>
> 5. Making mental models explicit
>
> 6. Integrating qualitative with quantitative measures of performance
>
> 7. Providing a shared experience for decision making and problem analysis.
>
> When claim managers integrate the systems thinking approach into their own decision making, they accelerate the changes that need to occur in the organization (Bergin and Prusko 1990, 35).

Many managers report the CLL to be their most meaningful training experience. Although it is too early to judge the long-term effects, managers are beginning to develop a language for discussing interactions between workload, quality, and costs. Follow-up study (Kim 1989) shows that some managers continue to use the mapping tools after the CLL. Causal diagrams are becoming commonplace inside Hanover. Experiments with new policies and strategies are starting. One recent participant reports:

> When I came back from the learning laboratory, I had a much better understanding of what the important issues were. Before the lab, I would have said that lack of quality was the only important factor. After the lab, it was obvious to me that productivity was also a key issue. So I restructured some units to enhance their ability to settle claims. After I saw dramatic increases in productivity [in the real organization], I applied pressure to improve quality—and I have seen a difference (Bergin and Prusko 1990, 35).

While further evaluative study is needed, the learning lab seems to serve both goals outlined above: Managers learn about the dynamics of a particular issue of great importance, and learn skills that may help them with other issues. This "double-loop" learning is the real goal of the research.

LESSONS: ELEMENTS OF EFFECTIVE
LEARNING LABORATORY DESIGN

Experiences at Hanover and elsewhere point to three lessons for designing effective learning laboratories: (1) focus on conceptualization; (2) design opportunities for reflection; (3) beware the computer.

Conceptualization. Most of the first half of the CLL is spent in a series of conceptualizing exercises. Managers discuss basic questions such as "What determines adjuster productivity?" and "What influences investigation quality?" to help them identify interdependencies. They gradually build up a causal map of the relevant feedback processes. The mapping accomplishes several goals. First, the participants participate—they discuss the issues of concern to them rather than receiving wisdom transmitted from the workshop leaders. Of course, the importance of participation and the perception of control over process and content have long been recognized in education, organization development, and psychology. We stress that introduction of systems thinking and computer simulation does not require taking control away from participants. Indeed, well-designed flight simulators enhance participants' control over the learning process. Second, cognitive mapping tools are introduced as a language for systems thinking. The participants learn causal diagramming in the process of mapping their own mental models. Finally, the mapping process brings to light many of the relationships in the simulation. When the computer is introduced, it is no black box—the relationships in the model have already been discussed.

Reflection. In early tests of the simulation we found the manager-players were thoroughly engaged within fifteen minutes. They were, literally, on the edges of their seats. They argued with one another about the next decision. They bragged about cost reductions they achieved. But afterwards none could articulate a significant new insight about claims management. They had played to win without pausing to reflect or to formulate and test theories about the causes of the problem.

These managers had fallen victim to the "video game" syndrome. To enable managers to experience the long-term side effects of decisions, simulations compress space and time. Good simulations also enable rapid trials with different strategies. But these very capabilities allow people to play without careful experimentation and without reflecting on the causes of the outcome. The players try a strategy; if it doesn't produce the desired outcome in a few months, they improvise. Rather than a series of controlled experiments, managers tend to vary multiple factors simultaneously. Instead of sticking with a strategy to see its long-term consequences, people quit a game that is going badly and start another (Moissis 1989). They behave the same way they do in real life. Trial and error produces little insight, whether performance is good or bad. Treated as a game, simulations can reinforce the misperceptions of feedback and cognitive errors in dynamic decision making (Brehmer 1980; Hogarth 1987; Dörner 1989).

To compensate for the managers' tendency to undermine their own learning, simple learning scenarios are used to introduce the game. The learning scenarios help develop disciplined strategic analysis and scientific method. Working in teams to encourage articulation of their reasoning, players are presented with a problem such as an unanticipated increase in incoming claims. They are first directed to focus only on the work flow and rebalance the pending pool. Each method of controlling work flow (hiring adjusters, increasing workweeks, or allowing quality standards to drop) is tried separately to isolate the different feedbacks and side effects associated with each. Before playing, the managers must state their strategy and what they expect to happen. After playing, they compare the actual results to their expectations and explain any discrepancies using their map of the causal relationships, then present their analysis to the group. The process of reflecting on discrepancies between expectations and outcomes establishes a discipline the managers then carry forward to experiments with new strategies. Without such discipline, simulation all too quickly becomes mere game playing.

The Computer. The participants in the Claims Learning Lab do not see the computer for the first day and a half. For many people, the computer is a predictive tool, a source of information, or a means of control (Orlikowski 1988; Weizenbaum 1976). It is not often seen as a tool for learning. In a successful learning laboratory, managers must perceive that the process is about their ways of thinking, their strategies, their problems—not about the computer. When the computer is introduced, the problems of the claims organization are the focus of attention.

Learning laboratories such as the CLL represent what Donald Schön calls a "virtual world," "a constructed representation of the real world." Schön (1983b) shows how virtual worlds play a critical role in learning among professionals. Constraints on experimentation are reduced. The pace of action can be varied. Actions that are irreversible in the real world become reversible. Changes in the environment can be eliminated. Complexity can be simplified. But Schön cautions that "the representational reliability of the virtual world has its limits." Learning always involves experimentation and reflection in the virtual world *and* the real world.

Herein lies a next major challenge for firms seeking to promote organizational learning. We must learn how to design and manage the process whereby managers move continually between the virtual world of the learning laboratory and the real world of management practice. Experiments in the virtual world should lead to hypotheses that are tested through measurement and experimentation in the real world. Conversely, actions taken in the real world will continually provoke new questions and present new puzzles that can be illuminated in the virtual world.

Current research concerns the transferability of the lessons of early experiments with learning laboratories to new organizational settings. The process and modeling tools described here arc now used successfully by organizations in diverse industries, including oil, chemicals, finance, health care, heavy manufacturing, consumer products, computers, and high tech. The library of microworlds embodying different general theories of business dynamics is gradually growing (Sterman 1988a; Graham et al. 1992 and Chapter 9 of this work). Experiments with learning laboratories in firms and universities are leading to improved methods for team learning.

Managers and organization theorists often point to high-performing teams in sports or the performing arts as role models of flexibility, learning, and consistent quality. Yet most firms, unlike a basketball team or symphony, have no practice fields where managers' skills can be developed and team competencies enhanced. Opportunities to reflect, to experiment, to challenge and revise mental models may be even more important for learning in firms than in sports or the arts. While much further research is needed, learning laboratories are becoming an important tool that helps organizations create meaningful practice fields to accelerate team learning. Simulation is increasingly important in re-creating the full range of interpersonal and substantive challenges that confront managers attempting to think globally while acting locally.

REFERENCES

Argyris, C. (1985), *Strategy, Change, and Defensive Routines*, Boston: Pitman.

Argyris, C. (1982), *Reasoning, Learning and Action*, San Francisco: Jossey-Bass.

Argyris, C., and D. Schön (1978), *Organizational Learning: A Theory of Action Approach,* Reading, Mass: Addison-Wesley.

Argyris, C., B. Putnam, and D. Smith (1986), *Action Science,* San Francisco: Jossey-Bass.

Axelrod, R. (1976), *The Structure of Decision: The Cognitive Maps of Political Elites,* Princeton: Princeton University Press.

Bakken, B. (1990), "Transfer and Learning in Simulated Dynamic Decision Environments," Working paper D-4017, System Dynamics Group, Sloan School of Management, MIT, Cambridge, Mass.

Beckhard, R., and R.T. Harris (1987), *Organizational Transitions: Managing Complex Change*, Reading, Mass.: Addison-Wesley.

Bergin, R., and G. P. Rusko (1990), "The Learning Laboratory," *The HealthCare Forum Journal* 33, no. 2: 32-36.

Brehmer, B. (1980), "In One Word: Not from Experience," *Acta Psychologica* 45: 223-41.

Brehmer, B. (1989), "Feedback Delays and Control in Complex Dynamic Systems," in P. Milling and E. Zahn, eds., *Computer-Based Management of Complex Systems,* Berlin: Springer-Verlag, 189-96.

Camerer, C. (1987), "Do Biases in Probability Judgment Matter in Markets? Experimental Evidence," *American Economic Review* 77, no. 5: 981-97.

Checkland, P. (1981), *Systems Thinking, Systems Practice,* Chichester, U.K.: Wiley.

Cooper, K. G. (1980), "Naval Ship Production: A Claim Settled and a Framework Built," *Interfaces* 10, no. 6: 20-36.

Diehl, E., and J.D. Sterman (1993), "Effects of Feedback Complexity on Dynamic Decision Making," Working Paper, Sloan School of Management, Cambridge, Mass.

Dörner, D. (1989), "Managing a Simple Ecological System," Working Paper, Lehrstuhl Psychologie II, University of Bamberg.

Dyer, W.G. (1987), *Team Building: Issues and Alternatives* (2d ed.), Reading, Mass: Addison-Wesley.

Eden, C., S. Jones, and D. Sims (1983), *Messing About in Problems,* Oxford: Pergamon Press.

Forrester, J.W. (1961), *Industrial Dynamics,* Portland, Ore.: Productivity Press.

Forrester, J.W. (1971), "Counterintuitive Behavior of Social Systems," *Technology Review* 73, no. 3: 52-68.

Forrester, J.W. (1969), *Urban Dynamics,* Portland, Ore.: Productivity Press.

de Geus, A.P. (1988), "Planning as Learning," *Harvard Business Review,* March-April: 70-74.

Graham, A., J. Morecroft, P. Senge, and J. Sterman (1992), "Model-supported Case Studies for Management Education," *European Journal of Operational Research* 59, no. 1: 151-66; also Chapter 9 of this volume.

Hall, R.I. (1976), "A System Pathology of an Organization: The Rise and Fall of the Old Saturday Evening Post," *Administrative Science Quarterly* 21: 185-211.

Hall, R.I. (1984), "The Natural Logic of Management Policy Making: Its Implications for the Survival of an Organization," *Management Science* 30: 905-27.

Hall, R.I. (1989), "A Training Game and Behavioral Decision Making Research Tool: An Alternative Use of System Dynamics Simulation," in P. Milling and E. Zahn, eds., *Computer-Based Management of Complex Systems,* Berlin: Springer-Verlag, 221-28.

Hayes, R.H., S.C. Wheelwright, and K.B. Clark (1988), *Dynamic Manufacturing: Creating the Learning Organization,* London: Free Press.

HealthCare Forum (1990), *The HealthCare Forum Journal* 33, no. 2.

Hogarth, R. (1987), *Judgement and Choice* (2d ed.), Chichester, U.K.: John Wiley.

Huber, P. (1987), "Injury Litigation and Liability Insurance Dynamics," *Science* 238, no. 2: 31-36.

Kahneman, D., P. Slovic, and A. Tversky (1982), *Judgment Under Uncertainty: Heuristics and Biases,* Cambridge: Cambridge University Press.

Katz, D., and R.L. Kahn (1978), *The Social Psychology of Organizations*, New York: John Wiley.

Kim, D. (1989), "Learning Laboratories, Designing Reflective Learning Environments," in P. Milling and E. Zahn, eds., *Computer-Based Management of Complex Systems,* Berlin: Springer Verlag.

Kleinmuntz, D. (1985), "Cognitive Heuristics and Feedback in a Dynamic Decision Environment," *Management Science* 31, no. 6: 680-702.

Kluwe, R.H., C. Misiak, and H. Haider (1989), "Modelling the process of complex system control," in P. Milling and E. Zahn, eds., *Computer-Based Management of Complex Systems,* Berlin: Springer-Verlag, 335-42.

Levitt, B., and J. March (1988), "Organizational Learning," *Annual Review of Sociology* 14: 319-40.

Lorange, P., M. Scott Morton, and S. Ghoshal (1986), *Strategic Control Systems*, St. Paul, Minn.: West Publishing Co.

MacNeil-Lehrer Report (1989), *Risky Business—Business Cycles*, Video, Public Broadcasting System, aired October 23, 1989.

Mason, R., and I. Mitroff (1981), *Challenging Strategic Planning Assumptions,* New York: Wiley.

Meadows, D.L. (1989), "Gaming to Implement System Dynamics Models," in P. Milling and E. Zahn, eds., *Computer-Based Management of Complex Systems,* Berlin: Springer-Verlag, 635-40.

Milling, P. and Zahn, E., eds. (1989), *Computer Based Management of Complex Systems,* Berlin: Springer-Verlag.

Moissis, A. (1989), *Decision Making in the Insurance Industry: A Dynamic Simulation Model and Experimental Results*, S.M. thesis, Sloan School of Management, MIT, Cambridge, Mass.

Morecroft, J. (1982), "A Critical Review of Diagramming Tools for Conceptualizing Feedback Models," *Dynamica* 8, no. I: 20-29.

Morecroft, J. (1988), "System Dynamics and Microworlds for Policymakers," *European Journal of Operational Research* 35: 301-20.

Nyhart, D. (1988), "Computer Modeling in Dispute Resolution—An Overview," *Dispute Resolution Forum,* April: 3-15.

Nyhart, D., and D. Samarasan (1989), "The Elements of Negotiation Management: Using Computers to Help Resolve Conflict," *Negotiation Journal* 5, no. 1: 43-62.

Orlikowski, W. (1988), "Computer Technology in Organisations: Some Critical Notes," in D. Knights and H. Willmott, *New Technology and the Labour Process,* London: Macmillan, 20-49.

Paich, M., and J.D. Sterman (1993), "Boom, Bust, and Failures to Learn in Experimental Markets," *Management Science* 39, no. 12: 1439-1458.

Perrow, C. (1984), *Normal Accidents: Living with High Risk Technologies,* New York: Basic Books.

Richardson, G. P., and A. Pugh (1981), *Introduction to System Dynamics Modeling with DYNAMO,* Portland, Ore.: Productivity Press.

Richardson, G. P., and P. Senge (1989), "Corporate and Statewide Perspectives on the Liability Insurance Crisis," in P. Milling and E. Zahn , eds., *Computer-Based Management of Complex Systems,* Berlin: Springer-Verlag, 442-57.

Richmond, B. (1987), *The Strategic Forum: From Vision to Operating Policies and Back Again*, High Performance Systems, 45 Lyme Road, Ste. 300, Hanover NH 03755.

Richmond, B., S. Peterson, and P. Vescuso (1987), *An Academic User's Guide to STELLA,* High Performance Systems, 45 Lyme Road, Ste. 300, Hanover NH 03755.

Roberts, E.B., ed. (1978), *Managerial Applications of System Dynamics*, Portland, Ore.: Productivity Press.

Schein, E. (1969), *Process Consultation: Its Role in Organization Development*, Reading, Mass.: Addison-Wesley.

Schein, E. (1987), *Process Consultation* (Volume II), Reading, Mass.: Addison-Wesley.

Schein, E. (1985), *Organizational Culture and Leadership,* San Francisco: Jossey-Bass.

Schön, D. (1983a), "Organizational Learning," in G. Morgan, ed., *Beyond Method,* London: Sage.

Schön, D. (1983b), *The Reflective Practitioner*, New York: Basic Books.

Senge, P. (1990a), *The Fifth Discipline,* New York: Doubleday.

Senge, P. (1990b), "Catalyzing Systems Thinking in Organizations," in F. Masaryk, ed., *Advances in Organization Development,* Norwood, N.J.: Ablex.

Simon, H. A. (1979), "Rational Decision-Making in Business Organizations," *American Economic Review,* 69, 493-513.

Simon, H. A. (1982), *Models of Bounded Rationality,* Cambridge: MIT Press.

Smith, V., G. Suchanek, and A. Williams (1988), "Bubbles, Crashes, and Endogenous Expectations in Experimental Spot Asset Markets," *Econometrica* 56, no. 5: 1119-1152.

Solomon, J. (1989), "Now, Simulators for Piloting Companies," *Wall Street Journal,* 31 July, B1.

Stata, R. (1989), "Organizational Learning—The Key to Management Innovation," *Sloan Management Review* 30, no. 3: 63-74.

Sterman, J. (1989a), "Misperceptions of Feedback in Dynamic Decision Making," *Organizational Behavior and Human Decision Processes* 43, no. 3: 301-35.

Sterman, J. (1989b, "Modeling Managerial Behavior: Misperceptions of Feedback in a Dynamic Decision Making Experiment," *Management Science* 35, no. 3: 321-39.

Sterman, J.D. (1988a), *People Express Management Flight Simulator,* software and briefing book available from the author, Sloan School of Management, MIT, Cambridge MA 02142.

Sterman, J.D. (1988b), "A Skeptic's Guide to Computer Models," in L. Grant, *Foresight and National Decisions,* Lanham, Md.: University Press of America, 133-69.

Wack, P. (1985), "Scenarios: Uncharted Waters Ahead," and "Scenarios: Shooting the Rapids" (two-part article), *Harvard Business Review,* September-October and November-December.

Weick, K.E. (1979), *The Social Psychology of Organizing*, Reading, Mass.: Addison-Wesley.

Weil, H. (1980), "The Evolution of an Approach for Achieving Implemented Results from System Dynamics Models," in J. Randers, ed., *Elements of the System Dynamics Method,* Portland, Ore.: Productivity Press.

Weizenbaum, J. (1976), *Computer Power and Human Reason: From Judgment to Calculation,* San Francisco: W.H. Freeman.

PART 3

LEARNING FROM MODELING AND SIMULATION

9

MODEL-SUPPORTED CASE STUDIES FOR MANAGEMENT EDUCATION

ALAN K. GRAHAM, JOHN D.W. MORECROFT,
PETER M. SENGE, AND JOHN D. STERMAN

ABSTRACT: There is growing interest in combining computer simulation models with conventional case studies to create learning environments for management education. "Model" here denotes an endogenous theory of business dynamics, a simulation microworld, and not merely a spreadsheet or multimedia computer environment. Model-supported case studies promise improvement in strategic thinking skills and better integration of modeling with policy and strategy formation. Two examples are presented (People Express Airlines and the Intecom PBX) to show explicitly how cases and system dynamics models are combined and used. Finally, we explore research questions that arise in conjunction with such work: (1) how to teach effective inquiry skills, (2) how to teach conceptualization skills, and (3) how to enhance the ability to transfer insight to new situations.

INTRODUCTION: THE ROLE OF MODELS IN CASE-BASED EDUCATION

To understand where system dynamics models, especially models-with-cases, may contribute to management education, consider first how business policy and strategy are traditionally taught. Case studies are the cornerstone. The objective is to develop skills to "think strategically," "view the business as a whole," or "adopt the perspective of the general manager." A typical case is 20 to 30 pages in length and contains about 10,000 words of text, plus diagrams and numerical information, often financial reports and market data. Usually, cases provide a brief history of the company, a description of its products or services, and descriptions of competitors. Depending on the purpose the case may describe details of manufacturing, marketing, and distribution, or delve into human resource policy, systems of administration and control, organizational structure, company traditions and values, management style, leadership, or personalities. Case teachers use such descriptive and numerical information to trigger classroom discussion about the business, its administration, and its strategic options. But how and what do students learn?

Case teachers do not teach answers. They offer instead frameworks that guide class discussion and help learners organize case information and form opinions. For example, Porter's (1980, 1985) competitive analysis framework is now widely used to guide discussion about business unit competitive strategy. Whether the subject is supercomputers, water meters, airlines, or fashion watches, Porter's framework prompts critical thinking about questions such as, "Is this an attractive industry to be in? What stops competitors from entering? What motivates customers to buy? Are suppliers or distributors in a position to siphon off the firm's profits?" It encourages close examination of the activities upon which a company builds and sustains its competitive edge. The framework provides the case teacher with a checklist of thought-provoking questions, and graphics with which to collect and select participants' comments.

At the end of a typical case discussion, students typically see several chalkboards of material, based mostly on their own comments, with a visual layout controlled by the teacher. What has been the pedagogical value of the process? First, learners feel involved—their opinions and comments have received attention. Second, the instructor has imposed discipline on the discussion through the use of the framework, but not a heavy discipline. The framework provides broad brush questions and accommodates a wide range of comments. With practice and perhaps some lectures on competitive analysis, learners begin to be able to use the framework. Third, the class as a whole has a shared focus for debate—the information displayed on the board. (The same learning benefits occur when strategic frameworks are used to organize management team discussion of live business problems, as in Morecroft 1994.)

However the case method has limitations. Chief among these is the impossibility of testing hypotheses the participants offer as to the effects of alternative actions. To evaluate the consequences of policies other than those described in the case, and even to attribute the actual outcomes to particular causes, one must conceptualize a model of the system described in the case and perform mental simulations to infer its likely dynamics. But people face formidable problems in formulating appropriate models of complex environments and correctly relating system structure to behavior. Extensive research in behavioral decision theory and other fields documents the bounds on human rationality that create persistent judgmental biases and systematic errors in complex settings (Simon 1979; Kahneman, Slovic, and Tversky 1982; Hogarth 1987).

Research in dynamic decision making and system dynamics shows that environments characterized by multiple feedback processes, side effects, time delays, and nonlinearity are particularly troublesome. Experiments show students and managers alike suffer from persistent "misperceptions of feedback," which result in extremely poor performance and slow or no learning (Sterman 1989a, b; Senge and Sterman 1992; Diehl 1989; Kleinmuntz 1985; Brehmer 1990). The very skills required for effective learning in the case method are precisely those for which the human mind is ill-suited. The result is an inability to assess the validity of alternative strategies. In the case method one cannot separate insight from hindsight.

We believe simulation methodologies such as system dynamics help overcome the misperceptions of feedback that plague managers in the real world. System dynamics offers a framework for conceptualizing complex business (and other) situations, tools to identify the physical, organizational, and decision-making structure of the systems, and simulation methods to infer correctly the dynamics of these structures. In the following, we define a model-supported case study as a traditional case supported by a simulation model and/or modeling tools. By model we mean a behavioral theory of the feedback structure of the business setting that endogenously generates the problematic behavior described in the case. We do not consider cases supported by spreadsheets portraying the financial reports or other exhibits typically found in the back of a case. Nor do we consider cases in which the written text is supplemented or replaced by hypertext, videodisc, or multimedia technologies. These developments, while promising, do not address what we consider to be the central deficiency of the case method—the need for a simulated microworld that can provide realistic feedback to the learner on the consequences of alternative strategies. Note that we are not proposing the use of simulation models to provide "the answers" but as the cornerstone of an environment for learning about business dynamics.

For which aspects of business strategy curricula may such model-supported cases be useful? Business policy and strategy courses cover topics in several dimensions, from strategies for the business unit/single business firm to the complex multidivisional, multibusiness firm. Issues range from the competitive and economic forces that shape strategic options to administrative and organizational constraints. Different frameworks develop different dimensions of strategic thinking. For example, McKinsey's "7 S" framework (a simple diagram showing 7 labeled and inter-linked bubbles, Hax and Majluf 1984, 94-96) helps trigger thinking about constraints on strategy—the fit between strategy and structure: Do the firm's structure, employees, administrative systems, capabilities, knowledge base, organization structure, and culture support or hinder the strategy? Portfolio frameworks like the famous growth-share matrix of the Boston Consulting Group (Hax and Majluf 1984, Chapter 7) can guide discussion about corporate portfolio management—what businesses should a firm be in, how should corporate resources be allocated, what criteria should management use to evaluate and compare business unit performance, how should one segment the business for strategic planning purposes?

Model-supported case studies retain a strong process flavor. They stimulate and guide discussion, without stifling it. Like other frameworks, the model, along with the systems thinking concepts that accompany it, shapes the case discussion. In addition, models-with-cases allow "what-ifs" and role-playing in a feedback system that captures side-effects and other attributes of reality, adding important new process dimensions that cannot be replicated in the conventional case method. Learners are drawn into the case by taking the role of key decision makers, exercising choice and judgment, and experiencing the consequences of their actions.

System dynamics models are particularly suited to understanding the coordination between strategy and operating policies—how to distinguish goals from strategies designed to achieve goals, and how to design a set of policies and programs that support rather than frustrate strategic objectives. In addition, at the business unit level, models can illuminate the administrative issues (goal formation, incentives, motivation, time allocation, information availability, etc.) as well as market, economic, and political environment issues. Models-with-cases provide an important link between strategy formation and implementation at the operations management level. Models-with-cases do not, however, have across-the-board applicability to all strategic issues. Rather, model supported cases make unique and much needed contributions to the development of strategic thinking skills for operating policy design (but see Merten, Löffler, and Wiedmann 1987 for one example of system dynamics used to support a multinational firm's dynamic portfolio management).

CASE STUDY: PEOPLE EXPRESS AIRLINES

The Rise and Fall of People Express

One of the most popular Harvard Business School cases of recent years describes People Express Airlines (Whitestone 1983). People Express went from startup in 1981 to the fifth-largest U.S. airline and annual revenues in excess of $1 billion by 1986. Behind its meteoric rise were deep discount prices, making air travel competitive with the bus on many routes; a host of innovative "new management" policies, such as universal employee ownership, work teams, and job rotation; and a charismatic founder, Don Burr. But PE's spectacular early success was matched by equally spectacular failure. In the first nine months of 1986 the firm lost $245 million, and, in September 1986, the firm was purchased by Texas Air for only $125 million (Figure 9-1; Table 9-1). The People Express case is widely used to examine a broad range of issues in growth management, industry deregulation, human resources, organizational structure, and executive hubris.

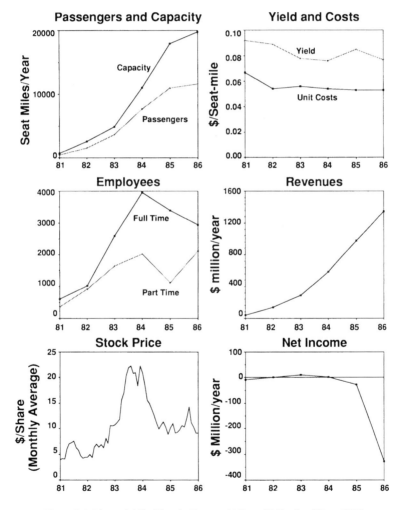

Figure 9-1. Rise and fall of People Express Airlines (Holland and Beer 1990)

Table 9-1. History of People Express Airlines (Sterman 1988)

April 1981	Service begins
March 1983	Fleet of 20 grows to 40 aircraft
May 1983	Expansion: Service to London
July 1985	2nd Quarter profits of $13 million
October 1985	Frontier purchased for $307 million
December 1985	Britt Airways purchased
February 1986	Record loss $32 M in 4th Q 1985
May 1986	Loss of $58 million in 1st Q 1986 Approval to buy PBA
June 1986	Deep fare cuts Don Burr puts PE up for sale
July 1986	Texas Air offers $314 million UAL offers $146 million for Frontier
August 1986	UAL deal falls through Frontier files Chapter 11
September 15, 1986	PE sold to Texas Air for $125 million

A Strategy Model

The People Express Management Flight Simulator (Sterman 1988) is an interactive simulation game based on a system dynamics model of the firm. Interestingly, Sterman developed the first version of the model before the demise of the company in 1986 (helping to address concerns about the prospective use of models). The model integrates the operations, human resources, organizational structure, and philosophy of People Express with the structure of the U.S. air-travel market and competitive environment of the early 1980s (Figure 9-2). In addition to "hard" variables such as fleet size, flight schedule, aircraft capacity, and a full set of financial reports, the model includes a variety of "soft" variables including hiring and training lags, the effects of overtime, fatigue, and stock price changes on morale, productivity, and employee turnover, and the effects of service quality on reputation and customer demand. The model differentiates between the quality-sensitive and price-insensitive business travelers and the price-sensitive, quality-insensitive discretionary travelers (what People Express veterans called the back-packers). Following standard marketing models, demand is driven by both advertising and word of mouth. Potential customers respond to the flight schedule and availability of service, fares, service quality, and "service scope" (the range of services offered). The model includes competitor price response based on PE's market share and fares. The stock price varies endogenously as PE's earnings, growth, and financial position change.

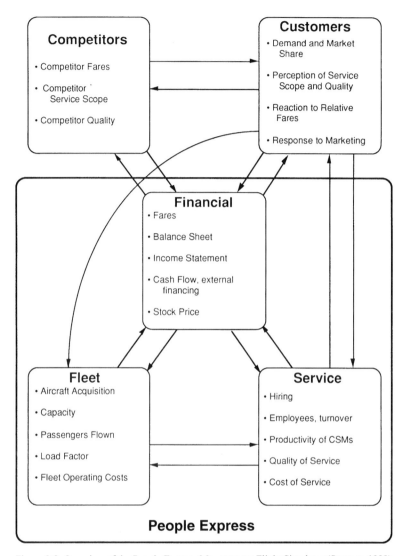

Figure 9-2. Overview of the People Express Management Flight Simulator (Sterman 1988)

The Management Flight Simulator and Workshop

For educational purposes, the model has been converted into a decision-making simulation, the People Express Management Flight Simulator, which puts each participant in the role of the top management. As in a traditional case format, participants prepare by reading the Harvard Business School case and a twenty-page briefing book summarizing the assumptions of the model and giving instructions on use of the software (Sterman 1988). Rather than merely discussing the reasons for the failure of People Express and offering untestable suggestions for strategies that might have succeeded, the Management Flight Simulator allows, indeed requires, participants to formulate and implement their own strategies for the success of People Express. Each quarter year, participants must set fares and decide how many planes to buy, how many customer service managers (CSMs) to hire, how much to spend on marketing, and what scope of services to offer. (The simulation is available for Macintosh and IBM-compatible computers. The model was developed in STELLA [Richmond, Vescuso, and Peterson 1987]. The gaming interface is implemented in MicroWorlds, an environment described in Chapter 15 of this work.) After entering their decisions for the quarter, participants receive feedback on the results and must make decisions for the next quarter (Figure 9-3). The participants may go bankrupt or may grow to dominate the market.

Instructors at different institutions have developed many different ways to use the simulator. One format, developed by Sterman, has proven effective in workshops ranging from a few hours to several days. The workshop begins with a short review of the history of People Express. Next, students view a brief video clip dating from 1985 in which Don Burr speaks about his philosophy (Harvard Business School 1985), a clip that invariably stimulates vigorous discussion including issues of leadership and underlying values such as the purpose of a corporation (to make

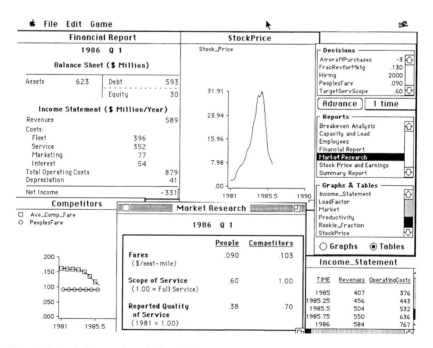

Figure 9-3. Typical screen from the People Express Management Flight Simulator (Sterman 1988)

money, or, as Don Burr argues, to "make a better world"). The workshop here resembles a traditional case discussion, with participants offering their own theories to explain the failure of the firm. The discussion concludes with participants' suggestions of strategies that would have succeeded. It is critical for people to "go public" with their own suggestions here so they can compare their initial thoughts to those they develop after managing the simulated company (see Senge and Sterman 1992 [Chapter 8 of this work] for discussion). Even in groups as large as 250, the introductory phase, including the video, can take as little as an hour. Next participants are instructed in the use of the simulator. While the model is quite complex, the interface for the simulator is straightforward and requires no prior training or computer skills. Students and senior managers without any computer experience have been able to begin testing their own strategies for People Express in about twenty minutes. No special training is required for the instructor.

During the next few hours participants run their own airlines. Teams of two or three are recommended to encourage debate and discussion of proposed strategies. The teams are encouraged to experiment systematically rather than always trying to maximize performance. Indeed, their first task is to agree on what they seek to accomplish (profits were the last of six major goals People Express sought to achieve). In the course of a few hours most teams are able to run the simulator several times. Nearly all teams experience bankruptcy at least once; by the end of the session nearly all also find a successful strategy. Participants are also encouraged to critique the model. To encourage such critical reflection, Sterman tells participants "this model is wrong." By explicitly identifying the simplifying assumptions and limitations of the model, participants are moved to consider how their strategies would perform in the real world. Telling participants up front that the model is imperfect avoids adversarial debate about the merits and shortcomings of the simulation model and stimulates joint inquiry into the realism of the results.

Successful game play, however, is not enough. The workshop continues with discussion to elicit and articulate the lessons learned by the participants. In our experience the level of discussion is always much deeper than the case discussion at the start of the workshop. First, participants appreciate how difficult it is to manage such a system. Many express admiration for Don Burr's achievement despite the eventual sale of the company. Participants are more aware of the side effects, counter-reactions, time delays, and tradeoffs they face. The simulator does seem to be effective in increasing participants' sensitivity to the feedback structure and dynamics of the system. Suggestions for strategies are also more specific and implementable than those typical of the earlier case discussion.

To illustrate, it is common in the initial discussion for participants to suggest that People Express could have succeeded if they had "maintained service quality." While perhaps desirable, "maintaining service quality" is a goal and not an actionable, implementable policy. After playing the game, participants articulate a more highly developed understanding of the time lags and counterpressures that may frustrate quality improvement programs. For example, in the context of People Express' rapid growth, hiring still more customer service managers (CSMs) to increase the organization's service capacity and counteract the decline in customer service further dilutes the average skill and experience level of the workforce and requires experienced CSMs to spend more time in hiring and training and less in serving the customers. Declining service quality reduces morale and productivity, increasing turnover and further reducing service resources; the remaining CSMs may have to work additional overtime, leading to fatigue, burnout, turnover, and falling productivity, further exacerbating quality problems. If lagging productivity causes profits to fall and the stock price drops, the plunging net worth of the employees further hurts morale and increases turnover, in a vicious cycle. Even if service improves, given People Express' low fares, the result is only to attract still more would-be customers, causing even more busy signals on reservations lines, congestion in the terminal, overbooking, and other problems that drag service quality down again. Participants are rarely able to identify and integrate all these effects without experiencing them as they run their own airline in the simulator. After playing they are much better able to do so. They volunteer examples of similar dynamics from personal experience or other cases, thus developing understanding of an important generic structure and successfully transfering the lessons to other situations.

In some workshops Sterman uses the STELLA model embodied in the Flight Simulator to test strategies suggested during the discussion. These tests, projected for all to see as a decade-long simulation unfolds in seconds, further cement the business lessons and systems thinking principles. In workshops designed to teach systems thinking as well as principles of business strategy, participants often go on to map the feedback structure of People Express through causal-loop diagrams (on causal diagramming techniques see Richardson and Pugh 1981). The simulated experience of running the company tends to produce causal maps of much higher quality compared to those of similar groups who draw only on the case and discussion.

The Lessons

A case as rich as People Express can be used to illuminate many issues. The core issues center around the reasons such spectacular success so quickly became failure. Was it their innovative philosophy, human resource policies, and organization design? Was it external competitive reaction? Was it top management ego? And, most importantly, how transferable are the lessons of the case to other firms and industries?

At the heart of People Express' demise were inherent contradictions between its innovative human resource policies on the one hand and its pricing policies and rapid growth on the other. Don Burr wanted to demonstrate "a new way to run an airline," to show that a nonhierarchical structure, democratic principles, trust, and shared economic risks and rewards would produce a vastly more productive organization. He also was intent on becoming a major player in the airline business in a few years, to which end he offered exceedingly low fares, attracting customers in droves and driving breakneck growth from 3 to over 75 aircraft in just 5 years.

Don Burr's creative innovations did indeed produce an organization much more productive than the industry average. Coupled with the savvy purchase of used aircraft, use of then-ignored Newark as a hub, and no-frills service, he created an organization that was profitable at fare levels less than half of the competition. However, the rapid growth—more than 100 percent per year—caused by the low prices was inconsistent with a hiring process that carefully screened prospective employees for their fit to a radically new culture (slowing the staffing process) and an organization in which individuals were largely self-managing and rotated among different jobs (slowing the learning process). The result was staffing shortages, skill dilution due to inadequate time to develop management skills, falling service quality, declining morale, and burnout. People Express soon had overloaded reservations lines, high rates of lost luggage, delayed flights, the highest overbooking rates in the industry, and led the industry in consumer complaints. When the competition, prodded by the success of People Express and similar post-deregulation startups, finally developed the capability to match PE's low fares, the company's sole remaining competitive advantage disappeared, ridership fell, and losses mounted, ultimately forcing the sale to Texas Air to stave off bankruptcy.

The simulation experience allows people to test other theories about the collapse of the company. For example, a common interpretation of PE's failure cites as the cause the innovative use of information technology by competitors, notably American Airlines. The SABRE system allowed American to match PE's fares despite higher costs (through yield management) and to dominate the chief distribution channel (travel agents), thus negating PE's price advantage while still offering full service and higher quality. The effect of yield management was indeed dramatic. However, the feedback framework developed through the simulator experience encourages students to see this stunning technological development as an endogenous competitive reaction to the price advantage and rapid growth of People Express rather than an unforeseen external event. Students are motivated to test this theory in the simulation by asking, for example, what might have happened if American's investment in yield management had failed or been delayed (higher competitor prices would have further increased PE's demand, pushing service quality still lower and increasing PE's vulnerability to price competition; competitors would have worked harder to find other ways to match PE's fares, etc.). Participants begin to design more effective strategies by asking how PE's own strategy provoked the competitors' response. Through such experimentation many propose a strategy of somewhat higher fares to control excessive growth of demand, thus preventing quality erosion and vulnerability to price competition caused by loss of the price-insensitive but quality-sensitive business traveler. They go on to debate issues such as whether slower growth and higher prices would reduce or delay price cuts by competitors; whether slower growth would have given PE management the time to scan the competitive environment and identify these threats earlier; whether slower growth and higher margins would have provided PE with the resources to develop their own yield management system in time (PE's own efforts to develop a yield management system were plagued with problems—their system came on line the day Don Burr announced the sale to Texas Air[1]). The simulator provides ways to test alternative theories, to reach a deeper understanding of the sources of difficulty, and, most importantly, of management's leverage in preventing or influencing the response of actors such as competitors who seem at first glance to be outside management control.

Uses, Users, and Student Evaluation

The People Express Management Flight Simulator was first used at the MIT Sloan School of Management in September 1988 as a day in a week-long orientation program for incoming master's students. Figure 9-4 summarizes the student evaluations. The People Express workshop was the highest rated session of the orientation program. The workshop has been repeated each year, involving 250 students and 90 Macintosh computers in each session. It is also used in courses on service operations management, behavioral decision making, and system dynamics.

[1] Don Burr, personal communication.

Figure 9-4. Student evaluations of People Express Management Flight Simulator as used in the orientation workshop for the incoming master's class at the Sloan School of Management, MIT, September 1988. Ratings in subsequent years have been similar.

The People Express Management Flight Simulator has now been adopted by dozens of universities including the Harvard Business School, University of Texas, Stanford Law School, London Business School, Notre Dame, University of Southern California, Queen's University (Ontario), IMD (Lausanne), IESA (Venezuela), and many others around the world. It is used for both orientation programs and in courses as diverse as strategy, marketing, operations management, simulation modeling, organizational behavior, human resource management, and economics. It has also seen wide use in management training at all levels of management in industries including air travel, telecommunications, computers, and manufacturing.

The success of the People Express Management Flight Simulator has led to the development of additional model-supported cases, including cases on strategy for durable goods such as consumer electronics, toys, and chain saws (Paich and Sterman 1993), commercial real estate, the international oil tanker market (Bakken 1990), Sun Microsystems (Brau 1990), and others.[2]

CASE STUDY: INTECOM AND THE PBX MARKET

An Industry in Transition

In the early 1980s the AT&T operating companies (such as New England Telephone and New York Telephone) were converting their highly profitable base of electromechanical telephone switching systems (known as PBXs) to new electronic PBXs, in an increasingly competitive market. A key issue facing senior managers was how to retain a high share of the installed base of PBX systems while customers migrated from the old to new technology. The strategy for managing the migration required executives to think about pricing, the size, motivation, and compensation of the salesforce, and the actions of competitors. In the event, some of the operating companies lost 60 percent of their market share during the migration while others lost only 20 percent!

The Model and Case

A management team from one operating company commissioned a system dynamics project to help them design the migration strategy. The model (Morecroft 1984) is combined with the Intecom case (Ghemawat 1986) to replicate for students the insights gained from the project. The Intecom case deals with the entry of Intecom, a new company affiliated with Exxon, into the top-end of the U.S. PBX market. Most of the case is devoted to describing switching products, PBX technology, customers, channels of distribution, installation, service, and manufacturing. The

---

[2] Contact John Sterman for additional information on these cases. The People Express and product life cycle simulation (B & B Enterprises) are available for Macintosh and IBM compatible computers running Windows.

case also provides information on competitors and deregulation. The appendices contain industry-level data on the installed base, line shipments, market shares, manufacturing costs, and corporate financial performance. The case provides a wealth of background information on the industry, thereby mimicking the experience base of the AT&T management team. Students are asked to read the case in advance and think about the following questions: What is a relevant measure of market share in the PBX market? How do you set reasonable sales objectives for a migration strategy? What pricing options would you consider for old and new systems?

The case discussion lasts for three hours and is organized around three STELLA maps (Richmond et al. 1987) of increasing complexity that represent the migration strategy visually (Figure 9-5). The maps are displayed on a Macintosh computer linked to a large-screen projection system. The first map shows a base of electro-mechanical PBXs (represented as a single stock) depleted by migration flows into a base of electronic PBXs shared between competitors and the operating company (represented as two stocks). The case teacher can use this very simple model to clarify the near-monopoly starting position of the operating companies, to trigger discussion of the changing regulatory environment, and to think about market share definitions (share of base or share of sales?). He can also introduce simulation by posing a question, eliciting suggestions, and then testing those suggestions by simulating the model. Thus students receive feedback on the accuracy of their mental models.

The case teacher then sets aside the computer and reverts to conventional chalk talk in order to help the class think carefully about the customers. Who are they, why should they migrate, what factors influence their decisions, what are their motives and incentives? Here the behavioral underpinnings of system dynamics (Morecroft 1985 and 1994; Sterman 1989a, b, 1987) provide a checklist of suggestive questions to structure the discussion and record people's comments. The second STELLA map incorporates the main features of the chalk talk and shows explicitly how sales effort, price, and customer behavior influence migration.

Class discussion next turns to the sales force. What is it like to be a systems salesperson? How might you spend your time? How do you set priorities? What motivates you? These questions help the class probe the vital issue of the determinants of sales effort. The final step is to talk about the competition. The critical feedback process brought out here is the self-reinforcing growth of the competition (in the aggregate) as competitors use increasing sales to expand marketing efforts and develop production experience and technical know-how, thus generating still greater sales. The structured discussion lasts about two hours and leads into the third STELLA map, which incorporates sales effort, price, sales time allocation, customer behavior, and competitor growth.

The students are now divided into teams and sent away for half an hour to devise their own migration strategy. The "levers" they have at their disposal are

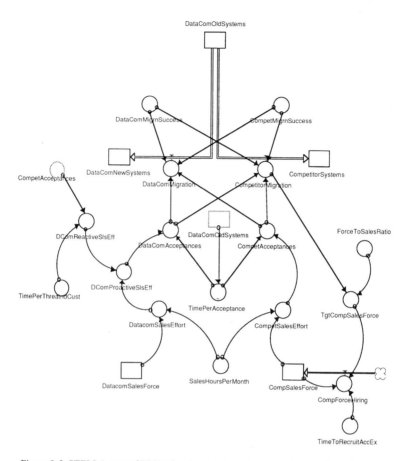

Figure 9-5. STELLA map of PBX migration problem, showing migration flows from base of leased electromechanical systems to purchased, electronic systems divided between the firm and the competition. Decision structure focuses on the strategy of the competitors and the allocation of the firm's salesforce effort between proactive and reactive selling.

price (for both old and new systems), and sales force size (a subset of the real levers available to AT&T management). Each team is given graph paper on which they can draw time profiles for price and sales force. The teams are asked to justify their choice of these policy levers and predict the likely development of market share, competitor sales, and sales expense to revenue ratio. Thus they must make explicit both their strategies and the results of their mental simulations regarding their effects, avoiding the "video-game" mentality where participants play enthusiastically but fail to reflect upon their experience (Senge and Sterman 1992 and Chapter 8 of this work). During the remaining time as many teams as possible are given the chance to explain their customer migration strategy and to simulate it online in the classroom.

The Lessons

Simulations show a wide range of outcomes (Figure 9-6). Some teams lose market share rapidly and also incur high sales expenses. Others maintain a much higher market share with low expense to revenue ratio. This diversity resembles the outcomes of the real AT&T operating companies. The successful teams recognized that a high lease price for the old base can be very profitable (milking the old base) but also creates vulnerability if competitors aggressively market the new technology.

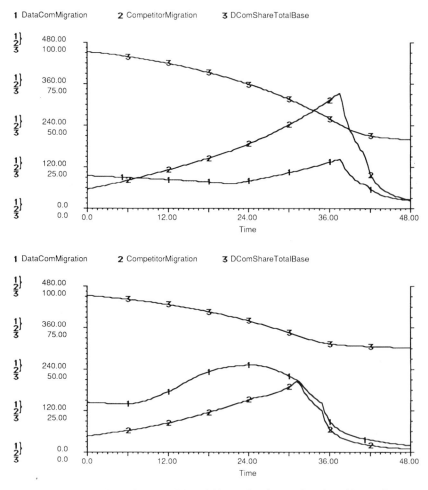

Figure 9-6. Simulations of PBX model. Variable 1: Migration rate from leased base to firm. Variable 2: Migration to competitor. Variable 3: Firm's share of installed based. Top: Firm's share of installed base falls under 50% when firm tries to retain profitable lease-base customers as competitors grow rapidly and conversion effort of the firm's highly stressed sales force is primarily defensive. Bottom: Firm retains a higher share when it expands sales force and seeks early conversion of existing customers to new systems, slowing competitor growth.

However, by using some of the extra funds from the old base to finance sales force expansion, competitor growth is restricted and the expense-to-revenue ratio is reduced. Like the People Express simulator, the model deepens the level of discussion by allowing students to experience the long-term consequences of their suggested strategies.

CONTRIBUTIONS OF MODEL-SUPPORTED CASES TO MANAGEMENT EDUCATION

We turn now to the contributions we expect system dynamics and computer-based case studies to make in teaching management and in development of effective systems thinking for business policy and strategy.

There seem to be at least three elements in the design of a strategy. Asking the right questions to discover the most important issues might be called *investigation.* Organizing some of the data into a new framework while downplaying other aspects is *conceptualization* or *framing.* Finally, one must select and apply past experience or an appropriate theoretical framework to help solve the current problem. Thus managers must *transfer* prior learning to the new situation. How do model-supported cases assist in investigation, conceptualization, and transfer?

Investigation / Learning Strategy

The primary contribution of model-supported case studies is creation of an environment in which investigation can occur. Morecroft (1988) describes simulation models and model-based games as *microworlds,* which are simpler and create outcomes faster than reality, a theme developed in other domains by Schön (1983) and Papert (1980). In complex dynamic systems, such as business systems, effective investigation of cause and effect requires a model representation of the business environment in which long-term consequences can be simulated. As argued above, the traditional case method must rely on faulty mental simulations for this function.

A second contribution model-supported cases can make to investigative skills is to develop skills in scientific method—hypothesis formation, experimental design, and critical evaluation of results. Computer simulations can be used to execute meaningful experiments designed to illuminate the structure and dynamics of the business environment, or to search for winning strategies with no idea as to why those strategies are effective. Many authors (Mass 1991; Senge 1990) suggest that effective learning depends on formation of clear expectations for the behavior of key variables *before* playing, coupled with careful explanations of discrepancies between expected and actual behavior *after* playing. Indeed, participants in the Sloan School's People Express exercise are asked to state explicit predictions (hypotheses) about the effects of policies, and discuss results afterward, and "Strategy Record Sheets" are provided for the purpose, much as scientists use lab notebooks.

Likewise, students in the Intecom case must specify in writing the dynamics they expect their strategies will generate before simulating them on the computer.

A third contribution of system dynamics to investigation is furnishing conceptual tools and results. System dynamics provides theory to explain how problems in complex systems arise, a language to describe them, and tools to relate system structure to behavior (Richardson and Pugh 1981; Lyneis 1980). These aid conceptualization of unfamiliar issues and often increase the effectiveness of investigation by providing a portfolio of archetypal structures that explain common system pathologies. For example, persistent cyclicality of production should prompt the analyst to seek negative feedback loops with significant delays between action and response (Sterman 1989b).

Finally, an important side effect of effective microworlds is fun. The learning process incorporates discovery, enjoyment, play, and sometimes competition. People can sustain interest in the subject matter, and the learning experience is more powerful and enduring.

Conceptualization and Abstraction

One advantage of the case study method is the real-life detail. Different types of information (numbers, descriptions, anecdotes, quotes, etc.) are mixed together. Information is available at many levels of analysis. The ability to deal with such information is critical to effective problem solving. But if the case materials have a truly realistic amount of detail, learning from the case becomes as difficult as learning from life. The primary contribution system dynamics makes to conceptualization skills is a set of well-developed tools and methods for moving between detailed descriptions of a situation and abstract representations. These tools include reference modes (graphs of the problematic behavior), causal-loop diagrams, stock-and-flow diagrams (such as those produced by STELLA), and policy structure diagrams (Richardson and Pugh 1981; Morecroft 1982).

The People Express case handles the conceptualization and abstraction process through a series of transitions from the detailed to the abstract: It begins with the written case (rich in detail, but little theory), moves to the briefing book (almost as rich in detail, but organized to show cause-and-effect structure more clearly), and then immerses learners in the simulation game (in which players control only a subset of the policy levers available to the real managers). The instructor may then analyze simulations (where decisions are replaced by decision rules and examination of the state of affairs at particular points in time is replaced by examination of system behavior over time), and finally, discuss behavioral principles.

The Intecom PBX case similarly uses a series of transitions, beginning with the detail-rich case and moving through stock-and-flow diagrams and policy structure diagrams that focus discussion on customer, sales force, and competitor behavior. The process likewise moves from the specific to the general: from small group discussion of migration strategy, to instructor-led consideration of simulations, and finally, to strategic lessons that relate simulated behavior to system structure. Recent experiments to involve management teams in conceptualization and model-based learning have also made specific use of transitions using conceptualization tools—moving from loosely structured discussion, to mapping, "friendly algebra," and ultimately simulation (Morecroft, Lane, and Viita 1989; Senge 1990).

Theory Application / Transfer Skills

Cases are taught not as exercises in historical analysis but so students may learn general principles applicable to new situations. Students must somehow extract general lessons from the cases they study and transfer them appropriately to problems they face as managers. Prior research suggests transfer of concepts from one situation to another is difficult, though some are more optimistic than others (Nisbett et al. 1987). A large literature suggests the traditional case method is not well suited to teaching systemic thinking and the ability to transfer insights from one problem to another (Kardes 1987; Nisbett et al. 1987; Bakken, Gould, and Kim 1992).

Both the People Express and Intecom workshops are designed to emphasize the applicability of the insights gained to other industries or firms. System dynamics provides tools that facilitate appropriate transfer of management insights. It emphasizes the importance of transfer and trains people to recognize the archetypal structures that explain common patterns of dynamic behavior in diverse systems (Graham 1977, 1988; Paich 1985). Just as the Porter or BCG frameworks supply generic strategies and structures that can be applied to a variety of different situations, the generic structures identified in system dynamics provide the student with interrelated templates they can transfer to actual cases. The conceptualization and analysis skills taught in system dynamics aid people in the prospective design of strategy by providing tools to highlight problematic patterns of dynamics, diagnose causes by identifying the generic feedback processes at work, and transfer insight about effective policies from these archetypal situations into the particular case.

EVALUATING THE EFFECTIVENESS OF MODEL-SUPPORTED CASES

Are model-supported case studies effective in teaching principles of business strategy analysis and systems thinking? Are they more effective than other methods? The closest analog to the model-supported cases described here are traditional management games. The purpose, protocols for, and technologies used in these games differ in significant ways from the model-supported case method presented here. Nevertheless, it is instructive that the literature on the effectiveness of management games paints a decidedly mixed picture. While many studies report favorable effects of games compared to traditional methods, others argue that games have no beneficial effect. Wheatley, Hornaday, and Hunt (1988), for example, found that students enjoy standard management games but argue that performance in the classroom and later life is not enhanced by games.

A key finding emerging from this literature is that game play alone is not sufficient for lasting learning. Neuhauser (1976) argues that the value of games comes from the process of building the model used in the game; thus the game designers find them interesting and useful while the learners who merely play the games may become bored and disenchanted. Toval and Flores (1987) make the same claim, and argue it is the process of model building that generates deep knowledge of the systems under study. Certainly this is the experience of professional model builders. Indeed, what emerges from the People Express, Intecom, and other model-supported cases is that learning comes from the full model-building experience, not primarily from simulation or game play. Model-building experience here means the full range of conceptualization, formulation, and testing that goes on, whether one employs a formal simulation or mental model. The People Express, Intecom, and other model-supported cases developed using system dynamics were explicitly designed to promote such modeling. Thus the negative results of many evaluations of prior management games do not apply. New evaluations of effectiveness are needed. Work on measurement methods is progressing in several projects. A number of evaluative studies are under way at MIT, including both students in the classroom and managers in organizations (Moissis 1989; Bakken 1989; Bakken, Gould, and Kim 1992 [Chapter 10 of this work]). The Educational Testing Service is currently attempting to define metrics for systems thinking to evaluate the effectiveness of system dynamics in high school curricula including physics, chemistry, and social studies (Mandinach and Cline 1993). Pilot programs are underway in several school districts in the United States (see the articles in "Systems Thinking in Education," a special issue of the *System Dynamics Review* edited by Janet Gould-Kreutzer [vol. 9 (2), Summer 1993] for a survey of approaches).

CONCLUSION

Effective management education is important to individuals, corporations, educational institutions, and ultimately, society in general. The preceding discussion strongly suggests that considerable improvement is available in management education. Computer-based case studies—models-with-cases—seem to offer considerable potential.

Moving forward with model-supported case studies will require collaboration among numerous stakeholders, including corporations and managers to fund, to serve as test sites for, and in some instances, to be final users of model-supported cases. Modelers and researchers are needed to create the cases and do the painstaking measurement necessary to establish their effectiveness. Universities must provide institutional support for research into management education and for integrating model-supported cases into the curriculum. The need is pressing; the prototypes already developed in universities and the private sector suggest the feasibility of the approach.

REFERENCES

Bakken, B. (1989), "Learning in Dynamic Simulation Games: Using Performance as a Measure," in P. Milling and E. Zahn, eds., *Computer-Based Management of Complex Systems,* Berlin: Springer-Verlag, 309-16.

Bakken, B. (1990), "Transfer of Learning in Cyclical Markets: An Experimental Approach," Working paper D-4166, System Dynamics Group, Sloan School of Management, MIT, Cambridge, Mass.

Bakken, B., J. Gould, and D. Kim (1992), "Experimentation in Learning Organizations: A Management Flight Simulator Approach," *European Journal of Operational Research* 59, no. 1: 167-82; also Chapter 10 of this work.

Brau, K. (1990), "A Computer-Based Case Study of Sun MicroSystems," MS Thesis, Sloan School of Management, MIT, Cambridge.

Brehmer, B. (1990), "Strategies in Real-Time, Dynamic Decision Making," in R. Hogarth, ed., *Insights in Decision Making,* Chicago: University of Chicago Press, 262-79.

Diehl, E.W. (1989), "A Study of Human Control in Stock-Adjustment Tasks," in P. Milling. and E. Zahn, eds., *Computer-Based Management of Complex Systems,* Berlin: Springer-Verlag, 205-12.

Graham, A. (1977), "Principles on the Relationship between Structure and Behavior of Dynamic Systems," Ph.D. Thesis, Department of Electrical Engineering and Computer Science, MIT, Cambridge.

Graham, A. (1988), "Generic Models as a Basis for Computer-based Case Studies," *Proceedings of the 1988 International System Dynamics Conference*, La Jolla, California. Also available as MIT System Dynamics Group Working Paper D-3947.

Ghemawat, P. (1986), "Intecom Teaching Note," Case Teaching Note 5-386-109, HBS Case Services, Boston, Mass.

Harvard Business School (1985), "People Express: Don Burr, Chairman and CEO, Question and Answer Session with an MBA Class," Video Tape 885-516, HBS Case Services, Boston, Mass.

Hax, A.C., and N.S. Majluf (1984), *Strategic Management: An Integrated Perspective,* Englewood Cliffs, N.J.: Prentice-Hall.

Holland, P., and M. Beer (1990), "People Express Airlines: Rise and Decline," N9-490-012. HBS Case Services, Boston, Mass.

Hogarth, R. (1987), *Judgment and Choice* (2d ed.), Chichester, U.K.: John Wiley.

Kahneman, D., P. Slovic, and A. Tversky (1982), *Judgment under Uncertainty: Heuristics and Biases,* Cambridge: Cambridge University Press.

Kardes, F. (1987), "The Case Method of Instruction and Managerial Decision Making," Working Paper, Sloan School of Management, MIT, Cambridge.

Kleinmuntz, D. (1985), "Cognitive Heuristics and Feedback in a Dynamic Decision Environment," *Management Science* 31, no. 6: 680-702.

Lyneis, J. (1980), *Corporate Planning and Policy Design*, Cambridge, Mass.: Pugh-Roberts Associates.

Mandinach, E., and H. Cline 1993), "Systems, Science, and Schools," *System Dynamics Review.* 9, no. 2: 195-206.

Mass, N. (1991), "Diagnosing Surprise Model Behavior," *System Dynamics Review* 7, no. 1: 68-86.

Merten, P., R. Löffler, and K.P. Wiedmann (1987), "Portfolio Simulation: A Tool to Support Strategic Management," *System Dynamics Review* 3, no. 2: 81-101.

Moissis, A. (1989), "Decision Making in the Insurance Industry: A Dynamic Simulation Model and Experimental Results," MS Thesis, Sloan School of Management, MIT, Cambridge.

Morecroft, J. (1982), "A Critical Review of Diagramming Tools for Conceptualizing Feedback System Models," *Dynamica* 8: 20-29.

Morecroft, J. (1984), "Strategy Support Models," *Strategic Management Journal* 5, no. 3: 215-29.

Morecroft, J. (1985), "Rationality in the Analysis of Behavioral Simulation Models," *Management Science* 31, no. 7: 900-16.

Morecroft, J. (1988), "System Dynamics and Microworlds for Policymakers," *European Journal of Operational Research* 35, no. 5: 301-20.

Morecroft, J. (1994), "Executive Knowledge, Models, and Learning," Chapter 1 of this work.

Morecroft, John D.W., David C. Lane, and Paul S. Viita (1989), "Modelling Growth Strategy in a Biotechnology Startup Firm," *System Dynamics Review* 7, no. 2: 93-116.

Neuhauser, J. (1976), "Business Games Have Failed," *Academy of Management Review* 1, no. 4: 124-29.

Nisbett, R., et al. (1987), "Teaching Reasoning," *Science* 238, no. 30: 625-31.

Paich, M. (1985), "Generic Structures," *System Dynamics Review* 1: 126-32.

Paich, M., and J.D. Sterman (1993), "Boom, Bust, and Failures to Learn in Experimental Markets." *Management Science* 39, no. 12: 1439-1458.

Papert, S. (1980), *Mindstorms*, New York: Basic Books.

Porter, M. (1980), *Competitive Strategy*, New York: Free Press.

Porter, M. (1985), *Competitive Advantage*, New York: Free Press.

Richardson, G.P., and A. Pugh (1981), *Introduction to System Dynamics Modeling With DYNAMO*, Portland, Ore.: Productivity Press..

Richmond, B., P. Vescuso, and S. Peterson (1987), *STELLA for Business*, High Performance Systems, 45 Lyme Road, Ste. 300, Hanover NH 03755.

Schön, D. (1983), *The Reflective Practitioner*, New York: Basic Books.

Senge, P. (1990), "Catalyzing Systems Thinking in Organizations," in F. Massaryk, ed., *Advances in Organization Development* , Norwood, N.J.: Ablex, 197-246.

Senge, P., and J. Sterman (1992), "Systems Thinking and Organizational Learning: Acting Locally and Thinking Globally in the Organization of the Future," *European Journal of Operational Research* 59, no. 1: 137-50; also Chapter 8 of this work.

Simon, H.A. (1979), "Rational Decision-Making in Business Organizations," *American Economic Review* 69: 493-513.

Sterman, J.D. (1987), "Testing Behavioral Simulation Models by Direct Experiment," *Management Science* 33, no. 12: 1572-1592.

Sterman, J. (1988), "People Express Management Flight Simulator," software and documentation available from J. Sterman, Sloan School of Management, MIT, Cambridge MA 02142.

Sterman, J. (1989a), "Misperceptions of Feedback in Dynamic Decision Making," *Organizational Behavior and Human Decision Processes* 43, no. 3: 301-35.

Sterman, J. (1989b), "Modeling Managerial Behavior: Misperceptions of Feedback in a Dynamic Decision Making Experiment," *Management Science* 35, no. 3: 321-39.

Toval, A., and M. Flores (1987), "Computer Systems Simulation in Education: Description of an Experience," *Computers and Education* 11, no. 4: 293-303.

Wheatley, W., R. Hornaday, and T. Hunt (1988), "Developing Strategic Management Goal-Setting Skills," *Simulation and Games* 19, no. 2: 173-85.

Whitestone, D. (1983), "People Express (A)," HBS Case Services, #483 - 103, Cambridge, Mass.

10

EXPERIMENTATION IN LEARNING ORGANIZATIONS: A MANAGEMENT FLIGHT SIMULATOR APPROACH

Bent Bakken, Janet Gould, and Daniel Kim

ABSTRACT: Managers' real-life experiences will need to be supported by new learning tools as external environments and internal dynamics of organizations become more complex. This need for simulated managerial experience has come from a trend towards fewer hierarchical levels in organizations. Managerial competency that was once achieved by progressing through many layers needs to be obtained through other means. This article shows how management flight simulators can enhance learning by allowing managers to compress time and space, experiment with various strategies, and learn from simulated deployments by reflecting on the outcomes. We focus on three aspects of the use of such simulators: (1) the design of a generic learning *process*—learning laboratories—to address service quality management issues in a variety of industrial settings; (2) how dimensions of this learning can be operationalized and *measured*; and (3) an experimental study that shows the *transfer* aspect of learning and how different learning strategies affect the way in which participants *transfer* learning across domains.

INTRODUCTION

Organizational decision making is highly complex and managerial choices are far from trivial. The fact that people have a hard time learning from real-life experiences compounds the problem, especially when the decisions and their consequences are separated in time and space. One of New England's largest banks provides an illustration of how difficult learning from experience can be. The bank's aggressive pursuit of ship-owning clients in the seventies led to huge losses in shipping portfolios in the early eighties. Massive losses led the bank to liquidate its entire shipping portfolio. At the same time, however, they aggressively expanded into risky real estate developments. In the late eighties, their real estate ventures resulted in quarterly losses of up to one billion dollars. These losses eventually caused the bank's ultimate demise in 1991. Although shipping and real estate markets share many structural features and are unstable for similar reasons, this bank was apparently unable to learn from their mistakes in shipping and repeated them in real estate (Bakken 1990).

This example not only highlights how difficult it is to learn causal relations in one decision environment, but also shows that decision makers do not easily draw appropriate lessons from failures. Certainly, people must simplify their decision environments into manageable chunks, lest decision making be impossible (Simon 1956, 1978). Yet, these simplifications do not work very well—people are poor intuitive judges and tend to violate almost all rules of rationality and consistency (Kahnemann and Tversky 1974). Decisions are prone to error even in quite simple contexts (Brehmer 1989; Sterman 1989). People often fail to grasp the power of exponential growth and pay too little attention to supply line information.

In experiments as well as in real organizational settings, decision makers have access to feedback about the appropriateness of actions (Einhorn and Hogarth 1978). As our bank example shows, however, the feedback interpretation in slowly evolving environments is far from straightforward. Many causal inferences are possible, and only an experimental approach can sort out the many competing explanations. Unfortunately, organizational life does not lend itself readily to experimental testing, leaving organizations and their members to construct meanings out of what they experience. Many organizational researchers have come to the same conclusion—organizational environments and meanings are not given, but constructed. In this construction process, intra-organizational defense mechanisms come into play, and as a consequence, people bias their choice of information sources (Argyris and Schön 1978; Weick 1977) thus preventing learning from taking place.

The use of feedback can be effective only if cause and effect are closely related in time and space, but real decision environments lack this closeness between decisions and meaningful feedback. In real estate markets, for example, it takes three to four years from the time a decision to build an office building is made until people can move into the building. In the meantime, markets may have changed significantly. Although the Total Quality movement has successfully capitalized on feedback information by making cause and effect closer in time and space (Kim 1989), there are many instances where shortening feedback cycle times is difficult. As the real estate case shows, there are important physical constraints on how fast feedback can become available.

Current changes in corporate structuring, such as de-layering of management levels, suggest that learning from real-world experience will become increasingly more problematic. A beneficial outcome of such recent trends toward flatter organizational structures is that feedback delays are shortened, making organizations more responsive. Fewer hierarchical levels, however, mean that there are fewer "training steps" on the corporate ladder. Instead of spending decades in the same organization at various levels of responsibility, the "lean and mean" organization catapults the typical manager into decision-making authority much sooner and without the extensive experience typically associated with senior decision makers.

Thus, problems inherent in learning from unguided organizational experience are compounded by ever scarcer time available for learning at a time when increasing interdependencies make learning more important. The problem is further heightened in cases where real-life feedback cycles are much longer than the decision-making cycle. In such cases, computerized management flight simulators can provide virtual worlds in which assumptions, relationships, and outcomes can be tested, thereby shortening the feedback cycle time in situations where delays are inherently long.

A management flight simulator is a learning tool that allows managers to compress time and space, experiment with various strategies, and learn from making rounds of simulated decisions. Embedded in specially designed learning environments called learning labs, these simulators can be designed to provide organizational "practice fields" (Senge 1990) where managers can experiment and learn in environments that allow failure and reflection.

PHILOSOPHY OF THE LEARNING ORGANIZATION AND THE ROLE OF FLIGHT SIMULATORS

Increasingly, attention is being focused on finding ways to make corporations more responsive to customers and enable them to provide higher quality products (de Geus 1988; Stata 1989). A "learning organization" is characterized by its attention to enhancing thinking processes that lay behind decision making. Furthermore, learning is encouraged through experimentation and testing in virtual worlds (Senge 1990). Although learning organizations have attributes along many dimensions, the interesting point for our purposes is that (a) they have an exploratory attitude, and (b) current solutions and processes are open to questioning (Argyris and Schön 1978). Organizations need to experiment in both production and management processes while balancing the need to be as close to the implementation world as possible.

As mentioned earlier, management flight simulators can be used in situations where real-life experimentation is unfeasible because of cost considerations, time involvement, or both. They can be regarded as a framing tool for dynamic issues, often referred to as transitional objects (Papert 1981). Moreover, thinking can be more structured and discussions more productive, since discussions can be focused around a computer model that helps depersonalize assumptions and makes them less threatening.

For the same reasons that we find flight simulators appealing—they are low cost, allow compression of time and space, and are conducive to reflection—there is a long tradition in the arts, sciences, and professions of using similar "virtual worlds" (Schön 1983). In fact, in technical professions, while "virtual worlds" have always existed, recent advances in simulations and other tools have made them ever more powerful. With the exception of spreadsheet analysis on personal computers, however, little has been made of virtual worlds for improving managerial practice. This lack of the widespread use of management simulators may be attributable to two flaws—most are either too simplistic to feel "real" or too complex to learn from. Simulators based on system dynamics overcome these polar extremes by providing a framework with which participants can make sense of complexity and by producing realistic and challenging dynamics (Vennix 1990). Management flight simulators can help in sorting out competing explanations by allowing participants to conduct experiments and learn from them.

In this chapter, we provide an in-depth look into the organizational processes by which simulator learning can be achieved. In doing so, we emphasize the need to provide a nonthreatening environment. The section below shows our underlying theory for designing and running simulator-based workshops. A generic service-quality, management flight simulator is used as a tool for questioning assumptions that impede learning in the real organizational setting. In the section titled "Measurement of Flight Simulator Learning," we define the dimensions of simulator-based learning and how to measure the learning. Several types of instruments are described. In the final section, "Transfer of Insights," we focus on the transfer dimension of such learning.

DESIGNING A REFLECTIVE LEARNING ENVIRONMENT

In order for management flight simulators to be effective learning tools, they must be designed into an environment that is conducive to learning. Without such an environment, the simulators become more of a management video game, and the goal becomes one of beating the highest score. The goal of a learning laboratory is to provide an environment that will help enrich managers' mental models using tools such as the management simulators. Learning laboratories help managers leverage their domain-rich knowledge by allowing them to play through simulated years, reflect on their actions, modify their mental models, then repeat the process. By compressing time and space, flight simulators can accelerate learning by enabling them to conduct many such cycles of action and reflection.

The impetus for designing such a learning laboratory originally came out of a study conducted at a major property and casualty insurance company. (Geraldine Prusko and Robert Bergin of Hanover Insurance were largely responsible for the overall design of the initial learning laboratories at this insurance company.) The goal of the design team was to create an environment in which managers could step out of day-to-day demands to reflect on their decision making (for a complete description, refer to Senge and Sterman in this work, Chapter 8). In addition, managers would also develop a common language, learn new tools for thinking systemically, discuss operational objectives and strategies in an open forum, test operating assumptions, experiment with new ideas about managing a claims office, and have fun while doing it.

A Generic Learning Laboratory Design

To leverage the benefits derived from a case-specific lab, such as the insurance claims learning lab, both the computer game and the workshop design were modified to be more generally applicable. What follows is a description of a generic learning laboratory on service quality management that has been adapted from the original claims learning laboratory design. This generic design can be used as the basis for creating other learning laboratories in domains outside the insurance industry. In addition to design issues, process points are also included to help the reader gain a better feel for the learning laboratory experience.

The overall design of the service quality management learning laboratory has four distinct stages: context setting, conceptualization, experimentation, and reflection. Each of the stages will be described.

Context Setting. Workshop leaders in the learning laboratory are positioned from the outset as "enablers," not authority figures. The participants are encouraged to challenge the assumptions of the model that underlies the simulators used in the learning lab. This openness to challenge and to test is critical for establishing a common understanding between workshop leaders and participants. The learning laboratory is positioned not as an answer generator but as a useful vehicle for illuminating and communicating issues of importance. Participants are also encouraged to share any reservations or concerns they may have about the laboratory with the rest of the group. These steps emphasize the experimental aspect of the laboratory and encourage participants to challenge their own operating assumptions.

In small groups, participants are asked to identify a specific industry setting where service quality management is important. The service can be an internal service or one with external customers. There are five key variables that the participants must fill in with specific factors that are relevant for their chosen industry setting. They must identify the personnel and customers, the service, and the direct costs and cost of poor quality. For example, in a banking industry context (see Table 10-1), personnel would be loan officers, the customers would be individual or business borrowers, the service "product" would be various types of loans, the direct costs would be personnel expenses including overhead, and the cost of poor quality would result in expenses resulting from loan delinquencies.

Table 10-1. Examples of various contexts used in a generic learning lab on Service Quality Management

Variables	Context			
	Insurance claims office	Bank Loan office	Engineering department	Internal training and development
Personnel	adjusters	loan officers	engineers	sales training staff
Customer	claimants	individuals, companies, developers	internal producers of designed components	world sales management group
Service	adjusting losses	loans	engineer traction control systems	comprehensive dynamic training
Direct costs	employee salaries, and overhead	employee salaries, ovwerhead, transaction	salaries, testing time, prototype materials, testing equipment	sales training budget, participant travel expense
Cost of poor quality	high settlement costs, including litigation expenses	non-performing loans, defaults	re-do job, missed schedules customer satisfaction, warranty costs, cost overruns	wasted time of attendees, poor sales service to external customers, lost sales

Working in small groups, the participants are asked to brainstorm and come up with the setting and variables described above. The overall purpose of this exercise is to have everyone think in terms of specific issues that they can personally relate to and establish a common understanding of the industry setting the learning laboratory is intended to address.

Conceptualizing the Issues. The groups of participants are asked to define what quality is within the context they have chosen and to identify the key factors that determine quality. Causal-loop diagramming tools are introduced as a way of representing the interconnectedness of a system. With each round of conceptualizing, small portions of the causal structure embodied in the simulator model are presented as a way of connecting the tool to the issues at hand.

Participants then focus on a particular issue (such as one of the decision variables in the flight simulator) and (1) determine the key factors that affect that variable; (2) sketch patterns of behavior; (3) provide structural explanations (using causal-loop diagrams); and (4) identify possible intervention points. One person in each group is responsible for presenting the work to the entire group. This process is then repeated, addressing a different issue.

Conceptualizing these variables, the participants draw from their domain-specific experience and explicate their mental models. At the same time, the participants are replicating part of the model-building process, making it easier to accept and identify with the pre-developed model as it becomes less and less of a black box. Each presenter "tells a story" with a causal-loop diagram and illustrates with a real-world example, if possible. This process helps participants develop the ability to articulate causal structures to other people. The overall objective in this stage is to have the group cover all the major issues contained in the management flight simulator and have a chance to challenge and test the interrelationships that different people within the group may propose.

Experimentation and Reflection: "Flying" the Flight Simulator. Participants are then grouped in teams of two and are instructed to pursue a single-minded goal where they are accountable for meeting one particular goal (e.g., maintaining headcount). In these planned scenarios, they are told in advance that there will be a one-time 20 percent step increase in workload. For each simulated month, three decisions must be made—hiring, desired production, and quality goal. The hiring decision is for adding or reducing the number of personnel. Setting desired production at 1.00 translates into asking the employees to have the outflow of work equal the inflow of new work received for each month. A productivity goal of less than 1.00 means the backlog of customers is growing since we are servicing less than the number coming in. The quality goal can be entered directly as a decision point where a quality level of 1.00 is simply a starting reference point against which one can gauge improvements or deterioration.

These planned scenarios allow the group to gain experience slowly by trying a very focused strategy through which they can get a feel for the dynamics of the simulator. Optimally, the debriefing structure encourages more reflection in every phase of the process—strategizing, managing within the simulator, and debriefing the outcomes. A more important underlying purpose is to begin addressing particular organizational issues through appropriate choices of planned scenarios—continually connecting refinements in mental models back to their work domain.

In later sessions, the participants manage their simulated offices where they have no *a priori* knowledge of how the stream of new customers is going to change. In both the planned scenarios and the free plays, each team is asked to do the following for every trial: (1) Plan a strategy and commit to it on paper; (2) predict the consequences of executing the strategy by sketching in behavior over time of some key variables; (3) play the game; and (4) debrief the game results and explain them to the rest of the group.

The discipline of planning a strategy and sketching out anticipated behavior in advance is important because it forces them to get in the habit of making their mental models explicit. The written records also provide a basis for comparing the actual outcome of each trial. By making such comparisons, gaps in thinking or failures to follow through an intended strategy are highlighted.

Surfacing Hidden Assumptions

If we view learning as a process where an *action —> result —> reflection —> learning* leads back to further *action,* flight simulators can facilitate learning by shortening the delay between *action—>result.* The simulator also demands structural explanations of the *action—>result* link that will force participants to search for a better understanding of the underlying forces that produce a given set of outcomes. The design of the learning laboratory also increases *reflection* and enhances *learning* out of which better decisions can arise.

How can the learning laboratory be used to engage the participants in what Argyris and Schön (1978) refer to as double-loop learning? *Double-loop learning* is defined as "those sorts of organizational inquiry that resolve incompatible organizational norms by setting new priorities and weightings of norms, or by restructuring the norms themselves with associated strategies and assumptions." Double-loop learning involves surfacing and challenging deep-rooted assumptions and norms of an organization that have previously been inaccessible.

The learning laboratory can help advance double-loop learning by providing a unique forum in which operating norms and assumptions can be questioned in a nonthreatening way, by experimenting with the computer simulator. For example, in a company that professedly emphasized pursuing high quality standards, the behavior in the simulator trials showed that controlling expenses dominated people's actions. One manager remarked that while playing the game "I kept telling myself, 'don't add to staff,' even though there is no one telling me not to *and* knowing that I really need to!" In many cases, when people discovered they had extra capacity, they chose to cut staff or push for more production to reduce expenses, instead of pushing for quality.

When given an office setting where quality was twice as high as in all previous scenarios, the vast majority decided to cut staff. In the short term, they reaped the benefit of lower expense costs, but those savings were dwarfed by the heavier losses incurred due to poor quality. In the insurance company claims learning lab, when asked why they had decided to cut staff, most replied that they felt the office was like a country club. They pointed to the number of claims in "backlog per adjuster" and number of "claims settled per adjuster" and stated that the workload was incredibly light. They expressed matter-of-factly that the right numbers should be twice what they were. When asked what made those the right numbers, they invariably paused, and replied sheepishly with the only answer that they coulf, "Because it's always been that way." In that instant, they realized how an unquestioned assumption had driven their decision making and may have contributed to poor performance.

The use of management flight simulators in learning laboratories advances double-loop learning by providing people with a framework for clarifying their mental models. Through the process of cycling through many rounds of decision making and rethinking their mental models, managers gain insights into their domain-specific issues. Although we have only anecdotal evidence linking "better management thinking" to better total cost or profit numbers, learning laboratories have great potential for helping managers reassess the way they think about their business. In the following section, we begin to address the measurement of this potential.

MEASUREMENT OF FLIGHT SIMULATOR LEARNING

Although the learning laboratories appear to have helped managers be more aware of their own mental models, further evidence is needed to determine the effectiveness of management flight simulators in improving actual decision making. A three-day system dynamics seminar for managers, held at a major computer manufacturer, has provided the opportunity to pilot test a number of instruments that were designed to gather experimental data about learning transfer after exposure to a system dynamics seminar and learning laboratory. The goal of the system dynamics seminar is for the managers to learn the concepts and then transfer them back to the work place.

Learning Objectives

The managers used the People Express Airline Management Flight Simulator (see Graham et al. in Chapter 9 of this work for a description of this simulator) during the seminar. They also read the case materials, and were taught to use causal loop diagrams to conceptualize about the feedback structure of People Express organization and its competitive environment. We expected to observe three levels of learning: understanding of the People Express case issues, understanding of the underlying feedback structure, and transferring insights to another domain.

Attaining the first level of learning means that managers have identified the basic organizational issues that led to the failure of People Express. They may explain, for example, that the low price offered by People Express created a huge demand for flights that could not be fulfilled with their existing service capacity. Their failure to expand service capacity rapidly led to poor service quality that eventually resulted in the demise of People Express.

The second level of learning requires managers to explain at a deeper level, linking the observed behavior to the underlying feedback structure of People Express. They should be able to articulate short-term versus long-term tradeoffs in the system and recognize the link between system structure and dynamic behavior.

At the third level of learning, managers should be able to transfer the systems insights gained from studying People Express to other cases. For example, they should be able to recognize the same "attractiveness principle" (described later) that operated in the People Express case when it surfaces in another case with a different cover story (i.e., not about an airline). For this article, we focus on this third level of learning and the role of the management flight simulator.

Effectiveness

The issue of effectiveness of the seminars and learning laboratory arises because we do not understand *which* thinking processes change or *how* they are changed by the training intervention. Unlike basic skills training, such as typing or computer repair, where success is measured by the student being able to perform the task, learning of system dynamics principles is not as easily evaluated. System dynamics training encompasses multiple levels of knowledge acquisition, from the basic skills level to higher levels of abstraction.

Measuring learning along certain dimensions is easier than along others. At a basic skills level, instruments can be used to measure a manager's ability to create a simple causal-loop diagram. At a more abstract level, determining the manager's understanding of a complete feedback structure and his ability to transfer that knowledge to another case is difficult to measure. In the People Express management flight simulator, cumulative net income is a good indicator of *game* performance, but *management* performance is not easily quantified in this way. Management performance is multifaceted and dynamic. Measurements must capture the skills developed from the basic to the abstract, as well as the transformation of the mental model as new skills are learned.

The research on simulation and games has generated controversy about the role and effectiveness of simulations in management education. Effectiveness of simulations is not yet proven. Early research on the transfer of case knowledge, in which no simulation or game is used, has shown that little transfer occurs when analogous problems are presented concurrently. Even less transfer may occur when problems are separated by a span of months or years. This suggests that prior experience in solving problems may not be used by managers faced with new manifestations of analogous problems. Also, knowledge gained from experience may be misapplied because irrelevant associations may be formed between a term mentioned in a case problem and a term in an existing problem (Kardes 1987).

Case analysis alone may not be sufficient for transfer of learning, but we suggest that a case analysis coupled with a game or simulator may improve the likelihood of transfer. Other evidence has suggested that participation in a management game provides increased learning, more favorable attitude, and higher levels of interest and motivation that are not achieved when working with a case alone (Raia 1966). Further research will determine the degree to which a game approximates real-world policy making situations, whether students learn the "right" things from the game experience, and whether game knowledge is efficiently transferred to the real world (Wolfe 1976).

According to Wolfe, effectiveness research must deal with all the different situation variables that have an impact on the gaming application. These include

1. game design characteristics, such as single function versus functionally integrative, complexity, algorithm validity/face validity, and random events;

2. administration characteristics, including starting position, team size, team selection, team accountability, duration, pacing, trial or practice runs, debriefing, within-course placement, and learning objectives;

3. player and group characteristics, consisting of motivation, aptitude and achievement, attitude, cognitive style, participation, decision-making method, and team structure; and

4. administrator characteristics, such as game experience and involvement, motivation, and subject matter familiarity.

Instrument Design

The system dynamics seminar, the People Express simulator, and the instruments were designed to respond to many of Wolfe's criticisms of earlier effectiveness research. For example, the People Express game was tested with many managers and students to make the interface both simple to use and realistic in emulating a typical management information system. The set-up of the seminar allowed for random assignments of teams and debriefings at each transition. Surveys and questionnaires were used to gather data about player characteristics (age, education, and prior systems experience), measure attitude, and gather some data on cognitive style. The seminar and game administrators were specifically chosen for their substantial system dynamics teaching experience and their high level of motivation.

The instruments used included surveys, questionnaires, strategy sheets, verbal protocols during game plays, game performance data, and causal-loop diagrams. The instruments have been designed to gather data on:

1. prior experience with system dynamics;

2. case understanding (using a written examination that measured knowledge of the People Express domain);

3. performance in the People Express management flight simulator (for example, a comparison between groups of the average cumulative net income at the end of a game);

4. verbalization of systems concepts using protocol analysis while playing the game;

5. strategy sheets used while playing the game, which can demonstrate the use of the system dynamics framework when other measures may not;

6. a team's development of causal-loop diagrams (representing their understanding of the feedback structure);

7. the transfer of systems insights about People Express to other cases; and

8. reflections on learning after participating in the entire seminar (Gould 1989).

The Three Questionnaires

Although many instruments were used, we limit our discussion to three specific questionnaires designed to test for learning transfer. Table 10-2 shows the sequence of the seminar and when the questionnaires (Q1, Q2, and Q3) were administered. The difficulty of transferring insights from the People Express case to other cases increases with each subsequent questionnaire.

The first questionnaire was designed to capture the manager's ability to recognize the most important issues faced by People Express after reading the case study materials and participating in a discussion. The manager was then expected to transfer the lessons learned from the People Express case materials to another case. Examples of the questions used in the questionnaires are found below.

The second questionnaire was administered after Group A conceptualized about People Express (i.e., created the causal-loop diagrams) and after Group B played the People Express game. Questionnaire 2 was designed to demonstrate the manager's ability to apply knowledge of the system dynamics framework to People Express as well as transfer the framework to another case. Each Group had a different experi-

Table 10-2. The two-group, pretest/posttest research design

Group A	Introduction to systems thinking	Q1	Introduction to People Express	Conceptualize	Q2	Play game	Q3	Advanced causal-loop diagramming session
Group B				Play game		Conceptualize		

ence before they answered questionnaire 2. This design allows us to compare the results based on each group's experience with the system dynamics framework. The conceptualizing process makes the framework an explicit part of the discussion. Playing with the management flight simulator does not include a discussion of how the flight simulator was designed using the system dynamics framework.

The third questionnaire was used after each group had conceptualized and played the game. This allows us to determine any effects from the sequence of experience using the system dynamics framework.

There are fourteen questions on the three questionnaires. There are four different types of questions as diagrammed in Table 10-3. We would expect that the quadrant II and III questions would be easier for the manager to answer correctly than quadrant IV questions. Each question was designed to measure the transfer of the system dynamics framework from the original People Express case to the new cases.

It is expected that questions with the same cover story and feedback structure encourage transfer more than questions with a different cover story and different feedback structure. Questions with a similar cover story but a different feedback structure may result in a misperception of the feedback structure because of the similarity of the cover story. When the cover story is different, but the feedback structure is the same, the managers may have trouble transferring their knowledge of the feedback structure because they are misled by the new cover story. When the cover story and feedback structure are different from the original case, the new case may be perceived to be an entirely new problem with no relationship to the original case, and thereby may decrease the likelihood of transfer.

In addition to the four types of questions in Table 10-3, the first question on each questionnaire was:

Why did People Express fail?

This question was used to measure any changes in response resulting from participation in the different phases of the seminar.

Each case example on the questionnaires was designed to reveal an underlying system dynamics feedback structure. The managers were taught about the "attractiveness principle" structure of People Express by participating in the discussions in the seminar and by playing the game. The "attractiveness principle" states that compensating changes in the components of attractiveness explain many past failures; frequently one aspect of a system is improved only to discover that other aspects have become worse. In the People Express case an increase in the availabil-

Table 10-3. Types of questions asked of the participants of the seminar

	Same cover story	Different cover story
Same feedback structure	I	II
Different feedback structure	III	IV

ity of flights reduced the quality of service because of the increased demand and shortage of service capacity. Because organizational resources are limited, it is impossible to increase the quantity and quality of everything for everyone. It is only through the deliberate manipulation of counterbalancing effects that control can be gained over the changing system. The attractiveness of flying People Express led to exponential growth in demand for seats. Many pressures develop to stop growth; some we can influence others we cannot. If pressures are alleviated where possible, growth will continue until it produces a further rise in the pressures that cannot be controlled (Mass 1974).

If people actually learned the attractiveness principle, we would expect them to apply that knowledge to the other cases on the questionnaires. Examples of two questions used in the questionnaires follow.

Each question on the questionnaires was designed to be an example of a short case. The following question is an example of a question from quadrant II. It has a similar feedback structure to People Express ("attractiveness principle"), but a different cover story (i.e., not about an airline).

> Commuting by car to downtown Boston from the suburbs takes much longer now than it did a decade ago. The state is now planning to construct a new expanded highway system to increase access to the downtown area. What effects will this have on the commute time? Is this case related in any way to the People Express Case? Explain.

An adequate response to this question would show an understanding of the "attractiveness principle," and would lead the manager to suggest that overcrowding will be reduced in the short term, but in the long run the highway will again be crowded because of the increased attractiveness of commuting on the new highway.

The question below is an example of a question from quadrant IV. It has a similar cover story to People Express, but a different feedback structure.

> Northeast Airlines has a small fleet that serves passengers traveling to small airports throughout the New England, New York, Pennsylvania and New Jersey area. Northeast is known as a high quality airline, but has grown very slowly during the past decade. The Vice President just left the company after a dispute with the CEO. The VP had tried to persuade the CEO to expand into an airport that was to be available soon in southern New Hampshire. This region was not served by Northeast. The CEO resisted. An Air Force base in southern New Hampshire will be decommissioned soon, and will be converted for civilian use. Commercial airlines will be able to lease terminal space. The landing field will accommodate planes as large as a DC8. Northeast has enough lead-time for planning their entrance into the market. Preliminary market research shows that Northeast has a good reputation within the new market. Northeast will need to add staff and purchase more planes for a total expansion of about 50 percent. The CEO thinks this expansion is too big for the company to absorb. He believes Northeast's high quality over the past decade is a result of his cautious, slow growth strategy. Should the CEO have listened to the VP's advice? Explain. Is this case related in any way to the People Express case? Explain.

Unlike People Express, where the "attractiveness principle" dominates, the former VP of Northeast Airlines may have suggested the correct policy. By expanding capacity before the increase in expected sales of seats, the VP may have expected that attractiveness in a new market with the proper advanced planning would lead to a successful business and lessen the immediate effect of the "attractiveness principle."

Preliminary Results

Pilot testing the instruments described above has helped identify areas of weakness and opportunities for improvement. The method of repeating the same question on each questionnaire (i.e., Why did People Express fail?), for example, led the managers to believe that a change in their response was expected on each questionnaire and could therefore bias the results. The wording of the simple case questions, which were designed to measure transfer, could be misleading. For example, not all managers would agree that the People Express and the Northeast Airlines cases represent examples of organizations with a similar cover story, but a different underlying structure. The instruments need further refinements to address these issues.

Despite these problems with the instruments, an initial review of the questionnaires shows that some managers are able to use the system dynamics feedback terminology and demonstrate evidence of system dynamics thinking. For example, the question about the Boston highway expansion yielded this response from one manager:

> In a short time more cars will fill the highway with a minimal decrease in commute time. It may even take longer as better highways increase housing development.

As anticipated, the response to the Northeast Airlines question showed little transfer.

In addition to the problems with the instrument design itself, the corporate setting creates many measurement control problems. The shortage of computers requires that managers work in teams while playing the game. The team discussions may improve performance for some managers and not for others. Managers frequently leave the seminar to respond to inquiries. Therefore, there is no assurance that all managers receive the same treatment. These issues further compromise our ability to separate the effects of playing the game versus conceptualizing. Although evidence of transfer appears on the questionnaires, instrument redesign and a controlled research setting may further our understanding of the effects of the system dynamics framework on management performance.

The next section of this paper uses management flight simulators with managers and students in a laboratory setting, which improves the experimental control. The simulators and debriefings are the only intervention and therefore allow us to determine more precisely the effect of the simulator on the transfer of learning across different settings.

TRANSFER OF INSIGHTS

Enriching professionals' mental models as far as dynamic interactions are concerned is not an end in itself. On the contrary, we can only argue that increasing people's ability to grasp dynamic complexity is desirable if it serves some concrete purpose. The purpose is, of course, increased competency and improved organizational decision making. Both benefits assume that people can transfer insights achieved in a laboratory situation. There are two dimensions to this transfer, transfer from workshop to work place and transfer from one workshop environment to another. The first transfer dimension depends on, but is not limited to, the second. In this section, we describe an experiment that investigates how students and professionals transfer differently from one management flight simulator to another.

MBA students and young professionals interacted with real estate and oil tanker simulators in an experimental study. These two markets were chosen for several reasons. First, time lags create substantial delays between desired and actual stocks of capacity in both cases. Second, both markets exhibit a short-time decision focus. Third, learning is problematic and market instabilities may persist for long periods of time (Hernandez 1991).

Experimental and Real Markets

Two computerized decision-making games were designed with cover stories depicting them as a world market for oil tanker transportation and an office real estate market. The feedback structures underlying both games (shown in Figure 10-1) are identical. The dynamic behavior arises from the fact that investors invest when expected operating profits are high and, conversely, do not invest when low profits are expected. Instabilities in these markets are accentuated by participants not accounting sufficiently for assets under construction (Hernandez 1991; Sterman 1989). In both markets demand is insensitive to price fluctuations whereas supply is very price sensitive. This causes instability and overinvestment.

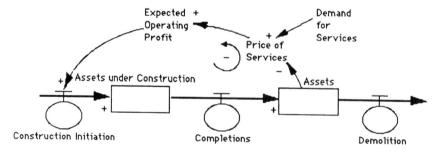

Figure 10-1. The main feedback structure of the market. The negative "loop" indicates that it is goalseeking, i.e., there is a tendency to balance demand and supply of services.

The simulated markets were identical with the exception of variable names and parameter values. One such difference is the higher substitutability in the real estate market, which makes this market more stable than the tanker market. Another difference is the average completion time for "Assets under Construction," which is longer in the tanker market. As a consequence, the shipping market exhibits more pronounced fluctuations. Though the construction cycle is far from a well-tuned pendulum clock, Figures 10-2 and 10-3 show that the element of industry cyclicality has persisted over the years. The results generated in the flight simulators were very similar to these historical time series.

The market for oil tanker transportation exhibits dynamics that are similar to those of the real estate industry, but instabilities are more dramatic. Prices show periods of calm when there exists slack capacity. However, when capacity utilization creeps above equilibrium, prices become highly erratic. In fact, when capacity utilization is low, the market is equilibrated by "mothballing" tankers, but when capacity utilization is high, transportation rates fluctuate to clear the markets.

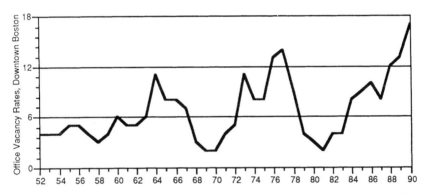

Figure 10-2. Office vacancy rates in percent, Boston (Boston Redevelopment Authority 1989)

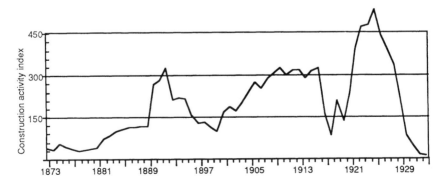

Figure 10-3. Construction activity in Chicago (percent of long-run trend) (Hoyt 1933)

Procedure

In the study reported here, the players were mostly current or future MBAs. Seventeen were students at MIT's Sloan School of Management. The students participated *individually* and were paid according to their performance. The other group consisted of 32 professionals from major corporations. Most had two to ten years' work experience in addition to an MBA degree. Several had long experience in one of the two markets. They played in *teams of two,* and the results of the 16 teams are included here.

The students were given monetary incentives, whereas the professionals took part in day-long seminars where the game-playing was an early, yet integral part of reflective exercises that culminated in a discussion session. Since these discussions took place after game-playing, the game-playing procedure itself was identical and comparable across both groups.

All participants first read a two-page newspaper article about market conditions portrayed in the first game. In addition, all subjects read a briefing book about the simulator before interacting with the computer. Then the game-playing started. Subjects were randomly assigned to the real estate or the oil tanker condition. Players were instructed to start again in the event of bankruptcy. If they did not go bankrupt, they continued until the game stopped. All full trials lasted 40 periods (the players were not informed in advance about the length of a trial). Two complete trials were completed within the first market condition. After a break, all players were given a two-page article about the other market, i.e., the transfer market, and asked to participate in that market until they had completed at least one full trial.

All participants were asked to maximize profits in each game. The student players were rewarded for average performance in all games they played ($4 per hour). In addition, they were given a performance bonus that amounted to $110 for the participant with the highest average profit. Instead of monetary rewards, the professionals had to announce their results publicly to their peers after the sessions, and that was apparently a strong incentive to perform well.

Results

Game performance can be a good indicator of how well players understand a cyclical market. Research in a similar setting has shown a positive relationship between performance and understanding of underlying feedback structure (Bakken 1990). In Figure 10-4, we see that students go bankrupt twice as frequently as professionals before they finish their first full, 40-decision, trial. Analysis of other potential differences, such as real-world experience in the simulated market, did not make any difference in game-playing strategy or outcome. Additionally, results showed no difference between subjects who started with Real Estate and continued with Oil Tankers and those who played the games in the reversed order.

Figure 10-5 shows that average performance in early trials is similar for both groups, and that both groups have transferred insights from the first to the second simulator. Transfer performance among the students, however, is markedly better than the professionals. The higher number of bankruptcies by the student group indicates that a different strategy was employed. In general, players who go bankrupt make more decisions than people who succeed in finishing a full round without going bankrupt. A high number of bankruptcies indicates that a player has an exploratory attitude and a willingness to make risky decisions. Bankruptcies impede performance initially, but provide valuable decision-making experience. In the long run, this exploratory decision-making style helps develop a deeper understanding that proves beneficial in the transfer game.

Why Are Professionals Less Exploratory?

What explains the apparent differences in decision-making strategy between the students and the professionals? One reason could be that students played individually while professionals played in teams of two. Since aversion to risk is higher in

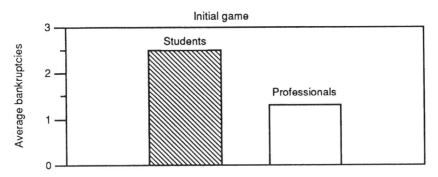

Figure 10-4. Students go bankrupt more often

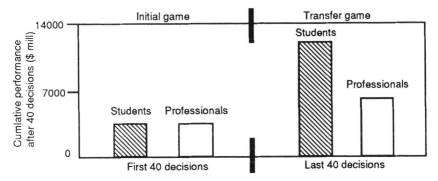

Figure 10-5. Students do as well as professionals, initially, and transfer better

team decision making, the consensus needed for team decision making reduces risk to the most risk-averse of the team players. In addition, our experimental results indicate that although every effort was made to ensure a nonthreatening environment, professionals still feel restricted. As we mentioned in the previous section, participants tend to use known (real-world) strategies to anchor their decisions. The same embedded routines that hinder exploration in the real world can also prevent exploration and learning in the simulated environment.

Another possible explanation for the difference in exploratory attitude is that the simulated environment poses more threat to professionals than to students. A hidden underlying assumption appears to be: "I know a lot about this market, so I just do in the game what I do in real life." Though fairly safe, such an attitude is counterproductive to learning since it fails to benefit from the experimental approach facilitated by the laboratory setting. Students' game playing strategy, on the other hand, seems to be more playful. They appear to use the information available in the game as a springboard for investigation into the causal dynamics. Not surprisingly, students take the exercise more as a learning experience. In the very short run they suffer and go bankrupt; in the long run they improve their performance.

The simulated environment is threatening enough for professional participants to limit their decision repertoire and impede learning as well as the ability to transfer. Threat has the general effect of narrowing options considered. Thus, without embedding the management flight simulator in a context that makes the simulator less threatening (such as a learning lab), the results indicate that real-world learning disabilities will be reproduced in a simulated world.

Poor Transfer of Learning; What Can and Should Be Done?

The professionals spent several hours in directed discussions after the experimental game-playing sessions that helped remedy some of the transfer shortcomings of the simulator. First, experiences were shared among the teams, enabling those who had followed conservative strategies to benefit from those who had pursued more adventuresome decisions. In a very compressed time interval, the discussion revealed that markets that seem to be different, in fact, share many commonalties. Participants could quickly perform mental what-if analyses due to the intense common experience of the simulator.

The simulator experience appeared to facilitate the sharing of real-life experiences. For example, professionals in one learning laboratory with real estate experience in the northeast region questioned the fact that asset values in the simulator could swing as much as 40 percent between peaks and troughs. During the last ten years, they argued, asset values had never declined, and they knew of no other instance where values had dropped by more than 10 percent. Interestingly, there were people who had lived through depressed market conditions in the southern states in the same session. They questioned the validity of the simulated asset

Figure 10-5 shows that average performance in early trials is similar for both groups, and that both groups have transferred insights from the first to the second simulator. Transfer performance among the students, however, is markedly better than the professionals. The higher number of bankruptcies by the student group indicates that a different strategy was employed. In general, players who go bankrupt make more decisions than people who succeed in finishing a full round without going bankrupt. A high number of bankruptcies indicates that a player has an exploratory attitude and a willingness to make risky decisions. Bankruptcies impede performance initially, but provide valuable decision-making experience. In the long run, this exploratory decision-making style helps develop a deeper understanding that proves beneficial in the transfer game.

Why Are Professionals Less Exploratory?

What explains the apparent differences in decision-making strategy between the students and the professionals? One reason could be that students played individually while professionals played in teams of two. Since aversion to risk is higher in

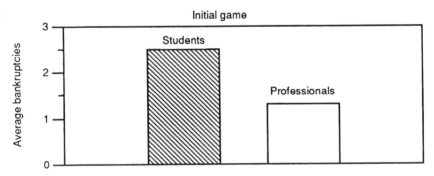

Figure 10-4. Students go bankrupt more often

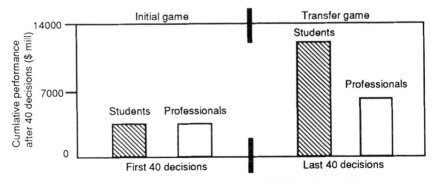

Figure 10-5. Students do as well as professionals, initially, and transfer better

team decision making, the consensus needed for team decision making reduces risk to the most risk-averse of the team players. In addition, our experimental results indicate that although every effort was made to ensure a nonthreatening environment, professionals still feel restricted. As we mentioned in the previous section, participants tend to use known (real-world) strategies to anchor their decisions. The same embedded routines that hinder exploration in the real world can also prevent exploration and learning in the simulated environment.

Another possible explanation for the difference in exploratory attitude is that the simulated environment poses more threat to professionals than to students. A hidden underlying assumption appears to be: "I know a lot about this market, so I just do in the game what I do in real life." Though fairly safe, such an attitude is counterproductive to learning since it fails to benefit from the experimental approach facilitated by the laboratory setting. Students' game playing strategy, on the other hand, seems to be more playful. They appear to use the information available in the game as a springboard for investigation into the causal dynamics. Not surprisingly, students take the exercise more as a learning experience. In the very short run they suffer and go bankrupt; in the long run they improve their performance.

The simulated environment is threatening enough for professional participants to limit their decision repertoire and impede learning as well as the ability to transfer. Threat has the general effect of narrowing options considered. Thus, without embedding the management flight simulator in a context that makes the simulator less threatening (such as a learning lab), the results indicate that real-world learning disabilities will be reproduced in a simulated world.

Poor Transfer of Learning; What Can and Should Be Done?

The professionals spent several hours in directed discussions after the experimental game-playing sessions that helped remedy some of the transfer shortcomings of the simulator. First, experiences were shared among the teams, enabling those who had followed conservative strategies to benefit from those who had pursued more adventuresome decisions. In a very compressed time interval, the discussion revealed that markets that seem to be different, in fact, share many commonalties. Participants could quickly perform mental what-if analyses due to the intense common experience of the simulator.

The simulator experience appeared to facilitate the sharing of real-life experiences. For example, professionals in one learning laboratory with real estate experience in the northeast region questioned the fact that asset values in the simulator could swing as much as 40 percent between peaks and troughs. During the last ten years, they argued, asset values had never declined, and they knew of no other instance where values had dropped by more than 10 percent. Interestingly, there were people who had lived through depressed market conditions in the southern states in the same session. They questioned the validity of the simulated asset cycles because they had themselves experienced asset value reductions of 50 percent over a period of a few years! The discussion then turned towards the preconditions for such a fall and what it meant for the northeast region.

From an organizational learning viewpoint, it is interesting that the colleague with exposure to the market with the 50 percent drop had not previously shared his experiences. Presumably, he had, until the simulated experience, thought that the southern market was so unique that it was irrelevant to current colleagues. The management flight simulator gave added credibility to viewing these markets as cyclical. Furthermore, the learning laboratory provided a framework where both commonalties and differences between cyclical markets could be integrated. This was done by the facilitator when the feedback structure depicted in Figure 10-1 was shared among the participants.

One real estate development company used the learning laboratory to instigate changes in its incentive structure. These changes were predicated on expected future difficulties induced by the cyclical nature of their business. Until then, it had been hard to convince junior partners that focusing exclusively on developing real estate was problematic. The lesson taken from professionals with three to ten years of experience was, "An investment missed today is millions lost in unearned capital gain tomorrow." The robustness of such a lesson is greatly reduced if the relevant time horizon is 30 to 40 years rather than 5 years. The cyclical experiences and emotionally laden bankruptcies improved the receptiveness for organizational change.

Theoretical Interpretation

Work on simple algebra word problems has shown that people have difficulties applying problem-solving insights from one domain to another. Risking oversimplification, one can say that research on transfer in this tradition has shown that though difficult to achieve, transfer of insights and strategies does occur. To transfer successfully, people need to possess a generic framework as well as experience in its use.

Frameworks are generic tools for a problem area, such as economics or statistics (Nisbett et al. 1986). But, a framework only helps transfer if its relevance is clear to a problem-solver. In general, that is not the case; people do not see the relevance of general frameworks when decision situations arise. In our case, the students do not seem to grasp the relevance of the framework when they play the first trial of the first game. However, when they are exposed to later trials of the first game, they slowly realize the system structure. Bankruptcies increase decision exposures. When the second market is presented to them, the student players appear to understand the generality of underlying causal forces and act accordingly. Numerous studies in transfer of problem solving (Bassok and Holyoak 1989; Gick and Holyoak 1983; Gilden and Profitt 1989; Newell and Simon 1972; Simon and

Hayes 1982) show that people can indeed apply a framework but only after being prompted or after repeated exposures to a given problem structure.

There exists evidence that if people are exposed to a problem area under many different conditions they may develop their own frameworks if given time and if they see the relevance of doing so. As an example (Gentner and Toupin 1986), most subjects are unable to recognize the relevance of a recently solved isomorphic problem when faced with a second one. However, when the subjects see a third isomorphic problem they "see a light" and realize that the two former problems shared structural characteristics and those are the same as the structure of the third problem.

CONCLUSION AND FUTURE RESEARCH

We have seen that management flight simulators can be integrated into learning laboratories to foster inquiry skills. Such skills are critical to a learning organization (Argyris and Schön 1978; de Geus 1988; Stata 1989). People need richer mental models for domains where such mental models tend to be deficient. Deficiencies typically occur if decision making and feedback about the appropriateness of those decisions are remote in time and space. We have seen that by designing nonthreatening learning laboratories, and by fostering experimentation in other ways, genuine reflection and experimentation may result. The effect of such experimentation is increased transfer, especially if accompanied by frameworks that can function as a vehicle for applying insights to new domains. The measurement of increased transfer and higher order thinking processes is complicated. However, we have shown that such measures are possible.

The results reported here are not entirely conclusive. Further methodological refinements of the measurement instruments need to be made. In addition, more decision making, learning, and transfer of learning data need to be collected to substantiate and validate the tentative conclusions presented in the previous section. These validations are currently under way and will be made available from the first author in the coming months.

REFERENCES

Argyris, C., and D. Schön (1978), *Organizational Learning: A Theory of Action Perspective*, Reading, Mass.: Addison-Wesley.

Bakken, B. (1990), "An Interview with a Thoughtful Shipping Investor," Working paper D-4167, System Dynamics Group, Sloan School, Massachusetts Institute of Technology, Cambridge.

Bassok, M., and K.J. Holyoak (1989), "Inter-domain Transfer between Isomorphic Topics in Algebra and Physics," *Journal of Experimental Psychology; Learning, Memory, and Cognition* 15, no. 1: 153-66.

Boston Redevelopment Authority (1989), *The Boston Class A Office Market*, 363.

Brehmer, B. (1989), "Feedback Delays and Control in Complex Dynamic Systems," in Milling and Zahn, eds., *Proceedings of the 1989 System Dynamics Conference,* Berlin: Springer-Verlag.

Einhorn, H.J., and R.M. Hogarth (1978), "Confidence in Judgment: Persistence of the Illusion of Validity," *Psychological Review* 85, no. 5: 395-416.

Gentner, D., and C. Toupin (1986), "Systematicity and Surface Similarity in the Development of Analogy," *Cognitive Science* 10, no. 3: 277-300.

de Geus, A. (1988), "Planning as Learning," *Harvard Business Review,* November-December.

Gick, M., and K.J. Holyoak (1983), "Schema Induction and Analogical Transfer," *Cognitive Psychology* 15: 1-38.

Gilden, D.L., and D.R. Profitt (1989), "Understanding Collision Dynamics," *Journal of Experimental Psychology; Learning, Memory, and Cognition* 15, no. 2: 372-83.

Gould, J.M. (1989), "Tools for Learning to Manage a Complex Environment," Working notes D-4051, System Dynamics Group, Sloan School, Massachusetts Institute of Technology, Cambridge.

Hernandez, K.L. (1991), "Learning in Real Estate: The Role of the Development System in Creating Oversupply," Unpublished M.S. thesis, Sloan School of Management, MIT, Cambridge, Mass.

Hoyt, H. (1933), *One Hundred Years of Land Values in Chicago,* Chicago: University of Chicago Press.

Kahnemann, D., and A. Tversky (1974), "Judgment under Uncertainty," *Science* 185: 1124-1131.

Kardes, F. (1987), "The Case Method of Instruction and Managerial Decision Making," Working paper, Sloan School, Massachusetts Institute of Technology, Cambridge.

Kim, D. (1989), "Learning Laboratories: Designing Reflective Learning Environments," in Milling and Zahn, eds., *Proceedings of the 1989 System Dynamics Conference,* Berlin: Springer-Verlag.

Mass, N. (1974), *Readings in Urban Dynamics*, Portland, Ore.: Productivity Press.

Newell, A., and H. Simon (1972), *Human Problem Solving,* Englewood Cliffs, N.J.: Prentice-Hall.

Nisbett, R., G. Fong, D. Lehman, and P. Cheng (1987), "Teaching Reasoning," *Science* 238: 625-31.

Papert, S. (1981), *Mindstorms,* New York: Basic Books.

Raia, A.P. (1966), "A Study of the Educational Value of Games," *Journal of Business* 39, no. 3: 339-52.

Schön, D.A. (1983), *The Reflective Practitioner: How Professionals Think in Action*, New York: Basic Books.

Senge, P.M. (1990), *The Fifth Discipline,* New York: Doubleday.

Simon, H. (1956), *Administrative Behavior,* New York: Wiley and Sons.

Simon, H. (1978), "Rationality as Process and Product of Thought," *American Economic Review* 68.

Simon, H., and J.R. Hayes (1974), "Understanding Written Problem Instructions," in L.W. Gregg, ed., *Knowledge and Cognition,* Potomac, Md.: Lawrence Erlbaum.

Stata, R. (1989), "Organizational Learning: The Key to Management Innovation," *Sloan Management Review* 30, no. 3: 63-74.

Sterman, J. (1987), "Testing Behavioral Simulation Models with Direct Experiment." *Management Science* 33: 1572-1592.

Sterman, J. (1989), "Misperceptions of Feedback in Dynamic Decision Making," *Organizational Behavior and Human Decision Processes* 43: 301-35.

Vennix, J. (1990), "Mental Models and Computer Models," Ph.D. dissertation, Center for Cognition and Information Research, University of Nijmegen, Nijmegen, Netherlands.

Weick, K.E. (1977), "Enactment Processes in Organizations," in Staw and Salanchick, eds., *New Directions in Organizational Behavior*, Chicago: St. Clair Press.

Wolfe, J. (1976), "The Effects and Effectiveness of Simulations in Business Policy Teaching Applications," *The Academy of Management Review* 1, no. 2: 47-56 (April).

11

OVERCOMING LIMITS TO LEARNING IN COMPUTER-BASED LEARNING ENVIRONMENTS

WILLIAM ISAACS AND PETER M. SENGE

ABSTRACT: The theoretical perspective of action science is applied to computer-based learning environments (CBLEs) in order to diagnose and help overcome individual, group, and organizational anti-learning pressures that may diminish CBLE effectiveness.*

* The authors would like to thank Robert Putnam and Dan Kim for their comments. The figures showing CBLE learning dynamics were developed with the help of John Sterman.

INTRODUCTION

Computer-based learning environments (CBLEs) can be important tools for fostering fundamental changes in policy makers' and managers' underlying assumptions and actions, and for enhancing strategic planning and decision making (Senge 1989, 1990; Kim 1989; Morecroft 1988). Researchers using these environments are also seeking to incorporate and test new insights from cognitive science about the nature of learning, the tendencies towards misperception, the occurrences of cognitive distortion, and the uses of heuristics in decision making (Sterman 1989; Kahneman, Tversky, and Slovic 1988). CBLEs can enhance organizational learning by making explicit the assumptions and logical inconsistencies in the operating policies of an organization, by fostering shared understanding of complex organizational processes and systems, and by exposing gaps between the ways managers believe they behave and the ways they actually behave. CBLEs make this analysis accessible to rational public scrutiny, experimentation, and change (Vennix 1990; Senge and Sterman 1992).

Paradoxically, the very success and explicitness with which CBLEs may achieve these ends brings into view a new set of challenges that are endemic to efforts to produce fundamental change and learning. The thesis of this article is that there exist individual, group, and organizational counterpressures that will limit the success of first-generation CBLEs in producing significant, enduring organizational learning. At the same time, because CBLEs can make these pressures far more visible, they are also made more accessible to study and to change. A new generation of CBLEs can be designed that take these anti-learning forces into account and help in overcoming them. This article explores these challenges, proposing a theoretical framework with which to view them, and indicating directions for redesign that takes them into account.

Learning challenges develop in CBLEs at the individual, group and organizational levels. At the individual level, recent research and theory suggest that confronting management problems that are complex, nonroutine, and counterintuitive, such as CBLEs pose, can create embarrassment and threat, and tend to trigger a set of self-fulfilling and self-sealing behaviors that diminish learning and the likelihood for change (Argyris 1990; Putnam 1990; Argyris, Putnam, and Smith 1985; Argyris and Schön 1978). Under these conditions, people may unwittingly defend prior positions, select information and arguments that confirm already established views instead of looking for reasons to change their views, attribute unreason and error to views that differ from their own, and often seek to "win," not learn (Argyris 1990; Putnam 1990; Senge 1990). Indeed, early studies have reported tendencies to approach CBLEs as games to be mastered rather than as learning tools (Kim 1989; Senge 1989).

In addition, CBLEs hold out the promise that new thinking and new insight will generate new ways of acting. Yet research also indicates that there is a significant gap between insights and new behavior, particularly when it concerns problems that are complex, nonroutine, and threatening. People have skillful ways of sustaining old behaviors that thwart efforts to learn new ones. (Argyris and Schön 1974). Evidence also suggests that people (both practitioners and researchers) tend to disregard or remain unaware of this gap (Argyris and Schön 1990; Argyris 1983).

Second, though CBLE research has tended to focus on individual understanding and individual cognitive limits, the locus of decision making in organizations tends to be "teams," groups of people who need one another to act (Senge 1990). For example, senior-level decisions are often made within groups, or require the support of groups to enact. If anything, reliance on teams—cross-functional teams, product development teams, and other types of problem solving teams—is increasing today as organizations attempt to harness diverse points of view and break down barriers to communication across traditional organizational boundaries. Increasingly, individual learning is irrelevant if not translated into team learning. However, this also complicates the learning challenge and embeds it within the study of group dynamics and group learning.

There is a rich history of research in social psychology and sociology on group cohesiveness and group effectiveness in organizations. This research stresses the immense influence of groups on the nature of the decision-making processes, the productivity and quality of work, the diffusion of social norms, and the self-esteem of organizational members (Zander 1979). Research on the dysfunctions of groups has also shown that besides the well-known cognitive limits of individual actors, groups present a range of additional constraints on the quality of decision making (March and Olsen 1980; Janis 1989, 1972; Cyert and March 1963). Groups can be dominated by internal politics, can factionalize, can insulate members from conflict, and can bias information.

As CBLEs begin to focus on group learning, they must be designed to take into account how group interactions can subvert inquiry and undermine needed changes. Failing to do so may cause CBLEs to produce a number of unintended effects. They may fail to encourage individuals to reflect on and challenge the impact of group norms on the quality of inquiry. Thus, they may reinforce conformity, such as everyone "agreeing" that the CBLE is useful, yet no one changing their views. CBLEs may suggest new views that are especially threatening to some group members. If people are not comfortable surfacing disagreements and have not been taught how to negotiate differences in views, this threat can intensify frictions within the team and call forth heightened defensiveness in response to these frictions. Lastly, CBLEs may provide participants with new understandings but not the underlying skills required to translate these new understandings into new actions, reinforcing group cynicism about the effectiveness of such change efforts.

Finally, efforts to alter decision making or learning at a local level in an organization often have significant impact on the larger organizational learning system. Organizations, like individuals, have preferred modes for learning—ways of handling interpersonal interaction, rules for managing or suppressing conflict, and ways of inferring meaning from experience. Designers of CBLEs, moreover, have their own "model" of learning, and need to recognize that their interventions may pit two distinct and incompatible learning models against one another. For example, systems-oriented CBLEs usually encourage a long-term view of policy and strategy issues. Yet, prevailing management systems may discount the long term in favor of short-term financial results. CBLEs may encourage policies that trade off narrow functional objectives for systemwide improvement—yet, organizational measures and rewards are predominantly functionally oriented. Although the goal of a CBLE may be to introduce an alternative mode of operation into the mainstream learning system, the host organization may reject the new approach the way an immune system rejects foreign bodies in any complex organism. Designers of CBLEs need to consider the nature of the organizational learning system with which they are interacting, the impact of their interventions on this system, and the strategies required for insuring that learning in fact takes place and is sustained.

The remainder of this paper presents a theoretical perspective that can begin to illuminate some of these anti-learning forces, and their implications for CBLEs. We then suggest ways CBLEs can be redesigned and expanded to foster collaborative learning skills as well as substantive policy insights. Our focus here is on individual and group limits to learning with the intention of building a foundation for subsequent examination of organizational limits to learning.

THE LEARNING THEORY UNDERLYING COMPUTER-BASED LEARNING ENVIRONMENTS

The central purpose for CBLEs is to provide decision makers with new opportunities for learning through conceptualization, experimentation, and reflection that are not easily achieved in everyday management activities. CBLEs may assist in conceptualizing new information, eliciting a shared language for a management team, or providing a structured way of thinking about complex problems (Morecroft 1988; Richmond 1987).Through simulation and gaming, they may allow experimentation with new policies that would be difficult or impossible to attempt in practice, in order to develop new insights into the nature of the system within which one is operating, and with new skills for managing that system. For researchers, CBLEs allow a window on individual and team learning patterns that can help in diagnosing managerial learning disabilities and designing improved learning processes.

In effect, CBLEs are "practice fields" for managers and management teams. Little learning would be possible for the sports team without regular practice sessions, or for the symphony orchestra or theater troupe without rehearsal. The continuous movement between practice and performance enhances individual skills, group understanding, establishes norms for coordination, and refines sensibilities toward the mechanics and aesthetics of group functioning. "Practice fields" embody the principles of what Donald Schön (1983) calls "virtual worlds," learning environments where time can be slowed down or speeded up, complexity can be simplified, irreversible actions made reversible, and the risks of experimentation eliminated.

Managers and their teams rarely, if ever, have the opportunity to practice—to experiment with alternative decisions without the uncontrollable presence of shocks from the environment, political manipulation, time pressure, and bewildering interdependency. Consequently, it becomes impossible in most management settings to formulate and test hypotheses. It is equally difficult to test the merits of different views, let alone synthesize broader views. In effect, managers are expected to learn through "performance only," through making decisions where the stakes are high, the time lags long, and opportunities for feedback and correction limited.

CBLEs build on a long tradition of experiential education theory pointing to the significance of learning through direct experience (as opposed to learning through "instruction"). In this work, learning is said to occur through the resolution of conflicts over different ways of dealing with the world. Lewin's model, for example, emphasizes two different sets of tensions: between concrete experience and abstract conceptualization, and between observation and action (Piaget 1970; Lewin 1951; Dewey 1938). According to Kolb (1984), the ideal learning process includes each of these elements, moving continually from concrete experience to reflective observation, to abstract conceptualization, to active experimentation, and finally back to concrete experience (Kolb 1984; Argyris and Schön 1978). In their work Argyris and Schön (1978) have described this process as moving from discovery of problems to invention of solutions, to production of solutions in action, to reflection on the impact of these actions, and then back to discovery (see Figure 11-1).

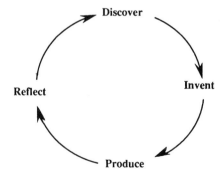

Figure 11-1. Argyris and Schön's (1978) learning cycle

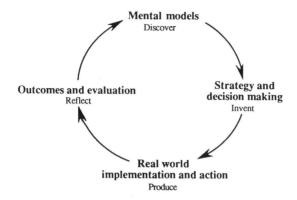

Figure 11-2. CBLE learning cycle

This basic learning cycle as it might operate in management situations can be redrawn as shown in Figure 11-2.

If this learning cycle operated effectively, new insights about the real world would be continually discovered and embedded in improved mental models, decisions would be invented based on new mental models, those decisions would be enacted, and then outcomes would be reflected upon to produce new insights.

Designers of CBLEs argue that this ideal learning cycle fails to operate effectively in organizations because of limits at each point in the cycle. First, decision makers have diverse and typically tacit mental models, making the development of strategies a process of negotiation among competing recommendations, not a rational comparison and testing of alternative assumptions. Second, delays between when decisions are made and their impact may be very long, often many years for strategic decisions. Third, additional delays between action and perceived consequences arise because of the time needed to collect, disseminate, and interpret data. The high degree of interdependence within organizations means that actions taken in one area may have significant effects in distant parts of the system, effects obscure to the original actors. The offshoot of this is that decision makers cannot see the consequences of their decisions in order to learn from them. Finally, differences in mental models held by decision makers can lead to widely different interpretations of available data, the sources of which are rarely investigated and tested. In addition, confounding factors, such as uncontrollable and unanticipated changes in markets, technology, economic conditions, or competitor actions inevitably alter the impact of decisions, especially over the long time spans relevant to organizational actions. All of this suggests that the ideal learning cycle breaks down (see Figure 11-3).

Designers of CBLEs believe their learning tools and models can mitigate some of the most basic limits to learning by providing rapid, unambiguous, and systemic

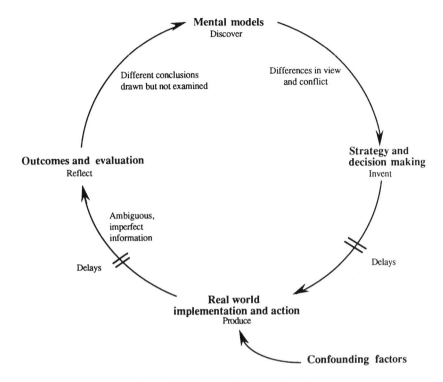

Figure 11-3. Managerial learning obstacles

feedback on actions taken, and by providing a relatively low-risk setting in which differences in mental models can be explored and tested. CBLEs constitute new media that can reflect back previously tacit assumptions and can provide insight into the nature of the complex interactions that determine the consequences of managerial decisions. For example, actions that have obvious, desired short-term benefits may have less than obvious, undesired longer term effects. The latter may be obscured in real life but visible through CBLEs (see Figure 11-4).

A THEORETICAL PERSPECTIVE ON LIMITS TO LEARNING IN CBLES

Despite their potential, CBLEs are likely to trigger "anti-learning" forces because of the type of learning they attempt to foster. Specifically, one purpose of CBLEs is to foster what learning theorists call *double-loop learning*. Argyris and Schön (1978) define double-loop learning as learning that seeks to encourage inquiry into and promote changes in an actor's or organization's "underlying norms, policies, and objectives," and that confronts gaps between beliefs and action (Argyris and Schön 1978). They contrast this with *single-loop learning,* which

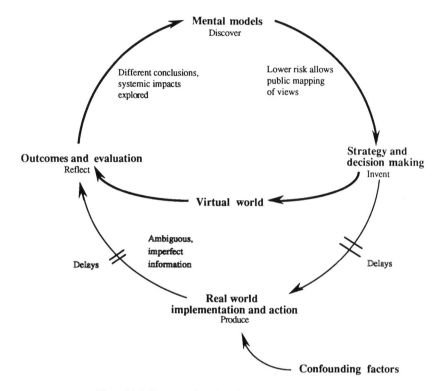

Figure 11-4. Impact on learning obstacles using virtual world

involves producing changes in behaviors and strategies in order to achieve desired outcomes in the face of environmental changes. Rather than merely adjust the strategies used to accomplish a particular goal, double-loop learning aims to alter the implicit or explicit goals themselves, and associated tacit structures of perception, thinking, and action. Double-loop learning is required when gaps between intention and outcome cannot be corrected without a change in underlying values, perceptions, and assumptions that gave rise to the gaps. This has bearing on CBLEs in two respects: either when the new understanding a CBLE conveys challenges fundamental assumptions held by a participant, or when participants seek to enact new understandings in practical settings.

CBLEs are often designed to help people see and understand the complex interactions that are producing persistent problems or thwarting efforts at improvement. In system dynamics terms, problematic system behavior arises from the feedback structures underlying behavior, especially the "operating policies" whereby information is converted into action (Senge 1989). Moreover, operating policies differ from official or "espoused" policies about how one ought to make decisions, and are usually partly or largely tacit for the actors in a system. Thus the type of learning required for fundamental improvement involves discovering how established policies are creating an organization's problems and inventing new policies to improve behavior—a classic problem of double-loop learning. Such learning challenges trigger a predictable set of reactions in individuals, including the effort to save face, one's own and others, to try to win and avoid losing, to appear rational whatever the actual status of one's reasoning, and to suppress emotion. To make matters more difficult, individuals typically use these strategies and reactions skillfully but remain unaware that they are doing so. In effect, people seem to act in ways that prevent them from learning about fundamental gaps between their intentions and actions (Argyris 1990, 1983; Argyris and Schön 1978).

Extensive research on the difficulties of double-loop learning and its implications for social organizations has been conducted by Chris Argyris and Don Schön and their colleagues over the past twenty years, and provides a useful perspective for understanding these effects in CBLEs (Argyris 1990; Argyris and Schön 1990, 1978; Schön 1983; Argyris, Putnam, and Smith 1985; Argyris and Schön 1974). Their approach, which they call "action science," has its roots in Lewin's participatory action research and attempts to both describe and alter social behavior, while creating knowledge that is usable by practitioners (Whyte 1989; Lewin 1951).

Action science focuses on the implementation of ideas. Drawing upon the ideal learning cycle discussed in the last section, it brings to light an additional difficulty to the ones raised there. It holds that there is no straightforward path between the invention of new strategies and their production, particularly when it comes to situations that involve double-loop learning. Under the threat or potential embarrassment of questioning basic assumptions and values, "individuals frequently produce actions contrary to their inventions *and* are often unaware of the discrepancy" (Argyris and Schön 1990: 19) (see Figure 11-5). Argyris and Schön suggest that this behavior is due to the skillful adherence to underlying rules of behavior and social virtues learned early in life (Argyris and Schön 1990: 20).

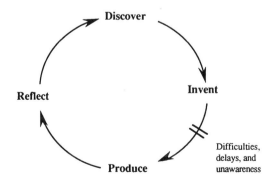

Figure 11-5. Obstacles in Argyris and Schön's learning cycle

These self-defeating rules form a general pattern that appears when actions and consequences appear to be nonroutine, complex, and contain threat or embarrassment, which they call "Model I" (Argyris and Schön 1990: 26). Model I is an example of a "theory-in-use," a set of underlying rules of behavior that inform actual behavior, which we may distinguish from "espoused theories," which are the reasons people give to explain their behavior. Model I is characterized by win/lose behaviors, face-saving, unilateral control, defensiveness, repression of emotion, and the attempt to appear rational (Argyris and Schön 1978). Numerous field studies have shown that, using Model I behaviors, people advocate their views, but take the reasoning for their views for granted, assume others will as well, and discourage inquiry into their views. Model I may also be characterized by apparent submission to opposing views in order to avoid examining the underlying beliefs that one has. The offshoot of Model I theory-in-use is limited capacity to confront one's own or others' thinking, and a tendency to either conceal what one really thinks, or raise what one thinks in a unilateral fashion.

Although Argyris and Schön argue that the majority of people utilize Model I social norms and behaviors, they claim that people can be trained to utilize "Model II." They constructed Model II as an explicit alternative to Model I, noting that it is rarely found in practice. Model II consists of underlying norms of valid information, free and informed choice, and internal commitment to that choice. Model II behavior is characterized by advocacy of one's views, done in such a way that inquiry into one's own and others' views is also encouraged. Model II skills can be taught in successive stages that gradually build competence, although high levels of expertise generally require several years of instruction and practice (Putnam 1990).

As indicated above, Model I behavior is not only observable in individuals and groups but is built into the socialized values commonly found in many societies and in most western organizations. Many social practices—like face-saving, protectiveness, the appearance of individual strength, and the suppression of feelings of vulnerability—are based in Model I theory-in-use and reinforce it. Individuals are so enmeshed in a defensive social milieu, of which they may be partly or completely unaware, that other forms of behavior may be hard to conceive of let alone enact, regardless of whether such behaviors might support deeper learning. Table 11-1 describes some of the social virtues and the Model I and Model II norms that characterize them (Argyris 1990: 106-107).

In summary, action science holds that, in addition to the difficulties of understanding in organizational settings arising from systemic factors, long delays between actions and consequences, misinformation, ambiguity, and systemic consequences that cannot be readily discerned, there are difficulties in the ways human beings move from new understandings to new behavior. These difficulties are greatest when necessary new understandings involve insights into the counterproductivity of basic assumptions and values. Thus, even if CBLEs can remove sys-

Table 11-1. Model I and Model II social virtues

Model I Social Virtues	Model II Social Virtues
Help and Support	
Give approval and praise to others. Tell others what you believe will make them feel good about themselves. Reduce their feelings of hurt by telling them how much you care, and if possible, agree with them that others acted improperly.	Increase others' capacity to confront their own ideas, to create a window into their own mind, and to face their unsurfaced assumptions, biases, and fears, by acting in these ways toward other people.
Respect for Others	
Defer to other people and do not confront their reasoning or actions.	Attribute to other people a high capacity for self-reflection and self-examination without becoming so upset that they lose their effectiveness and their sense of self-responsibility and choice. Keep testing this attribution.
Strength	
Advocate your position in order to win. Hold your own position in the face of advocacy. Feeling vulnerable is a sign of weakness.	Advocate your position and combine it with inquiry and self-reflection. Feeling vulnerable while encouraging inquiry is a sign of strength.
Honesty	
Tell other people no lies, or tell other people all that you think.	Encourage yourself and other people to say what they know yet fear to say. Minimize what would otherwise be subject to distortion and cover-up of the distortion.
Integrity	
Stick to your principles, values, and beliefs.	Advocate your principles, values, and beliefs in a way that invites inquiry into them and encourages other people to do the same.

temic factors that confound learning, this will not guarantee that appropriate new policies will be recognized or implemented.

IMPLICATIONS FOR COMPUTER-BASED LEARNING ENVIRONMENTS

Action science's findings have several implications for CBLEs. We focus here on those that apply at the individual and team levels.

At an individual level, they help explain some of the more commonly observed difficulties in CBLE research. One example is the "video-game" mentality, where individuals tend to treat computers as a video game and rapidly try many different actions with no reflection on why their actions fail to produce intended outcomes; they simply keep experimenting until "their score" improves (Kim 1989; Senge 1989). Treating a threatening object as a game to beat can be seen as an attempt to control the outcome of the encounter, a strategy consistent with Model I. The "video game" syndrome is the tip of the iceberg in this domain. Individuals have a wide range of tacit defense mechanisms that they will employ to maintain control in computer-based learning environments.

Observation of CBLEs suggests that participants tend to one of two extremes: They use the CBLE selectively to discover ways to reinforce their prior views, or they treat the computer as an oracle that has all the answers. In one case, for example, a CBLE-generated counterintuitive result took the managers involved over a year to take seriously enough to begin designing real-world tests of the new view. Unquestioning acceptance of a CBLE can be equally problematic, because of the tacit and embedded nature of Model I learning rules. For example, people may espouse a systems perspective, but be as unilateral and unskilled in reciprocal inquiry as they were with a "linear" perspective. The furniture of conceptual explanation will have been slightly rearranged, but the worldviews underlying policies and strategies , and moreover the process by which they come to those views will be unchanged.

At a team level, Model I theories-in-use produce limited ability to inquire into differences of opinion, distancing from problems, and control or avoidance dynamics. In such a setting, individuals with new, more systemic views may end up either withholding those views or advocating them unilaterally. When team members interact within a CBLE, they may suppress fears of their own inadequacy triggered by the threat of computer models or the complexity they portray, unilaterally reject computer-based learning, or accept the process without questioning it while keeping their own assumptions from being exposed.

The same defensive dynamics may also be found in intergroup conflict in organizations. Organizational defensive patterns co-opt learning advances. In one setting that we studied, two senior management groups in a single organization had a long tradition of conflict and animosity towards the other. One group engaged in computer-based learning. This activity was seen by the other group as overly technical, insensitive to human needs, and a power play. The learning intervention heightened the conflict between these groups: The more one group began to operate with a different view, the more threatening it became.

Some CBLEs have been designed to help structure the espoused theories of management teams (Morecroft 1988). While helping teams conceptualize their views of complex issues, enhance communication, and focus debate, such CBLEs also raise important questions. In particular, CBLEs that focus exclusively on restructuring espoused views fail to draw attention to gaps between espoused

behavior and theories-in-use, and the real difficulties that underlie attempts to produce new nonroutine or complex behaviors. Because people are generally unaware
of these gaps and become defensive if they are brought to awareness, people have
tendencies to "bypass" them, avoid exploring them, and so allow inconsistent or
ineffective theories-in-use to prevail. If CBLEs intentionally or unintentionally col-
lude with this general tendency, they may subtly reinforce systematic gaps between
espoused theory and theory-in-use.

Finally, researchers and interventionists themselves may, and very often do,
unwittingly exacerbate the problems. They typically operate in Model I ways by
developing views that they advocate unilaterally, see their task as imposing their
view on the "client," and seek to protect their image as "experts." If so, they may
unwittingly undermine the effectiveness of the learning environment that they are
seeking to foster. For example, they may act unilaterally in the design of the learning environment, giving little freedom to participants. This will create defensiveness and lessen the ownership of participants in the overall process. They may
unwittingly suggest that there is a way to win and not lose in the experience, activating Model I responses. Or they may fail to provide adequate opportunity for participants to test the underlying assumptions in the model that is used, thereby
behaving in the very way that they wish to correct in participants. The underlying
message communicated by the style and learning rules of the interventionist can
overwhelm the intended learning effects of their intervention (Argyris and Schön
1990; Argyris 1972).

CBLEs may be used in the service of Model I or Model II values. Table 11-2
summarizes these options.

Table 11-2. Protective and reflective uses of CBLEs

Protective	Reflective
CBLEs used to:	CBLEs used to:
• Prove a point	• Increase practical experimentation
• Keep assumptions hidden	• Promote inquiry into "whys"
• Validate own predispositions	• Challenge predispositions
• Make selective use of data	• Encourage open testing and public criteria for testing
• Give predetermined answer, cover-up predetermination and remain unaware of doing so	• Develop internal commitment to objectivity, actively encouraging inquiry into own views
or...	
• Act like an oracle	• Experience the system and the assumptions in it as the cause of behavior

Because of the nature of the problems addressed by CBLEs, participants tend to behave in Model I ways. Whether or not these tendencies predominate depends on *the extent to which these behaviors are discussible and alterable.* This is particularly challenging, since unskilled attempts to raise or discuss such matters are likely to reinforce the protective, nonlearning behaviors one is seeking to eschew. For example, confronting people on their defensiveness usually evokes a defensive response, rather than an alternative behavior. On the other hand, as will be discussed below, it may be possible to design CBLEs in such a way as to begin to recognize such behaviors in nonthreatening ways and thereby enhance conditions for double-loop learning.

REDESIGNING CBLES TO ENHANCE LEARNING

We believe that it is possible to design CBLEs to enhance individual and team learning and ability to transfer insights from CBLEs to the workplace. CBLEs can introduce participants to the discipline of reflecting on their own behavior and assumptions, to perceiving gaps between their intentions and model outcomes, and also to seeing gaps between their beliefs and their actual behavior. Designers of CBLEs can also begin to use action science tools to achieve these goals. But to do so, they must become publicly reflective about their own approach, making it accessible to inquiry.

First, CBLEs should adopt explicitly the goal of helping managers develop individual and collective skills required to surface and test their assumptions. These skills have often been taken for granted. Designers of CBLEs have tended to focus on the policy issues at hand and to ignore the effort individuals and teams must make in order to develop learning skills. CBLEs should be modified to help participants reflect on the learning theory that governs their own actions, and to begin to try out elements of Model II theory.

We believe that a methodology for practicing Model II skills can be woven into the fabric of CBLEs. This will require in part that participants learn systems conceptualization skills and conduct computer experiments with care and adequate time for reflection. Conceptualization skills can be developed through exercises embedded in the CBLE that emphasize basic competencies in the language of feedback processes and "systems archetypes" (Senge 1990; Kim 1989). This is the basic language used in constructing the computer models employed in CBLEs, and familiarity with it enables participants to make explicit their espoused theories concerning the system in question.

Once they have mastered basic conceptualization tools, the participants can discover gaps between their expectations of system behavior based on their conceptualized views of system interactions, and the behavior that actually arises. The behavior of complex systems is very often surprising, even when we are fully aware of the basic interdependencies within those systems (Forrester 1971). After participants in a CBLE have conceptualized the basic interactions in the computer model, an important part of their espoused view has been explicated: their view of how the system is structured.[1] However, managers also have views about what types of policies or strategies are needed to achieve desirable behavior in the system as a whole. When they play out these strategies and policies in the CBLE, often the outcome is *not* what they expect, even though they "understand" the interactions in the system. This reveals inner contradictions in their espoused theory. The actions they advocate do not produce the outcomes they expect, even when the underlying assumptions in the computer model match their very own assumptions. This discovery can be a powerful catalyst for learning.

For example, in a CBLE designed to understand causes of escalating settlement costs in property and liability insurance, most insurance managers discover that the policies they believe are needed to control the system actually produce steadily rising costs. But in order to make this discovery, managers must have a disciplined approach to the computer experiment. They must state explicitly their expected outcomes prior to executing their strategy. Then, they must carefully note and explain the gap between their expected outcome and actual outcome, after executing their strategy. Enforcing this discipline is not easy, precisely because managers are unschooled in such disciplines, and because the act of making one's thinking explicit can be threatening, leading to Model I behaviors (Kim 1989).

A second gap, between managers' espoused decision making and their actual behavior, can also be revealed unambiguously in CBLEs, given some learning discipline. This gap arises when managers state the policy or strategy they believe is necessary to achieve successful outcomes and then fail to follow that strategy. This usually happens when the strategy is a radical departure from what is the norm in their organization. In other words, this gap usually reveals an implicit "organizational theory-in-use." The CBLE reveals the theory-in-use more unambiguously than is possible in real life.

A powerful example occurred in the development of the same insurance CBLE. The design team responsible for developing this particular CBLE gradually developed a new espoused theory that significant improvement in the system required large scale investment in skilled human resources (hiring, training, increased pay, and enhanced stature for a particular professional function). They came to believe this strategy so strongly that they made speeches advocating the strategy. Yet, when they developed a computerized "flight simulator" and had the opportunity to play out their strategy, each invested only modestly. In a series of 10 separate experiments by each of the 3-person teams, not a single simulation included more than a

---

[1] In CBLEs using a model based on research conducted in advance, participants' conceptualizations may differ from that of the model. This can allow for interesting reflections on the participants' and model builders' views, identification of tests to resolve differences, and still better models.

modest increase in professional head count. The reason that eventually surfaced was that each of the managers was strongly conditioned to control expenses. They could not bring themselves to a large increase in hiring that would increase expenses, *even though* their espoused theory told them that the increased labor expense, eventually, would be more than compensated for by improved quality and reductions in other costs. Once they realized this gap between their own "understanding" and their behavior, they decided to design an experiment into the subsequent CBLE to help other managers discover the same gap.

To build on these conceptualization skills, and help participants diagnose and change their own anti-learning tendencies, CBLEs might employ a redesigned version of one of the central tools of action science, the "case" methodology (Argyris 1990, 1983; Senge 1990; Argyris and Schön 1974). This tool asks participants to examine dialogue of a problematic situation they experienced, distinguishing what they and the others involved said, and what they were thinking or feeling but not communicating. This tool provides a window on the theories-in-use that an individual employs as he or she crafts responses to a problem, and can be a source for rich reflection and learning.

We believe that the action science case method can be adopted for use in CBLEs. Instead of dialogue, participants would write a log of their decisions on the right hand column of a paper, and write what they are thinking and feeling on the left. This log could be written during or after playing out a simulation. If written afterward, participants could use the actual record of their decisions, as stored by the computer, so as to have an accurate record to reflect on. In the left hand column they would record the internal dialogue that accompanied their decision making—for example, the reasons behind their decisions, their expected outcomes, and any problems they expected their decisions to generate. They would also be encouraged to write any other thoughts they had about the exercise at the time. This would begin to bring to light the taken-for-granted lens through which participants viewed the problem, and their strategies for defining and managing it. Participants would then be asked by a coach to explore their thinking about their decisions, so that they would be forced to question the assumptions underlying them. Each participant would periodically switch roles between being coached and coaching.

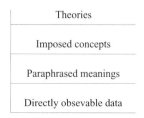

Figure 11-6. Ladder of inference

The questions asked by the coach could be guided by the application of another well-established tool of action inquiry, the ladder of inference (Argyris 1990) (see Figure 11-6). This tool attempts to reconstruct and make explicit the way the mind makes inferences and abstractions. Directly observable data, such as might be recorded on a video or tape recorder, is distinguished from paraphrased meanings of that data, and from the imposed concepts and theories drawn from the data. At each step on the ladder, the participant is asked to make his reasoning process explicit. For example, the directly observable data might be that someone arrives at 2:15 P.M. for a meeting. Several others, thinking the meeting was to begin at 2:00, think he is "late." Another person thinks that he "doesn't care about this work." A number of abstractions have been made from relatively little data, reflecting a range of assumptions about prior agreements, what "late" means, and the internal state of the person involved. Most importantly, people are unlikely to surface these abstractions because of the possible conflicts that might ensue. Rather, they treat the abstractions *as if they were data* and simply act on them—form conclusions about the person, not invite him to subsequent meetings, or simply treat him as someone with low commitment. In fact, the person might have had a different expectation regarding the meeting time, might have been in an accident, or might indeed have placed less priority on the meeting. The possibilities would need to be explored. As this example reveals, people interpret events and act in specific ways, making inferences in split seconds that they never test.

When used in conjunction with the case methodology, the ladder of inference can be used to "unpack" assumptions and inferences being made in CBLEs, in order to foster deeper learning. For example, in one CBLE we observed, we found people making decisions based on inferences about the behavior of the competition as the cause of the problems when, in fact, the underlying model did not take the competition into account. The players decisions actually interacted to produce the problems that they wished to attribute to exogenous forces. Using the case methodology, a coach could use the ladder of inference to ask questions that would cause the participants to recognize their inference, see the "data" upon which it was based, and discover *why* they had jumped from that data to an erroneous assumption. Questions like the following could be relevant:

- What was the decision you made?

- What did you expect to happen? What led you to think so?

- Why did/didn't that occur? What were you thinking about at the time?

- What impact did the prior behavior of the system or others have on you at the time?

- What past experiences, if any, in actual settings influenced your decision and the assumptions behind it?

By developing discipline at stating espoused theories and observing both systemic consequences and actual decision making, and then compelling reflection on why gaps appear, CBLEs can enhance managers' learning skills. They can also begin to produce change, we believe not only in the espoused theories of participants, but in their theories-in-use.

It is not enough that such cases should be written and reflected on mechanically. The way in which this reflection is done is likely to invoke defensiveness that prevents learning unless participants, designers, and facilitators in the CBLE genuinely desire to move toward a Model II approach. This requires everyone to begin to learn how to make their thinking more explicit, make perceived errors discussable, and learn how to encourage others to inquire into their thinking. By explicit, we mean illustrating with relatively directly observable data the experiences that lead to conclusions being drawn.

The behavior of designers and facilitators is especially important because they not only establish ground rules in CBLEs but are role models. If they are unaware of their own Model I behaviors, they will have little ability to foster Model II in the CBLE. On the other hand, if they operate in a spirit of genuine curiosity and openness, they will contribute to just such an atmosphere in the CBLE. As this atmosphere develops, CBLEs can enable managers to experiment with alternative learning behaviors at relatively low risk, just as they can experiment with alternative policies and strategies.

For the above changes in approach to succeed, designers of CBLEs must also be nonprotective about the models that have been developed to underlie CBLEs. In our experience, most system dynamicists are perfectly willing to make their assumptions explicit but still often fail to do so in CBLEs because of the time required or because of not knowing how to expose assumptions effectively (i.e., how to keep from creating a boring monologue on "what the model assumes and why"). We have found that the best approach is to design ways for the participants to conceptualize important relationships in the model themselves. Ways to guide such conceptualization are gradually being developed (see Kim 1989; Senge 1990). As CBLEs become directed and facilitated by more managers from within the organization itself, this can actually become easier. Facilitators who are *not* expert model builders tend to take less for granted and better appreciate the dilemmas of a manager who is learning systems thinking. Such facilitation by members of the organization is essential if the issues addressed must be understood by large numbers of people within the organization.

Can these new elements of CBLEs help with group Model I limits to learning? We believe they can. When team members begin to interact in CBLEs in Model II ways, they begin to break down habitual patterns of interaction. Norms can begin to be changed as debate and dialogue in CBLEs is facilitated by individuals becoming more skilled in Model II behavior, and where participants are provided opportunity to reflect as a group on the nature of their social learning skills. But our contention remains to be tested. Future research should focus on the efficacy of the steps outlined above in undermining entrenched group behavior patterns, not only within but subsequent to experience in CBLEs.

CONCLUSIONS AND IMPLICATIONS FOR RESEARCH

Several conclusions may be drawn from this analysis. First, computer-based learning environments are interventions into an existing learning system, which includes the tacit rules individuals bring to double-loop learning problems, the nature of team interaction, and the processes of intergroup and organizational learning. CBLEs should be designed to empower individuals to act effectively within each level of this system. Second, computer models may be used in ways that *limit* learning, not extend or enhance it, because both interventionists and participants bring Model I ways of operating into these settings. Third, because critical decisions are made and enacted by teams, CBLEs have especially great impact if they foster the skills required for collaborative learning about complex issues. Finally, CBLEs can be redesigned to incorporate reflection upon espoused theory, through developing conceptualization skills and theory-in-use, through deliberate reflection on the actions taken in computer experiments, and through exploration of the reasons for these actions. Further group learning may be enhanced as CBLEs are designed to encourage reflection on group learning skills.

This analysis also suggests a number of directions for further research, so that CBLEs may be used both to discover more completely the nature of managers' theories-in-use concerning complex situations, and as tools to produce changes in these theories-in-use. These directions include:

- Further identification of the generic ways in which individuals and groups respond to learning environments of this sort.

- Examination of the ways in which differences in the level of inquiry skill, and amount of interpersonal interaction affect CBLEs.

- Study of the ways that people bring their own learning "model" into these interactive learning environments. Research methods might include utilizing "thinking aloud" protocols or "action science maps" (Argyris 1990; Ericsson and Simon 1984) of the key features of the individual's theory-in-use, and collaborative inquiry into the impact of the experience.

- Examination of what people take away from CBLEs and attempt to put into practice in their working environments. Research would investigate the extent and nature of changes in theories-in-use altered in work settings. What is the range and type of errors in learning behavior of which people are aware before and after the CBLE? Research methods might include before and after interviews about the usability of the knowledge gained, observation and interviews of team meetings, and analysis of decisions made before and after experience.

• Exploration of the impact of CBLEs on organizational defensive patterns. How do individuals and the organization deal with these patterns? Methods might include representative case studies of comparable organizations that have had and that have not had such trainings, pre-CBLE and post-CBLE comparisons within the same organization, and collaborative action inquiry into the nature of the learning systems in these companies (Putnam 1990) .

The primary intention of this paper has been to expand the mission of CBLEs to embrace the need to enhance learning skills as well as shed light on complex policy and strategy issues. While there are many learning problems with CBLEs, these problems *are not created by CBLEs.* They are problems that inhere in the way individuals, teams, and organizations approach difficult learning issues. When CBLEs are most effective they become microcosms of the larger organization's learning processes. By bringing the behaviors and values that limit learning to the surface, CBLEs have unique potential to help change these behaviors and values. Hopefully, the ideas presented above can help realize that potential.

REFERENCES

Argyris, C. (1972), *Inner Contradictions of Rigorous Research,* New York: Academic Press.

Argyris, C. (1983), *Reasoning, Learning and Action*, San Francisco: Jossey-Bass.

Argyris, C. (1990), *Overcoming Organizational Defenses*, Boston: Allyn and Bacon.

Argyris, C., R. Putnam, and D.M. Smith (1985), *Action Science,* San Francisco: Jossey-Bass.

Argyris, C., and D. Schön (1974), *Theory in Practice: Increasing Professional Effectiveness*, San Francisco: Jossey-Bass.

Argyris, C., and D. Schön (1978), *Organizational Learning: A Theory of Action Perspective,* Reading, Mass.: Addison-Wesley,

Argyris, C., and D. Schön (1990), "Conceptions of Causality in Social Theory and Research: Normal Science and Action Science Compared," mimeo, Harvard University. Also in Argyris, C. (1993), *Knowledge in Action,* San Francisco: Jossey-Bass, Appendix A: "Design Causality," 149-85.

Cyert, R.M., and J. March (1963), *A Behavioral Theory of the Firm,* Englewood Cliffs, N.J.: Prentice Hall.

Dewey, J. (1938), *Education and Experience,* Kappa Delta Pi.

Ericsson, K.A., and H. Simon (1984), *Protocol Analysis* , Cambridge: MIT Press.

Forrester, J.W. (1971), "Counterintuitive Behavior of Social Systems," *Technology Review* 73, no. 3: 52-68.

Forrester, J.W., and P. Senge (1980), "Tests for Building Confidence in System Dynamic Models," *TIMS Studies in the Management Sciences*, 14: 209-28.

Janis, I. (1972), *Victims of Groupthink* , Boston: Houghton Mifflin.

Janis, I. (1989), *Crucial Decisions,* New York: Free Press.

Kahneman, D., P. Slovic, and A. Tversky, eds. (1982), *Judgement under Uncertainty: Heuristic and Biases*, Cambridge: Cambridge University Press.

Kim, D. (1989), "Learning Laboratories: Designing a Reflective Learning Environment," in P. Milling and E. Zahn, eds., *Computer-Based Management of Complex Systems*, Berlin: Springer-Verlag.

Kolb, D. (1984), *Experiential Learning*, Englewood Cliffs, N.J.: Prentice-Hall.

Lane, D., J. Morecroft, and P. Viita (1989), "Modelling Growth Strategy in a Biotechnology Startup Firm," London Business School working paper.

Lewin, K. (1951), *Field Theory in the Social Sciences,* New York: Harper and Row.

March, J.G., and J. Olsen (1980), *Ambiguity and Choice in Organizations*, Universitetsforlaget, Bergen, Norway.

Morecroft, J. (1988), "System Dynamics and Microworlds for Policy Makers, "*European Journal of Operational Research* 35: 301-20

Morgan, G. (1986), *Images of Organization* , Beverly Hills: Sage.

Piaget, J. (1970), *Genetic Epistemology,* New York: Columbia University Press.

Putnam, R. (1990), "Putting Concepts to Use: Re-Educating for Organizational Learning," unpublished doctoral dissertation, Harvard University, Cambridge.

Richmond, B. (1987), *The Strategic Forum: From Vision to Strategy to Operating Policies and Back Again*, High Performance Systems, 45 Lyme Road, Ste. 300, Hanover NH 03755.

Schön, D. (1983), *The Reflective Practitioner*, New York: Basic Books.

Senge, P. (1990), *The Fifth Discipline: The Art and Practice of the Learning Organization*, New York: Doubleday.

Senge, P. (1989), "Organizational Learning: A New Challenge for System Dynamics," in P. Milling and E. Zahn, eds., *Computer-Based Management of Complex Systems*, Berlin: Springer-Verlag.

Senge, P., and J.D. Sterman (1992), "Systems Thinking and Organizational Learning: Acting Locally and Thinking Globally in the Organization of the Future," *European Journal of Operational Research* 59, no. 1: 137-50; also Chapter 8 of this work.

Sterman, J.D. (1988), "A Skeptic's Guide to Computer Models," in L. Grant, ed., *Foresight and National Decisions*, Lanham, Md.: University Press of America.

Sterman, J.D. (1989), "Modeling Managerial Behavior: Misperceptions of Feedback in Dynamic Decision-Making," *Management Science* 35, no. 3: 321- 39.

Vennix, J. (1990), "Mental Models and Computer Models: Design and Evaluation of a Computer-Based Learning Environment for Policy Making," Ph.D. dissertation, University of Nijmegen, Nijmegen, Netherlands.

Whyte, W.F., ed. (1989), "Action Research for the 21st Century: Participation, Reflection and Practice," *American Behavioral Scientist* 32, no. 5: 502-12.

Zander, A. (1979), "The Study of Group Behavior During Four Decades," *Journal of Applied Behavioral Science* 15, no. 3: 272-94

PART 4

NEW IDEAS IN REPRESENTATION AND SOFTWARE

12

SOFTWARE FOR MODEL BUILDING AND SIMULATION: AN ILLUSTRATION OF DESIGN PHILOSOPHY

STEVE PETERSON

ABSTRACT: The article illustrates a philosophy for model building and simulation software design. In addition, it suggests areas in which evolution of model-building and simulation software will occur.

INTRODUCTION

For the past seven years, individuals at High Performance Systems have been engaged in the design, development, and marketing of model-building and simulation software for the Apple Macintosh computer. Since early 1993, we have been involved in the development of such software for the IBM PC and compatible computers. During that time, a design philosophy—an evolving set of design principles—has emerged. The philosophy informs and guides our development effort. This article illustrates our design philosophy.

A graphical user interface provides the basis for one design model that supports both expert and less-skilled practitioners of the modeling process. This design model provides a multilevel, hierarchical environment for the construction, analysis and consumption of a simulation model. Each layer in the environment is described. Building blocks and tools within each layer are illustrated. Finally, emerging tools are identified. As these become incorporated into the software environment for modeling and simulation, the fruits of the modeling process will become available to an even wider audience.

GRAPHICAL TOOLS ARE REQUIRED FOR A WIDE AUDIENCE

As other articles within this volume illustrate, the modeling process provides a systematic mechanism for the modeler to understand, and improve the performance of, dynamic systems. This process comprises four distinct, yet interrelated stages: conceptualization, model construction, model simulation analysis, and communication. The purpose of model-building and simulation software is to support the user at each stage of the modeling process.

For both expert and novice in systems thinking, the design and implementation of model-building and simulation tools can impact effectiveness in applying the modeling process. For example, less-skilled practitioners can find their effectiveness constrained when software does not support the visualization of assumptions within a given model. In a similar vein, even an expert modeler may find it difficult to communicate insights from a model, if the model itself looks too complex for the intended audience to easily understand at first glance.

For a wide audience, one that varies both in technical expertise and in modeling proficiency, effective software will minimize both technical and conceptual requirements. One design model that lowers both the technical and the conceptual burden provides a hierarchical, multilayer environment incorporating graphical tools to support conceptualization, construction, analysis, and communication activities. This design model is incorporated into the ithink™ and STELLA® II software (Richmond, Peterson et al. 1993). At any level in the hierarchy, both construction tools and consumption tools are provided. Construction tools aid the user in the conceptualization and construction stages of the modeling process. Consumption tools aid the user in the analysis of simulation results. An overview of the environment follows. Then, each layer in the environment is discussed in detail.

AN OVERVIEW OF THE OPERATING ENVIRONMENT

It's trite but true: A picture is worth at least a thousand words. Figure 12-1 provides an overview of the operating environment in the STELLA II and ithink software.

As Figure 12-1 indicates, STELLA II is a multilevel, hierarchical environment for constructing and interacting with models. The environment consists of two major layers: the High-Level Mapping & I/O layer, and the Model Construction

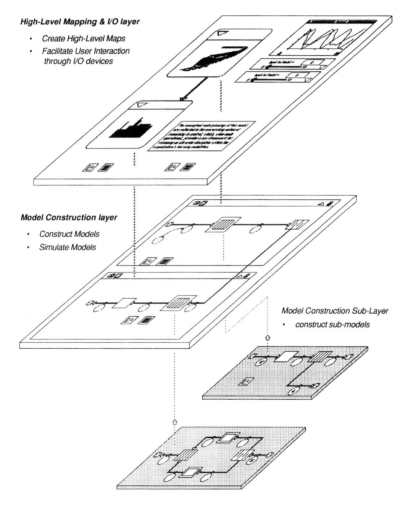

Figure 12-1. A pictorial overview of the environment

layer. Within the Model Construction layer, it is possible to "drill down" to create sub-models. Sub-model spaces are tightly coupled with the Model Construction layer, which in turn is tightly coupled with the High-Level Mapping & I/O layer.

The purpose of the layering is to manage complexity—both for producers and for consumers of models. For producers, the environment fosters a top-down approach to model development. Using tools and objects on the High-Level Mapping & I/O layer, modelers can create a high-level system map. Then, on the Model Construction layer, they can develop a more detailed representation of the relevant processes. Finally, the microlevel structure of specific processes can be represented within sub-model spaces. Because the software facilitates seamless navigation between layers, someone who is constructing a model need not be distracted by extraneous details. The net result is that one can stay in control of the effort—the environment facilitates a seamless movement among conceptualization, construction, analysis, and communication activities.

For consumers of a model, the benefits of the layered environment are even more palpable. Model consumers can begin on the High-Level Mapping & I/O layer, gaining an overview of the model's structure, and interacting with the model through the use of catchy input and output devices (the optional Authoring version of STELLA II and ithink provides a wealth of these latter devices). Working at their own pace, consumers can then move down to the Model Construction layer to work with a more detailed view of the system. As required, they can go even further into the details by exploring sub-model spaces. Because of layering, details can be revealed at a controlled pace. As such, consumers will learn the lessons from the model, without becoming overwhelmed by complexity.

THE HIGH-LEVEL MAPPING & I/O LAYER

The High-level Mapping & I/O layer was designed to facilitate conceptualization, high-level mapping, and model input/output. On this layer, building blocks aid conceptualization and facilitate high-level mapping of a formal model. Objects provide concrete mechanisms for user interaction. These building blocks and objects are shown in Figure 12-2.

Building Blocks for High-Level Mapping. At present, model conceptualization is largely an art rather than a science. In the conceptualization stage, the modeler defines a purpose for the model, and focuses on a pattern of behavior over time that the model is to explain. Then, the modeler simplifies reality, by selecting and lumping together those interrelationships that are seen as essential for achieving the model purpose. To help the user focus the modeling effort, the software provides three high-level mapping tools: the process frame, the bundled flow, and the bundled connector. Since these building blocks are less detailed than stock, flows, or

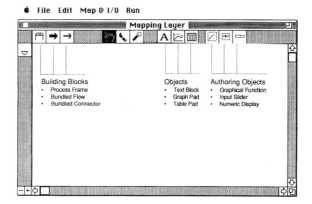

Figure 12-2. The High-Level Mapping & I/O layer

equations, they provide a conceptual bridge between the mental model and the formal model. The resulting map—consisting of key system processes, as well as the material and informational flow channels between them—can make it easier for a novice to understand the overarching structure of the model. A simple high-level map is shown in Figure 12-3.

It's important to note that the high-level map is more than simply a static picture of the system. As one creates a high-level map using the process frame, the bundled flow, and the bundled connector, sector frames are created automatically on the Model Construction layer. These frames will house the Stock/flow structure of the process under investigation. Navigational controls allow users to drill down to the details of a specific model sector. Finally, as material flow and information connections are made between sectors on the Model Construction layer, the high-level map will be updated automatically to reflect these connections. The high-level map thus will always be "in sync" with the underlying detailed representation.

Nonabstract Objects for Input and Output. The second salient feature of the high-level mapping layer is its collection of objects. In the first set of objects, the text block enables one to use text to describe the map as desired. The graph pad and

*Large boxes indicate Sectors. Dark arrows indicate material flows
between sectors. Shaded arrows indicate information flows.*

Figure 12-3. A high-level map

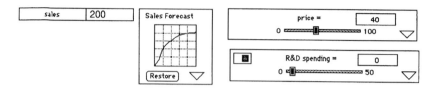

Figure 12-4. Using mapping objects to create a simple control panel

table pad facilitate the collection of model output as graphs and tables. The second set of high-level objects are available only in the Authoring version of the software. The Graphical Function Input and Editing device, input slider, and numeric display provide compelling, nonabstract mechanisms for users to interact with a model. These objects are illustrated in Figure 12-4.

As suggested by the figure, the authoring objects make it possible to develop learning environments and management practice fields in which users can enhance their mental models by interacting directly with a formal model. The Graphical Function Input and Editing Device, for example, makes it possible for model consumers to sketch a model relationship, without requiring them to work with the detailed structure of the formal model. The slider enables consumers to change input parameters, either while a model simulation is paused or while it is running. The slider also allows consumers to override model equation logic. It thus makes it possible for consumers of a model to compare the results of their own decision rules against the output of decision rules that have been embedded in the model. Finally, the numeric display reports out the current value of selected model variables, providing consumers with a sense for the current state of the system as the model simulation progresses.

Preliminary tests with interactive model-based environments (Peterson 1989) suggest that individuals become intellectually and emotionally involved with a model as they use such devices. In particular, real-time "gaming" of a model raises the emotional stakes. Ease of use and emotional involvement translate into user accessibility. Through the use of concrete input and output devices, consumers are far more likely to learn from a model experience than might otherwise be the case.

THE MODEL CONSTRUCTION LAYER

The graphical approach to construction and analysis extends down to the Model Construction layer. On this layer, a modeler will use a set of modeling building blocks to construct the formal model. Again, a collection of objects facilitates analysis and interaction with the model. These building blocks and objects are shown in Figure 12-5. As an illustration of design philosophy, the discussion will focus on building blocks.

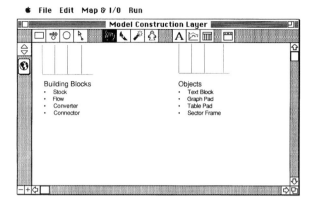

Figure 12-5. The model construction layer

Building Blocks for Model Construction. The stock, flow, converter, and connector are the structural building blocks that the modeler uses to construct a formal model. These building blocks are derived from Forrester's diagramming conventions (Forrester 1961). Once selected from the tool kit, each building block is positioned within the diagram, and then hooked together with other elements as desired to reflect the structural relationships under investigation. Associated with each building block is a set of structural and procedural rules. These rules prevent the user from making typographical and syntactic mistakes. They also remove much of the technical tedium traditionally encountered in constructing a formal model.

For example, as the user creates a structural map using stocks and flows, the software infers the difference equation structure required for simulation. This equation structure is available as a separate window for user examination. However, there is never a need to write a difference equation. Instead, the user can spend time in the graphical domain, representing the relationships that govern particular flow processes.

The user adds flesh to this structural skeleton by using converters and connectors. Converters represent constants, time series inputs, and algebraic conversions of other model variables. In addition, converters are used to represent graphical functions—graphically constructed table look-up functions. Connectors indicate logical or causal connections between model elements. Only realistic connections are allowed. For example, the software will not allow the user to connect converters only to form a feedback loop—an intermediary stock is required. Similarly, the software will not allow the user to drag a connector into a stock—stocks can only change through the movement of their associated flows.

Once a stock/flow map has been developed, it's possible to "drill down" to another level of detail by creating sub-models. A simple sub-model is shown in Figure 12-6. As the figure illustrates, sub-models can be selectively displayed.

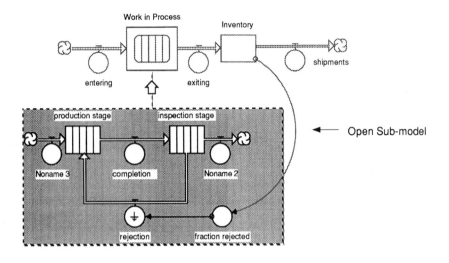

Open Sub-model

Closed Sub-model

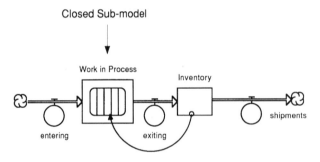

Figure 12-6. Sub-models

Selective display enables a modeler to manage the complexity associated with a formal model.

Within each stock, flow, and converter is a repository for storing equation logic and documenting assumptions. The user accesses this repository by double-clicking on an element. Defining an equation simply requires pointing and clicking with the mouse—there is no need to type variable names, and hence no chance for typographical errors. A sample equation dialog is shown in Figure 12-7.

There are several aspects of this dialog to consider. First, the user defines the equation using the list of required inputs. These inputs are required, because they have been indicated on the model diagram. The software thus enforces a one-to-one correspondence between the structural map and the equation logic that drives the simulation. Second, the equation is defined in isolation. The user can focus on the specifics of a particular process, without being distracted by other aspects of the model. Third, special built-in functions (steps, ramps, boolean operations, distribu-

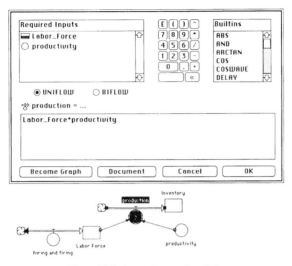

Figure 12-7. A sample equation dialog

tions, etc.) are available from within the dialog. The user can simply choose from among these as needed. Finally, space for documenting each relationship is available. Documentation may be left extant within the dialog, or may be hidden from view. In either case, the verbal description is available to both the producer and the consumer of the model in a contextually sensitive manner.

CONCLUSION: INTEGRATING EXISTING AND EMERGING TOOLS

Software such as STELLA II and ithink provide extensible environments that make the formal modeling process accessible to an audience of expert and neophyte modelers, as well as an audience of model consumers. These environments are highly evolved relative to the command-line environments of the 1960s, and will continue to evolve to meet the needs of mental modelers in industry, education, and government. Trends in computation power and graphical user interface design make possible a variety of evolutionary trajectories. Below are listed a set of emerging construction and consumption tools. Each is in an early stage of development. As these tools become integrated in modeling and simulation software, we can expect to see a larger portion of the thinking populace make use of the power of the modeling process.

Less Abstract, Object-Oriented Model Conceptualization Frameworks. The stock/flow framework for model conceptualization is rigorous and precise. It also is abstract, and in many cases is not a "natural" way for the less-proficient modeler to think about system structure. The layered approach outlined here offers one solution to this difficulty. Object-oriented programming concepts may form the basis for another approach.

For example, instead of distributing managerial decision rules as flow processes throughout a model, an object-oriented approach would lead to the conceptualization of a manager as a single object. Within that object would be a set of response engines—a set of stocks and flows synthesized through the construction of the object. Each "engine" would receive, process, and respond to relevant pressures within the system. The resultant activity and information would feed to other objects within the system, each containing its own set of response engines.

Model Analysis Tools. Graphs, tables, animations, and numeric displays provide useful insight into model behavior. But the question of why a model behaves as it does is often difficult for even the expert modeler to answer. Analytical techniques, such as eigenvalue analysis, are currently too demanding for the general user. Software tools that can dynamically sense and then display graphically the strength of selected model feedback mechanisms hold much promise. Currently, such tools are in their infancy.

Concrete Model Input Tools. The collection of input objects described here go far to facilitate user interaction with a model. Emerging technologies such as voice input hold much potential for making user input to a model even easier to accomplish.

Concrete Model Output Tools. Current technologies enable a personal computer to display stunning animation sequences, to synthesize speech, and to play full-motion video. We have begun to merge these technologies with modeling and simulation software (process frames and sector frames, for example, are capable of sequencing movies based on model output). The technology is only in its infancy, however, and performance can be quite sluggish. As the technology evolves, it opens the door to the creation of virtual realities. In these environments, the structure of the simulation model, as modified by user input, would generate a compelling, visceral learning experience for all users.

REFERENCES

Forrester, J.W. (1961), *Industrial Dynamics,* Portland, Ore.: Productivity Press.

Peterson, S. (1990), *A User's Guide to STELLA® Stack,* High Performance Systems, 45 Lyme Road, Suite 300, Hanover, NH 03755.

Richmond, B., S. Peterson et al. (1993), *STELLA® II Documentation,* High Performance Systems, 45 Lyme Road, Suite 300, Hanover, NH 03755.

Richmond, B., S. Peterson et al. (1993), *ithink™ Documentation,* High Performance Systems, 45 Lyme Road, Suite 300, Hanover, NH 03755.

13

THE SYSTEM DYNAMICS APPROACH TO COMPUTER-BASED MANAGEMENT LEARNING ENVIRONMENTS: IMPLICATIONS AND THEIR IMPLEMENTATION IN POWERSIM

PÅL I. DAVIDSEN

ABSTRACT: Modell Data AS; the Department of Information Science, University of Bergen; and Stord College of Education, Norway, have developed a number of interactive, computer-based learning environments for system dynamics modeling and simulation. Applications range from relatively general training simulators for Der Rütli, a German management institute, and the Norwegian Naval Academy, to production and market management simulators for Norwegian enterprises in a variety of domains ranging from the aluminum industry to fish farming, and to tanker, helicopter, and airplane simulators for pilot training. These applications have been developed using the associated MS Windows™-based modeling and simulation software, PowerSim™.

PowerSim by itself is a general purpose learning environment for the investigation of dynamic systems. In this paper, we will focus on the general principles of its application to specific domains and, for now, we reserve the concept "computer-based learning environment" for that purpose. The system dynamics approach implies a series of requirements that are generally not satisfied by current computer-based learning environments, often called "management flight simulators." This paper outlines some of these requirements and documents how we use PowerSim to satisfy these requirements. Moreover, we indicate trends in the utilization of PowerSim to support just-in-time open learning.

FROM DECISION MAKING TO POLICY DESIGN
AND STRATEGY COMPOSITION

Although system dynamics-based learning environments can be used to learn domain specific decision procedures, the purpose of developing and using such environments is more general. When managing dynamic systems, the implementation of operating procedures should be thought of as a result of a strategy formulation (Forrester 1986). A strategy is composed of a well-balanced set of domain-specific policies, such as production, inventory, marketing, sales, personnel, and capital management policies. Moreover, there is the tactical selection and adaptation of strategy leading up to operational decision procedures.

The system dynamics approach supports the management of dynamic systems at all these levels by helping us understand the intimate relationship between structure and behavior in such systems. The higher the level of administration on which we operate, the wider is the time horizon, the more complex are the systems in question, and the greater is the need for an approach of this kind.

Although presented as strategic, most simulation-based learning environments do not support the design and evaluation of policies and strategies. For an environment to do so, three requirements must be satisfied. The learner must be allowed to (1) investigate the underlying assumptions, (2) formulate alternative policies, and (3) evaluate these policies before deciding to continue. Moreover, this must be done repeatedly so that the experience gained from evaluating a strategy can form the basis for investigations, and the formulation and evaluation of alternative strategies. Current "management flight simulators" have not provided an option for hypothetical strategies to be subjected to simulation-based evaluations, whereupon the simulator reverts to current time. Using PowerSim™, we have built in this capability in the Rütli Management Simulator. Thus, we facilitate double-loop learning (Senge and Sterman 1992, and Chapter 8 of this work) implemented in the form represented in Figure 13-1.

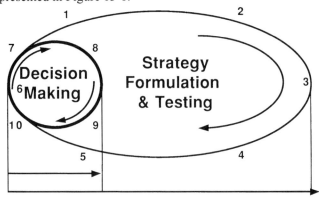

Figure 13-1. Two modes in which to run the simulator

There are, in other words, two modes in which the simulator can be run interchangeably:

- an operational mode in which final decisions are being made and submitted to a model that responds with a state projection over the assigned *operational* horizon (e.g., one year);

- a strategic mode in which strategies may be developed and submitted along with user-defined assumptions about the environment (e.g., competitors) to a model that responds with a state projection over the assigned *strategic* horizon (e.g., five years).

Computer-based learning environments should support off-the-shelf computer networks. The PowerSim software has been designed to do so. Consequently, the simulator may be run in a single-user mode, i.e., on a local computer, or in a computer network against other participants—some or all of which may be simulated by the computer. Throughout the network, additional computers can join a running simulation so as, for instance, to portray a new competitor entering the market. Such a competitor may typically be formed by a team of managers that break away from existing competing teams.

The procedure for running a management simulator designed in PowerSim is summarized in Figure 13-1 and is the same whether participants run solely against a local computer or in a network of computers. In the latter case, identical simulations models are stored on each of the participating local computers as well as on the server, although they are applied for different purposes. The phases in the two modes of running the simulator are as follows:

1. Make assumptions about the environment. One of the major challenges in the design of computer-based learning environments intended for strategic purposes is the fact that during strategy formulations, there is no environment available to provide input to the model. The participants are operating into the future, and must make assumptions about the environment in which they are operating. In some cases, this will be an aggregate environment, typically portrayed by the local computer, or an environment represented by participants acting as teams of managers in a computer network. In any case, there are two ways of characterizing that environment. One is to make assumptions about the behavior (i.e., the dynamics) of the environment. Another way is to characterize the policies governing its behavior. In the Rütli Management Simulator, these assumptions concern the price, functionality, lifetime, and image of the products supplied by competitors in a market, and their corresponding delivery delays.

A technique has been developed that allows the simulator to select between "real input" from the computer model or other actors while in operational mode, and user-defined assumptions while in test mode.

2–3. Formulate and submit a strategy to the computer. Secondly, the participants must formulate their policies. In the Rütli Management Simulator, there are altogether 26 decisions to be made that make up the price, inventory, quality, personnel, capital, advertising, and finance policies.

Having done so, the participants press "Try Decisions" in a control panel to submit their assumptions and strategies to their local computer.

4. Let local computer compute the behavioral consequences. That local computer is now ready to project the model across the strategic horizon. The simulation can be made to halt at a certain frequency or under specific conditions so as to allow for the modification of assumptions or strategy.

5. Evaluate effects of strategy. Using a number of simulation reports, the participants can then evaluate the effects of their assumptions about the environment and their corresponding strategies.

6. Revert to current time. If desired, they can modify their assumptions and/or their policies, run another test, and through a systematic analysis of the results decide upon a combination of policies. Or the participants may decide to go ahead and implement their strategy. In any case their local model must be brought back to current state at current time. To do so, the participants press "Revert" in a control panel.

7–8. Make and submit an operative decision to the computer. Having found a policy to be applied and reverted the model, the participants are ready to enter the operative mode. In accordance with their strategy, they then formulate the corresponding operative decisions that apply to the current operative time horizon.

Having done so, they press "Make Decisions" in a control panel to submit their operative decisions to their local computer.

9. Let computer compute the behavioral consequences. In cases where the participants run solely against their local computer, that computer simulates the consequences of all decisions across the operative decision horizon. In cases where a network is set up, the decisions are transmitted to the server, which awaits decisions from all participants and projects the model based upon these inputs. In such cases, all decisions are forwarded to all local computers to form the basis for updating the state of the simulation models stored locally.

10. Evaluate effects of decisions. Using the available simulation reports, the participants can now evaluate the effects of their collective decisions and, when desired, reenter the strategic mode.

TRANSPARENCY AND MODIFIABILITY; REPRESENTING THE INTEGRATION OF STRUCTURE AND BEHAVIOR

The learning environment must effectively support strategic investigation, formulation, and evaluation. This implies that the model, embedded in the learning environment, must be available for inspection and modification whenever required. Consequently, the learning environment must offer a smooth transition from tools used to model and set up simulations in general, to the kind of "management flight simulators" currently marketed, where the model is often hidden and where there is minimal support for analysis.

Users investigate the underlying simulation model of the learning environment by inspecting the structural assumptions embodied in that model and by utilizing the test mode to reveal their behavioral consequences. Using PowerSim, we can open the model for inspection. We do so by iconizing views of the model to be opened by the user, the result of which would typically look like Figure 13-2.

These model views can represent the model in the form of a stock-and-flow diagram (Figures 13-3a, b) where the user is allowed to inspect the underlying equations. Also, the model can be represented in the form of a feedback loop diagram (Figure 13-3c) and in the form of text. Moreover, there are icons that can be opened to specify input or define tactics using slide-bars (Figure 13-3d), or opened to study the resulting model behavior.

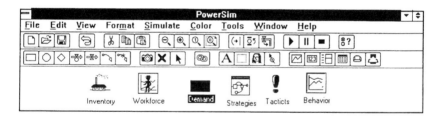

Figure 13-2. Iconized sector and management windows

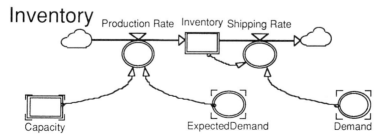

Figure 13-3a. Opening "Inventory"

Workforce

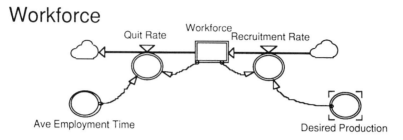

Figure 13-3b. Opening "Workforce"

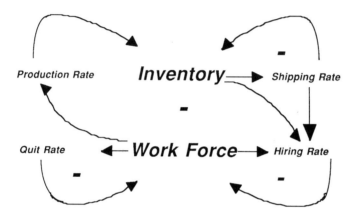

Figure 13-3c. Opening a feedback-loop representation

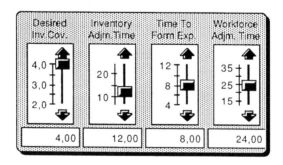

Figure 13-3d. Opening a window for tactical adaptation

To facilitate investigation, we integrate into the structural representation of the simulation model, whether in the form of stock-and-flow diagrams (Figure 13-4a) or feedback-loop diagrams (Figure 13-4b), "live" graphs and/or numbers representing the model behavior. We also embed such miniature graphs directly in text.

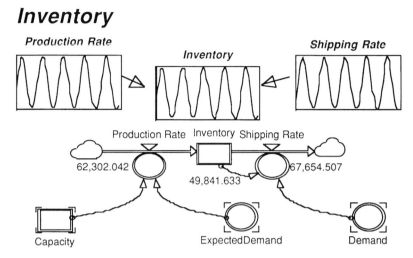

Figure 13-4a. Linking descriptions of behavior into stock-and-flow diagrams

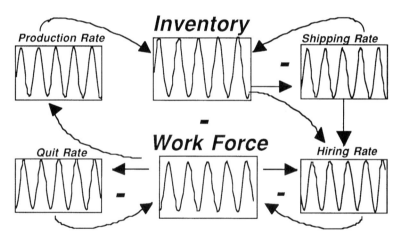

Figure 13-4b. Linking descriptions of behavior into feedback-loop diagrams

Thus, using the graphical editing tools of PowerSim, we let the structural documentation in the learning environment come alive during simulation. In that way, behavior is linked closely to the underlying structure and becomes self-explanatory.

Strategic formulations typically require structural reformulations of the model. To facilitate that, we open up windows on the underlying model that focus on policies to be designed by participants as parts of a new strategy (Figure 13-5).

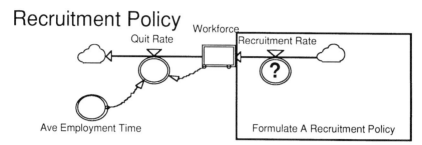

Figure 13-5. Window opened for recruitment policy formulation

NETWORKS OF CO-MODELS

In most cases, we analyze systems into subsystems and synthesize models from sub-models representing these subsystems. Using PowerSim, we define these models in the form of co-models to be integrated in any super-model. Co-models are interrelated using "chains" that indicate the transfer of variable values from one model to variables in any of its co-models during the course of the simulation.

We specify the synchronized simulation of all co-models in a main model—just another co-model. For each co-model, we may define individually a start and stop time as well as an integration interval synchronized with of the main model. In our design of learning environments, we make extensive use of co-models. Here are some examples.

We usually define the control panels and all reports in one or more co-models, the most essential of which are often contained as part of the main model. Other co-models may be used to emphasize various aspects of the relationship between structure and behavior, such as the ones portrayed in Figure 13-4. Note that we can define views that encompass a variety of controls and reports. Thus we can supply information relevant to the formulation of a policy in the form of numerical or graphical reports related to the control panel for that policy. In Figure 13-6, we indicate how information about current costs, historic competitor prices, and historic price components are being used as a background for price setting.

We can also use co-models to initiate and phase out main models. A Navy project may consist of a 5-year construction and acquisition phase that partly overlaps with a 25-year operation phase, which again overlaps with a 5-year phase-out. The first 5-year period may be represented by one or several co-models that supply the main model with a fleet, initial supplies, infrastructure, and trained personnel of a certain quality that, in part, determine the operational characteristics of the fleet, represented by the main model. The final 5-year period is portrayed in a second co-model that gradually takes over and phases out all of the components listed above.

Moreover, co-models with longer integration intervals can be used to sample variable values from any model, and can typically be used to support or represent

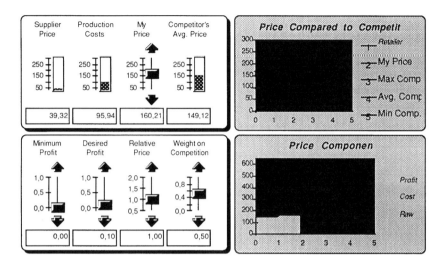

Figure 13-6. Window opened for setting and evaluating price policies

information systems with their biases and delays, e.g., a financial sector or a user interface. A model can also supply any of its co-models with empirical information—one of which may compare this information with the sampled behavior of the simulation model.

Carefully defined and individually run co-models constitute an important educational resource. In many cases, they can effectively supplement an introduction to the model as a whole. The Rütli Management Simulator is equipped with co-models representing an order- and supply-line with a co-flow of quality, the structure of work force and capital, the market and marketing, and the financial sector—each of which are used in a two-day simulation-based introduction.

In the case of applying computer networks, co-models are typically used to create an interface between the administrator of such multiuser learning environment and the server model so that she can set up the environment with a well-initialized model and investigate the policies of all participants and their dynamic consequences. Other co-models are developed to form an interface between each of the participants and their local models. These interfaces filter out information that the participants should not share involuntarily, e.g., financial information.

POWERSIM FEATURES THAT FACILITATE THE DESIGN OF MODELS AND LEARNING ENVIRONMENTS

The PowerSim software utilizes MS Windows™ facilities extensively. Consequently we can easily custom design and organize our system dynamics models and learning environments using a variety of graphical tools supported by MS

Windows. A precise and consistent use of colors contributes significantly in that respect. For educational purposes, we can hide parts of the model by assigning the background color to the symbols we want our students to identify on their own. Alternatively, we can use a "show what" menu item to hide any class of symbols in the model (levels, rates etc.) and in the learning environment (graphs, slide-bars, etc.).

In some cases, we may want to modify certain model or interface components or to protect such components from unauthorized editing. In that case, we can use a password to lock the model and the associated environment in simulation mode so that no editing can take place. The same password can be used to gain access to the model, to disclose hidden components, and to modify the result.

PowerSim allows us to define models or model components as arrays. Such a transition is relatively straightforward. Arrays are indicated by model components equipped with double border lines. Range variables with sub-ranges can be defined and utilized as index variables. A well-formulated grammar and a library of special functions help modelers define complex operations on arrays. An extensive series of consistency checks warn against and prohibit dimensional inconsistencies.

The library of special functions consists of a set of sub-libraries and is open for user-supplied additions written in the form of dynamic link libraries (DLLs). Each simulation generates new results. These results can be saved automatically, enumerated, plotted, and compared.

SYSTEM DYNAMICS-BASED EDUCATIONAL TECHNOLOGIES IN A "JITOL" LEARNING ENVIRONMENT: LOOKING INTO THE NEAR FUTURE

Within the EEC project JITOL (Just in Time Open Learning), Norway contributes both in the technical (WP 1), the evaluative (WP 2), and the application-oriented (WP 3) work packages. In WP 3, our purpose is to train educators in the use of information technologies relevant to their needs. Among the courses currently under development is one on system dynamics modeling, one on computer-based learning environments for system dynamics, and one on management simulators.

In the JITOL project we teach professional educators to analyze, build, and utilize simulation models as a basis for interactive hypermedia productions. The software environment in which this education will take place consists of three electronic books: a textbook, one of assignments, and a workbook. They are all related in the form of hypertext. There are hyperlinks to PowerSim models that constitute a platform of examples from which students can work. Winix™ network software allows the student to participate in conferences or communicate directly with the advisor, including sending graphical material and models as appendices. Since the modeling process itself is so crucial, it will be possible to record annotated modeling sessions and send them on the network for consultation. Using picture and moving icons (picons/micons), participants can exchange illustrative references at low transmission costs, pending efficiently transmitted source material. In this section, we focus on some of these requirements that must be satisfied to facilitate distance education in system dynamics in the form of JITOL.

The JITOL student is typically challenged to identify a dynamic problem, to model the problem, and to suggest and test solutions to that problem. Initially he turns up with a problem-behavior associated with the well-known inventory-work force-production cycle.

The advisor offers an explanation for why the system exhibits an oscillatory behavior illustrated in Figure 13-7. First, she creates her own model and annotates the resulting simulation: At carefully selected points, she stops the simulation, inserts comments, and resumes the simulation. When the student receives the annotated version of the model, the model itself will be hidden by the advisor who has assigned the background color to the model components and prohibited editing, using a password. When the student runs the model in annotated mode, the simulation stops at the appropriate points in time to provide access to the teacher's annotations.

The student is then challenged to create his own model of the system, i.e., a theory that explains the behavior in detail (Figure 13-8). Note that, as part of the annotations, the advisor electronically transmits icons that refer to underlying source material illustrating the problem—in this case video footage and a textbook that will appear upon a double-click. These icons appear (and possibly disappear) at appropriate times during the simulation. The simulation will pause when such a reference is activated through a double-click, or can optionally be made to stop once an icon appears. In the next section, we will return to the utilization of icons in various forms as references in a simulation-based hypermedia production, and to their significance in long-distance education.

Following a discussion of the fundamental relationships between stocks and flows representing the states and the state-transitions in dynamic systems, the student comes up with a stock-and-flow diagram in which a reference is made to an

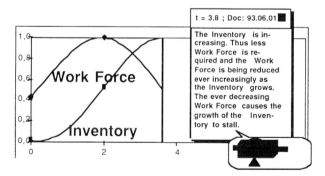

Figure 13-7. The explanation (advisor's annotations)

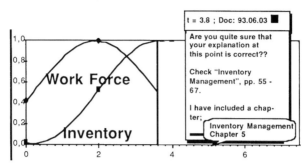

Figure 13-8. The challenge (student's model)

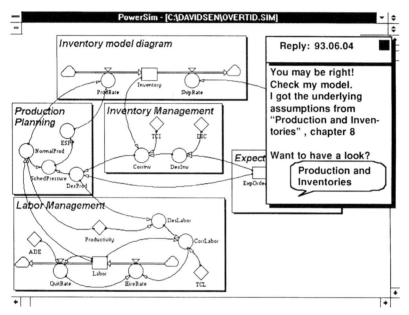

Figure 13-9. Annotated stock-and-flow diagram of the model

article on inventory management (Figure 13-9). Using behavior and structure annotations as illustrated, the JITOL sessions can be turned into rich, learner-directed interactions, whereby texts and references to a variety of hyper-media-based source materials are exchanged.

HYPERMEDIA ACCESS

Three kinds of technologies are associated with system dynamics modeling. The core technology encompasses the model editor and the run-time system required to simulate any model. The auxiliary technology constitutes mathematical and graphical libraries required to analyze and display the dynamic models. Both kinds of libraries can be embedded in the model editor or run-time systems to support the model building, the simulation, and the portrayal of results during the simulation. This is true as well for a third kind of library that provides access to or from peripheral technology.

Peripheral technology is hardware and software that are not built into or embedded in the primary technology. It serves three kinds of purposes: It extends our mathematical and graphical capabilities. It contains and provides access to reference or source materials relevant to the model under development and use. It also enables us to create a software environment, such as a "management flight simulator," in which the underlying assumptions can be presented, the simulation can take place, and the results can be displayed to facilitate and enhance the interpretation of the model.

For the purpose of understanding complex, dynamic systems, we have traditionally utilized graphical techniques. Therefore, we need to integrate a representation of behavior into one of structure—or vice versa (Davidsen 1991). Modern window management technology allows us to create embedded multidimensional, and colored time-plot, vector, and state-space diagrams.

We face a major challenge in search for illustrations that can be applied for practical purposes across a wide variety of disciplines and over an extensive period of time: On the one hand, we need to attain a certain level of generality by utilizing abstractions. On the other hand, we want to be specific, i.e., to minimize the discrepancy between our perception of real issues and the way we represent (model) these issues: To facilitate model conceptualization and avoid misinterpretations, we must be concrete. It is useful to employ a series of representational forms—some of which allow us to consider reality from a distance, and some of which bring us very close to real issues, in order to strike the requisite balance between abstraction and concreteness. System dynamics diagrams are typically abstract. They are ideal for describing generic components, but less suited for triggering real life associations. They offer students a relatively limited expressive power with which to portray their vision of reality. To some students, such a high degree of abstraction may constitute an insurmountable threshold.

The introduction of animation constitutes an additional dimension that may cause students to associate their model observations with real phenomena. We operate in animation with interactive interface objects that can attain properties such as size, color, position (both absolute and relative to each other), speed, and direction of movement, etc. We can make extensive use of animation to portray the relationship between structural components, their individual behavior, and their interactions. The major advantage of animation is the precise relationship that we can establish between the dynamics of a model and the corresponding animation.

Moreover it can contribute significantly as overlays on interactive video-productions. On the other hand, there are two disadvantages. The creation of an animated production is the job of a highly skilled specialist and demands relatively large amounts of resources. And, though they do trigger associations, animations are seldom close enough to reality to substitute for video. Note that though animation is inherently dynamic, few languages have been developed that describe dynamic behavior. The system dynamics language is one that we can use to provide substance to our animations.

Video productions have become intimately integrated with computer technology in the form of interactive video. Such video productions allow the individual student to explore visual, textual, and audible materials that form a hyperspace. Digitization techniques facilitate the creation of p[icture]icons and m[oving] icons, icons that contain picture or film material. We can include picons/micons in the structural or behavioral presentation of models, as references to the original material stored on peripheral technology. As an illustration of structure, picons/ micons would typically be superimposed on top of the elements of stock-and-flow or feedback diagrams (or some animated version of such diagrams). By double-clicking on the picons/micons, the underlying material, which illustrates levels and rates and the relationships between them, is brought onto the screen in full size. The video material may also illustrate the typical behavior produced by selected structural components of the system in isolation. Likewise, during the simulation, picons/micons may appear, triggered by the behavior of the model, referring to material that illustrates the behavior mode currently exhibited by the model or the dominant structure underlying current model behavior. By carefully defining the conditions for the appearance of picons/micons, their position, and the duration of their appearance, we may integrate references to structure and behavior in a way that clearly illustrates the relationship between the two. In view of the critique raised against the symptomatic approach represented by the "flight simulators," it should be stressed that the interactive video approach thus offers an opportunity to associate the two systems aspects, not only as they are portrayed in the model, but also as they appear in reality.

By utilizing overlay technology, we can combine real life references in the form of video footage with traditional diagrams and animation. We can use overlay to emphasize important structural relationships that produce the dynamic behavior illustrated in a video sequence. Or we can use the technique to animate the behavior, created by the interaction of components, appearing in the video. Full motion video digitization with compression and decompression enable us to download, manipulate, and retrieve video in real time, using a minimum of space so that video and sound will appear as data types, stored on digital media along with textual and numerical information. The representation of all forms of information on a common platform facilitates the integration of these forms to support the illustration of dynamic systems properties. More importantly, it allows students to use cam-corders to document their models and to apply their own footage annotations, to link this reference material into their models at their convenience, and to combine it the way they find most useful. This enhances learner participation, adds to the meaning of interactivity and opens up new, learner-defined ways to understand complex behavior.

REFERENCES

Davidsen, P.I. (1991), "The Structure-Behavior Graph: Understanding the Relationship Between Structure and Behavior in Complex, Dynamic Systems," Department of Information Science, University of Bergen, Bergen, Norway; System Dynamics Group, Massachusetts Institute of Technology, Cambridge.

Forrester, J.W. (1987), "Lessons from System Dynamics Modeling," *System Dynamics Review* 3, no. 2: 136-49.

Senge, P., and J.D. Sterman (1992), "Systems Thinking and Organizational Learning: Acting Locally and Thinking Globally in the Organization of the Future," *European Journal of Operational Research* 59, no. 1: 137; also Chapter 8 of this volume.

14

THE SYSTEM DYNAMICS MODELING PROCESS AND DYSMAP2

BRIAN DANGERFIELD

ABSTRACT: Recent work on the practice of strategic policymaking has highlighted how a model can be introduced to make the process more effective. System dynamics models are particularly appropriate for inclusion in this emerging framework for the debate of policy issues. The procedural framework integrates ideas from group decision support systems, boardroom systems, and scenario generation, and requires particular features in the system dynamics modeling software employed. Consideration is given to those specific features of the DYSMAP2 software that meet the need of senior managerial groups faced with the resolution of policy issues.

INTRODUCTION

A central tenet of system dynamics is that problematic behavior in our systems arises from the complex interaction of nonlinear feedback processes, coupled with our inability to understand these dynamics intuitively. System dynamics modelers have therefore stressed the need for formal models, solved by computer simulation, from the inception of the field (Forrester 1958).

While some have developed roles for qualitative mapping and modeling using various diagrams to represent feedback structure (Wolstenholme and Coyle 1983; Wolstenholme 1990), and these tools are often useful, intuition is simply not capable of reliably inferring the dynamics of a complex nonlinear system. Computer simulation is required.

In the light of this unique dependency between computer and method, it is incumbent on the developers of system dynamics software to ensure that they offer as many features as are needed to support good modeling and, indeed, to enhance the quality of the modeling and policy design processes. This paper sets out important features of the DYSMAP2 system dynamics modeling software (Dangerfield and Vapenikova 1987; Vapenikova 1986, 1989) insofar as such features contribute to the ease with which a formal computer model can be incorporated into the process of policy debate.

MODELS IN THE POLICY PROCESS

It is only relatively recently that practitioners of system dynamics have sought to define the appropriate role for a model in the process of supporting strategic policy (Morecroft 1988; Lane 1989; Dangerfield 1991). This role is perhaps best described as strategic counseling through the medium of a model.

Senior managers and directors engage in a series of interactions with an emerging model. It is hoped that their perceptions are sharpened and better policy actions result, based on an improved understanding of the system. Policymakers' mental models are challenged and enlarged; maybe their attitudes are softened. De Geus (1988) sets out what he sees as the advantages of this process in an elegant description of his experiences within the Royal Dutch/Shell group of companies. Put at its starkest the thesis is simple: Senior managers will have far better mental maps as a result of their experiences with a computer-based model than would result from not having been exposed to such a process.

These statements of the role of a system dynamics model, shifting the emphasis from content to process, are extremely timely. Many management scientists cannot easily place system dynamics in a taxonomy of modeling methods. Indeed, it is often omitted altogether from textbooks on the subject whereas many other model-based techniques, with little to offer in the way of supporting strategic policy, are given significant coverage (see also de Geus' foreword to this volume).

DYSMAP2: A SOFTWARE TOOL FOR SYSTEM DYNAMICS MODELING

To appreciate how DYSMAP2 can be employed as part of this process of using model-based scenarios to confront senior managers' mental models it is necessary to embrace two related lines of development within management science. These are the ideas of group decision support systems and boardroom systems.

Group decision support systems have been the subject of an emerging literature culminating recently in a book by Eden and Radford (1990), which included seven pages of references. Such systems focus on how best to manage organizational issues of strategic significance. They are based on the premise that, at the strategic level in an organization, "answers" are not likely to be found for what are ill-structured and many-faceted problems commonly involving tradeoffs. Instead, the emphasis switches to the design of a strategic thinking process. This may well presage a shift in organizational culture. Of course, these ideas mesh nicely with the role of a system dynamics model as described above, for one of the ways to structure the thinking process is to introduce a computer model that captures the issues at stake.

The group decision support process involves a facilitator who, in the current context, would be a management scientist familiar with system dynamics modeling and the DYSMAP2 software. At the stage of model conceptualization the facilitator would employ an ordinary pedagogic piece of hardware, namely a whiteboard. It should be as large as possible consistent with the size of the room being used for the session. For group construction of influence and flow diagrams this is arguably a superior approach to doing the same thing directly on a monitor screen.

Numerous revisions to the emerging diagrams can be expected, and the flexibility provided by a large whiteboard, colored pens, and an eraser wins over direct construction via a monitor, where size limitations render text and diagrams less legible.

Moreover, the use of a computer at this stage will not encourage participants to amend or enlarge the evolving diagrams with the same ease that they can pick up a board marker. If the session is going well, they should need no encouragement to contribute directly in this way. Vennix et al. (1990) describe the effective use of a whiteboard at this stage of the process in their description of the construction of a system dynamics model of a health care issue. Direct copying from a whiteboard (though not yet in color) is now possible; this offers considerable utility for participants who can then be provided with hard copy as a primer for further contemplation in advance of the next session.

At a suitable point the facilitator will convert the model from its diagrammatic form to its equation-based analog, obtaining the cooperation of the client group for the assessment of suitable parameter values. In particular, here, the table functions available in DYSMAP2 allow the group to capture "soft" issues or relationships based on judgment and belief, that are incapable of being verified directly using formal statistical methods. This is a powerful feature not so readily available with other modeling paradigms and is one that has considerable utility for dealing with policy-level issues.

Although equations are formulated by the facilitator outside of the plenary conferencing process, there is no reason why the model should be a black box to the participants. DYSMAP2 allows long variable names (up to 32 characters including underscore) and this permits user-friendly algebra. A typical equation might be:

$$Sales\_rate\_of\_XYZ.kl = Normal\_Sales.k * Effect\_of\_Advertising.k$$

With one equation for each variable in the model, which can be put in any order in the listing, it is easy for participants to relate the detail of the model to the diagrams they have helped to produce beforehand, which they each have a personal copy of.

Sharp and Price (1984) have offered the view that the syntax of system dynamics models is cumbersome. This may well be a reference to the postscripts required in DYSMAP2 after all variable names, wherever they are used. There seems no reason why the postscript requirements should inhibit the acceptability of the model to the user. The letters J, K, and L relate to past, present, and future time points, respectively. It is easy to understand how these are relabeled on completion of each time step so that the simulation advances through time. Furthermore, the rigor provided by the use of postscripts prevents absurd formulations such as

$$Rate1.kl = Rate2.jk$$

and participants can be apprised of how such statements would violate the normal laws of equation formulation should one of them suggest such a change.

Collaboration with the client management group in the early stages of model construction is vitally important in the context of the entire policy support process. While the qualitative phase of strategic modeling can itself yield benefits (Naylor 1986; Wolstenholme 1990), the most exciting phase is likely to be associated with running the assembled model and subsequent consideration of various policy-oriented scenarios. Since the greatest added-value, in a managerial learning sense, is likely to occur at this stage in the process, the payoff from client involvement in the earlier model construction phase is now realized. While debate surrounding the scenario projections is a healthy sign of interest and enthusiasm and is a testimony to the model "doing its job," it would be disastrous if, on the other hand, there were to be unanimous rejection of the model by the client group. However, this is much less likely to happen when the group members have directly contributed to model construction. The notion of the consultant preparing his own DYSMAP2 model and then turning up to demonstrate its capabilities is one that should never be entertained.

Prior to public explorations with the model, the analyst should satisfy himself as to its internal consistency. The DYSMAP2 dimensional analyzer is a useful tool here in that it subjects each equation to a test of dimensional consistency using the user-supplied definition statements. In themselves these are an extremely important component of the set of model statements, not least for labels on graph plots. The units of measure can be extracted from each definition statement and a dimensional check performed on every active equation in the model. A further check is provided by an optional tabulation of all the maximum and minimum values reached by each variable during the course of the simulation. Thus, without plotting out every single model variable, the results of, for instance, extreme condition tests can be inspected at a glance.

Because it has been implemented as an interpreter rather than a compiler (Vapenikova 1986), model execution is one continuous uninterrupted process with DYSMAP2. The user would normally opt to be put into the Interactive Command Processor environment immediately on completion of a successful run of a model. Various forms of color graph plot can then be presented, with a maximum of six plots on one graph. By default *all* variables' values are stored during execution for possible subsequent plotting. Requests to SAVE variables for plotting are unnecessary unless the model is so large that disk storage of the data is compromised. It is at this stage that the dialectic role of the model comes into its own. The reaction of the participants to the scenarios is rarely neutral, especially if representatives from separate functional areas are present.

In order to ensure the fullest participation a certain hardware configuration is recommended. While this must always be considered as one aspect of the wider issue of physical room layout, as described for instance by Huxham (1990), it is nonetheless of fairly central importance. Appropriate hardware is a large wall-screen and an RGB projector, usually fitted to the ceiling, which allows all participants an unfettered sight of the screen displays. Here we recognize the contribution provided by the ideas of "boardroom systems" mentioned earlier. Such systems emerged in the U.K. in the late 1980s and are described by Preedy and Bittlestone (1985). These systems are promulgated with a view to providing an extremely rapid and effective way of presenting information to senior managers and directors. But the ideas also fit in well with the notion of group decision support systems and system dynamics modeling for managerial learning. It can be only a matter of time before boardroom systems embrace a modeling capability; this is perhaps a significant opportunity for system dynamics to forge a niche as *the* management science tool for use at the strategic level in organizations.

DYSMAP2 offers three forms of graph plot: up to six variables from one run (with a single Y-axis or multiple Y-axes), a single variable across a maximum of six policy runs, and finally, one variable against another instead of against time. The facilitator can request a time-based graph to be zoomed to allow clearer representation of the system behavior at crucial time periods. In addition, the automatic selection of scales on the vertical axes can be overridden if necessary.

A graph that allows a single variable to be plotted over a number of runs (a comparison or co-plot) is highly informative. The participants can appreciate the effects of policy alternatives far more quickly. Consider the DYSMAP2 co-plots shown as Figures 14-1 and 14-2. These are derived from a simple generic production planning model for a consumer goods manufacturing firm. Figure 14-1 depicts a co-plot of the behavior of the finished goods inventory after an exogenous 10 percent step increase in sales at day 120 followed by an equivalent decrease 150 days later. It is quite clear from the figure that the longer the correction time for finished goods stock and the averaging time for the sales rate, the further the stock level falls, and for a longer period. In terms of the supply position for its customers, the longer the adjustment time, the worse the firm's performance.

By contrast, the co-plot of the production rate (Figure 14-2) reveals that the least destabilizing response to the sales rate changes (and therefore one that would best suit the firm's production manager) occurs when the longest adjustment time is adopted. A trade-off between the effects on the finished goods stock position and production rate stability must be contemplated, and the very nature of these graphs draws this out clearly. It is not possible to define a policy, based only on stock correction and sales averaging time, that simultaneously stabilizes both finished goods inventory and the rate of production.

Within the Interactive Command Processor the co-plot command is simply CO_PLOT <variable name> although, as with all the interactive commands, an abbreviation (in this case CP) is acceptable. A color plot of the variable's behavior

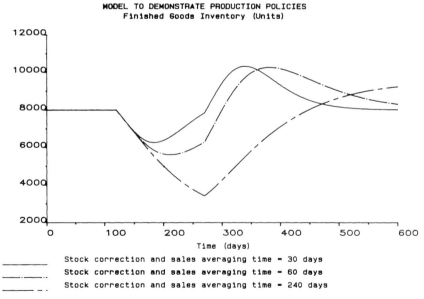

Figure 14-1. Co-plot of the finished goods inventory over three different adjustment times

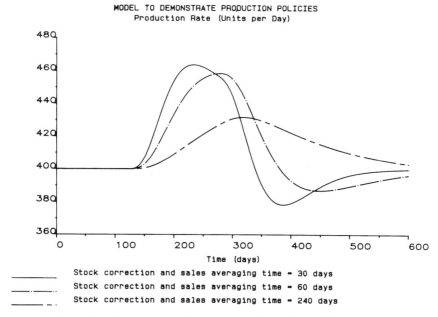

Figure 14-2. Co-plot of the production rate over three different adjustment times

across the first six runs executed is then displayed. If it is desired to restrict the display to a more specific subset of runs then a variation of the PLOT command can be used. For example

PLOT X/1 X/4 X/6

will produce a co-plot of variable X across runs 1, 4, and 6.

The design of the command processing environment fits in well with group decision support and its manifestation in decision conferencing. Besides the generation of graph plots, participants may request the alteration of a parameter value or even a posited relationship as a prelude to another run. This can be accomplished through the CHANGE (C) command, available together with other facilities, such as a listing of runs conducted in the session, hard copy versions of the graphs, a screen list of variables available for plotting, and, if necessary, the individual model equations together with their definitions. Movement between different runs is simplicity itself using the SELECTRUN (SR) command. Provided the large screen projection facilities are available and the personal computer is powerful enough (relative to the size of the model and the simulation run length), there are no other technical limitations to employing DYSMAP2's command processor environment as a forum through which policy issues can be confronted and debated.

FUTURE DEVELOPMENTS

Apart from the implementation of a WINDOWS-based version of DYSMAP2 (something that will take it away from the keyboard-driven approach to computing and more in line with modern applications software in management science) there are perhaps two main features that would enhance its utility specifically in the context of managerial learning. These are facilities for optimization and gaming.

Optimization can be employed in one of two ways: either for the improvement of system performance or for achieving the best fit of model variables to past time series data. A modified version of the original DYSMAP program, called DYSMOD (Luostarinen 1982) which has now been ported to a PC environment and retitled as DYSMOD/386, has been used by Keloharju (1983) to demonstrate both of these purposes.

A facility to enable data fitting would expedite the model's acceptance by the participants who often expect to see good agreement between simulated behavior and past time series data. Such a feature also yields the subsidiary benefit of offering a further source of information in the quest for suitable parameter values. The estimates that result from the fitting process can be compared with those emerging in discussions with relevant managers or from statistical analysis of empirical data.

Of possibly more direct relevance to enhanced learning by the participants is a gaming capability. The value of system dynamics models in a gaming environment has been stressed by Meadows (1989). Engaging in business games may not be something that very senior people are likely to do. As de Geus (1988) comments, "We didn't feel we could go to executives who run some of the biggest companies in the world and say, 'Come on, let's have a little game.'" However, for some senior managers who take decisions within a given policy framework, game play can help them understand the consequences of their particular role in the operations of their firm. An ideal arrangement would involve a single group of managers watching the behavior of the selected system variables on a color screen and then interrupting the run *at any time* in order to revise their decisions. This is in sharp contrast to the ormal way of conducting business games which calls for responses concerning a specific subset of decision variables and only at pre-set intervals (Duke 1980; Hall 1987).

There are dangers in operating with competing teams since "playing to win" may replace the goal of "playing to learn." To obviate the dysfunctional aspects of competition in gaming, a better procedure would be to carry out a number of runs with the same group striving to improve on their previous best performance. Further, suppose separate functional groups have been restricted to separate screens showing only their own relevant set of graph plots, but created from a common model. It would be an interesting experiment then to ascertain to what extent actions taken by each of the functional groups, affording "improvement" based on their own criteria, was consonant with overall system improvement.

All of these ideas pose problems for the software developer. Real-time graph plotting is called for alongside an "interrupt and change" facility. The choice of scales for the vertical axes is made difficult when the entire array of values is not yet known. Rather than wanting to achieve as fast a run time as possible there is now a desire to slow the entire program down so as to allow the human mind to digest what is happening. Coding the sort of specifications described would require the resolution of a number of problems but they should not be regarded as insuperable.

However, a more immediate agenda for practitioners of system dynamics surely centers around a consideration of how to promote widespread endorsement of the *practice* of strategic policy debate organized around a model. Existing software capabilities are already sufficient to underpin the group decision support process. Let us digest the results of considerably more practical experience in the fiery crucible of real-life strategic policy making before we decide what further effort should be put into software development.

REFERENCES

Dangerfield, B.C. (1991), "System Dynamics Models in the Process of Corporate and Public Policy," unpublished Ph.D. Thesis, University of Salford, Salford, U.K..

Dangerfield, B.C., and O. Vapenikova (1987), *DYSMAP2 User Manual*, University of Salford, Salford, U.K.

de Geus, A. (1988), "Planning as Learning," *Harvard Business Review* 66 (March-April): 70-74.

Duke, R.D. (1980), "A Paradigm for Game Design," *Simulation and Games* 11: 364-77.

Eden, C., and J. Radford, eds. (1990), *Tackling Strategic Problems: The Role of Group Decision Support*, London: Sage Publications.

Forrester, J.W. (1958), "Industrial Dynamics: A Major Breakthrough for Decision Makers," *Harvard Business Review*, July-August, 37-66.

Hall, R.I. (1987), *Magazine Publishing Game Player's Manual*, University of Manitoba.

Huxham, C. (1990), "On Trivialities in Process," in C. Eden and J. Radford, eds., *Tackling Strategic Problems: The Role of Group Decision Support*, London: Sage Publications, 162-68.

Keloharju, R. (1983), *Relativity Dynamics*, Helsinki School of Economics, Helsinki.

Lane, D.C. (1989), "Management Learning by Simulation," in D. Murray-Smith, J. Stephenson, and R.N. Zobel (eds.), *Proceedings of the Third European Simulation Congress*, Edinburgh: Simulation Councils Inc., 321-39.

Luostarinen, A. (1982), *DYSMOD User's Manual,* Helsinki School of Economics, Helsinki.

Meadows, D. (1989), "Gaming to Implement System Dynamics Models," in P.M. Milling and E.O.K. Zahn, eds., *Computer-Based Management of Complex Systems*, Berlin: Springer-Verlag, 635-40.

Morecroft, J.D.W. (1988), "System Dynamics and Microworlds for Policymakers," *European Journal of Operational Research* 35: 301-20.

Naylor, D. (1986), "Scenarios for European Telecommunications," Unpublished paper presented at the *Eighth European Conference on Operational Research*, Lisbon.

Preedy, D.K., and R.G.A. Bittlestone (1985), "O.R. and the Boardroom for the 90s," *Journal of the Operational Research Society* 36: 787-94.

Sharp, J.A., and D.H.R. Price (1984), "System Dynamics and Operational Research: An Appraisal," *European Journal of Operational Research* 16: 1-12.

Vapenikova, O. (1986), "The Development of DYSMAP2," in J. Aracil, J.A.D. Machuca, and M. Karsky, eds., *Proceedings of the 1986 International Conference of the System Dynamics Society*, Seville, Spain, 19-24.

Vapenikova, O. (1989), "DYSMAP2/386 - DYSMAP2 Implementation on 80386-based PCs," in *Proceedings of the European Simulation Multi-Conference*, Rome: Simulation Councils Inc.

Vennix, J.A.M., J.W. Gubbels, D. Post, and H.J. Poppen (1990), "A Structured Approach to Knowledge Elicitation in Conceptual Model Building," *System Dynamics Review* 6: 194-208.

Wolstenholme, E.F. (1990), *System Enquiry*, Chichester, U.K.: Wiley.

Wolstenholme, E.F., and Coyle, R.G. (1983), "The Development of System Dynamics as a Methodology for System Description and Qualitative Analysis," *Journal of the Operational Research Society*, 34: 547-56.

15

MANAGERIAL MICROWORLDS AS LEARNING SUPPORT TOOLS

Ernst W. Diehl

ABSTRACT: MicroWorld Creator software facilitates experiential learning by making simulations more participatory in two important ways: It increases the user's control over the input to the simulation, and it displays output in formats that are familiar to the user. Equally important, it allows a user to probe deeper and deeper into any variable in a report that he or she is curious about. Its unique lens functionality opens the model's equations for inspection and allows users to interact directly with the model in a way that is not intellectually overwhelming—one equation at a time. The software encourages repeated exploration of simulation models by providing a consistent environment that enables simulation users to orient themselves quickly when moving from one simulation to the next, and enables simulation developers to create different simulation interfaces in a short amount of time.*

* This article is an edited compilation of two previous articles: Diehl 1992 and Diehl 1993.

INTRODUCTION

System dynamics and the computer industry have shared similar histories. Twenty years ago, computers were accessible only to a "priesthood" of technical experts. Since then, progress in hardware and software has given millions of people the ability to "interface," or interact, with computers. Although few people might be interested in actual programming, many have become savvy consumers. They are able to choose the appropriate off-the-shelf software or customize existing software to suit their needs.

System dynamics likewise began with a core group of technical experts. Over the years, system dynamics simulations also have profited from progress in the computer industry—the emergence of microcomputer hardware and more powerful machines has gradually made simulations faster and less expensive to use. However, simulation software—the decisive complementary component—has not yet enabled people to interface simulations. Consequently, they have not yet become intelligent consumers of simulations: Managers faced with an eroding service capacity are not "simulation savvy" enough to recognize what dynamics are involved, and therefore do not know what type of simulation to explore in order to understand the situation better.

DESIGN CRITERIA FOR MICROWORLD CREATOR (S**4)

Meadows has identified seven levels of system dynamics expertise as illustrated in Table 15-1 (Meadows 1989). When considering the use of simulations for facilitating learning in any of these levels, we can divide Meadows' chart into two parts: exploration of existing models (levels 1–4) and creation of new simulation systems (levels 5–7). Although current software tools are sufficient to enable experts to interface with simulations in all seven areas, novices have been left frustrated by limited software and extensive prerequisite knowledge required. STELLA, a software program introduced in 1985, was the first successful attempt to close this gap (Richmond 1985).

Table 15- 1. Meadows' seven levels of system dynamics expertise*

Level	Competence
1	Understand the system
2	Carry out a specific decision
3	Implement a recommended policy
4	Modify a mature model
5	Construct a new model
6	Teach others to build new models
7	Guide organizational change

*Source: Meadows 1989

The interface provided by MicroWorld Creator (S**4) is designed to enable general users without simulation background to participate and profit from the exploration stage of learning. It can enable novices to interact with simulations in order to (1) understand the system in which they operate; (2) carry out a specific decision in a "microworld" setting to test the results; and (3) implement a recommended policy based on the outcome of the simulation.

The development of MicroWorld Creator (S**4) grew out of a need to make simulations more accessible to general users. The Hanover Insurance case provides a well-documented example (Bergin and Prusko 1990; Senge and Lannon 1990; Senge 1990, pp. 325 ff.; Senge and Sterman 1992 and Chapter 8 of this work). In 1986, a system dynamics consulting project was underway at Hanover Insurance Company. N. Forrester and Senge were working closely with an in-house team developing a model of claims operation.

Once the model was finished, the team discussed how they could enable the rest of the company to work with the simulation. Traditionally, this would be done by a consultant, who would translate the insights gained from the software to managers, or in a report that summarized the learning experience. Neither option seemed desirable: relying on consultants is time consuming, and written reports do not have the interactive and exploratory nature of simulations. Instead, the team was looking for an experiential approach towards organizational learning. Meadows (1989) stresses the importance of experiential learning by quoting an old Chinese proverb: "When I hear, I forget. When I see, I remember. When I do, I understand." The team felt that the best way to recreate the model-building experience would be to let other managers directly interact with the simulation. The team decided to implement the simulation as a "microworld," using MicroWorld Creator (S**4) to design the interface.

The microworld is at the core of a three-day workshop at Hanover Insurance. In the computer microworld, the participants are put in charge of their own claims office (see Figure 15-1). On a monthly basis, they input the same decisions they make in a real claims office: how many people to hire, desired productivity, and desired size of settlement payments. Likewise, since production ratios are used to track the "health" of a claims office, the reports give managers information on pending claims, number of adjusters, settlement size, and other pertinent information. The similarities between the microworld and the managers' "macroworld," in terms of the decisions made and the reports received, allow the managers to draw parallels between the simulation and their reality.

Why is the Hanover microworld successful? The workshop combines two powerful elements that enhance the learning experience: (1) a tool (MicroWorld Creator S**4) that allows the participants to gain experiential knowledge about claims management; and (2) an effective learning setting, where the participants have the opportunity to repeatedly interact with the microworld environment.

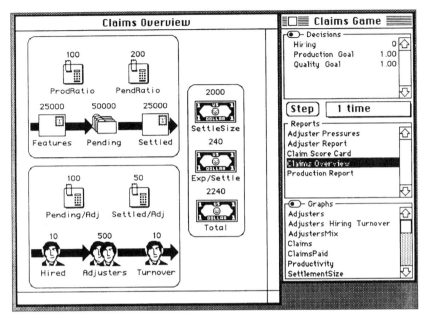

Figure 15-1. Interface of the Hanover Insurance claims game

The Hanover microworld has all of the elements of a typical simulation, but its gaming format increases user participation and experiential understanding of the system. The user is drawn into the simulation through increased participation in terms of *input* (decisions), and the familiarity of the *output* (reports). MicroWorld Creator (S**4) is explicitly designed to increase the accessibility of simulations by utilizing these two strengths of games.

USER INPUT AND USER CONTROL

Traditional simulation software allows the user to influence the system only at the beginning of the simulation run. Having set the parameters, the user then sits back and waits until the simulation has run its course. By contrast, MicroWorld Creator (S**4) allows continuous user input during the course of the simulation. The user can react immediately to a change in market share or service quality. Rather than being a passive observer, the user becomes a player in the simulation. The ability to stop the simulation after a time step and change the parameters puts the user in control of the simulation.

The user is not only in control of selected decision variables but is also in control of simulation time. The user can either intervene on a round-by-round basis or take a more strategic outlook and evaluate his "game plan" on a year-by-year basis.

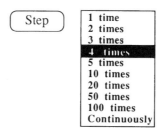

Figure 15-2. Simulation time control

Furthermore, the user can go back in time to revisit crucial turns in the simulation. The Step button on the screen allows users to decide how often they want to review their decisions—every time period, every other time period, etc. (see Figure 15-2). The user also has the option of letting the microworld run as a straight simulation by choosing "Continuously" from the menu. In this instance, the user will see the results at the end of the simulation. With the Step control, users can interact with the simulation as often—or as seldom—as they desire.

SALIENCY AND FAMILIARITY OF OUTPUT

Traditional simulation software displays the outcome in tabular format and charts against time. This output format is sufficient for simulation experts, since they are trained to translate the numbers into meaning. However, typical users, when confronted with a table of numbers, might have difficulty understanding the underlying dynamics as they evolve over time. MicroWorld Creator (S**4) increases the saliency of the output because familiar reports, such as income/loss statements and balance sheets, create a bridge between the simulation and the user's own decision-making environment.

The philosophy behind MicroWorld's software is that whatever reports the manager uses in her "macroworld" should be made available to her in the emulated "microworld" as well. This feature provides the user with ready identification with the information. However, traditional graphs and tables are just as accessible as reports, if the user wishes to view them.

ANALYTICAL LENS ANALYSIS

There is, however, an inherent limit in preformulated reports. While reports can be designed to support anticipated lines of inquiry, even the most experienced analyst can anticipate only some of the questions that might arise during the course of a strategic debate. MicroWorld (S**4) provides a unique tool to increase the bandwidth

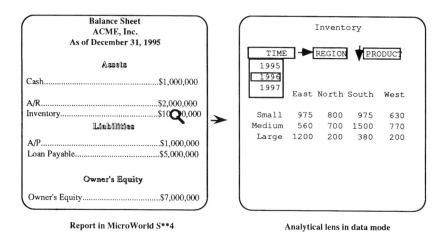

Report in MicroWorld S**4   Analytical lens in data mode

Figure 15-3. MicroWorld (S**4)'s analytical lens

of data analysis and to create dynamic reports. Clicking on any variable in a report will access an "analytical lens" that is built into the program (see Figure 15-3).

The analytical lens extends the analysis seamlessly across time and across dimensions such as competitors, product lines and regional markets. Any report thus can be a starting point for questions such as: "How did inventory behave in previous years? What are our inventory estimates for competitor X in Europe?"

The analytical lens provides not only a framework for historical data analysis, but perhaps more importantly a framework for what-if analysis. What-if analysis can only have an impact if its underlying assumptions have credibility within the management team and if it avoids any mysterious black-box assumptions. To truly support the testing of assumptions, the system needs to be open enough to allow in-depth exploration of the model, without requiring extensive technical expertise. MicroWorld (S**4) is based on the principle that any assumption in the simulation should be open for inspection and should easily be changed. Clicking on any vari-able brings up the underlying model assumption (see Figure 15-4).

The analytical lens can be used as a starting point for exploring the model assumptions and allows both causal backward drilling or causal forward drilling. For example, having inspected the equation for inventory the manager might want to explore what the underlying assumptions are for production or sales, the inputs used in the equation, and so might drill further backward. Similarly the manager might want to inspect how inventory influences other parts of the model. Clicking on any variable name in the "Uses" box or in the "Is Used For" box turns the focus of the lens on the particular variable.

The analytical lens allows a manager to probe deeper into any variable in a report that he feels uneasy about. The underlying assumptions are there to be

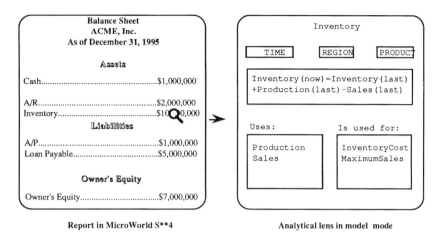

Report in MicroWorld S**4   Analytical lens in model mode

Figure 15-4. Underlying model assumptions revealed by the analytical lens

explored in a way that is not intellectually overpowering—one equation at a time. In this way, the lens allows managers to interact directly with the model. With the use of MicroWorld (S**4)'s lens, managers can understand assumptions when they are ready to rather than being overwhelmed by large listings of equations. Exploring the equations one at a time allows managers the opportunity to fully understand assumptions about the connections between the different variables.

INTERFACE DEVELOPMENT: THE DESIGNER'S POINT OF VIEW

Microworlds provide the participants with a fail-safe practice field where time and space are compressed. Managers can "practice" or experiment with different strategies and scenarios repeatedly and compare the different outcomes. Simulations by their very nature derive their main value from repeated use. To encourage repeated use, Microworld Creator (S**4) provides a simple and consistent user interface.

The simplicity of the MicroWorld interface design makes it easy for the user to orient herself in the microworld environment. Beginning in 1988, the incoming master's students at the Massachusetts Institute of Technology Sloan School of Management have experimented with the People Express computerized case study, which was designed with MicroWorld Creator (see Chapter 9 of this work). Experience has shown that even students who have never used a Macintosh before take only five to ten minutes to master the mechanics of the game. From that time on, they are engaged in strategic discussions about the game content rather than the mechanics.

In addition, the basic microworlds environment is consistent across simulations. By providing the user with the same environment it is much easier to move from one simulation to the next. Users can also benefit from interacting with different models in the same "family" that share a similar interface. A consistent interface format enhances the similarities between the underlying models by taking the user's mind off the simulation environment and letting her focus on the model itself.

The People Express Management Flight Simulator interface (Figure 15-5), for example, shares the same MicroWorlds interface as the Hanover Insurance Claims Game (Figure 15-1). While the different screen displays in both interfaces reflect the particularities of the two applications, the simulation "cockpit" at the right remains the same. In the upper right corner, decisions are entered. The middle section provides reports that are updated each time period of the simulation. The lower box provides charts and tables to track the performance over time.

To keep up with the need for users to move easily from one simulation to another, it is essential that interface design take hours, rather than days or weeks. MicroWorld Creator (S**4) was developed with the purpose of making it easy to create new simulation interfaces. From the developer's point of view, rapid interface development opens up an additional application area: MicroWorld Creator (S**4) can be used as a knowledge acquisition tool and be used early on in the development of the model itself. Often a modeler needs feedback from managers while the model is still in its infancy (Vennix, Gubbels, Post, and Poppen 1990). A

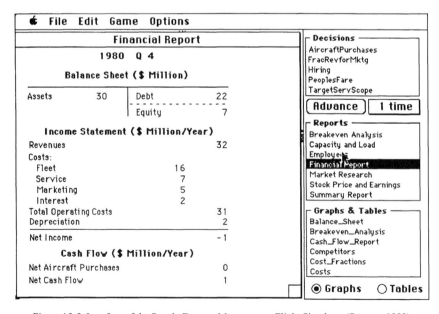

Figure 15-5. Interface of the People Express Management Flight Simulator (Sterman 1988)

nontechnical interface provides a medium through which managers can interact with the model at different stages of development and give the modeler valuable feedback on the relationships expressed in the model and the parameters used.

To facilitate rapid interface development, MicroWorld Creator (S**4) does not require any programming knowledge on the part of the designer other than specifying the model equations in "friendly algebra." Instead, common picture-drawing programs such as MacDraw are used to construct the reports. For example, when creating a report, the symbol "@" followed by a variable name can be used in the report as a placeholder for the actual variable in the simulation model. The report can then be pasted into a MicroWorld Creator (S**4) file using the Import Report command. Once the report is imported, MicroWorld Creator (S**4) substitutes the actual value for each variable (see Figure 15-6). Within the given parameters of the MicroWorlds environment, the designer is given the freedom to craft a unique "look and feel" for the simulation. Both the reports and the charts can be custom-designed to fit the requirements of individual models.

FUTURE DIRECTIONS IN INTERFACE DEVELOPMENT: THE ROLE OF REALISM

When designing an interface it is important to keep in mind what type of interface the intended audience needs, and what setting is appropriate to the type of learning required. What information needs to be explored? What format will best convey the core insights of the model? What learning setting will enhance the lessons?

These questions must be addressed when discussing the use of sound and animation to increase the realism of a simulation. The fundamental question to be

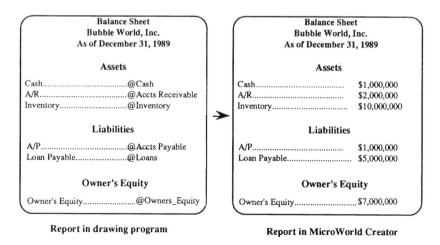

Figure 15-6. Importing a Report into MicroWorld Creator

guided by is "Does realism enhance the learning environment?" Sound and animation, if used, should increase the insight the users get out of the simulation, not just heighten the realism. For example, animation may be used effectively to help the manager see how the simulation reflects her reality. Seeing a video of a screaming customer throwing a product back with a loud bang might bridge the gap between simulation and reality better than seeing a number on the screen that says service quality is zero. But when overused, graphics can inhibit user participation in the simulation. A manager accustomed to reading and analyzing profit/loss statements may be annoyed by an interface that represents such data in terms of dollar bills piling up in a bank vault. A user may become annoyed at an interface that continues to offer "helpful" suggestions about playing the game long after such advice is needed.

Adding "realism" for realism's sake is misguided. The HoloDeck of the Starship Enterprise (Star Trek 1990) should not be the ultimate goal of microworl designers. Once the simulation becomes as complex as reality itself, the user faces the same difficulty of seeing the interdependencies in the simulation as in reality.

The basic task of the interface is to ensure that the user gets relevant information in a fast, clear and unambiguous way. Sound and animation, if used in the right setting, may help provide that information. In a situation where the user has very little time to interact with the simulation, and the learning objective is to gain a cursory understanding of the dynamics, visual aids may help the user gain a quick grasp of the system elements under study. However, when the user has more time and wants to gain deeper understanding of how structure influences behavior, those same interface elements could become a distraction.

MicroWorld Creator (S**4) is explicitly designed to address learning on levels 1-4 of Meadows' schema. Ultimately, our objective is to create the support technologies that put Meadows' levels 5–7 into the reach of the everyday user.

Major work lies ahead to deliver learning and decision support software that is truly supports individual, team, and organizational learning. While the steps toward this end are not entirely clear, we will know that we have arrived once managers start to frown, "How can you have meaningful organizational learning without learning support software?" just as one might hear today, "How can you do financial analysis without a spreadsheet?"

REFERENCES

Bergin, R.S., and Prusko, G.F. (1990), "The Learning Laboratory," *Healthcare Forum* 33, no. 2: 32-36.

Diehl, E.W. (1993), "The Analytical Lens, Strategy-Support Software to Enhance Executive Dialog and Debate," *American Programmer* 6, no. 5: 26-32.

Diehl, E.W. (1992), "Participatory Simulation Software for Managers: The Design Philosophy Behind MicroWorld Creator," *European Journal of Operational Research* 59, no. 1: 210-15.

Diehl, E.W. (1990), *MicroWorld Creator™, Software and User Manual*, Cambridge, Mass: MicroWorlds, Inc.

Diehl, E. (1991). *MicroWorld S**4™, Software and User Manual,* Cambridge, Mass: MicroWorlds, Inc.

Meadows, D. (1989), "Gaming to Implement System Dynamics Models," in P.M. Milling and E.O.K. Zahn, eds., *Computer-Based Management of Complex Systems,* Berlin: Springer-Verlag, 635-40

Richmond, B. (1985), "STELLA: Software for Bringing System Dynamics to the Other 98 Percent," in M.E. Warkentin, ed., *Proceedings of the 1985 International Conference of the System Dynamics Society* (Keystone, Colo.), 706-18.

Senge, P.M. (1990), *The Fifth Discipline: The Art and Practice of the Learning Organization*, New York: Doubleday.

Senge, P.M., and C. Lannon (1990), "Managerial Microworlds," *Technology Review* 93, no. 5: 62-68.

Star Trek — The Next Generation (1990), TV Motion Picture Series, Paramount Pictures.

Sterman, J. (1988), *People Express Management Flight Simulator* (software and briefing book), available from the author, Sloan School of Management, MIT, Cambridge MA 02142.

Vennix, J.A.M., J.W. Gubbels, D. Post, and H.J. Poppen (1990), "A Structured Approach to Knowledge Acquisition in Conceptual Model Building," *System Dynamics Review* 6, no. 2: 194-20.

16

UNDERSTANDING MODELS WITH VENSIM

ROBERT L. EBERLEIN AND DAVID W. PETERSON

ABSTRACT: Vensim®* (the Ventana Simulation Environment) is an interactive software environment that allows the development, exploration, analysis, optimization, and packaging of simulation models. It was created to increase the speed with which models could be developed, and the quality of the resulting models. Vensim has a variety of capabilities that directly speed up key tasks by an order of magnitude, making time for more complete and thorough model analysis. The higher speed indirectly increases model quality, by allowing more thorough exploration of model structure and behavior. To improve model quality directly, Vensim offers both statistical tools and automatic testing (Reality Checks). Models packaged with Vensim's application language can be easily accessed as decision support systems, instructional models, or open-structure games.

* Vensim is a registered trademark and Causal Tracing, Reality Check, Venapp, and Ventana are trademarks of Ventana Systems, Inc. Patents are pending in the United States and elsewhere relating to portions of the Vensim software.

MOTIVATION: SPEED AND QUALITY

Numerical simulation of dynamic systems preceded the modern computer by centuries. In the intervening years there have been continual advances in the hardware and software supporting such simulation models. However, the fundamental difficulty of understanding the models and their behavior has remained a major stumbling block to the more widespread use of models.

Vensim® was developed in response to a need to have more flexibility in developing models and more power in the analysis that follows. Though originally motivated by large and complex models, Vensim's tools for understanding model structure and behavior have proved useful for small models as well. Even for simple pedagogical models it can take many hours to uncover the range of behavior they can generate, and the reasons for the behavior. Vensim allows thorough analysis in a fraction of the time normally required, and opens the door to new insights and more complete understanding.

Because the behavior of a dynamic system, especially a social system, is often counterintuitive (Forrester 1971), simulations can result in surprises. Just as frequently, it is errors and omissions in simulation models, which we refer to as bugs, that result in surprises. Fortuitously, what is required to find the sources of counterintuitive behavior is substantially the same as what is required to find bugs. In essence, what is required is a fast and easy way to gain deep understanding of a model.

THE VENSIM WORKBENCH: TOOLS FOR RAPID ACCESS TO MODEL STRUCTURE AND BEHAVIOR

Although a great deal of work has been done on theoretical ways of gaining understanding of model behavior, the practical limit on model understanding is often the simple, mechanical inefficiency of finding out what the model is doing. Most simulation packages require users to specify graphs or reports in advance of simulations. To explore details, the simulation must be repeated with additional output specified. Recognizing this, we have, through evolution and multiple fresh starts, made the things that were time consuming and tedious fast and fun.

First, Vensim stores the complete behavior of each simulation in a rapid-access database format. Therefore, the user need not specify any output before performing a simulation, and simulations need never be repeated to see more detail. Second, Vensim provides a variety of tools to access the simulation database with great speed and convenience. Both of these objectives are achieved within a visually oriented, mouse-driven environment, which provides rapid access not only to simulations, but also to the structure of the model.

The look and feel of the Vensim software is based on a workbench-toolbox metaphor. A typical workbench is shown in Figure 16-1. The current model (d:\writing\world.vmf) is named on the top title bar. Simulation runs and data are placed on

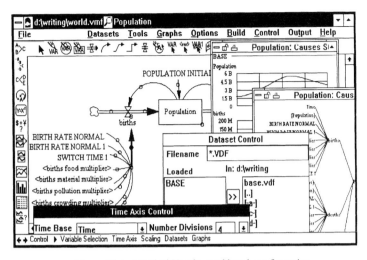

Figure 16-1. A typical Vensim workbench configuration

the workbench, and are controlled through the dialog box labeled "Dataset Control." The model construction is done using stock-and-flow or causal-loop diagramming techniques. The output from analysis is also placed onto the workbench.

Running down the left hand side of Figure 16-1 is a column of icons, providing rapid access to a set of tools. These tools are drawn from the toolbox as shown in Figure 16-2 and are customized to perform a specific action. For example, the first tool in Figure 16-1 is a "Tree Diagram" tool (the first in the leftmost column of Figure 16-2) configured to show a variable and its causes. Many of the tools oper-

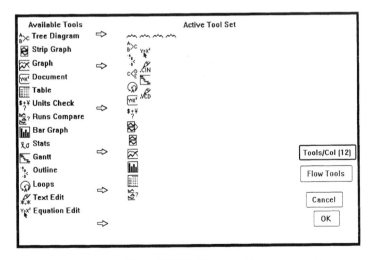

Figure 16-2. The Vensim toolbox

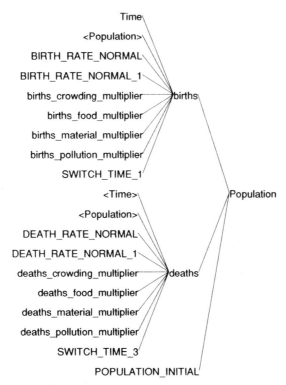

Figure 16-3. Tree showing the causes of population

ate on one variable of the model at a time; this current "focus" variable may be quickly chosen from the entire model in a variety of ways, and its current identity is displayed in the top title bar, to the right of the magnifying glass icon. In Figure 16-1, the variable Population has been selected as the focus variable.

Understanding comes about by running the model under different conditions and then looking at the results. This can be done with a click of the mouse. For example, clicking on the first tool in Figure 16-1 would generate the output shown in Figure 16-3. Alternatively, clicking on the seventh tool in Figure 16-1 (this is a "strip graph" tool) gives the output shown in Figure 16-4. Both of these tools provide information about a variable and its causes, but in different formats and with different detail. The ability to click and see allows more experimentation and investigation, dramatically improving both quality and understanding.

CAUSAL TRACING: "WHY-IF" ANALYSIS

The workbench-toolbox metaphor gives information about the model in its current position very quickly. The added ability to reposition the model by double-

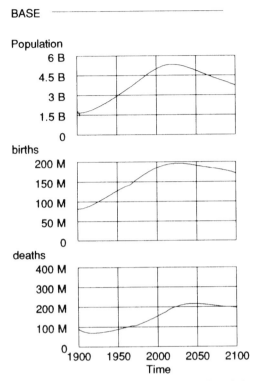

Figure 16-4. Strip graph showing the causes of population

clicking on the output of other tools allows an automated form of Causal Tracing™ (Patent Pending, 1989; see also Eberlein, Peterson, and Wood 1990). Simply put, Causal Tracing starts with some behavior of interest, and looks at the causes of that behavior, then the causes of the causes and so on. At each step we are looking for something that is interesting because it is spurious or surprising. The spurious or surprising thing is often the key, or one of the keys, to the true cause of the interesting behavior. The causal tracing process traces out the structure (subset of the model) that generates the behavior of interest.

Figures 16-3 and 16-4 show population and its causes. In Figure 16-4, the population overshoots and begins to decline in about the year 2020. Double-clicking (clicking twice in quick succession) on "deaths" in this figure makes "deaths" the focus variable. The next activation of the causes strip graph tool yields the results shown in Figure 16-5. Double-clicking on "deaths material multiplier" and invoking the causes strip graph again would show us the causes of this variable, and so on. Very quickly we are led to the underlying cause of behavior (depletion of natural resources leading to declining population in this case). Incorrect choices will still

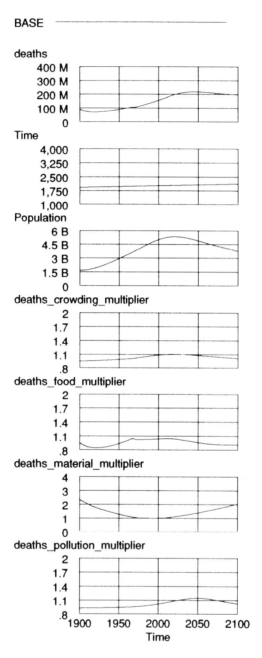

Figure 16-5. Strip graph showing the causes of deaths

be made, but the whole process is so fast and convenient that seconds or minutes, rather than hours or days, will be lost tracing these down.

REALITY CHECK: AUTOMATIC ROBUSTNESS TESTING

Reality Check™ is a powerful technology available in Vensim that allows you to test simulation models against your understanding of a problem. Reality Checks are statements about conditions and the consequences that must follow, such as "If there are no workers, we do not produce anything," or "If production is constant, sales cannot continue to grow." Reality checks are thought experiments about the behavior of the system being modeled, and they constitute a powerful knowledge base for testing the validity and robustness of any model.

Once Reality Checks have been set up, Vensim exercises the model by forcing the conditions specified in Reality Checks to come true, and testing to see if the logical consequences also result. Violations are reported, allowing the user to identify and correct errors in the model structure.

Reality Checks add powerful new validation possibilities to the modeling process. They are behavioral in nature, and can be formulated by experts in the domain the model addresses rather than experts in the modeling process. They can address both boundary conditions and incremental changes. Most importantly, they are focused on the system being modeled, not the model. Once Reality Checks have been specified for a modeling situation, they can be used again and again as the model evolves. Changing the exact equation structure in a model, the number of intermediate variables, and so on, does not require the rewriting of Reality Checks.

Reality Checks are another important example of providing the ability to do things that are possible but not practical using other techniques. When Reality Checks are activated, Vensim manages the implicit logical switching that is necessary to implement them. It is not necessary to enter elaborate test equations that obscure understanding and make updating a model difficult. Because Reality Checks are divorced from model structure it is possible to build up a collection of Reality Checks that can be used to test any model of a particular problem. In this manner the Reality Checks can serve as a test-bed against which different models can be compared and their failings uncovered.

VENSIM APPLICATIONS: CUSTOM-MADE INTUITIVE INTERFACES

While Vensim is well suited to developing, modifying, and understanding models, there are many situations, especially learning situations, in which the flexibility Vensim provides is neither required nor appropriate. For these situations, Vensim provides the facility to package applications in a user interface that is appropriate for a specific audience.

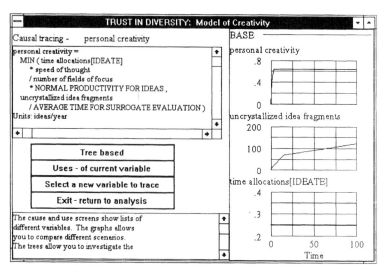

Figure 16-6. Typical Venapp screen showing causal tracing

The model and user interface together are referred to as a Vensim Application, or "Venapp." A Venapp is a microworld in which the user can interact with a model in a simple easy-to-use interface. Venapps can be created to make use of models interactively in a gaming mode, or to run multiple scenarios. A typical Venapp screen is shown in Figure 16-6. This is a causal tracing screen and double-clicking on a variable will automatically bring up the causes of that variable in the same format.

The biggest difference between Vensim Application and other available microworlds is the ability to perform causal tracing and to use the analysis tools available in Vensim. Because all tools can be accessed from within the application, models no longer need to remain "black box." The structure and even equations can be made available for inspection by nontechnical users. This allows those using the applications to study in detail the assumptions underlying the model, improving acceptance and preventing the spread of myths relating to model structure.

FUNCTIONALITY IN PERSPECTIVE

Vensim is an interactive software environment that supports the entire modeling process, from conceptualization through to optimization and application packaging. The sketch tool allows representations of feedback and causality to be built simply and with a minimum of restrictions as either stock-and-flow or causal-loop diagrams. Data are easily added into the system, and data-based conceptualizations are supported using the sketch tool. The modeling language is simple, but has a number of advanced features that support complex structures. The system includes optimization for the purposes of calibration, sensitivity testing, and policy analysis.

Vensim is an evolutionary step in the development of a system that allows unskilled modelers, with no professional assistance, to develop and understand models addressing important problems. As it now stands Vensim provides an intuitive and straightforward, but flexible, method of building models from stock-and-flow or causal-loop diagrams, and powerful tools for analyzing simulation results. In our view the key aspect that sets Vensim apart from most other simulation systems is the ability to quickly gain deep understanding of a model.

APPLICATION TO LEARNING ENVIRONMENTS

A necessary piece of any learning environment is the ability to impart understanding. To do so typically requires a great deal of human effort, either from a teacher or from a skilled debriefer. The causal tracing features and other capabilities of Vensim can lessen this reliance on human effort, allowing faster and cheaper dissemination of understanding.

When the learning process is designed around the development of models Vensim provides a simple method for building models and analyzing their results. The workbench-toolbox metaphor allows users to switch easily between structure and behavior and to understand how the two are related.

When the learning process is designed around exploration and analysis of existing models, a great deal of structure can be added to the model exploration process. Using Venapp scripts, it is possible to control which parameters can be modified, suggest different parameter combinations as interesting scenarios, and even lead students through specific scenarios and the causal tracing process.

EXTENSIONS

Vensim is one step toward a system that allows the modeling novice to gain the insights and understanding now available only to experienced modelers. In any such long-term development there are tradeoffs. For the beginner, simplicity and a set of predefined steps are key. Providing a packaged model (Venapp) as an environment for beginners is an interim solution.

Ultimately, we believe that the development of high-quality models will be possible without extensive training by experts. Reality Checks are a significant step in this evolutionary process. The entire modeling process needs to be refined and tuned to human rather than technical skills. Understanding and explanations need to be concrete, and supported by available data. Eventually, we hope, the distinction between model builders and model consumers will disappear.

REFERENCES

Eberlein, R.L., D.W. Peterson, and W.T. Wood (1990), "Causal Tracing: One Solution to the Modeling Dilemma," *Proceedings of the 1990 International Conference of the System Dynamics Society,* Boston, Mass., 341-54

Forrester, Jay W. (1971), "Counterintuitive Behavior of Social Systems," *Technology Review* 73, no. 3: 52-68; also in *Collected Papers of Jay W. Forrester,* Portland, Ore.: Productivity Press (1975), ch. 16, 211-44.

17

PROFESSIONAL DYNAMO: SIMULATION SOFTWARE TO FACILITATE MANAGEMENT LEARNING AND DECISION MAKING

JAMES M. LYNEIS,
KIMBERLY SKLAR REICHELT, AND
TODD SJOBLOM

ABSTRACT: The new Professional DYNAMO allows the building of sophisticated systems around DYNAMO models in the familiar Windows environment. These easy-to-use interfaces facilitate understanding of the relationship between system structure and behavior, and thereby provide the means to improve managerial decision making.

INTRODUCTION

From its inception, the purpose of the DYNAMO family of simulation software has been to support the development and use of system dynamics models for solving real-world business and social problems. Emphasis has been on responding to the consulting and research needs of Pugh-Roberts Associates and the MIT System Dynamics Group. This has led to very powerful software for the creation and analysis of (often) large models. DYNAMO software is recognized for its capabilities, including:

- equation capacity

- computation speed

- use of arrays

- extensive error checking

- ability to interface with spreadsheets

- ability to store and compare results from simulation experiments conducted previously, including "data models"

Pugh-Roberts has also recognized the need of clients to feel ownership of these models, and to use them internally. In the mid-1980s, we developed DYNEX as a first step toward meeting this need. DYNEX enabled model users, who were not advanced model builders, to conduct simulation experiments. The advent of microcomputers and the popularization of "systems thinking" accelerated both the technology for bringing sophisticated models to manager's desks, as well as the perceived need to do so. Increasingly, our software development has focused on making models more accessible and understandable to managers. Professional DYNAMO, a Microsoft Windows-based product, is the result of that effort.

FACILITATING LEARNING AND DECISION MAKING

We believe that there are two dimensions to using models to improve managerial decision making: first, to improve managers' "systems thinking" skills; and second, to provide the means to make better decisions in a specific situation. Both are necessary. The first provides the intellectual underpinnings for the second.

"Systems thinking" skills involve the recognition that:

- information feedback, delays, and accumulations are the building blocks that define the interactions between parts within the system; and

- the system's structure, that is, how the building blocks are put together, determines the system's behavior.

Understanding these concepts gives managers the confidence and intuitive grasp necessary for making better decisions (e.g., taking counterintuitive actions, such as adding capacity when sales are declining so that it will be operating when the next upturn begins).

The learning that underlies this understanding is, of course, an interactive process. Analyses with a model can provide a quick and effective means of achieving this learning. One tries something, sees how it works, understands how the system structure facilitated or defeated the action, and then tries again. Learning also involves applying the lessons learned to the real system, and thereby validating or improving the model.

But an intuitive grasp alone is insufficient. Managers need to know, for example, how much capacity to add, and when. Once the intellectual underpinning is achieved, models can be used to develop policy guidelines and specific decisions. These will change over time as conditions change, and must be updated appropriately.

THE "WHAT-IF...?" ENVIRONMENT

The Professional DYNAMO environment, set up in the "What-if...?" mode, has a number of features that facilitate management learning and decision making:

1. *The ability to easily define alternative scenarios and policy tests.* As illustrated in Figure 17-1, the input screens are clear and easy to use; one can build off of a "base case" or off of any previous simulation test.

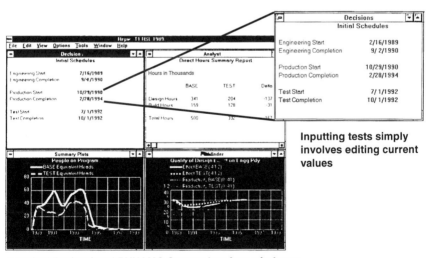

A typical Professional DYNAMO System has four windows: a Decisions window in the upper left, and three output windows.

Figure 17-1. A typical interface layout and input screen

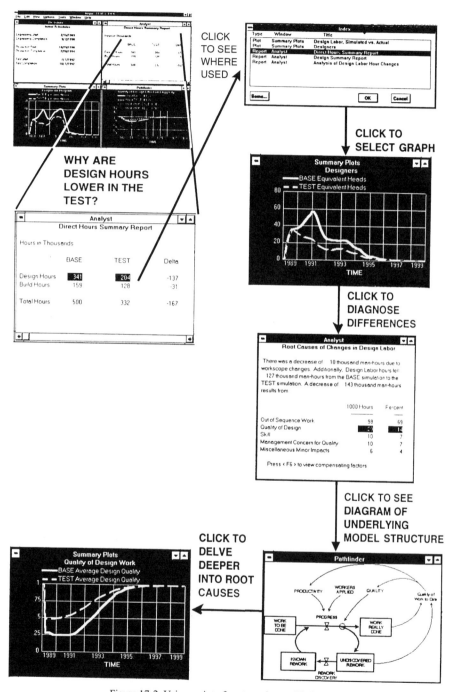

Figure 17-2. Using an interface to understand behavior

2. *Tools that guide the user through the process of understanding how the structure of the system produces the observed results.* These tools include reports that compare and highlight the key differences between simulation tests, graphical plots, and model diagrams. These reports, plots, and diagrams are automatically linked so that the user can literally trace back through causal structure. Figure 17-2 illustrates how a user might trace through a Professional DYNAMO system to determine the causes of behavior.

3. *DYNAMO's Interactive Documentor.* This feature enables a more sophisticated user to access the model's underlying equation structure quickly and easily. By double-clicking on a variable, the user is shown all uses of the variable. Also, the definitions for all variables used in the equation are shown. The user can then double-click on any variable shown, and move to the definition for the selected variable. For example, in Figure 17-3 the equation for "ISTAFF" (indicated staff) is shown. One component of indicated staff is time left to do the required work ("TLEFT"). By double-clicking on TLEFT, the user is shown the equation for TLEFT. The user can move quickly between the equations and the output corresponding to the variable through this "clicking" procedure. The process of relating structure to behavior is thereby facilitated.

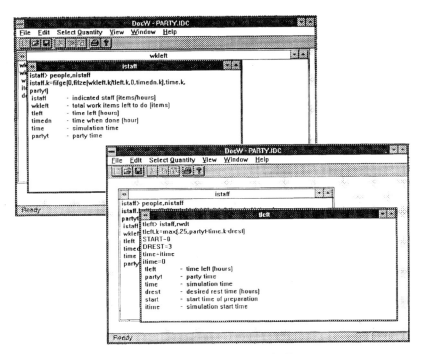

Figure 17-3. An example use of the Interactive Documentor

4. *Decision support.* In the end, managers must make specific decisions. Professional DYNAMO's ability to quickly conduct a large number of analyses and construct graphs showing key performance tradeoffs as a function of a given decision facilitates this process. This capability allows managers to develop policy guidelines; for example, the tradeoff between schedule and cost on a large construction or software project illustrated in Figure 17-4. Often there is an optimal range for a given decision. The analysis tools described above help managers understand why such a range exists, and gives them confidence to make the necessary decisions.

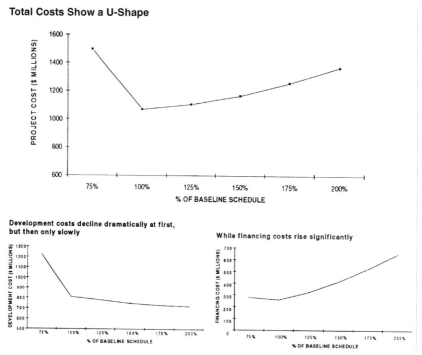

Figure 17-4. A typical cost-schedule tradeoff

THE GAMING ENVIRONMENT

A somewhat different process of learning occurs when using models in "gaming" mode. Here, rather than entering policy rules (e.g., that production rate depends in a specified way on forecast sales, inventory, and backlog adjustment), users input specific decisions (e.g., the production rate for the next quarter). Gaming mode corresponds more closely to the decision-making environment. It is meant to re-create that environment in a "flight simulator" environment that allows experimentation and learning.

In gaming mode, learning occurs during two periods. First, when actually playing the game, managers learn by experimentation—making decisions and seeing their consequences. And second, managers learn in a post-game wrap-up when the results of their decisions can be analyzed against other teams, or against "ideal" decision sets. Two capabilities of Professional DYNAMO facilitate that learning:

1. *The ability to create very realistic "flight simulators,"* including reports that correspond to actual company reports, including situation-dependent memoranda. This realism helps managers to identify with the situation, and causes them to take the exercise seriously, and not as "just a game." For example:

   • Appropriate memos, drawing on information from the current state of the simulation, are generated every decision interval (see Figures 17-5 and 17-6).

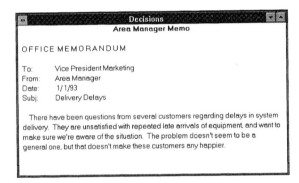

Figure 17-5. Area manager memo

```
                        Decisions
                  Area Manager Memo

OFFICE MEMORANDUM

To:       Vice President Marketing
From:     Area Manager
Date:     1/1/93
Subj:     Delivery Delays

   There have been questions from several customers regarding delays in system
delivery. They are unsatisfied with repeated late arrivals of equipment, and want to
make sure we're aware of the situation. The problem doesn't seem to be a
general one, but that doesn't make these customers any happier.
```

```
                        Decisions
                Competitive Situation Report

OFFICE MEMORANDUM

To:       Vice President Marketing
From:     Marketing Research Director
Date:     1/1/93
Subj:     Competitive Situation Report

Our industry association has compiled its triennial market report. Key market
statistics are:

                              Estimated
   Competitor               Market Share

       A                        14.3
       B                        13.1
       C                        11.5
 Systems Division                9.6
       D                         9.3
   All Others                   42.2
```

Figure 17-6. Competitive situation report memo

- Reports like the pro forma income statement in Figure 17-7 show historical data and current budgets; the forecasts are updated as the user inputs decisions.

Decisions				
Income Statement				
Year Ending	1991 Actual	1992 Actual	1992 Budget	1993 Forecast
Revenue (thousands of dollars)	186,259	210,139	220,334	301,923
Cost of Goods Sold - Parts	38,329	41,627	53,162	59,838
Cost of Goods Sold - Manufacturing	47,588	59,791	49,880	75,497
Marketing & Sales	38,496	43,756	42,922	63,017
Technical Services	22,024	25,689	24,870	30,396
Depreciation	10,232	10,725	10,366	12,090
Total Expenses	156,670	181,589	181,198	240,838
Net Earnings Before Taxes	29,589	28,550	39,136	61,085
Return on Sales (percent):				
Actual	+15.9%	+13.6%	+17.8%	+20.2%
Target	+15.0%	+15.0%	+15.0%	**+15.0%**
←– No Decision Required				

Figure 17-7. Pro forma income statement

- And entering decisions is a straightforward process of editing or typing over current values (see Figure 17-8; all decisions are shown in bold font).

Decisions				
Pricing and Return on Sales				
Year Ending:		1990	1991	1992
Price (per equivalent system sold):				
Actual (Average for Year)		127,487	128,929	128,598
Actual (End of Year)		129,193	127,867	130,170
Typical Competitor (End of Year)		118,014	118,600	117,245
Percent Higher Than Competitors		+9.5%	+7.8%	+11.0%
Return on Sales (percent):				
Actual		+13.4%	+15.9%	+13.6%
Target		+15.0%	+15.0%	+15.0%
Recent Unit Cost	111,271			
Your Implied Unit Cost	99,710			
Staff Recommended Markup:	+17.7%			
Staff Recommended Price:	131,018			
ROS Implied By:				
Staff Recommended Price:	+23.9%			
Your Price Target:	+20.2%			
Recent ROS:	+14.2%			
125000 ←– Your Target Price				
+15.0% ←– Your Target ROS				

Figure 17-8. Pricing and return on sales — decision inputting

2. *Post-session analysis and comparison.* In the post-session wrap-up, an instructor or facilitator uses Professional DYNAMO's analysis tools to relate differences in behavior to the system structure and decisions made. Typically, the results for several teams, or earlier experiments for the same team, are

compared. The process is similar to that described above for the "What-if...?" analyses, and involves using reports, plots, and diagrams to interactively trace differences.

The ability to compare the decisions made by different teams is critical to this process, especially in a classroom environment. In this way, differences in performance and in behavior can be traced back to differences in decisions. For example, Figure 17-9 compares two decisions from the results of an actual exercise. As can be seen, Team 2 set more aggressive market share targets than Team 1, and was more successful in achieving those targets because they acquired the necessary resources to do so (as indicated by the greater hiring of service reps in Figure 17-9). These comparisons, in conjunction with model diagrams, help drive home the concept of "self-fulfilling prophecy" dynamics. Other comparisons show how teams amplify cycles by failing to recognize delays in feedback loops and by not maintaining balance among resources, and how "experience" spirals can adversely affect productivity and costs. We have found that these comparisons help to internalize the relationship between system structure, decisions, and behavior.

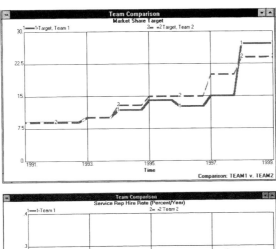

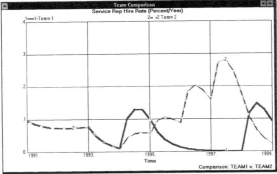

Figure 17-9. Sample comparison of team decisions

INTERFACE DEVELOPMENT FROM THE BUILDER'S PERSPECTIVE

Professional DYNAMO was designed to provide system builders with a powerful tool for building easy-to-use systems that facilitate user understanding of why behavior occurs. With Professional DYNAMO, system builders can:

- get automatic linkage among plots, reports, and diagrams;
- range-check decisions, and have allowable ranges for decisions depend on other decisions or variable values;
- add menus to the menu bar;
- write macros to perform keystrokes automatically;
- use FOR loops to write many plots and/or reports in a single statement;
- click-to-build, i.e., add statements to a plot file "on the fly";
- put diagrams in an interface;
- use generic code to apply to all models for quick, but complete, ready-made systems;
- update the on-line help offered to users.

These features provide managers and students with a powerful tool for learning and decision support.

18

HEXAGONS FOR
SYSTEMS THINKING

ANTHONY M. HODGSON

ABSTRACT: This article describes an approach to bridging the gap between the generalist thinking of decision makers and the specialized thinking of modelers by concentrating on the preliminary issue conceptualization stage of modeling. A new type of visual facilitation is described using hexagons as a flexible mapping technique to bridge the gap between thoughts and models. A typical team application is described, and a link is also made to creative thinking techniques, including the use of cognitive color coding. These techniques are supported by new use of magnetic hardware and a specially designed mapping software. In conclusion, the idea of the transitional discipline is introduced as a way in which a variety of specialist decision support methods can be made more user friendly.

HEXAGONS FOR SYSTEMS THINKING

Picture a group of senior executives of a major company standing around a whiteboard and debating intensely where brightly colored hexagons should be placed in relation to one another on the board. Is this speculation or a real working session? Actually, events like this are becoming more frequent. They are a manifestation of a new approach to systems thinking that is finding favor with managers faced with high levels of system complexity combined with high levels of uncertainty; in brief—fuzzy problems.

In this discussion I will explore some of the underlying theory and technique that makes such an unlikely activity a potent method for advancing executive thinking, especially in teams. But first, let's look at the activity in a little more detail.

AN EXAMPLE OF A WORKSHOP PROCESS

A leader (typically a chief executive or functional head) and team identify that there is an area of challenge they face and for which their stock of past responses is not adequate. New ground needs to be broken. Recognizing that breaking new ground will require the stimulus of nontraditional methods, the group appoints a facilitator consultant who takes on the role of designing and carrying out a group process, usually in the form of a workshop.

The facilitator realizes that, given a relatively undefined arena of discussion of some complexity (which has been identified more by intuition than analysis), each team member will have implicit mental models of that arena. These implicit models represent an untapped wealth of data, understanding, and judgment that is hidden and not shared. Furthermore, the facilitator realizes that the normal level of conversation in a management meeting will be unlikely to tap into more than a small fraction of this potentially rich picture. A process that visually shares mental models will be more effective.

To prepare for the workshop each member of the team is interviewed briefly on his or her initial reactions to the subject, and, through open-ended questioning, the first layer of deeper thought is mapped individually, giving the facilitator a feel for the emergent natural agenda and also the degree of congruence and dissonance between the mental models of the individuals. This helps tune up the entry into the workshop and establishes a psychological contract.

At the workshop, the facilitator introduces the main themes and tendencies in their thinking to date about the challenge. What then follows is a process we can call "issue conceptualization" (a term coined by Kees van der Heijden at Shell Group Planning). Often, the hardest part of modeling is to get a hold on what the issues really are. A process of elicitation is more effective than the customary methods of debate. The mood is more like that of creative thinking, where temporary suspension of judgment is encouraged until sufficient breadth of material has been aired. Concept mapping with hexagons is used as a technique.

Conversation, which happens in a linear way, leaving to memory the burden of recollecting patterns of connection, is an inefficient medium, unsupported by visual representation. We are all constrained here by the "magical number seven plus or minus two" as the inherent limit to short term memory and attention (Miller 1956). The recording of statements on flip charts or whiteboards has become customary to help limitations of attention and memory. This skill leaves us, however, with a memory that tends to be a checklist or a diagram of some kind, both of which are inflexible.

By using movable hexagons for capturing data, a simple visual medium is created for handling flexibly the content of conversation. To return to our team, as the statements come out in conversation the facilitator captures each distinct idea as a summary headline on a magnetic-backed hexagon, which can be placed initially at random on a large steel whiteboard, clearly seen and accessible to the group. Each point is checked, as it is written up, for mutual comprehension but without at this stage debate about its validity. The guiding principle is that if someone in a responsible team thinks it, there must be something in it.

In this phase, association and exploration are encouraged so that stones are not left unturned in the team members' minds. A layer deeper than that of the interviews begins to emerge through the mutual stimulation of different angles of approach. The phase draws to a close with anything from twenty to fifty or more hexagons arrayed on the board. There has been a kind of catharsis of the minds; a memory owned by the group has been formed and it is represented visually. But by now it is quite unmanageable conceptually. (Figure 18-1 shows a hypothetical example, constrained to twelve hexagons for ease of illustration.)

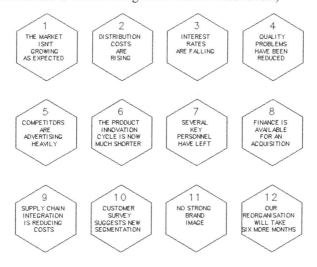

Figure 18-1. Brainstorming hexagons

Pressure now builds on the facilitator to come to the rescue by indicating some kind of order to remove the chaos. Yielding to this pressure, however, would remove the ownership of the process and the thinking from the executives. They are now challenged to explore their own mutual perception of order in the chaos. The simplest technique for doing this is to start grouping the hexagons, a process called clustering. It is at this stage that a pioneer in the group has to come forward and make a first step at introducing some order. This spurs other members of the group to differ, to join in by demonstrating alternatives, to reach agreement, and to express their reasons why. The conversation reaches a deeper level and brings implicit thinking into the open. At this stage also, well-worn theories may emerge as ordering principles (safe ways out of the chaos), but these are then seen to be leading round in circles giving opportunity for the facilitator to provoke exploration of alternative, more adventurous groupings. These new clusters, in turn, stimulate the formation of new higher-order concepts to embrace the combination within each cluster. Figure 18-2 shows how the hexagons in Figure 18-1 might end up from such a process, having been reshuffled a number of times.

What now emerges is an "issue map" that represents a quite new perception and grasp of the "vague concern" and provides a platform for the formulation of the next steps of thinking and decision making needed by the group.

The issue map will tend to point to the interconnectedness of things. The team will now have unearthed some of the systemic implications of the field and be set on a course that may well lead them to consider feedback or even further conceptualization of a system dynamics model. Such a course of development in the team's

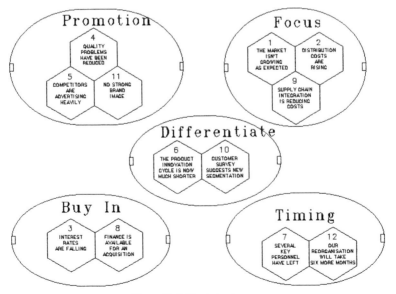

Figure 18-2. Clustering hexagons

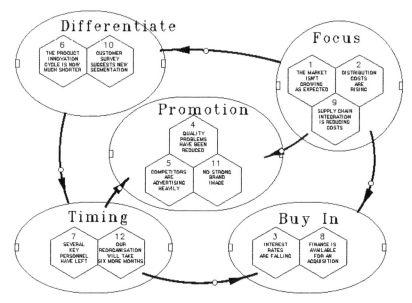

Figure 18-3. Influence diagramming

thinking could be represented with connecting arrows as shown in Figure 18-3. On the other hand, the issue map may lead to a number of other disciplines of group decision support (Rosenhead 1989).

GENERATIVE THINKING

The above account of a group thinking process that moves from implicit to explicit modeling assumes the outcome of the process to be of requisite quality. However, the impact of sharing the modeling process may not, of itself, lead to a breakthrough. Decision making increasingly needs a creative step for which structural thinking prepares the way but doesn't get there. Here it can be useful for modelers to use techniques that increase the chances of breaking out of an implicit mindset into new ground. This breakout is what we call "generative thinking" (to contrast it with deeper insight into what is already there).

For example, the hexagon method can be used with great effect as a tool for stimulating lateral thinking. The technique, which runs counter to our logical mindset, uses random association of what seem to be unconnected ideas to evoke the mind's rich store of associations and new ideas. Invention often proceeds along these lines. A simple example is shown in Figure 18-4.

In conventional brainstorming, we capture the ideas as they come out in bullet statements on flip charts. In the hexagon method we capture them as headlines on

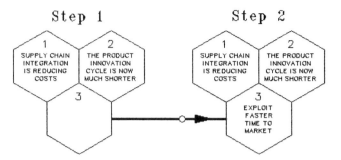

Figure 18-4. Generating new ideas

the magnetic hexagons which are then free to be moved into any paired association we choose at random. The third blank hexagon then invites a lateral thought (see Figure 18-4).

This method has proved very effective to trigger a new wave of ideas when a session "dries up" or when the quality of ideas is inadequate. It acts as an unblocking device. When a group doing this is asked to select the most interesting ideas, it usually chooses the second generation of laterally stimulated ideas.

There is a tendency to believe that only divergent processes are creative and that convergence is antithetical to creativity. This is at variance with creative design experience, where the creative act is often in synthesis.

The introduction of hexagon templates for creative convergence is a further technique we have found very powerful. This method uses the results from a "1 + 1 = 3" exercise as a building unit for several generations of thought as shown in Figure 18-5.

This is a "four-fold" generator, where "four-fold" refers to the number of selected starting ideas. In this case, from the brainstorming session and subsequent clustering, the four most interesting and diverse ideas were selected and then placed in the outer circle of the template. Then the blanks were filled by the search for new ideas which strongly embodied qualities from both source ideas. The central idea is a core insight. (Note that wording can be deceptive here to the reader outside the working session. Unknown blood, sweat, and tears will have gone into the consensus insight, which will be packed with all the associated ideas and experiences for that particular group. Meaning is not really transferable by wording alone.)

Generative thinking is lateral thinking plus intuitive judgment. As well as being a breakthrough device, it is a very powerful support tool for decision makers, particularly when time is scarce, the decision criteria are qualitative and the results of diverse advice need to be quickly synthesized. In the latter case it is the advice that is placed in the outer perimeter of the generator pattern.

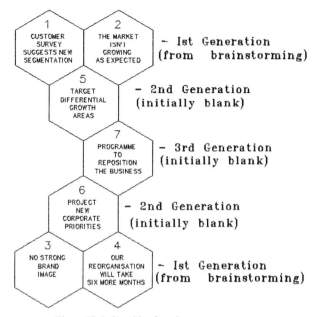

Figure 18-5. Core idea from hexagon generator

COLOR CODING COGNITIVE MAPS

So far we have considered the cognitive mapping process as a two-dimensional surface where all idons are equivalent. We can now introduce color coding. Codification is a crucial process in any effective thinking. The simplest scheme is a binary code such as accept/reject (green:red) or opportune/dangerous (yellow: black). By introducing a judgmental framework and color coding it, we can then assign colors to ideas and read a further layer of significance into our cognitive map. This also provokes a deeper layer of interchange in the working group.

One powerful application of color coding is to show working groups their style of thinking. There appears to be some correlation between the quality and effectiveness of strategic thinking and the extent to which a range of cognitive styles is invoked by the thinker. This is reflected, for instance, in Russo and Schoemaker's decision traps (Russo and Schoemaker 1990). The failure to exercise a cognitive mode may lead one into a trap.

In dealing with unknown situations we need, as well as flexibility, ways of directing mental energy to fruitful areas. This is where the cognitive pairs fulfill a role. We recognize that in assessing situations we find these pairings expressing themselves. For example we might elicit how far a client group perceived areas in a cognitive map (see Figure 18-6) as:

1. opportunities	yellow
2. problems	black
3. innovations	green
4. improvements	brown
5. environmental factors	blue
6. internal factors	orange
7. strengths	white
8. ambiguities	grey
9. strategic views	purple
10. tactical actions	red

The advantage of the color coding is that it gives a nonverbal signaling system that empowers the thinking of the team using it. Frequently the propensities of people in a team will bias the range of considerations going into a decision process; for example, over-focus on threats and tactics with neglect of externalities. The "color balance" of contributions will reveal these biases and enable the facilitator to carry out balancing activities.

Although developed pragmatically, evidence is accumulating that senior managers do indeed draw on a variety of cognitive capabilities—their mental portfolio—when making decisions and judgments (Isenberg 1987); some other practitioners have explored the use of color coding as the basis for practical methods of identifying and switching mental modes (Rhodes and Thame 1988; de Bono 1986).

lateral thinking	*yellow*	opportunity spotting
critical thinking	*black*	problem solving
imaginative thinking	*green*	innovation
judgmental thinking	*brown*	quality appraisal
holistic thinking	*blue*	environmental scanning
systems thinking	*orange*	designing
metacognition	*white*	thinking about thinking
chaotic thinking	*grey*	ambiguity
strategic thinking	*purple*	directing
decision thinking	*red*	action

Figure 18-6. A scheme for color coding cognition of models

The five pairs of cognitive styles also reflect the way the mind, in decision making, is a "dilemma resolution system" (Hampden-Turner 1990). The attribution of color codes to these modes has some basis in color psychology.

THE DYNAMIC REPRESENTATION PARADIGM

The above sketch is just one illustration of an emerging field that may be crucial to the wider acceptance and utilization of modeling, namely "dynamic representation." This is thinking with visual idea-representing icons that can be manipulated, combined, and re-arranged as a continuous process of formulating thought. The *idon* is a combination of idea and icon.

Idons can be realized in simple form by such things as magnetic plastic hexagons or in more complex form as a new type of representational software: idonic software, such as the CK Modeller.

Idons used in a combination are a powerful way for us to express the deeper layers of thought from our mental models. Up to now the expression of thought for interacting groups has been limited to blackboard and chalk and conversation, the two most user controllable media we have.

Modeling is considered to be one way of describing what we do in our minds, as a function of having cognitive capability. Language, mathematics, and drawing (of diagrams) are our traditional cultural ways of externalizing and communicating thought. We do not yet understand very well how the brain does this, how subjective constructs are generated and how internal models affect behavior. It does seem, however, that the brain operates with inductive rules and that complexes of these rules in some way form the mental models (Holland et al. 1990).

A further feature of expressing thought is that it has static and dynamic aspects. The static aspect is the encapsulation of knowledge as words, mathematics, or diagrams. This is the "known." This article and this work are examples of a static representation. The dynamic aspect is the process whereby we deal with the "unknown" through continuous exploratory behavior. Here we refer to word-ing, deriv-ing, doodl-ing. The "ing" is important here since it implies a process that is never finished. Where we are concerned with problem solving, decision making, and strategizing in the face of the unknown, it is this process side that needs to be paramount. This might be summarized in a phrase like, "How do I know what I think until I see what I am modeling?"

Our common culture sets for us here a peculiar trap that binds us, most of the time, to the static media. Thought or knowledge is expected to be presented as coherent and accurate and able to stand up to criticism. This forces thinking to be private and only so-called finished thoughts are overtly presented. Thus our verbal thinking is embodied in papers, our mathematical understanding is embodied in algebra, and our view of the way things work is drawn in diagrams. These in turn become fixed beliefs, objective laws, and representations of the way things are. Power relationships in hierarchies reinforce this state of affairs since to progress professionally and socially we need to be seen to be "right" more often than "wrong." This is not helpful for dealing with the unknown.

A dynamic representation medium inverts this state of affairs. It is not just a presentational gimmick. Dynamic media, by their nature, give permission for continuous change. In the presentational culture, it is seen as a weakness to change one's mind. In the explorational culture, it is a weakness to remain fixated. In the fixated state, statements become dogmas, equations become truths, and diagrams become "dogmagrams." But the map is never the terrain. And if the terrain itself is undergoing change then mapping as a process becomes more significant than any given map.

As an example, the hexagon method, using magnetic objects movable at will on a whiteboard surface, greatly facilitates dynamic representation. So do emerging examples of rapidly user-configurable softwares. But these are precursors of what will become a whole new range of dynamic media. The hexagon stands in relation to thinking as a brick does to building. It is simple and modular.

The core idea of the hexagon method is the "semantic unit," the atomic object of meaning. From the static paradigm we value the coherence whereby words are joined in sentences, symbols compute with each other, and parts are defined in diagrams of the whole. But we are now prisoners of syntax. In dynamic thinking we are dealing with chaoses of meanings, unconnected symbols, and fragmented thoughts. Beneath our conscious mind is also a chaos of mind as well as an order of mind. It is often out of this chaos of mind that creativity springs (Nonaka 1988).

CHAOS AND SYSTEM IN THE MIND

By acknowledging the chaos in our minds as a resource and not a failing, we can set out to catch, as butterflies in a net, odd thoughts, the significance of which we have yet to realize. We can state them in isolated hexagons without having any pre-determined order. We do this, for example, when we write associative checklists or bullet charts. But checklists do not support the emergence of the new order out of the chaos. With the freedom to move any object anywhere, we can re-iterate experiments forming different patterns and can develop new meaning. We challenge the mind to entertain new organizations of knowledge hitherto unattempted (de Bono 1990). The medium is the flexibility, not the unit itself.

So how does this notion of chaos relate to modeling, decision support, and systems thinking? The crucial connection is that our understanding of systems is more often buried in our subliminal mind than ready at hand in our surface mind. Both the chaos and the order of our mind are out of consciousness. They take place, so to say, in the backs of our minds. The generation of new thinking, by whatever means, requires that we tap into this reservoir of insight and information, and form new patterns of understanding from it. We need ways of continuously rendering the implicit explicit.

One area where we know this to be the case is in the development of expert systems. To create a knowledge based inference engine, we have to elicit rules from an expert. This elicitation of how the expert does what he does is never easy, since most of the effectual knowledge is implicit. Practical knowledge is often buried.

Modeling is essentially a dynamic activity of thinking out to the point where we can test our understanding, whether it be by simulation or by life itself. The tools of cognitive mapping, like hexagons, are a stepping stone from tacit mental perception to communicable mental work-in-progress. This work-in-progress notion is critical. Continuous improvement is the mark of a thinking environment.

SUMMARY OF ESSENTIAL TECHNIQUES

Concept mapping with idons is the process of rendering tacit models visible and sharable by the use of representational mapping. This mapping is done by means of a variety of techniques that are like "moving diagrams." They exploit the basic wisdoms that a picture is worth a thousand words and that thinking includes the power to influence patterns of ideas. Idons create a flexible medium where change of pattern is facilitated.

1. Each unit of meaning (statement, fact, opinion) is recorded on one single object, we call this an idon (from idea plus icon)

2. The idon object is persistent throughout the process and is movable at any time, thus encouraging flexibility.

3. Idons can be added, subtracted, revised, and moved at any time; they can be augmented with clusters, arrows, and text overlays.

4. Various conventions, particularly color, can be used to create additional layers of meaning, especially about connectivity and significance.

5. These conventions can carry meaning in terms of both frameworks of thought (e.g., a planning concept) and even of the nature of a particular thought (e.g., a cognitive mode).

6. The process can be carried out simultaneously by more than one person in collaboration, interrelating their thoughts in common models.

7. The representations of maps are practical control tools for:

   • live discussion;

- group memory;

- task organization;

- building shared models;

- decision support;

- information retrieval.

Thus concept mapping with idons, seen initially as something like an extension of brainstorming and mind mapping, turns out to be much deeper in its scope and implications.

Conceptual mapping with idons is a flexible medium that

- increases the brain's capacity to handle complexity;

- enables people in groups to share their thinking "aloud";

- provides a basis for new dynamic user-determined computer interfaces (for example, CK Modeller software);

- enables computer-based methods and information to be run from individually configured mindmaps.

The combination of these aspects in suitably designed methods, skills, and computer software, creates a new visual working environment that enables a bridge to be built between implicit mental models and conscious modeling techniques like system dynamics.

THE ROLES OF HARDWARE, SOFTWARE, AND ENVIRONMENT

The visual facilitation methods described here require a supportive environment that can accommodate a series of work processes from issue conceptualization to simulation. In the early stages, the use of physical tools such as colored plastic magnetic hexagons on whiteboards is excellent for gaining the "hands-on" involvement of a group. The hexagon is only one example of a range of symbols that include system dynamics symbols, circles, clouds, rectangles, triangles, and so on, each suitable for different thinking techniques.

However, this medium is most unsuitable for memory and documentation. Graphical software can provide tracking and memory as well as flexible feedback and review. Normal graphics software, however, does not lend itself to rapid and flexible manipulation. The CK Modeller software has been specially designed for this and its use also raises the potential for live, on-screen facilitation.

For example, clients have run conferences based on a room equipped with both large screen and 20" color monitors linked to a computer. A process facilitator takes them through the material. A skilled facilitator captures the key points and builds a group map on the screens. The executives take over and direct the structuring process. The intensity and productivity of the interaction is high and the captured data enables instant documented feedback of the deliberations.

Already the way is open for business teams to have group decision support systems transform the nature of the boardroom. Further, by using cognitive software to link boardroom to personal and institutional modeling databases and to conduct mapping and modeling via electronic mail and computer conferencing, the level at which telecommunicated decision-making processes can be conducted is greatly enhanced.

CREATING TRANSITIONAL DISCIPLINES FOR LEARNING

Effective decision making needs to be supported by both tentativeness and rigor, both elicitation and expertise, and both tactile and electronic technology. These are not either/or; they are both/and requirements. This paper has introduced a number of ideas and practical methods for bridging the gap between clients and practitioners. But there is a great deal more to do in this operation.

Once we have given ourselves permission to be chaotic, tentative, and provisional and to carry out work-in-progress, we can bring in all kinds of methods to support the bridging process. These methods can be related to various decision making disciplines, not just systems thinking or system dynamics. But, being dynamic, they encourage a different style of thinking than conventional modeling disciplines. They are more abbreviated, less rigorous and less expert dependent. The term we prefer for them is *transitional disciplines* and their symbolic tools are transitional objects.

The purpose and role of a transitional discipline is to provide a bridge between an area of specialist expertise and the mind of a generalist decision maker. In directing complex organizations, a senior manager cannot know all the expertise that may be relevant to a decision. Neither can he appreciate all the inputs supplied by experts, unless he has some way of making a conceptual link. A mental model generated by a manager or by a management team in a collaborative session provides the cognitive bridge that connects information with insight. Introduction of the transitional discipline in the right form and at the right time can accelerate that insight. An example is the use of archetypes (Senge 1990).

Through those links the necessary nourishment for the decision process can be obtained. Without it, the decision maker is at the mercy of the experts or his or her own arrogance, and so may equally either over-value or under-value given advice (de Geus 1988).

To communicate a transitional discipline to executives is not a matter for academic courses. Time and mental energy are too scarce. This is where the power of visual facilitation comes in. Through matching understanding of the task, selection of appropriate mental frameworks, use of flexible tools (such as idon methods), and interactive skills in stimulating and managing thinking processes in groups, we create an acceleration of learning that gets the job done.

The role of a transitional discipline is to act as a provocation for creative insight as well as a better-framed judgment. The transitional discipline has to provide scope for those using it to play with options and test innovations. There needs to be scope in modeling for creativity. This may take the form of innovative ideas or of deepening insights. The transitional toolkit serves the same role for the adult mind as the learning toy does for the child's mind. The scope to manipulate symbolic objects encourages free play. It is a kind of conceptual Lego kit. There is an imaginative design component to decision making (Friend and Hickling 1987). Imagination is an ingredient of entrepreneurial strategy. If our strategic modeling has no room for this then it will simply add to the list of predictable strategic methods that are vulnerable to more imaginative competition.

It is this need, especially in business management, to combine expert input, conceptualization, and imagination that makes the idon such a powerful tool. The range of symbolic objects—circles, rectangles, triangles, pentagons, and so on—can be tailored to correspond to particular decision support disciplines. In so far as it is also becoming codified as a set of effective practices, we can also look at creative thinking itself as a form of transitional discipline. There are many varieties of methods developed in this area (Adams 1986), but creative processes have been generally implemented through the traditional media of the blackboard and the chart pad. New tools, such as magnetic hexagons and other shapes, add dimensions of flexibility and speed to the constant rearranging that goes on when creative thinking is made visible.

Facilitation skill is the special expertise that supports people in representational thinking. In a formal discipline, sequences and procedures emerge that are part of the expertise, just as much as the knowledge content (Rosenhead 1989). Facilitation is more informal and has to do with matching well-designed procedures for thinking through a problem with the start points, concerns, and needs of the working team, so that a sequence and procedure can be found that works well for them. It is the art of empowering the team to engage properly and productively with the transitional discipline. The facilitator is required to be a catalyst for the interaction of expertise, conceptualization, and imagination. To do this he needs the corresponding techniques of frameworks, cognitive mapping, and creative thinking methods. This combination can be viewed as a cognitive bridge.

One of the functions of a transitional discipline is to provide a framework for facilitation. For example, a two-dimensional grid can be a framework for establishing relative positioning against two criteria; an interconnected set of "balloons" can be a system for the elicitation of the content of its components. The simplest form would be brainstorming against a list of categories.

Figure 18-8. The cognitive bridge

Such frameworks require the practitioner to have a firm grasp of the essentials of any discipline and understand the "cognitive gap" between the client group and that discipline. It also requires the innovative skills to create the transitional framework in such a way that (a) the compromise of the technical methodology is reduced to a minimum, and (b) the level at which it is pitched is not going to frustrate the client group. The role of the framework is not to show off the practitioner's grasp but to stimulate appropriate thinking in the client. Many of the papers in this work indicate that system dynamics expertise is reaching out to generalist decision makers and, through innovative processes and softwares, is generating its own transitional discipline.

REFERENCES

Adams, James L. (1986), *Conceptual Blockbusting,* Harmondsworth: Penguin.

de Bono, Edward (1986), *Six Thinking Hats*, New York: Viking.

de Bono, Edward (1990), *I Am Right, You Are Wrong,* New York: Viking.

CTI Publications (1990), *Thinking with Hexagons*, company publication, Idon, Ltd.

CK Modeller software (1990), Creativity Software Ltd.

Friend, John, and Allen Hickling (1987), *Planning Under Pressure,* Oxford, U.K.: Pergamon Press.

de Geus, Arie (1988), "Planning as Learning," *Harvard Business Review* March/April: 70-74.

Hampden-Turner, Charles (1990), *Charting the Corporate Mind,* Oxford, U.K.: Blackwell.

Holland, John H., Keith J. Holyoak, Richard E. Nisbett, and Paul R. Thagard (1987), *Induction— Processes of Inference, Learning and Discovery,* Cambridge: MIT Press.

Isenberg, Daniel J. (1987), "Inside the Mind of the Senior Manager," in Perkins, Lochhead, and Bishop, eds., *Thinking,* London: Erlbaum.

Miller, George A. (1956), "The Magical Number Seven, Plus or Minus Two; Some Limits on Our Capacity for Processing Information," *Psychological Review* 63: 81-87.

Nonaka, Ikujiro (1988), "Creating Organizational Order Out Of Chaos: Self-Renewal in Japanese Firms," *California Management Review* Spring: 51-53.

Rhodes, Jerry, and Sue Thame (1988), *The Colors of Your Minds,* London: Collins.

Rosenhead, Jonathan, ed. (1989), *Rational Analysis for a Problematic World,* New York: Wiley.

Russo, J. Edward, and Paul J.H. Schoemaker (1989), *Confident Decision Making,* London: Guild Publishing.

Senge, Peter M. (1990), *The Fifth Discipline,* New York: Doubleday/Currency.

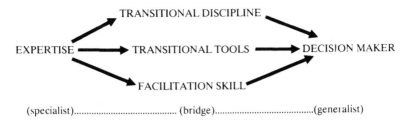

Figure 18-8. The cognitive bridge

Such frameworks require the practitioner to have a firm grasp of the essentials of any discipline and understand the "cognitive gap" between the client group and that discipline. It also requires the innovative skills to create the transitional framework in such a way that (a) the compromise of the technical methodology is reduced to a minimum, and (b) the level at which it is pitched is not going to frustrate the client group. The role of the framework is not to show off the practitioner's grasp but to stimulate appropriate thinking in the client. Many of the papers in this work indicate that system dynamics expertise is reaching out to generalist decision makers and, through innovative processes and softwares, is generating its own transitional discipline.

REFERENCES

Adams, James L. (1986), *Conceptual Blockbusting,* Harmondsworth: Penguin.

de Bono, Edward (1986), *Six Thinking Hats*, New York: Viking.

de Bono, Edward (1990), *I Am Right, You Are Wrong,* New York: Viking.

CTI Publications (1990), *Thinking with Hexagons*, company publication, Idon, Ltd.

CK Modeller software (1990), Creativity Software Ltd.

Friend, John, and Allen Hickling (1987), *Planning Under Pressure,* Oxford, U.K.: Pergamon Press.

de Geus, Arie (1988), "Planning as Learning," *Harvard Business Review* March/April: 70-74.

Hampden-Turner, Charles (1990), *Charting the Corporate Mind,* Oxford, U.K.: Blackwell.

Holland, John H., Keith J. Holyoak, Richard E. Nisbett, and Paul R. Thagard (1987), *Induction— Processes of Inference, Learning and Discovery,* Cambridge: MIT Press.

Isenberg, Daniel J. (1987), "Inside the Mind of the Senior Manager," in Perkins, Lochhead, and Bishop, eds., *Thinking,* London: Erlbaum.

Miller, George A. (1956), "The Magical Number Seven, Plus or Minus Two; Some Limits on Our Capacity for Processing Information," *Psychological Review* 63: 81-87.

Nonaka, Ikujiro (1988), "Creating Organizational Order Out Of Chaos: Self-Renewal in Japanese Firms," *California Management Review* Spring: 51-53.

Rhodes, Jerry, and Sue Thame (1988), *The Colors of Your Minds,* London: Collins.

Rosenhead, Jonathan, ed. (1989), *Rational Analysis for a Problematic World,* New York: Wiley.

Russo, J. Edward, and Paul J.H. Schoemaker (1989), *Confident Decision Making,* London: Guild Publishing.

Senge, Peter M. (1990), *The Fifth Discipline,* New York: Doubleday/Currency.

ANNOTATED BIBLIOGRAPHY

John D.W. Morecroft and John D. Sterman

The articles in this book provide references to many useful works relevant to those interested in the use of modeling and simulation for learning. However, the literature describing theory, examples, and evaluations of the effectiveness of tools and processes for model supported learning is growing rapidly. This bibliography surveys recent literature that complements the themes covered in this book. The bibliography draws on "Desert Island Dynamics: An Annotated Guide to the Essential System Dynamics Literature" (Sastry and Sterman 1993), a selection of system dynamics applications in all domains. We thank Anjali Sastry for allowing us to draw on her bibliography, and Paul Langley for assistance in adding to the bibliography.

Several papers listed here appear in recent proceedings of the International System Dynamics Conferences. In the annotated bibliography the proceedings are abbreviated to ISDC 1989, ISDC 1990, etc. The full references for the last five years' of these proceedings are:

ISDC 1989: Milling, P.M., and E.O.K. Zahn, eds., *Computer-Based Management of Complex Systems,* collected papers from the 1989 International System Dynamics Conference (Stuttgart, Germany), New York: Springer-Verlag, 1989.

ISDC 1990: Andersen, D.F., G.P. Richardson, and J.D. Sterman, eds., *Proceedings of the 1990 International System Dynamics Conference* (Chestnut Hill, Massachusetts, U.S.A., July 1990), available from the System Dynamics Society.

ISDC 1991: Saeed K., D. Andersen, and J. Machuca, eds., *Proceedings of the 1991 International System Dynamics Conference* (Bangkok, Thailand, August 1991), available from the System Dynamics Society.

ISDC 1992: Vennix, Jac A.M. et al., eds., *Proceedings of the 1992 International System Dynamics Conference* (Utrecht, The Netherlands, July 1992), available from the System Dynamics Society.

ISDC 1993: Machuca, J.A.D., and E. Zepeda, eds., *Proceedings of the 1993 International System Dynamics Conference: The Role of Strategic Modeling in International Competitiveness* (Cancún, Mexico, July 1993), available from the System Dynamics Society.

Copies of the 1990-1993 proceedings, along with some back issues of the *System Dynamics Review,* can be purchased from the System Dynamics Society. Contact: Julie Pugh, Executive Director, 49 Bedford Road, Lincoln MA 01773, U.S.A. Fax 617-259-0969.

The *System Dynamics Review* is a primary source for current developments in the field. Contact: Journals Subscription Department, John Wiley and Sons Ltd., Baffins Lane, Chichester, West Sussex, PO19 1UD, U.K.

•

van Ackere, Ann, Erik Reimer Larsen, and John D.W. Morecroft (1993), "Systems Thinking and Business Process Redesign," *European Journal of Management* 11, no. 4: 412-23 (December 1993).

Examines policy formulations and simulations of a model of the beer distribution game in order to demonstrate the connections between systems thinking, modeling and business process redesign.

Andersen, David F., Ik Jae Chung, George P. Richardson, and Thomas R. Stewart (1990), "Issues in Designing Interactive Games Based on System Dynamics Models," *ISDC 1990*, 31-45.

Documents the experience of two teams of experts — one a system dynamics modeling team and the other a team of psychologists expert in human judgment and decision making — as they interact to create a gaming simulation.

Bakken, Bent E. (1989), "Learning in Dynamic Simulation Games: Using Performance as a Measure," *ISDC 1989*, 309-16.

Reports experiments to measure learning that players transfer from one gaming simulation to another, when the simulators have identical underlying feedback structure but represent different industry situations. Learning is measured by comparing players' performance to the score of a control group, along with performance of simulated decision rules.

Bakken, B., and Sterman, J.D. (1993), "Commercial Real Estate Management Flight Simulator," available from John Sterman at MIT Sloan School of Management, Cambridge MA 02142.

An interactive management flight simulator in which the player manages a portfolio of commercial buildings, deciding when to build new buildings or trade existing buildings in a volatile market. Includes full documentation and instructions. Macintosh based.

Bakken, B., and Sterman, J.D. (1993), "International Oil Tanker Management Flight Simulator," available from John Sterman at MIT Sloan School of Management, Cambridge MA 02142.
> An interactive management flight simulator in which the player manages a fleet of oil tankers, deciding when to commission new ships or trade existing capacity in a volatile market. Includes full documentation and instructions. Macintosh based.

Barker, John, and Richard N. Tucker (1990), *The Interactive Learning Revolution*, New York: Kogan Page.
> Overviews interactive video technologies and their applications.

Bean, Michael P., Ernst W. Diehl, and David P. Kreutzer (1992), "Strategy Simulation and Scenario Planning: An Application of Generic System Structures," *ISDC 1992*, 69-77.
> Through case studies, the article describes how strategy simulations and the resulting scenarios can be useful tools for understanding the interrelationships of different elements within a competitive industry, and for identifying critical leverage points that may help a firm create competitive advantage.

The Beer Distribution Game
> This simple four-stage production-distribution board game provides compelling first-hand experience of fundamental principles of systems. Perhaps the most widely used and most effective introduction to system dynamics. Instructions, videos, analyses, and interpretive papers are available from John Sterman at MIT. The System Dynamics Society provides boards and other materials to run the game but only to members of the Society. For membership information contact Julie Pugh, Executive Director, 49 Bedford Road, Lincoln MA 01773, U.S.A. Fax 617-259-0969.

Bergin R., and G.P. Prusko (1990), "The Learning Laboratory," *The HealthCare Forum Journal* 33, no. 2: 32-36.
> Describes the design, use, and impact of a computer-based management flight simulator and learning laboratory to develop systems thinking and improved management policies at a leading insurance company.

Carroll, J.S., J.S. Sterman, and A.A. Marcus (1994), "Playing the Maintenance Game: How Mental Models Drive Organizational Decisions," in R.R. Stern and J.J. Halpern, eds., *Nonrational Elements of Organizational Decision Making,* Ithaca, N.Y.: ILR Press.
> Contrasts approaches to organizational learning to improve maintenance productivity and equipment reliability in the petrochemicals and nuclear power industries. The petrochemicals case focuses on the Du Pont Maintenance Game, an interactive board game based on a system dynamics model. Data show how

the game has led to higher reliability and lower maintenance costs for many Du
Pont plants.

Corben, D.A., and E.F. Wolstenholme (1992), "A Hypermedia Based Delphi Tool
for Knowledge Acquisition in Model Building," *ISDC 1992*, 117-26.
Describes a computer-based support tool to automate the application of the
Delphi method of expert opinion assessment. The tool facilitates the
development of causal-loop diagrams as a method to capture the mental models
of the group.

Cotton, Bob, and Richard Oliver (1993), *Understanding Hypermedia: From
Multimedia to Virtual Reality*, London: Phaidon.
Overviews multimedia technologies and applications.

Curry, B., and L. Moutinho (1992), "Using Computer Simulation in Management
Education," *Management Education and Development* 23, no. 2: 155-67.
Discusses the underlying educational principles on which computer-based
teaching and training should be based, and describes evidence on the
effectiveness of the computer-based approach.

Diehl, Ernst W. (1993), "Strategy Support Software: Enhancing Executive
Dialogue and Debate," *ISDC 1993*, 76-82.
Describes the use of Microworlds S**4 software to facilitate interactive
exploration of the structure and assumptions of simulation models.

Diehl, E., and Sterman, J.D. (1994), "Effects of Feedback Complexity on Dynamic
Decision Making," Working Paper 3608-93-MSA, Sloan School of Management,
MIT, Cambridge MA 02142.
Reports an experimental study in which subjects managed a simple production-
inventory system in the presence of different time delays and side-effect
feedbacks. Performance was systematically and significantly suboptimal.
Subjects tended to ignore the time delays and feedback processes. As the
dynamic complexity of the system increased, the deviation between the
subjects' decisions and the optimal policy increased.

European Multimedia Yearbook 1993, London: Interactive Media Publications, 67-69.
Overviews multimedia technologies, applications, and relevant issues
concerning the delivery, implementation, and evaluation of these technologies.

Forrester, J.W. (1987), "Fourteen 'Obvious Truths,'" *System Dynamics Review* 3,
no. 2: 156-59.
The core of the system dynamics paradigm, as seen by the founder of the field.

Forrester, J.W. (1985), "The Model Versus a Modeling 'Process,'" *System Dynamics Review* 1, no. 1: 133-34.

> The value of a model lies not in its predictive ability alone but primarily in the learning generated during the modeling process.

Geurts, Jac L., Ivo Wenzler, and Hans J.J. van Kuppevelt (1993), "Communicating Complexity Through Visualization: The Use of Schematics in Gaming Simulations," *ISDC 1993*, 171-80.

> Discusses visualization as a key tool in the related fields of gaming/simulation and system dynamics. Uses two gaming projects as examples to explain techniques and processes of visualization from the gaming discipline.

Gould-Kreutzer, Janet, ed. (1993), *System Dynamics Review—Systems Thinking in Education* 9, no. 2 (Summer 1993).

> A special issue of the System Dynamics Review including eight papers examining current issues relating to the role of system dynamics and systems thinking in education, especially pre-college education.

Gunz, Hugh (1988), "Information Technology in Management Education: Myths and Potentialities," *Personnel Review* 17, no. 5: 3-11.

> Examines the potential for, and limitations of, information technology in helping implement strategies to develop management education in the U.K. A case study illustrates the themes discussed.

Hennessy, Sara, and Tim O'Shea (1993), "Learner Perceptions of Realism and Magic in Computer Simulations," *British Journal of Educational Technology* 24, no. 2: 125-38.

> Discusses a key issue affecting the educational potential of interactive computer simulations — their possible lack of credibility. Puts forward some means of overcoming disbelief through manipulating the degree of reality inherent in simulations.

Homer, J.B., J.D. Sterman, B. Greenwood, and M. Perkola (1993), "Delivery Time Reduction in Pulp and Paper Mill Construction Projects: A Dynamic Analysis of Alternatives," *ISDC 1993,* 212-21.

> Describes the structure, results, and use of a large model to help a firm design policies to improve large-scale project management. Demonstrates that an interactive "modeling for learning" process focused on managers is compatible with the development of a large, detailed, data-intensive simulation model that is carefully tested and calibrated.

Huff, Anne Sigismund, ed. (1990), *Mapping Strategic Thought,* New York: John Wiley & Sons.
Describes the use of mapping methods to illustrate and analyze managerial cognition. Part 1 contains 9 papers describing field work to map managerial models in a wide range of industries including telecommunications, chemicals, automobiles, and consumer electronics. Part 2 describes a number of different mapping methods and how they are used, such as content analysis, repertory grids, strategic loops, and narrative semiotics.

Kampmann, C., and J.D. Sterman (1992), "Do Markets Mitigate Misperceptions of Feedback in Dynamic Tasks?" *ISDC 1992,* 285-94.
Experimental study of decision-making performance in environments with different levels of dynamic complexity (time delays, feedback loops) and different market institutions. Markets reduce but do not eliminate the "misperceptions of feedback" that lead to dysfunctional behavior in complex settings, but complexity degrades performance relative to optimal even in the presence of perfectly functioning market institutions.

Kemeny, Jennifer M., and W. Brian Kreutzer (1992), "An Archetype Based Management Team Flight Simulator," *ISDC 1992,* 303-10.
Describes an example of a Management Team Flight Simulator (MTFS) that supports team learning through a computer-based model combining hypertext, system archetypes, and simulation.

Keys, Bernard, and Joseph Wolfe (1990), "The Role of Management Games and Simulations in Education and Research," *Journal of Management* 16, no. 2: 307-36.
A review of the management gaming movement. Summarizes how the field has evolved to its current state. Several models of experiential learning applicable to gaming are explained. Projects future developments in the field.

Kim, D. (1989), "Learning Laboratories: Designing a Reflective Learning Environment," *ISDC 1989,* 327-34.
A case study of a process designed to convey dynamic insights to participants in a workshop setting designed around a management flight simulator game.

Kim, D.H. (1990), "Toward Learning Organizations: Integrating Total Quality Control and Systems Thinking," Working Paper D-4036, System Dynamics Group, Sloan School of Management, MIT, Cambridge MA 02142.
Argues that SD and Total Quality Management are complementary approaches to improvement and organizational learning. Systems thinking and modeling are needed to speed the improvement cycle for processes with long time delays.

Klein, R.D., and R.A. Fleck, Jr. (1990), "International Business Simulation/Gaming: An Assessment and Review," *Simulation & Games* 21, no. 2: 147-65.

> Reviews the gaming literature to identify strengths and weaknesses. Examines the roles that simulations can play in international business pedagogy. Reviews existing international business simulation games to determine what each game can contribute to the teaching of international business.

Kofman, F., N. Repenning, and J.D. Sterman (1994), "Unanticipated Side Effects of Successful Quality Programs: Exploring a Paradox of Organizational Improvement," Working Paper 3667-94-MSA, Sloan School of Management, MIT, Cambridge MA 02142.

> Analog Devices, Inc., a leading semiconductor manufacturer, implemented a highly successful Total Quality program. However, financial performance deteriorated. The paper uses a system dynamics model to explain the apparent paradox. It argues that improvement programs like TQM can generate negative side-effects and explores policies for improved implementation of quality programs and other programs designed to stimulate organizational learning.

Kreutzer, David P., and Janet M. Gould-Kreutzer (1993), "Designing Management Simulators," *ISDC 1993*, 222-30.

> Describes issues facing designers of simulators — the purpose of the interface, nature of the interaction, characteristics of the users, the context of use, and the style of presentation — and how they influence the design of the software application.

Lane, David C. (1993a), "The Road Not Taken: Observing a Process of Issue Selection and Model Conceptualization," *System Dynamics Review* 9, no. 3: 239-64.

> Describes a case study involving information technology managers within Royal Dutch/Shell and their new programmer recruitment policy. The processes of issue generation and selection and model conceptualization are described.

Lane, David C. (1993b), "From Discussion to Dialogue: How an Interactive Modeling Process Was Used with Managers to Resolve Conflict and Generate Meaning," *ISDC 1993*, 231-34.

> Case study of model-based dispute resolution within a management team.

Langley, Paul A. (1993), "Learning with Model-Supported Case Studies," *ISDC 1993*, 245-54.

> Discusses results from three experiments with undergraduate and postgraduate students that studied the efficacy of the learning experience using model-supported case studies and management flight simulators.

Langley, Paul A., and Erik R. Larsen (1993), "Multimedia Management Flight Simulators," *ISDC 1993*, 255-64.
Discusses the role that multimedia technologies can play in enhancing the design of gaming simulations, in both classroom and distance learning environments.

Langley, Paul A., and Erik R. Larsen (1994), "I Can't Believe It's a System Dynamics Model," Learning Centre Working Paper W-94-08, London Business School, London NW1 4SA, U.K.
Examines the possibilities for suing commercially available games in a system dynamics context. Demonstrates the opportunities with reference to "Sin City," a well-known commercial gaming simulation.

Larreche, Jean-Claude (1987), "On Simulations in Business Education and Research," *Journal of Business Research* 15: 559-71.
Reviews the history of business simulations and their use in education and research. Design characteristics and a typology of simulations are discussed.

Laurillard, Diana (1993), *Rethinking University Teaching—A Framework for the Effective Use of Educational Technology*, Routledge.
This book explores the potential of technological media to improve student learning and teaching efficiency, and discusses practical methodologies for the design, development, and implementation of educational technologies.

Linstead, Stephen (1990), "Beyond Competence: Management Development Using Computer-Based Systems in Experiential Learning," *Management Education and Development* 21, no. 1: 61-74.
Describes a technology-based course designed to create a more realistic environment for experiential insight transferable to the real organization. The course is currently in use in organizations as varied as commercial banking, software engineering, construction, brewing, retailing, and air passenger transport.

Machuca, Jose A.D., Miguel A.D. Machuca, Antonio Ruiz, and Jose C. Ruiz (1993), "Systems Thinking and Learning for Management Education," *ISDC 1993*, 298-307.
Describes work in progress at the Universidad de Sevilla to design learning laboratories for management education.

Mahmoud, Mohamed, and Peter Genta (1993), "Microworld of an Open University: A Strategic Management Learning Laboratory," *ISDC 1993*, 318-27.
Describes the work and experience gained by a team using a systems thinking approach to developing a microworld to support the strategic planning of Athabasca University, a fast-growing open university in western Canada.

Mandinach, Ellen B., and Hugh F. Cline (1994), *Classroom Dynamics: Implementing a Technology-Based Learning Environment,* Hillsdale, N.J: Erlbaum Associates.

History and evaluation of programs designed to introduce system dynamics and computer modeling as learning methods to enhance pre-college education. Reviews the approaches and results in a number of schools in the U.S., covering different subject areas, grade levels, and techniques. The authors are researchers at the Educational Testing Service of Princeton, N.J.

Mass, Nathaniel J. (1991), "Diagnosing Surprise Model Behavior: A Tool for Evolving Behavioral and Policy Insights," *System Dynamics Review* 7, no. 1: 68-86 (written in 1981).

Guidelines for learning from unexpected model behavior. Offers principles for scientific exploration and resolution of anomalous model results.

Meadows D.L. (1984), "*Strategem 1,* A Management Training Exercise on Long-Term Economic-Environment Interactions," Simulation game available from the Institute for Policy and Social Science Research, Hood House, University of New Hampshire, Durham NH 03824, U.S.A.

A computer-supported board game for groups focusing on sustainable development. Includes population, agriculture, resources, environment, economic activity, trade, etc. Widely used around the world, includes extensive briefing and debriefing materials.

Meadows D.L. (1989), "Gaming to Implement System Dynamics Models," *ISDC 1989,* 635-40.

Principles and examples for the successful development and use of interactive simulation games, by one of the leading experts in the field.

Meadows D.L., T. Fiddaman, and D. Shannon (1989), "*Fishbanks Ltd.,* A Microcomputer Assisted Simulation that Teaches Principles for Sustainable Management of Renewable Resources," game available from the Institute for Policy and Social Science Research, Hood House, University of New Hampshire, Durham NH 03824, U.S.A.

Computer-supported board game in which players manage a fishery. Illustrates principles for management of renewable resources. Widely used in education; certified by the U.S. Dept. of Education. Easy to play by everyone from high schools students to government officials.

Meadows, Donella H. (1989), "System Dynamics Meets the Press," *System Dynamics Review* 5, no. 1: 68-80.

Reviews the history of encounters between system dynamics and the media. Offers guidelines for effective communication to the public at large. Stresses the importance of communicating even the simplest system concepts.

Morecroft, J.D.W. (1982), "A Critical Review of Diagramming Tools for Conceptualizing Feedback System Models," *Dynamica* 8, no. 1: 20-29.
    Critiques causal-loop diagrams and proposes subsystem and policy structure diagrams as alternative tools for representing the structure of decisions in feedback models.

Morecroft, J.D.W. (1983), "System Dynamics: Portraying Bounded Rationality," *Omega* 11, no. 2: 131-42.
    System dynamics models represent decision making as boundedly rational. Reviews and contrasts the concept of bounded rationality as developed by Herbert Simon with system dynamics theory. Uses Forrester's Market Growth model to show how locally rational decision rules can interact to yield globally dysfunctional outcomes.

Morecroft, J.D.W. (1984), "Strategy Support Models," *Strategic Management Journal* 5, no. 3: 215-29.
    Models should be used as participants in the ongoing dialogue among managers regarding strategy formation and evaluation. Emphasizes processes for model development and use that enhance the utility of modeling for the design of business strategy.

Morecroft, J.D.W. (1985), "Rationality in the Analysis of Behavioral Simulation Models," *Management Science* 31, no. 7: 900-16.
    Shows how the intended rationality of decision rules in system dynamics models can be assessed, and how one analyzes a simulation model and output to understand the assumed bounds on rationality in dynamic models. A model of sales force effort allocation is used to illustrate.

Morecroft, J.D.W. (1988), "System Dynamics and Microworlds for Policymakers," *European Journal of Operational Research* 35, no. 3: 301-20.
    Reviews developments in system dynamics that underpin the "Modelling for Learning" approach, including the adoption of ideas from behavioral decision tgheory and improvements in methods of simulation analysis.

Morecroft, J.D.W. (1992), "An Introduction to the Oil Producers' Model," Learning Centre Working Paper W-94-09, London Business School, London NW1 4SA, U.K.
    Describes the structure of the Oil Producers' Model, building on archetypes and uses partial model simulations and "thought experiments" to build understanding of the model's dynamic behavior.

Morecroft, John D.W. (1992), "Design of a Learning Environment: The Oil Producers' Microworld," *ISDC 1992,* 465-74.

Describes a computer-based learning environment of the global oil industry, and how participants are briefed about the oil business, systems thinking, and the model's feedback structure. Illustrates the gaming interface and model-generated scenarios.

Morecroft, J.D.W., Linda E. Morecroft, and Erik R. Larsen (1992), "The Oil Producers' Model Equation Description," Learning Centre Working Paper W-94-11, London Business School, London NW1 4SA, U.K.

Describes the equation formulations underlying the behavioral decision function of the Oil Producers' Model as developed by a team in a "Modelling for Learning" project.

Morecroft, J.D.W., D.C. Lane, and P.S. Viita (1991), "Modeling Growth Strategy in a Biotechnology Start-up Firm," *System Dynamics Review* 7, no. 2: 93-116.

A case study of a start-up in which system dynamics modeling helps a management team to map the operating structure of their business and to explore, through simulation, the feasibility of growth plans.

Paich, M., and J.D. Sterman (1993), "Boom, Bust, and Failures to Learn in Experimental Markets," *Management Science* 39, no. 12: 1439-1458.

Reports an experiment with the "B & B Enterprises Management Flight Simulator" (Sterman 1991) in which players manage a new product in a competitive environment. People perform poorly relative to even simple strategies. Performance relative to potential deteriorates significantly as dynamic complexity increases. Repeated play did not allow players to develop better understanding of the system dynamics, posing a challenge to designers and users of simulations for learning about complex dynamic systems.

Peterson, Steve (1990), "Designing Learning Environments," *ISDC 1990*, 852-62.

Describes principles for the design of learning environments, based on experiences gained at High Performance Systems, Inc. Illustrated with two examples of learning environments designed in Hypercard.

Richardson, G.P. (1986), "Problems with Causal-Loop Diagrams," *System Dynamics Review* 2, no. 2: 158-70.

Causal-loop diagrams cannot show stock-and-flow structure explicitly and can obscure important dynamics. Offers guidelines for proper use and interpretation of CLDs. An important article for anyone seeking to use systems mapping tools.

Richmond, B. (1993), "Systems Thinking: A Critical Set of Critical Thinking Skills for the 1990s and Beyond," *System Dynamics Review* 9, no. 2: 113-34.
Proposes a process and skill set to teach systems thinking. The process relies on learner-directed learning. The skill set includes general scientific reasoning, operational thinking, and system dynamics, supported by simulation.

Ronchetto, John R., Tom A. Buckles, Robert M. Barath, and James Perry (1992), "Multimedia Delivery Systems: A Bridge Between Teaching Methods and Learning Styles," *Journal of Marketing Education*, Spring 1992: 12-21.
Describes current and emerging applications of electronic and computer technologies for marketing education, and proposes an organizing structure for choosing an appropriate multimedia delivery system.

Rosenhead, Jonathan, ed. (1989), *Rational Analysis for a Problematic World,* New York: John Wiley & Sons.
Papers describing six widely used problem structuring methodologies and their application. Includes contributions by Peter Checkland on soft system methodology; strategic options development by Colin Eden; the strategic choice approach by John Friend; and robustness analysis by Jonathan Rosenhead. Introductory and concluding chapters examine the unity among seemingly diverse problem structuring methods and prospects for these methods in practice.

Sastry, A., and J.D. Sterman (1993), "Desert Island Dynamics: An Annotated Guide to the Essential System Dynamics Literature," *ISDC 1993,* 466-75.
An annotated bibliography of key works in the field of system dynamics. Covers a wide range of applications, from business to physiology. While representing the authors' admittedly subjective opinions of what is "essential," it is a useful guide to the system dynamics literature.

Simons, Kenneth L. (1993), "New Technologies in Simulation Games," *System Dynamics Review* 9, no. 2: 135-52.
Stresses the importance of tools to help learners explore and test the underlying structure and assumptions of computer-based learning environments. Provides examples including a model of Lovelock's Daisy World (illustrating the Gaia hypothesis).

Senge, Peter M. (1990), "Catalyzing Systems Thinking within Organizations," in F. Masarik, ed., *Advances in Organization Development,* Norwood, N.J.: Ablex.
Presents a case study in which the use of system dynamics generated insights into a chronic business problem. Steps in generating, testing, and disseminating a system dynamics model are described.

Senge, Peter M. (1990), *The Fifth Discipline: The Art and Practice of the Learning Organization,* New York: Doubleday Currency.
Introduces systems thinking as part of a wider approach to organizational learning. Conveys basic system structures to a nontechnical business audience by means of anecdotes and archetypes.

Sterman, J.D. (1987), "Testing Behavioral Simulation Models by Direct Experiment," *Management Science* 33, no. 12: 1572-1592.
Principles for testing the decision rules in system dynamics models by converting the proposed model to a management flight simulator and exploring the decision-making behavior of managers operating the game. Uses a simple model of the Kondratiev cycle to illustrate.

Sterman, John D. (1988), *People Express Management Flight Simulator,* available from author, Sloan School of Management, MIT, Cambridge MA 02142.
An interactive simulation exercise that gives users first-hand experience at the controls of the airline company. It illustrates feedback effects and nonlinearities at work, providing participants with an experiential learning opportunity. One of the most widely used management flight simulators. Includes extensive instructions and briefing materials. Macintosh or IBM/Windows.

Sterman, John D. (1989), "Misperceptions of Feedback in Dynamic Decision Making," *Organizational Behavior and Human Decision Processes* 43, no. 3: 301-35.
Describes an experiment with a simple economic system in which subjects systematically generate costly oscillations. Estimates decision rules to characterize subject behavior. Finds that people systematically ignore feedbacks, time delays, accumulations, and nonlinearities. These misperceptions of feedback lead to poor quality decisions when dynamic complexity is high.

Sterman, J.D. (1989), "Modeling Managerial Behavior: Misperceptions of Feedback in a Dynamic Decision Making Experiment," *Management Science* 35, no. 3: 321-39.
Analyzes the results of the Beer Distribution Game. Misperceptions of feedback are found to cause poor performance in the beer game, as in other experiments. Estimates of the subjects' decision rules show they ignore time delays, accumulations, feedbacks, and nonlinearities. Simple models of subject decisions are estimated and found to replicate subject behavior well.

Sterman, J.D. (1991), "B & B Enterprises Management Flight Simulator," available from author, Sloan School of Management, MIT, Cambridge MA 02142.
Interactive management flight simulator in which a player manages a new product in a highly competitive environment including word of mouth, marketing, price effects, competition, learning curves, capacity acquisition

delays, and other realistic features of modern markets. Includes briefing materials and instructor's manual. Macintosh or IBM/Windows.

Sterman, J.D. (1992), "Teaching Takes Off: Flight Simulators for Management Education," *OR/MS Today*, October 1992, 40-44.
Overview of games and interactive management flight simulators for business education. Describes the effective use of such tools in the classroom and field.

Sterman, J.D., E. Banaghan, and E. Gorman (1992), "Learning to Stitch in Time: Building a Proactive Maintenance Culture at E.I. Du Pont de Nemours and Co.," case study available from John Sterman, Sloan School of Management, MIT, Cambridge MA 02142.
Case study describing the motivation for the development of the Du Pont Maintenance Game, an interactive system dynamics-based board game Du Pont has used successfully to improve maintenance operations (see Carroll, Marcus, and Sterman 1994, above).

Sterman, J.D., and T. Fiddaman (1994), "The Beer Distribution Game Flight Simulator," available from John Sterman, Sloan School of Management, MIT, Cambridge MA 02142.
Computer-based flight simulator of the beer distribution game allows players to operate any of the sectors in gaming mode or simulate the system with a wide range of policies. Also permits structural changes such as deleting links in the distribution chain, providing global information, etc. Includes extensive instructions and instructor's manual. Macintosh based.

Thatcher, D.C. (1990), "Promoting Learning Through Games and Simulations," *Simulation & Games* 21, no. 3: 262-73.
Introduces the notion of a learning system, and considers the active nature of learning from experience. Discusses the role of simulations and games in promoting learning, as well as the process of debriefing and its relationship to reflection.

Toval, Ambrosio, and Mariano Flores (1987), "Computer Systems Simulation in Education: Description of an Experience," *Computers in Education* 11, no. 4: 293-303.
Describes how the Spanish National Project for Computers in Education (Atenea) uses modeling and simulation, in particular how the applications using system dynamics techniques are used in the classroom.

Warren, Kim (1994), "Simulating the Effects of Regulatory Change in the U.K. Pubs Industry," Learning Centre Working Paper W-94-07, London Business School, London NW1 4SA, U.K.
    Describes how small feedback models depicting industry structure and structural change can be used to build shared understanding of the implication of regulatory change.

Wells, R.A. (1989), "A Review of Educational Technology for Management Development," *Journal of Management Development* 8, no. 2: 33-40.
    Outlines the use of new technologies, including microcomputers, video, and teleconferencing.

Wheatley, Walter J., Robert W. Hornaday, and Tammy G. Hunt (1988), "Developing Strategic Management Goal-Setting Skills," *Simulation & Games* 19, no. 2: 173-85.
    Presents both sides of the debate over the instructional value of gaming simulations, and offers some empirical evidence on the effect of gaming on goal-setting.

Williams, Edgar L. (1993), "Computerized Simulation in the Policy Course," *Simulation & Games* 24, no. 2: 230-39.
    Presents results from a survey of U.S. instructors teaching policy/strategy courses in business schools, examining the differences between courses that use simulations/games and those that do not.

Wolstenholme, E.F. (1990), *System Enquiry—A System Dynamics Approach,* Chichester, U.K.: John Wiley.
    Describes a research methodology for system dynamics analysis. Emphasizes causal-loop diagramming, mapping of mental models, and other tools for qualitative system dynamics.

Young, Showing H., Jenshou Yang, and Sy-Feng Wang (1992), "Enhancing the Learning Effects of Dynamic Decision Games on Systems Thinking—An Experimental Study," *ISDC 1992,* 847-56.
    Describes an experimental study to investigate the effects on learning and performance of different information displays in an interactive dynamic decision game.

ABOUT THE EDITORS

JOHN D. W. MORECROFT

John Morecroft is Associate Professor of Strategic Management at London Business School and was previously a faculty member at MIT's Sloan School of Management. He is a consultant to Royal Dutch/Shell and an adviser to McKinsey and Co. He is a leading expert in strategic modeling and system dynamics and has published widely in major academic journals such as the *Strategic Management Journal, Management Science, European Journal of Operational Research,* and the *System Dynamics Review.* In 1990 he received the Jay Wright Forrester award of the System Dynamics Society. Building on these ideas he runs the successful executive program *Systems Thinking and Strategic Modelling* and is Director of the Learning Centre at London Business School.

JOHN D. STERMAN

John Sterman is Professor of Management Science at MIT's Sloan School of Management and Director of MIT's System Dynamics Group; he also is a leader in the Sloan School's Organizational Learning Center. His research includes systems thinking and organizational learning, computer simulation of corporate strategy, and the theory of nonlinear dynamics. He has pioneered the development of "management flight simulators" of corporate and economic systems, now used by corporations and universities around the world. Professor Sterman has been awarded the Jay W. Forrester Prize for the best published work in system dynamics, and has three times won awards for teaching excellence from the students of the Sloan School. He has been featured on public television's *MacNeil/Lehrer News Hour,* National Public Radio's *Marketplace,* and CBC television, and in *Fortune,* the *Financial Times, Business Week,* and many other newspapers and journals.

INDEX

Books from Productivity Press

Learning Organizations
Developing Cultures for Tomorrow's Workplace
Sarita Chawla and John Renesch, Editors

The ability to learn faster than your competition may be the only sustainable competitive advantage! A learning organization is one where people continually expand their capacity to create results they truly desire, where new and expansive patterns of thinking are nurtured, where collective aspiration is set free, and where people are continually learning how to learn together. This compilation of 34 powerful essays, written by recognized experts worldwide, is rich in concept and theory as well as application and example. An inspiring followup to Peter Senge's groundbreaking bestseller *The Fifth Discipline*, these essays are grouped in four sections that address all aspects of learning organizations: the guiding ideas behind systems thinking; the theories, methods, and processes for creating a learning organization; the infrastructure of the learning model; and arenas of practice.
ISBN 1-56327-110-9 / 575 pages / $35.00 / Order LEARN-B115

Collected Papers of Jay W. Forrester
Jay W. Forrester

Industrial dynamics—the application of feedback concepts to social systems—offers a rational foundation to support the art of management. This collection includes provocative discussions of issues critical to manufacturing managers, including production-distribution systems, inventory and in-process order corrections, corporate growth patterns, and reducing research costs.
ISBN 0-262-06065-5 / 284 pages / $65.00 / Order XJFORR-B115

Introduction to Computer Simulation
Nancy Roberts, David Andersen, Ralph Deal, Michael Garet, William Shaffer

Simulation as an aid to solving problems has been a powerful tool for centuries. With the advent of the computer revolution, this tool has come within the reach of virtually everyone. This book is both an introduction to systems thinking—the critical element in problem solving for complex organizations—and a "how to" on building computer simulation models. Primarily developed as a classroom text, it is also a perfect vehicle for professionals in many different arenas (including business, government, and the social sciences) who want to reshape their organizations and their products or services by using system dynamics to solve complex problems. It provides a practical, concrete method for using computer simulation to model complex systems. No computer experience is required.
ISBN 1-56327-052-8 / 570 pages / $35.00 / Order XICS-B115

PRODUCTIVITY PRESS, DEPT. BK, P.O. BOX 13390, PORTLAND, OR 97213-0390
Telephone: 1-800-394-6868   Fax: 1-800-394-6286

Introduction to Urban Dynamics
Louis Alfeld and Alan K. Graham

This text explains the complexity of the urban system through examination of simpler urban subsystems. Sequential evolution of 10 urban models presents the assumptions, structure, behavior, and utility of urban dynamics models for urban policy analysis. Organized as a textbook with practice exercises at the end of each chapter, the book serves as an excellent starting point for teaching interdisciplinary courses on urban systems analysis and design.
ISBN 0-262-01054-2 / 337 pages / $45.00 / Order XINUDY-B115

Urban Dynamics
Jay W. Forrester

In this controversial book, Forrester presents a computer model describing the major internal forces controlling the balance of population, housing, and industry within an urban area. He simulates the life cycle of a city and predicts the effects of proposed remedies on an urban system. This book became the basis of a major research effort at M.I.T. that has impacted many government policy decisions for solving urban problems.
ISBN 1-56327-058-7 / 256 pages / $45.00 / Order XURBDY-B115

World Dynamics
Jay W. Forrester

This book interrelates population, industrialization, natural resources, food, crowding, and pollution to present an exploratory theory of man in the world ecology. The theory is case in a computer model that generates the dynamics of transition from growth to world equilibrium. Several alternate scenarios emerge from this world dynamics system. The present system apparently leads to the least desirable outcome. Industrialization may be a more fundamental threat than population. The book is the first step toward adapting the principles of system dynamics to the behavior of the forces involved in determining the transition from growth to world equilibrium. It has been adopted in many colleges and universities for teaching courses in such diverse fields as geology, zoology, life sciences, political science, ecology, and cybernetics. The book serves in its own right as well as a study complement to other books examining world environmental problems. (First published in 1971.)
ISBN 1-56327-059-5 / 142 pages / $35.00 / Order XWDYC-B115

Building a Shared Vision
A Leader's Guide to Aligning the Organization
C. Patrick Lewis

This exciting new book presents a step-by-step method for developing your organizational vision. It teaches how to build and maintain a shared vision directed from the top down, but encompassing the views of all the members and stakeholders, and understanding the competitive environment of the organization. Like *Corporate Diagnosis,* this books describes in detail one of the necessary first steps from *Implementing a Lean Management System:* visioning.
ISBN 1-56327-163-X / 150 pages / $45.00 / Order VISION-B115

PRODUCTIVITY PRESS, DEPT. BK, P.O. BOX 13390, PORTLAND, OR 97213-0390
Telephone: 1-800-394-6868   Fax: 1-800-394-6286

Dynamics of Commodity Production Cycles

Dennis L. Meadows

In this book Meadows addresses such questions as why price and production of commodities fluctuate; the common structure behind the cyclical behavior of different commodities, and the likelihood of predicting the influence of new policies. Professor Meadows finds the classical Cobweb Theorem and its modifications to be inadequate representations of dynamic relationships in actual commodity systems. Employing the system dynamics methodology, he develops a general dynamic model of the economic, biological, technological, and psychological factors which lead to the instability of commodity systems. With appropriate parameter values, the general model explains the hog, cattle, and chicken cycles observed in the real world. Experimental simulations of the model present surprising implications for current stabilization policies. (First published in 1970.)
ISBN 0-262-13141-2 / 116 pages / $35.00 / Order XDYCOM-B115

Dynamics of Growth in a Finite World

Dennis L. Meadows et al.

This book details the research on which The Club of Rome's first report, The Limits to Growth, is based. This technical report describes the purpose and methodology of the global modeling effort and presents the "World3" model equation by equation. The information provides a deeper understanding of the model, indispensable for individuals interested in either extending the study or constructing their own large-scale simulation models. It also provides technical material for multidisciplinary courses on population, the environment, natural resources, and economic development. Useful for people interested in studying or constructing their own models. (First published in 1974.)
ISBN 0-262-13142-0 / 637 pages / $60.00 / Order XDYGO-B115

Dynamo User's Manual (6th edition)

Alexander L. Pugh III

The software computer program DYNAMO, for IBM compatibles, interprets system dynamics models as used to represent business, social, economic, biological, psycho-logical, engineering, and other systems. DYNAMO is a computer language for simu-lating models of business, economic, social, biological, and engineering systems. Developed at MIT for people who are problem-oriented rather than computer-oriented, it permits easy communication with the computer and easier communication among modelers and can be mastered by nonprogrammers in days rather than the weeks or months required for most languages.
ISBN 0-262-66029-6 / 310 pages / $25.00 paper / Order XDYNUM-B115

PRODUCTIVITY PRESS, DEPT. BK, P.O. BOX 13390, PORTLAND, OR 97213-0390
Telephone: 1-800-394-6868   Fax: 1-800-394-6286

Elements of the System Dynamics Method

Jorgen Randers, ed.

Learn how models of dynamic systems are made. The authors give practical advice about choosing a problem that will yield interesting results, what to include in the model and what to leave out, the desirable amount of detail, selecting parameter values, knowing whether the model is "good," and how to make the model interesting to other people.

ISBN 0-915299-39-9 / 344 pages / $50.00 paper / Order XELEM-B115

Industrial Dynamics

Jay W. Forrester

A complete presentation of the system dynamics approach to the study of industrial systems, including the managerial viewpoint, classification of models, and advice to managers. The separate functions of management activity (cash flow, orders, materials, personnel, and capital equipment) are integrated by an information network. Critical system variables are revealed and policies for better management indicated. This first complete presentation of the system dynamics approach to the study of industrial systems explains Forrester's objectives, his personal classification of models, his views on testing model validity, and his advice to managers who are eager to capitalize on what industrial dynamics has to offer.

ISBN 0-915299-88-7 / 479 pages / $65.00 paper / Order XINDDY-B115

Readings in Urban Dynamics (vol. 1)

Nathaniel J. Mass, ed.

This collection of readings explores how urban model building can contribute to improving human judgment and decision making. This collection of 20 working papers explores and extends concepts introduced by Jay W. Forrester's *Urban Dynamics.* The books addresses basic issues raised by reviewers of *Urban Dynamics* and points out many of the current problems and controversies surrounding the construction of realistic urban models. Equally important, it helps to illustrate how the process of urban model building can potentially contribute to improving human judgment and decision making. Included in this volume are papers by Jay W. Forrester, Dennis L. Meadows, and John F. Collins (former mayor of Boston). Also included is a report on the application of urban dynamics theory to Lowell, Massachusetts. (First published in 1974.)

ISBN 0-262-13140-4 / 303 pages / $45.00 / Order XRVOL1-B115

Readings in Urban Dynamics, vol. 2

Walter Schroeder III et al., eds.

This second volume in a series arising from Jay W. Forrester's controversial *Urban Dynamics* addresses basic criticisms of Urban Dynamics and describes extensions of the original Urban Dynamics model. Individual chapters describe model extensions that examine such policy issues as land rezoning, housing abandonment, and city-suburb interactions. The urban dynamics models can be employed as a policy guide for urban planning, and extensions of the models can focus on specific urban issues such as education, transportation, and crime. The models also provide a better-informed perception of how different aspects of a city affect one another. (First published in 1975.)

ISBN 0-262-19170-9 / 305 pages / $55.00 / Order XRVOL2-B115

PRODUCTIVITY PRESS, DEPT. BK, P.O. BOX 13390, PORTLAND, OR 97213-0390
Telephone: 1-800-394-6868   Fax: 1-800-394-6286

Principles of Systems

Jay W. Forrester

A key text on system dynamics, this book introduces the concepts of system structure and shows by example how structure determines behavior. Covers feedback dynamics, models and simulation, equations and computation, flow diagrams, information links, integration, and more! The book contains ten chapters of text followed by workbook problems and answers. Although the problems are framed in a corporate context, the principles are general to many fields. Because the principles discussed are general in nature, the book is suitable for use in studying the dynamics of urban, ecological, corporate and other complex systems. This makes a perfect workbook companion to *Industrial Dynamics* and *Collected Papers* by Jay W. Forrester.
ISBN 0-915299-87-9 / 387 pages / $25.00 paper / Order XPRSYS-B115

Toward Global Equilibrium
Collected Papers

Dennis L. Meadows and Donella H. Meadows, eds.

This collection of 13 studies identifies specific issues connected with growth, particularly those critical areas of future research in the fields of population, resources, environment, and social ethics—including DDT and mercury pollution, natural resource depletion, and solid waste disposal. It provides policy suggestions which may alleviate these problems and examines the economic, political, and ethical implications of growth and the transition to equilibrium. (First published in 1973.)
ISBN 0-262-13143-9 / 358 pages / $45.00 / Order XGLOEQ-B115

Thoughtware
Change the Thinking and the Organization Will Change Itself

J. Philip Kirby and D.H. Hughes

In order to facilitate true change in an organization, its thinking patterns need to be the first thing to change. Your employees need more than empowerment. They need to move from doing their jobs to doing whatever is needed for the good of the entire organization. Thoughtware is the underlying platform on which every organization operates, the set of assumptions upon which the organization is structured. When you understand and change thoughtware, the tools and techniques of continuous improvement become incredibly powerful.
ISBN 1-56327-106-0 / 200 pages / $35.00 / Order THOUG-B115

PRODUCTIVITY PRESS, DEPT. BK, P.O. BOX 13390, PORTLAND, OR 97213-0390
Telephone: 1-800-394-6868   Fax: 1-800-394-6286

TO ORDER: Write, phone, or fax Productivity Press, Dept. BK, P.O. Box 13390, Portland, OR 97213-0390, phone 1-800-394-6868, fax 1-800-394-6286. Send check or charge to your credit card (American Express, Visa, MasterCard accepted).

U.S. ORDERS: Add $5 shipping for first book, $2 each additional for UPS surface delivery. Add $5 for each AV program containing 1 or 2 tapes; add $12 for each AV program containing 3 or more tapes. We offer attractive quantity discounts for bulk purchases of individual titles; call for more information.

ORDER BY E-MAIL: Order 24 hours a day from anywhere in the world. Use either address:
To order: service@ppress.com
To view the online catalog and/or order: http://www.ppress.com/

QUANTITY DISCOUNTS: For information on quantity discounts, please contact our sales department.

INTERNATIONAL ORDERS: Write, phone, or fax for quote and indicate shipping method desired. For international callers, telephone number is 503-235-0600 and fax number is 503-235-0909. Prepayment in U.S. dollars must accompany your order (checks must be drawn on U.S. banks). When quote is returned with payment, your order will be shipped promptly by the method requested.

NOTE: Prices are in U.S. dollars and are subject to change without notice.